Financial Management: A Risk Management Approach

Financial Management: A Risk Management Approach

Edited by Zachary Bell

STATES
ACADEMIC PRESS
www.statesacademicpress.com

States Academic Press,
109 South 5th Street,
Brooklyn, NY 11249, USA

ISBN: 978-1-63989-202-0

Cataloging-in-Publication Data

Financial management : a risk management approach / edited by Zachary Bell.
p. cm.
Includes bibliographical references and index.
ISBN 978-1-63989-202-0
1. Financial risk management. 2. Finance. 3. Finance--Management.
4. Risk management. I. Bell, Zachary.
HD61 .F56 2022
658.155--dc23

For information on all States Academic Press publications
visit our website at www.statesacademicpress.com

STATES
ACADEMIC PRESS

Contents

Preface ... VII

Chapter 1 **Surplus Sharing with Coherent Utility Functions** ... 1
Delia Coculescu and Freddy Delbaen

Chapter 2 **Application of Machine Learning to Mortality Modeling and Forecasting** ... 13
Susanna Levantesi and Virginia Pizzorusso

Chapter 3 **Optimal Bail-Out Dividend Problem with Transaction Cost and Capital Injection Constraint** ... 32
Mauricio Junca, Harold A. Moreno-Franco and José Luis Pérez

Chapter 4 **Pricing Options and Computing Implied Volatilities using Neural Networks** ... 56
Shuaiqiang Liu, Cornelis W. Oosterlee and Sander M. Bohte

Chapter 5 **Determining Distribution for the Product of Random Variables by using Copulas** ... 78
Sel Ly, Kim-Hung Pho, Sal Ly and Wing-Keung Wong

Chapter 6 **Risk Model Validation: An Intraday VaR and ES Approach using the Multiplicative Component GARCH** ... 98
Ravi Summinga-Sonagadu and Jason Narsoo

Chapter 7 **Credible Regression Approaches to Forecast Mortality for Populations with Limited Data** ... 121
Apostolos Bozikas and Georgios Pitselis

Chapter 8 **The W, *Z/v*, δ Paradigm for the First Passage of Strong Markov Processes without Positive Jumps** ... 143
Florin Avram, Danijel Grahovac and Ceren Vardar-Acar

Chapter 9 **Machine Learning in Banking Risk Management** ... 158
Martin Leo, Suneel Sharma and K. Maddulety

Chapter 10 **Can Sustainable Investment Yield Better Financial Returns: A Comparative Study of ESG Indices and MSCI Indices** ... 180
Mansi Jain, Gagan Deep Sharma and Mrinalini Srivastava

Chapter 11 **Efficient Retirement Portfolios: Using Life Insurance to Meet Income and Bequest Goals in Retirement** ... 198
Fangyuan Dong, Nick Halen, Kristen Moore and Qinglai Zeng

Chapter 12 **Model-Free Stochastic Collocation for an Arbitrage-Free Implied Volatility** **209**
Fabien Le Floc'h and Cornelis W. Oosterlee

Permissions

List of Contributors

Index

Preface

This book has been an outcome of determined endeavour from a group of educationists in the field. The primary objective was to involve a broad spectrum of professionals from diverse cultural background involved in the field for developing new researches. The book not only targets students but also scholars pursuing higher research for further enhancement of the theoretical and practical applications of the subject.

Financial management is the practice of planning, organizing, directing, and controlling financial activities such as procurement and utilization of funds in a business entity. It is concerned with the estimation of capital requirements, determination of capital composition, choices of sources of funds, investment of funds, etc. Risk management is the process of identifying, assessing and controlling threats to a company's capital and source of revenue. These threats can arise from a wide range of sources such as financial uncertainty, legal liabilities, strategic management errors, accidents, and natural disasters. The topics included in this book on financial management are of utmost significance and bound to provide incredible insights to readers. It picks up individual branches and explains their need and contribution in the context of a growing economy. This book is a vital tool for all researching and studying this field.

It was an honour to edit such a profound book and also a challenging task to compile and examine all the relevant data for accuracy and originality. I wish to acknowledge the efforts of the contributors for submitting such brilliant and diverse chapters in the field and for endlessly working for the completion of the book. Last, but not the least; I thank my family for being a constant source of support in all my research endeavours.

Editor

1

Surplus Sharing with Coherent Utility Functions

Delia Coculescu [1] **and Freddy Delbaen** [2,3,*]

1 Institut für Banking und Finance, Universität Zürich, Plattenstrasse 32, 8032 Zürich, Switzerland; delia.coculescu@bf.uzh.ch
2 Departement für Mathematik, ETH Zürich, Rämistrasse 101, 8092 Zürich, Switzerland
3 Institut für Mathematik, Universität Zürich, Winterthurerstrasse 190, 8057 Zürich, Switzerland
* Correspondence: delbaen@math.ethz.ch

Abstract: We use the theory of coherent measures to look at the problem of surplus sharing in an insurance business. The surplus share of an insured is calculated by the surplus premium in the contract. The theory of coherent risk measures and the resulting capital allocation gives a way to divide the surplus between the insured and the capital providers, i.e., the shareholders.

Keywords: coherence; monetary utility; insurance benefit; benefit sharing

---

1. Notation and Motivation

In the present work, we analyze a method to distribute the surplus of an insurance business between the different agents taking part in the risk exchange. The insured pay premia to an insurance company, and in exchange for this, the company takes over the risks, i.e., the company will pay out the claims that otherwise would have to be covered by the insured. Besides these two players, there is also the supervisor or the regulator. The task of the regulator is to make sure that the insurance business is fair. That means for instance that all companies play with the same rules so that competition can take place. The regulator must also see whether the companies have enough capital to cover the risks, since otherwise—in case of bankruptcy—a substantial portion of the risk would be transferred to society, i.e., to the tax payers or to other economic agents.

As already pointed out by Deprez and Gerber (1985), insurance premia should be dependent on the whole portfolio of insurance contracts. That would mean that the premium to be charged for a contract can only be calculated when all other contracts (signed or in the "pipeline") are known. In practice, this is impossible, and hence, premia are charged that are certainly higher than the fair allocation of the total premium to the individual contracts. The result is that the extra part must be seen as a contribution to the capital of the company and hence is entitled to a share in the eventual surplus.

In the present document, we will deal with a way to calculate the share of each economic agent, be it the capital providers or shareholders or the insured through their extra premium. The problem of how to fix the total amount of regulatory capital is the subject of joint ongoing work, which was initiated by Artzner and Eisele (2018).

We also restrict our analysis to a one-period model. The surplus share is particularly important for life insurance contracts, and handling these would necessitate a multi-period setup. The technical and conceptual problems are not easy, so we "postponed" it to further research.

We will use the language of probability theory, as is usually done in financial and actuarial mathematics. We will fix a probability space $(\Omega, \mathcal{F}, \mathbb{P})$ on which all random variables will be defined. In particular, the claims will be seen as random variables defined on this probability space. For simplicity, we will only work with bounded random variables. The vector space of bounded random variables is denoted by $L^\infty(\Omega, \mathcal{F}, \mathbb{P})$ or simply L^∞. The restriction to bounded random variables facilitates the modeling since we do not have to make assumptions on integrability, big tails, and so on. However, it triggers some extra mathematical problems. The solution of these problems will only be sketched, and for more details, we refer to Delbaen (2002, 2011). We assume that the insurance company makes decisions using a coherent utility function.

Definition 1. *A mapping $u\colon L^\infty \to \mathbb{R}$ is called a monetary utility function if the following properties hold:*

1. *if $0 \le \xi \in L^\infty$, then $u(\xi) \ge 0$;*
2. *u is concave, i.e., for all $\xi, \eta \in L^\infty, 0 \le \lambda \le 1$, we have $u(\lambda\xi + (1-\lambda)\eta) \ge \lambda u(\xi) + (1-\lambda)u(\eta)$;*
3. *for $a \in \mathbb{R}$ and $\xi \in L^\infty$, $u(\xi + a) = u(\xi) + a$;*
4. *if $\xi_n \downarrow \xi$ (with $\xi_n \in L^\infty$), then $u(\xi_n) \to u(\xi)$.*

If moreover for all $0 \le \lambda \in \mathbb{R}$, $u(\lambda\xi) = \lambda u(\xi)$, we call u coherent.

The number $u(\xi)$ can be seen as a risk-adjusted valuation of the future uncertain position ξ. Property (1) in the definition is therefore clear. Risk adverseness is usually translated by concavity properties, and it is believed that combinations are less risky than individual positions. This explains Property (2). Property (3) means that risk-adjusted valuations are measured in money units. Of course, money today (date of the valuation) is different from money at the end of the period. Introducing a deflator or discounting—as has been the practice in actuarial business for hundreds of years—solves this problem. It complicates notation, and as long as there is only one currency involved, it does not lead to confusion if one supposes that this discounting is already incorporated in the variables. The fourth property is a continuity property. Using monotonicity (a consequence of the previous properties; see Delbaen 2011), we can also require that $u(\xi_n) \downarrow u(\xi)$. In this text, we will use the stronger property where $\downarrow$'s are replaced by $\uparrow$'s; see Delbaen (2011). This avoids some mathematical problems that are easily overcome, but they obscure the philosophy of the approach. The homogeneity property is a strong property. Later in this paper, where we use commonotonicity, positive homogeneity is already satisfied.

Sometimes, the value $u(\xi)$ only depends on the distribution or law of the random variable ξ. In this case, we say "law invariant", "law determined", etc. An example of such a mapping is the distorted probability. These were introduced in insurance by Yaari (1987), Denneberg (1989), and Denneberg and Kaplan (1998). They were later used by Wang (2002). An example of such a utility function is (for $\xi \ge 0$) the Choquet integral $\int_0^\infty f(\mathbb{P}[\xi > t])\,dt$ where $f : [0,1] \to [0,1]$ is convex, $f(0) = 0, f(1) = 1$. See Delbaen (2011, 1974), Shapley (1972), and Schmeidler (1986) for more details and for the relations between convex games and commonotonicity. See also Remark 5 below, where we explain that our models cover the concave distortion as a subcase.

We say that a random variable ξ is acceptable if $u(\xi) \ge 0$. We remark that $\xi - u(\xi)$ is always acceptable. If u is coherent, then the acceptability set $\mathcal{A} = \{\xi \mid u(\xi) \ge 0\}$ is a convex cone. The continuity assumption allows one to apply convex duality theory and leads to the following representation theorem:

Theorem 1. *If u is coherent, there exists a convex closed set $\mathcal{S} \subset L^1$ (with L^1 being the vector space of random variables on $(\Omega, \mathcal{F}, \mathbb{P})$ that are integrable), consisting of probability measures, absolutely continuous with respect to $\mathbb{P}$, such that for all $\xi \in L^\infty$:*

$$u(\xi) = \inf_{\mathbb{Q} \in \mathcal{S}} \mathbb{E}_{\mathbb{Q}}[\xi].$$

Conversely, each such set $\mathcal{S}$ defines a coherent utility function.

Remark 1. *We identify an absolutely-continuous probability measure $\mathbb{Q} \ll \mathbb{P}$ with its Radon–Nikodym derivative $\frac{d\mathbb{Q}}{d\mathbb{P}}$.*

Remark 2. *Replacing the true or physical probability $\mathbb{P}$ by other measures is a practice that is well known in insurance. Standard techniques that can be described are, e.g., "tilting" and increasing or decreasing ages in* *life insurance contracts. To calculate premia, more weight is then given to unfavorable events, and favorable events get less weight. The existence of such a set $\mathcal{S}$ says that the change in probability is done in a systematic and consistent way.*

Remark 3. *We can show that the upward sequential continuity in the definition of coherent utility functions is equivalent to the existence of a minimizer $\mathbb{Q}_0 \in \mathcal{S}$. This equivalence follows from a deep mathematical result in functional analysis (the theorem of R.James), Delbaen (2011). That the* inf *can be replaced by* min *simplifies some of the proofs. We call this property the weak compactness property of $\mathcal{S}$.*

Definition 2. *We say that two random variables ξ, η are commonotonic if there exist a random variable ζ, as well as two non-decreasing functions $f, g \colon \mathbb{R} \to \mathbb{R}$ such that $\xi = f(\zeta)$ and $\eta = g(\zeta)$.*

Remark 4. *Loosely speaking, two risks are commonotonic if they are bets on the same event. Indeed, ξ and η being nondecreasing functions of ζ, neither of them is a hedge against the other, as both risks ineluctably move in the same direction. It is a non-trivial exercise to show that we can always take $\zeta = \xi + \eta$ (see Delbaen 2011, p. 20 for a proof of this result).*

Definition 3. *We say that $u \colon L^\infty \to \mathbb{R}$ is commonotonic if for each couple ξ, η of commonotonic random variables, we have $u(\xi + \eta) = u(\xi) + u(\eta)$.*

Remark 5. *Commonotonic concave monetary utility functions are positively homogeneous and hence coherent. In general, coherent utility functions satisfy $u(\xi + \eta) \geq u(\xi) + u(\eta)$. That means that by diversifying, the risk-adjusted valuation gets better. Commonotonic random variables form the opposite of diversification, as explained in Remark 4. Roughly speaking: what is worse for ξ is worse for η. The commonotonicity of u can therefore be seen as a translation of the rule: if there is no diversification, there is also no gain in putting these claims together. Including commonotonicity as an economic principle is desirable for the purpose of premium calculation or risk measurement in insurance, and many actuarial models are built on the assumption that the premium principles are commonotonic. For instance, the popular class of concave distortions mentioned above is comprised of commonotonic utilities; hence, they can be seen as particular examples fitting in the framework we develop below.*

2. Description of the Model

We use the following setup. There are N agents to be insured, indexed $i = 1, \ldots, N$. There is one insurer denoted by the index 0. There is also a "super"-reinsurer, whose role will be explained later. He/she will be denoted by r. The agents have liabilities that they want to insure. The liability for agent i is $X_i \geq 0$. Without insurance, his/her position will be $-X_i$. There are different premium principles, which will be described in the examples below. The utility functions of the agents are denoted by u_i. The coherent utility function of the insurer is u_0 and, to reduce complexity, supposed to be commonotonic. The utility functions of the agents are more restrictive than the insurer's utility function u_0; meaning: when a random variable is not acceptable for the insurer, then it is not acceptable for the agents. Equivalently, we can say that acceptable elements for the agent i are acceptable for the insurer. This is a translation of the fact that the agent i feels a need for insurance and that an insurer can fulfill this need. Because of the translation property, we then have for all ξ and all $i \geq 1$:

$$u_0(\xi) \geq u_i(\xi).$$

We assume the utilities $u_i, i = 1, \ldots, N$ to be monetary utility functions as in Definition 1 and satisfying the above inequality, with no further assumptions.

The insurer also brings in an initial capital k_0. He/she will take the insurance only if he/she can obtain a better outcome. Because u_0 is coherent, the total premium, π_0, must be at least $\pi_0 = -u_0\left(-\sum_{i=1}^N X_i\right)$. Indeed, the insurer takes the random variable $-\sum_i X_i$ and receives π_0. The deal is only acceptable for the insurer if $u_0(\pi_0 - \sum_i X_i) \geq 0$. We suppose that the scenario set for u_0, $\mathcal{S}_0$ is weakly compact so that there is a $\mathbb{Q}_0 \in \mathcal{S}_0$ such that:

$$\mathbb{E}_{\mathbb{Q}_0}\left[\sum_{i=1}^{N} X_i\right] = \sup_{\mathbb{Q}\in\mathcal{S}_0} \mathbb{E}_{\mathbb{Q}}\left[\sum_{i=1}^{N} X_i\right] = -u_0\left(-\sum_{i=1}^{N} X_i\right).$$

In case u_0 is commonotonic, we can (and shall) even choose $\mathbb{Q}_0$ so that for all Y commonotonic with $\sum_i X_i$ and such that the distribution of Y has no other points of increase as $\sum_i X_i$, we have $u_0(Y) = \mathbb{E}_{\mathbb{Q}_0}[Y]$. This applies for cases such as $Y = \min(R, \sum_i X_i)$ or $Y = (\sum_i X_i - R)^+)$, where $R \in \mathbb{R}$.

From Delbaen (2002, 2011), using the capital allocation principle, we find that the individual "fair" premia should be:

$$\pi_i = \mathbb{E}_{\mathbb{Q}_0}[X_i]. \tag{1}$$

In Delbaen (2002, 2011) it is shown that the allocation principle can also be obtained as an application of the marginal contribution of one agent. The latter was the approach given in Deprez and Gerber (1985). The equivalence requires some technical assumptions that go beyond the scope of this paper. What this means is that under these extra assumptions, we have:

$$\pi_i = \lim_{\varepsilon\downarrow 0}(-1)\frac{u_0(-\sum_j X_j - \varepsilon X_i) - u_0(-\sum_j X_j)}{\varepsilon}$$

The equality $\pi_i = \mathbb{E}_{\mathbb{Q}_0}[X_i]$ immediately implies:

$$-\pi_i = \mathbb{E}_{\mathbb{Q}_0}[-X_i] \geq u_0(-X_i) \geq u_i(-X_i).$$

For the agent i, this is a good deal, provided that the insurance pays entirely the claim X_i at Date 1, since $-\pi_i \geq u_i(-X_i)$. What he/she pays for insurance is better than paying X_i.

In the following, we propose four different models, that is four different ways in which the premia can be fixed by the insurer in situations where there is either a government guarantee or a reinsurance possibility. There is a distinction between the fair premia and what is actually charged, which may be higher. We argue that the difference should be regarded as a contributionto the capital by the insured agents, and be remunerated by a share of the surplus. We provide conditions that the deals are acceptable by all agents and the insurer. More precisely, we consider that a deal is acceptable for the insurer whenever the utility u_0 of the profit received by the insurer exceeds k_0. We say that the deal is acceptable for agent i whenever the insurance deal generates an increase in the agent's utility u_i, as compared with the situation without insurance.

3. Model 1

In this example, we suppose that the insurer has limited liability. We take for the total premium:

$$\pi_0 = -u_0\left(-\sum_{i=1}^{N} X_i\right).$$

We distinguish several cases:

1. $\sum_i X_i > \pi_0 + k_0$. In this case, the total claim size exceeds the available capital. The excess is supposed to be covered by, for instance, the government, and this at no cost. The initial capital should then be sufficiently high to make the deal acceptable for the government. The determination of this level is beyond the contents of this paper. We denote by A the set $A = \{\sum_i X_i > \pi_0 + k_0\}$.
2. $\pi_0 \leq \sum_i X_i \leq \pi_0 + k_0$. In this case, there is no surplus, and the insurer will lose part of his/her investment. We denote by B the set $B = \{\pi_0 \leq \sum_i X_i \leq \pi_0 + k_0\}$.

3. $\pi_0 > \sum_i X_i$. In this case, there is a surplus. The insurer will keep the surplus entirely. This can be defended since the agents already "gained" from the allocation principle, which is their share when entering the insurance. Furthermore, they do not take any risk. We denote by C the set $C = \{\pi_0 > \sum_i X_i\}$.

Theorem 2. *The deal is acceptable for the insurer.*

Proof. The insurer will accept the deal if:

$$u_0((\pi_0 + k_0 - \sum_i X_i)\mathbf{1}_{B\cup C}) \geq k_0.$$

This is easily proven. By the definition of π_0, we have $u_0(\pi_0 - \sum_i X_i) = 0$; hence $u_0(\pi_0 - \sum_i X_i + k_0) = k_0$; therefore, by monotonicity, $u_0\left((\pi_0 - \sum_i X_i + k_0)^+\right) \geq k_0$. □

Remark 6. *We remark that there must be a regulator, who requires a minimum capital k_0. Otherwise, the company would choose $k_0 = 0$, take the profit in the event C, and leave the trouble to "society" in the event A. As said in the introduction, the rules used by the regulators and the implementation in models is the topic of research by Artzner and Eisele.*

4. Model 2

This is almost the same as Model 1, but this time, we require a premium for covering the excess. We also assume that the reinsurer has no default. The reinsurance premium will be calculated by the same coherent utility function, i.e., the same set $\mathcal{S}_0$. It is here that we use the commonotonicity. The retention will be denoted by R, and this results in the splitting:

$$\sum_i X_i = \left(\sum_i X_i\right) \wedge R + \left(\sum_i X_i - R\right)^+.$$

The two terms are commonotonic, and hence, the premium satisfies:

$$\pi_0 = \pi^R + \rho^R; \quad \pi^R = \mathbb{E}_{\mathbb{Q}_0}\left[\left(\sum_i X_i\right) \wedge R\right]; \quad \rho^R = \mathbb{E}_{\mathbb{Q}_0}\left[\left(\sum_i X_i - R\right)^+\right].$$

The retention level needs to be chosen so that the claims are fully covered, that is the available funds (given by $k_0 + \pi^R$) are not below the retention level. We define the optimal retention R as the maximal retention level that results in the full coverage of the claims:

$$R := \max\{x \mid x \leq k_0 + \pi^R\}.$$

The existence and uniqueness of R follow from an easy analysis of the function Φ defined as:

$$\mathbb{R}_+ \to \mathbb{R}_+;\ x \to x - \mathbb{E}_{\mathbb{Q}_0}\left[\left(\sum_i X_i\right) \wedge x\right].$$

As $x - \mathbb{E}_{\mathbb{Q}_0}\left[(\sum_i X_i) \wedge x\right] = \mathbb{E}_{\mathbb{Q}_0}\left[(x - \sum_i X_i)^+\right] = \int_0^x \mathbb{Q}_0\left(\sum_i X_i \leq a\right) da$, the function $\Phi(x)$ is continuous, convex, strictly increasing after it leaves zero, is zero at zero, and tends to ∞ for $x \to +\infty$.

Hence, the optimal retention R satisfies:

$$R = k_0 + \pi^R,$$

that is, the available capital is R, which is also the maximum the insurer has to pay out. The surplus is therefore:

$$R - \left(\sum_i X_i\right) \wedge R.$$

The agents again do not take any risk, and hence, they should not participate in the surplus. The insurer finds it a good deal if:

$$u_0\left(R - \left(\sum_i X_i\right) \wedge R\right) \geq k_0.$$

However, the definition of R shows that $u_0\left(R - \left(\sum_i X_i\right) \wedge R\right) = k_0$. That means there is no incentive to do business, and the insurer must get all the profit to have an equivalent outcome.

5. Model 3

This is an extension of the previous models. The agents pay a premium equal to $p_i \geq \pi_i$, where π_i is the fair premium, introduced in Equation (1). This has the advantage that the insurer can announce the premium without having to calculate the total premium necessary to cover the total losses. Of course, this procedure should lead to a premium greater than the fair premium, as calculated in the previous models. An example of such a premium calculation could be the amount $\sup_{\mathbb{Q}\in\mathcal{S}_0} \mathbb{E}_{\mathbb{Q}}[X_i] = -u_0(-X_i)$. The extra premium $p_i - \pi_i$ can be seen as a contribution of agent i to the capital; hence, agents should be entitled to a share in the surplus. All investors must be treated in the same way, and hence, the share of agent i is proportional to his/her contribution, namely $\frac{p_i - \pi_i}{\sum_j (p_j - \pi_j) + k_0}$. The investor will get a proportion $\frac{k_0}{\sum_j (p_j - \pi_j) + k_0}$. These fractions are paid out regardless of having caused a claim or not.

The retention is now defined by the relation:

$$\sum_i (p_i - \pi_i) + k_0 + \pi^R = R.$$

The existence and uniqueness of R are proven in the same way. This time, we must see whether this is a good deal for the insurer, as well as for the agents.

Theorem 3. *The deal is acceptable for the insurer.*

Proof. For the insurer, we must check the inequality:

$$u_0\left(\frac{k_0}{k_0 + \sum_i (p_i - \pi_i)}\left(R - \sum_i X_i\right)^+\right) \geq k_0.$$

By positive homogeneity of u_0, this is the same as:

$$u_0\left(\left(R - \sum_i X_i\right)^+\right) \geq k_0 + \sum_i (p_i - \pi_i).$$

As in the previous example, this follows from the definition of R, which implies:

$$u_0\left(R - \left(\sum_i X_i\right) \wedge R\right) = R - \pi^R = k_0 + \sum_i (p_i - \pi_i).$$

□

Theorem 4. *The deal is acceptable for the insured as soon as* $p_i \le \sup_{\mathbb{Q}\in\mathcal{S}_0} \mathbb{E}_\mathbb{Q}[X_i]$.

Proof. For agent i, we must check:

$$u_i\left(-p_i + \frac{p_i - \pi_i}{k_0 + \sum_j (p_j - \pi_j)}\left(R - \sum_i X_i\right)^+\right) \ge u_i(-X_i).$$

This is equivalent to:

$$u_i\left(\frac{p_i - \pi_i}{k_0 + \sum_j (p_j - \pi_j)}\left(R - \sum_i X_i\right)^+\right) \ge u_i(p_i - X_i).$$

The left-hand side is positive, whereas the right-hand side is negative, provided the premium p_i is not too big. For instance, if $p_i \le \sup_{\mathbb{Q}\in\mathcal{S}_0} \mathbb{E}_\mathbb{Q}[X_i]$, we have $u_0(p_i - X_i) \le 0$ and, hence, also $u_i(p_i - X_i) \le 0$. □

Remark 7. *In any case, the agent i will not pay a premium p_i that is bigger than $-u_i(-X_i)$. Paying a higher premium and counting on surplus participation is not realistic since the surplus share also depends on the claims incurred through the other agents.*

6. Model 4

We continue the building of stepwise more complicated models. We suppose that there are two insurers. The first one has a utility function u_0, described by the scenario set $\mathcal{S}_0$. This insurer acts as the direct insurer. The second insurer acts as a reinsurer with utility function u_r described by the scenario-set $\mathcal{S}_r$. For a claim $0 \le \xi$, the reinsurer would charge a premium $\sup_{\mathbb{Q}\in\mathcal{S}_r} \mathbb{E}_\mathbb{Q}[\xi]$.

Both utility functions u_0 and u_r are supposed to be commonotone. Their scenario-sets are therefore determined as cores of convex games, say $v_0 \ge v_r$. For simplicity, we suppose that both scenario-sets $\mathcal{S}_0, \mathcal{S}_r$ are weakly compact. We can therefore suppose that there are elements $\mathbb{Q}_0 \in \mathcal{S}_0, \mathbb{Q}_r \in \mathcal{S}_r$, such that for all a:

$$\sup_{\mathbb{Q}\in\mathcal{S}_r} \mathbb{E}_\mathbb{Q}\left[\sum_j X_j\right] = \mathbb{E}_{\mathbb{Q}_r}\left[\sum_j X_j\right]$$

$$\sup_{\mathbb{Q}\in\mathcal{S}_r} \mathbb{E}_\mathbb{Q}\left[\left(\sum_j X_j\right)\wedge a\right] = \mathbb{E}_{\mathbb{Q}_r}\left[\left(\sum_j X_j\right)\wedge a\right]$$

$$\sup_{\mathbb{Q}\in\mathcal{S}_r} \mathbb{E}_\mathbb{Q}\left[\left(\sum_j X_j - a\right)^+\right] = \mathbb{E}_{\mathbb{Q}_r}\left[\left(\sum_j X_j - a\right)^+\right]$$

$$\sup_{\mathbb{Q}\in\mathcal{S}_0} \mathbb{E}_\mathbb{Q}\left[\sum_j X_j\right] = \mathbb{E}_{\mathbb{Q}_0}\left[\sum_j X_j\right]$$

$$\sup_{\mathbb{Q}\in\mathcal{S}_0} \mathbb{E}_\mathbb{Q}\left[\left(\sum_j X_j\right)\wedge a\right] = \mathbb{E}_{\mathbb{Q}_0}\left[\left(\sum_j X_j\right)\wedge a\right]$$

$$\sup_{\mathbb{Q}\in\mathcal{S}_0} \mathbb{E}_\mathbb{Q}\left[\left(\sum_j X_j - a\right)^+\right] = \mathbb{E}_{\mathbb{Q}_0}\left[\left(\sum_j X_j - a\right)^+\right].$$

The reinsurer is supposed to be default-free (it could be a government institution or a solidarity fund of the insurance industry). We suppose that the agents have access to this reinsurer. We assume that:

$$u_i \le u_r \le u_0 \text{ for all } i,$$

in particular $\mathcal{S}_0 \subset \mathcal{S}_r$. This reflects the fact that on the one hand, the agents are more risk-adverse than the insurers, and on the other hand, the reinsurer being default free, the premia for the reinsurer are higher than for the direct insurer.

The actions of the direct insurer are subject to the rule that after reinsurance, the claims must be covered completely. The direct insurer will therefore take a reinsurance with a retention R, to be determined later. For the retention level R, the cost of the reinsurance is given by (using the commonotonicity of u_r):

$$\rho^R := -u_r\left(-\left(\sum_j X_j - R\right)^+\right) = \mathbb{E}_{\mathbb{Q}_r}\left[\left(\sum_j X_j - R\right)^+\right].$$

To get full coverage of their risks without the input of any capital (that is, $k_0 = R = 0$), the agents should pay a total premium:

$$\rho^0 = -u_r\left(-\sum_j X_j\right) = \mathbb{E}_{\mathbb{Q}_r}\left[\sum_j X_j\right],$$

as the direct insurer can transfer the totality of the claims to the reinsurer at the cost ρ^0. Using the capital allocation principle, we deduce that the premium for such a coverage to be paid by agent j is:

$$\pi_j^r := \mathbb{E}_{\mathbb{Q}_r}\left[X_j\right].$$

For the moment, we consider the amounts π_j^r as the premium-input of the agent j; if they pay higher premia, p_j, the differences, $p_j - \pi_j^r$, are regarded as capital-input. In practice however, the direct insurer brings in a capital $k_0 > 0$ (again, we consider this to be fixed by a regulator), and hence, the retention R will not be zero. This means that whenever $R > 0$, the premia π_j^r that we are considering are not exactly the fair premia (see also Remark 8 below).

As the insurer participates with capital k_0, we must determine the retention level R; as before, we consider R to be the maximal retention level that results in full coverage. The full coverage condition is now given by: $R \le k_0 + \sum_j p_j - \rho^R$, so that the optimal retention is:

$$R = \max\{x \mid x \le k_0 + \sum_j p_j - \rho^R\}.$$

The full coverage condition can be written as: $R - \mathbb{E}_{\mathbb{Q}_r}\left[\left(\sum_j X_j\right) \wedge R\right] \le k_0 + \sum_j (p_j - \pi_j^r)$.

Therefore, the existence and unicity of optimal retention comes using identical arguments as before for Φ, but this time for the function Ψ, defined as:

$$\mathbb{R}_+ \to \mathbb{R}_+;\ x \to x - \mathbb{E}_{\mathbb{Q}_r}\left[\left(\sum_j X_j\right) \wedge x\right].$$

From now on, we always assume R to be the optimal retention, that is: $R = k_0 + \sum_j p_j - \rho^R$, or, alternatively:

$$\Psi(R) = k_0 + \sum_j (p_j - \pi_j^r).$$

In Remark 9, we analyze the dependence of the optimal reserve on the level of the capital.

With the capital input of the insurer being k_0 and the retention level R, the outcome (i.e., surplus) at the end of the contract is:

$$S := k_0 + \sum_j p_j - \rho^R - \left(\sum_j X_j\right) \wedge R \geq 0.$$

We denote by $\lambda_0 = \frac{k_0}{k_0+\sum_j(p_j-\pi_j^r)}$ the proportion of the surplus that the direct insurer is keeping and by $\lambda_i = \frac{p_i-\pi_i^r}{k_0+\sum_j(p_j-\pi_j^r)}$ the proportion of the surplus that agent i is keeping.

We now prove that this procedure of surplus sharing is beneficial for the insurer and for the insured. Let us fist check the utility for the direct insurer.

Theorem 5. *The deal is acceptable for the direct insurer.*

Proof. For the direct insurer, the deal is acceptable if and only if the utility of his/her share of the surplus is not less that k_0, that is $u_0(\lambda_0 S) \geq k_0$. The utility of his share is given by:

$$u_0(\lambda_0 S) = \lambda_0 \left(k_0 + \sum_j p_j - \rho^R - \mathbb{E}_{\mathbb{Q}_0}\left[\left(\sum_j X_j\right) \wedge R\right]\right).$$

This quantity is bigger than k_0 if and only if:

$$-\mathbb{E}_{\mathbb{Q}_0}\left[\left(\sum_j X_j\right) \wedge R\right] - \mathbb{E}_{\mathbb{Q}_r}\left[\left(\sum_j X_j - R\right)^+\right] \geq \sum_j(-\pi_j^r) = -\mathbb{E}_{\mathbb{Q}_r}\left[\sum_j X_j\right] = u_r\left(-\sum_j X_j\right).$$

The utility functions u_0 and u_r are commonotone, and therefore, we have that:

$$u_0\left(-\left(\sum_j X_j\right) \wedge R\right) = -\mathbb{E}_{\mathbb{Q}_0}\left[\left(\sum_j X_j\right) \wedge R\right]$$

$$u_r\left(-\left(\sum_j X_j - R\right)^+\right) = -\mathbb{E}_{\mathbb{Q}_r}\left[\left(\sum_j X_j - R\right)^+\right].$$

Therefore, the inequality is obvious, given $u_0 \geq u_r$. □

Theorem 6. *The deal is acceptable for the insured as soon as* $p_i \leq \sup_{\mathbb{Q}\in\mathcal{S}_r} \mathbb{E}_{\mathbb{Q}}[X_i]$.

Proof. To check the advantage for the insured i, we must show that $u_i(\lambda_i S - p_i) \geq u_i(-X_i)$, that is:

$$u_i(\lambda_i S) \geq p_i + u_i(-X_i)$$

The surplus being nonnegative, the left-hand side is nonnegative. The right side is negative provided the premium p_i is not too big. For instance, if $p_i \leq \sup_{\mathbb{Q}\in\mathcal{S}_r} \mathbb{E}_{\mathbb{Q}}[X_i]$, we have $u_r(p_i - X_i) \leq 0$ and, hence, also $u_i(p_i - X_i) \leq 0$. □

Remark 8. *For each agent, the cost* p_i *was split into two parts: premium-input* π_i^r *and capital-input* $p_i - \pi_i^r$*, with all premia-input summing up to* $\mathbb{E}_{\mathbb{Q}_r}[\sum_j X_j] = -u_r\left(-\sum_j X_j\right)$*. This is higher than the total required premium, which should be the cost of the reinsurance contract plus the cost of the direct insurance of the claims up to the retention level, given as:*

$$-u_r\left(-\left(\sum_j X_j - R\right)^+\right) - u_0\left(-\left(\sum_j X_j\right)\wedge R\right)$$

$$= \mathbb{E}_{\mathbb{Q}_r}\left[\left(\sum_j X_j - R\right)^+\right] + \mathbb{E}_{\mathbb{Q}_0}\left[\left(\sum_j X_j\right)\wedge R\right].$$

Indeed, from our assumptions on the utility functions, we have:

$$\mathbb{E}_{\mathbb{Q}_r}\left[\left(\sum_j X_j - R\right)^+\right] + \mathbb{E}_{\mathbb{Q}_0}\left[\left(\sum_j X_j\right)\wedge R\right] \le \mathbb{E}_{\mathbb{Q}_r}\left[\sum_j X_j\right].$$

Probably, a more fair way to split the cost p_i is to consider:

$$\pi_i = \mathbb{E}_{\mathbb{Q}_r}\left[X_i \mathbf{1}_{\{\sum_j X_j > R\}}\right] + \mathbb{E}_{\mathbb{Q}_0}\left[X_i \mathbf{1}_{\{\sum_j X_j \le R\}}\right]$$

as being the premium-input of agent i and the remaining $p_i - \pi_i$ as being the capital-input of agent i (provided this is positive). This different way of splitting the cost does not affect (of course) the way of computing the optimal retention level, nor the surplus S available after payment of all claims. It is only meant to provide an alternative rule for sharing the surplus: now, $\frac{k_0}{k_0+\sum_j(p_j-\pi_j)}$ is the proportion of the surplus that the direct insurer is keeping and $\frac{p_i-\pi_i}{k_0+\sum_j(p_j-\pi_j)}$ the proportion of the surplus that agent i is keeping. Nevertheless, for such allocations of the surplus, we did not find a simple condition for the premia p_i that ensures that the deals are acceptable for the agents, while respecting $p_i \ge \pi_i$. By a simple rule, we mean a condition on all p_i that does not involve the agent's utility directly.

However, the reader can easily check that for the direct insurer, any allocation among the insured agents of the quantity $\mathbb{E}_{\mathbb{Q}_r}\left[\left(\sum_j X_j - R\right)^+\right] + \mathbb{E}_{\mathbb{Q}_0}\left[\left(\sum_j X_j\right)\wedge R\right]$ leaves the insurer with an outcome that in u_0 utility is equivalent to the initial capital k_0. This is even independent of the retention limit.

Remark 9. *We will now show that with increasing capital k_0, the utility for the direct insurer goes up. Let us denote by $R(k_0)$ the solution of:*

$$R - \mathbb{E}_{\mathbb{Q}_r}\left[\left(\sum_j X_j\right)\wedge R\right] = k_0 + \sum_j (p_j - \pi_j^r).$$

We recall that the function $\Psi(R) = R - \mathbb{E}_{\mathbb{Q}_r}\left[\left(\sum_j X_j\right)\wedge R\right]$ satisfies $\Psi(0) = 0$ and is continuous with $\Psi'(R) = \mathbb{Q}\left(\sum_j X_j \le R\right)$. Hence, it is strictly increasing after it leaves zero and tends to ∞ when R tends to ∞. Furthermore, it is convex. These properties ensure that Ψ^{-1} is well defined on $(0,\infty)$ and is continuous, strictly increasing, and concave.

Furthermore, we recall, that we consider that all $p_j \ge \pi_j^r$ so that $\sum_j(p_j - \pi_j^r) \ge 0$. We can consider $k_0 > 0$, to ensure the positivity of the quantity $k_0 + \sum_j(p_j - \pi_j^r)$. The implicit function theorem then shows that $\frac{dR}{dk_0} \ge 0$.

The utility of the insurer's share of the surplus $u_0(\lambda_0 S)$ can be written as:

$$\begin{aligned}
&\lambda_0\left(k_0+\sum_j p_j-\mathbb{E}_{\mathbb{Q}_0}\left[\left(\sum_j X_j\right)\wedge R\right]-\mathbb{E}_{\mathbb{Q}_r}\left[\left(\sum_j X_j-R\right)^+\right]\right)\\
&=\frac{k_0}{k_0+\sum_j(p_j-\pi_j^r)}\left(k_0+\sum_j(p_j-\pi_j^r)-\mathbb{E}_{\mathbb{Q}_r}\left[\left(\sum_j X_j\right)\wedge R\right]-\mathbb{E}_{\mathbb{Q}_0}\left[\left(\sum_j X_j\right)\wedge R\right]\right)\\
&=\frac{k_0}{k_0+\sum_j(p_j-\pi_j^r)}\left(R-\mathbb{E}_{\mathbb{Q}_0}\left[\left(\sum_j X_j\right)\wedge R\right]\right)\\
&=\frac{k_0}{k_0+\sum_j(p_j-\pi_j^r)}\mathbb{E}_{\mathbb{Q}_0}\left[\left(R-\sum_j X_j\right)^+\right].
\end{aligned}$$

The first factor is clearly increasing in k_0, and the second factor is increasing in R, hence also in k_0. More important is the difference between this utility and the initial capital k_0:

$$\begin{aligned}
u_0(\lambda_0 S)-k_0&=\frac{k_0}{k_0+\sum_j(p_j-\pi_j^r)}\left(R-\mathbb{E}_{\mathbb{Q}_0}\left[\left(\sum_j X_j\right)\wedge R\right]\right)-k_0\\
&=k_0\left(\frac{R-\mathbb{E}_{\mathbb{Q}_0}\left[\left(\sum_j X_j\right)\wedge R\right]}{k_0+\sum_j p_j-\mathbb{E}_{\mathbb{Q}_r}\left[\sum_j X_j\right]}-1\right)\\
&=k_0\left(\frac{\mathbb{E}_{\mathbb{Q}_r}\left[\left(\sum_j X_j\right)\wedge R\right]-\mathbb{E}_{\mathbb{Q}_0}\left[\left(\sum_j X_j\right)\wedge R\right]}{k_0+\sum_j p_j-\mathbb{E}_{\mathbb{Q}_r}\left[\sum_j X_j\right]}\right).
\end{aligned}$$

This shows that when $k_0\to\infty$, the extra return tends to $\mathbb{E}_{\mathbb{Q}_r}\left[\sum_j X_j\right]-\mathbb{E}_{\mathbb{Q}_0}\left[\sum_j X_j\right]$, but also shows that the return on the initial capital tends to zero.

7. Discussion of the Models

There are different shortcomings of the models used. The premia paid by the agents are augmented by the administration or handling costs. Here, we might argue that in the case of a claim, the agents incur these costs themselves. In the handling costs, there is also included the commission paid out to the intermediaries, the brokers. These commissions should not be too high since otherwise, the agents could keep their liabilities or take insurance only for the larger part of the claims, the so-called tail of the distribution.

We believe that in general, the utility functions of the insured agents should not be supposed positively homogeneous. They should be concave. For this reason, we did not make any assumption on the utility function of an agent, except that it is more restrictive than that of an insurer, which seemed to us to be a realistic property. The inequalities $u_i \le u_r \le u_0$ can be verified in case u_0 and u_r are positively homogeneous and u_i is only concave. However, the inequality implies some geometric restrictions on the acceptability set of agent i. For instance, the function u_i cannot be differentiable at $0 \in L^\infty$. Note also that whenever commonotonicity is used, one must suppose that the utility functions are positively homogeneous, as this is a consequence of commonotonicity, Delbaen (2011). In the current paper, we only used coherence and commonotonicity for the utility functions of the insurer and the reinsurer, but these properties were not used for the insured (where we used only the monotonicity of the utility functions and the inequalities implied by the more restrictive utilities).

We supposed the presence of a reinsurer who is default free. In some cases, a government can provide a guarantee, but in general, we must include the possibility of default of the reinsurer.

Some countries require guarantees from the reinsurer either under the form of deposits or under the form of letters of credit issued by "bona fide" financial institutions.

In the case of liability insurance, there might be a rule that in case of the default of the insurer and of the reinsurer, the agent is not liable for the remaining losses. Especially in high-end insurance contracts, such rules and exceptions make the modeling extremely difficult.

In our models, there is a reward for those who take the risk. This is in contradiction with some life insurance practices, where only the amount of the total premium is important.

Author Contributions: These authors contributed equally to this work.

Funding: This research received no external funding.

Conflicts of Interest: The authors declare no conflict of interest.

References

Artzner, Philippe, and Karl-Theodor Eisele. 2018. Oral communication. Strasbourg.

Delbaen, Freddy. 1974. Convex Games and Extreme Points. *Journal of Mathematical Analysis and Applications* 45: 210–33. [CrossRef]

Delbaen, Freddy. 2002. *Coherent Risk Measures. Lectures Given at The Cattedra Galileiana at the Scuola Normale Superiore Di Pisa, March 2000.* Pisa: Scuola Normale Superiore di Pisa.

Delbaen, Freddy. 2011. *Monetary Utility Functions. Lectures Held in 2008 and Published in the Series "Lecture Notes of the University of Osaka"*. Osaka: Osaka University.

Denneberg, Dieter. 1989. Verzerrte Wahrscheinlichkeiten in der. Versicherungsmathematik, quantilabhängige Prämienprinzipen. In *Mathematik-Arbeitspapiere*. Bremen: Universität Bremen, vol. 34.

Denneberg, Dieter, and Dmitri Kaplan. 1998. Die Methode der verzerrten Wahrscheinlichkeiten in der Lebens- und Rentenversicherung. *Blätter DGVFM* 23: 473–87. [CrossRef]

Deprez, Olivier, and Hans U. Gerber. 1985. On convex principles of premium calculation. *Insurance: Mathematics and Economics* 4: 179–89. [CrossRef]

Shapley, Lloyd S. 1971. Cores of Convex Games. *International Journal of Game Theory* 40: 214–25. [CrossRef]

Schmeidler, David. 1986. Integral Representation without Additivity. *Proceedings of the American Mathematical Society* 97: 255–61. [CrossRef]

Wang, Tan. 2002. A Class of Multi-Prior Preferences. Working Paper. Available online: http://citeseerx.ist.psu.edu/viewdoc/download?doi=10.1.1.197.9509&rep=rep1&type=pdf (accessed on 20 December 2018).

Yaari, Menahem E. 1987. The dual theory of choice under risk. *Econometrica* 55: 95–115. [CrossRef]

2

Application of Machine Learning to Mortality Modeling and Forecasting

Susanna Levantesi [1,*] and **Virginia Pizzorusso** [2]

[1] Department of Statistics, Sapienza University of Rome, Viale Regina Elena, 295/G, 00161 Rome, Italy
[2] Ernst and Young Advisory, Via Meravigli, 12, 20123 Milano, Italy; virginia.pizzorusso@gmail.com
* Correspondence: susanna.levantesi@uniroma1.it

Abstract: Estimation of future mortality rates still plays a central role among life insurers in pricing their products and managing longevity risk. In the literature on mortality modeling, a wide number of stochastic models have been proposed, most of them forecasting future mortality rates by extrapolating one or more latent factors. The abundance of proposed models shows that forecasting future mortality from historical trends is non-trivial. Following the idea proposed in Deprez et al. (2017), we use machine learning algorithms, able to catch patterns that are not commonly identifiable, to calibrate a parameter (the machine learning estimator), improving the goodness of fit of standard stochastic mortality models. The machine learning estimator is then forecasted according to the Lee-Carter framework, allowing one to obtain a higher forecasting quality of the standard stochastic models. Out-of sample forecasts are provided to verify the model accuracy.

Keywords: mortality; forecasting; machine learning; Lee-Carter model

1. Introduction

During the 20th Century, mortality has declined at all ages, producing a steep increase in life expectancy. This decrease is mainly due to the reduction of infectious disease mortality (between 1900 and 1950), as well as cardio-circulatory diseases and cancer mortality (in the most recent decades). Knowledge of future mortality rates is an important matter for life insurance companies with the goal of achieving adequate pricing of their life products. Therefore, sophisticated techniques to forecast future mortality rates have become increasingly popular in actuarial science, in order to deal with the longevity risk. Among the stochastic mortality models proposed in the literature, the Lee-Carter model Lee and Carter (1992) is the most widely used in the world, probably for its robustness. The original model applies singular-value decomposition (SVD) to the log-force of mortality to find three latent parameters: a fixed age component and a time component capturing the mortality trend that is multiplied by an age-specific function. Then, the time component is forecasted using a random walk. More recent approaches involve non-linear regression and generalized linear models (GLM), e.g., Brouhns et al. (2002) assumed a Poisson distribution for deaths and calculated the Lee-Carter model parameters by log-likelihood maximization.

In recent years, machine learning techniques have assumed an increasingly central role in many areas of research, from computer science to medicine, including actuarial science. Machine learning is an application of artificial intelligence through a series of algorithms that are optimized on data samples or previous experience. That is, given a certain model defined as a function of a group of parameters, learning consists of improving these parameters using datasets or accumulated experience (the "training data"). Even though machine learning may not explain everything, it is very useful in detecting patterns, even unknown and unidentifiable ones, as well as hidden correlations. In this way, it allows us to understand processes better, make predictions about the future based on historical data, and categorize sets of data automatically.

We can distinguish between supervised and unsupervised learning methods. In the supervised learning methods, the goal is to establish the relations between a range of predictors (independent variables) and a determined target (dependent variable), whereas in the unsupervised learning methods, the algorithm sets patterns among a range of variables in order to group records that show similarities, without considering an output measure. While in the supervised method, the algorithm learns from the dataset the rules that are fed to the machine, in the unsupervised method, it has to identify the rules autonomously. Logistic and multiple regression, classification and regression trees, and naive Bayes are examples of supervised learning methods, while association rules and clustering are classified as unsupervised learning methods.

Despite the increasing usage in different fields of research, applications of machine learning in demography are not so popular. The main reason lies in the findings often being seen as "black boxes" and considered difficult to interpret. Moreover, the algorithms are not theory driven (but quite data driven), while demographers are often interested in analyzing specific hypotheses. They are likely to be unwilling to use algorithms whose decisions cannot be rationally explained.

However, we believe that machine learning techniques can be valuable as a complement to standard mortality models, rather than a substitute.

In the literature related to mortality modeling, there are very few contributions on this topic. The work in Deprez et al. (2017) showed that machine learning algorithms are useful to assess the goodness of fit of the mortality estimates provided by standard stochastic mortality models (they considered Lee-Carter and Renshaw-Haberman models). They applied a regression tree boosting machine to "analyze how the modeling should be improved based on feature components of an individual, such as its age or its birth cohort. This (non-parametric) regression approach then allows us to detect the weaknesses of different mortality models" (p. 337). In addition, they investigated cause-of-death mortality. In a recent paper, the work in Hainaut (2018) used neural networks to find the latent factors of mortality and forecast them according to a random walk with drift. Finally, the work in Richman and Wüthrich (2018) extended the Lee-Carter model to multiple populations using neural networks.

We investigate the ability of machine learning to improve the accuracy of some standard stochastic mortality models, both in the estimation and forecasting of mortality rates. The novelty of this paper is primarily in the mortality forecasting that takes advantage of machine learning, clearly capturing patterns that are not identifiable with a standard mortality model. Following Deprez et al. (2017), we use tree-based machine learning techniques to calibrate a parameter (the machine learning estimator) to be applied to mortality rates fitted by the standard mortality model.

We analyze three famous stochastic mortality models: the Lee-Carter model Lee and Carter (1992), which is still the most frequently implemented, the Renshaw-Haberman model Renshaw and Haberman (2006), which also considers the cohort effect, and the Plat model Plat (2009), which tries to combine the parameters of the Lee-Carter model with those of the Cairns-Blake-Dowd model with the cohort effect, named "M7" (Cairns et al. (2009)).

Three different kinds of supervised learning methods are considered for calibrating the machine learning estimator: decision tree, random forest, and gradient boosting, which are all tree-based.

We show that the implementation of these machine learning techniques, based on features components such as age, sex, calendar year, and birth cohort, leads to a better fit of the historical data, with respect to the estimates given by the Lee-Carter, Renshaw-Haberman, and Plat models. We also apply the same logic to improve the mortality forecasts provided by the Lee-Carter model, where the machine learning estimator is extrapolated using the Lee-Carter framework. Out-of-sample tests are performed for the improved model in order to verify the quality of forecasting.

The paper is organized as follows. In Section 2, we specify the model and introduce the tree-based machine learning estimators. In Section 3, we present the stochastic mortality models considered in the paper. In Section 4, we illustrate the usage of tree-based machine learning estimators to improve both the fitting and forecasting quality of the original mortality models. Conclusions and further research are then given in Section 5.

2. The Model

We consider the following categorical variables, identifying an individual: gender (g), age (a), calendar year (t), and year of birth (c). We assign to each individual the feature $\mathbf{x} = (g, a, t, c) \in \mathcal{X}$ with $\mathcal{X} = \mathcal{G} \times \mathcal{A} \times \mathcal{T} \times \mathcal{C}$ the feature space, where: $\mathcal{G} = \{males, females\}$, $\mathcal{A} = \{0, ..., \omega\}$, $\mathcal{T} = \{t_1, ..., t_n\}$, $\mathcal{C} = \{c_1, ..., c_m\}$. Other categorical variables could be included in the feature space X, e.g., the marital status, the income, and other individual information.

We assume that the number of deaths $D_{\mathbf{x}}$ meets the following conditions:

- $D_{\mathbf{x}}$ are independent in $\{\mathbf{x} \in \mathcal{X}\}$;
- $D_{\mathbf{x}} \sim Pois(m_{\mathbf{x}} \cdot E_{\mathbf{x}})$ for all $\{\mathbf{x} \in \mathcal{X}\}$.

where $m_{\mathbf{x}}$ is the central death rate and $E_{\mathbf{x}}$ are the exposures.

Let us define $d_{\mathbf{x}}^{\text{mdl}}$ as the expected number of deaths estimated by a standard stochastic mortality model (such as Lee-Carter, Cairns-Blake-Dowd, etc.) and $m_{\mathbf{x}}^{\text{mdl}}$ the corresponding central death rate. Following Deprez et al. (2017), but modeling the central death death rate instead of mortality rate ($q_{\mathbf{x}}$), we initially set:

- $m_{\mathbf{x}} = m_{\mathbf{x}}^{\text{mdl}}$
- $D_{\mathbf{x}} \sim Pois(\psi_{\mathbf{x}} \cdot d_{\mathbf{x}}^{\text{mdl}}), \qquad \text{with} \quad \psi_{\mathbf{x}} \equiv 1, \quad d_{\mathbf{x}}^{\text{mdl}} = m_{\mathbf{x}}^{\text{mdl}} E_{\mathbf{x}}$

The condition $\psi_{\mathbf{x}} \equiv 1$ means that the specified mortality model perfectly fits the crude rates. However, in the real world, a mortality model could overestimate ($\psi_{\mathbf{x}} \leq 1$) or underestimate ($\psi_{\mathbf{x}} \geq 1$) the crude rates. Therefore, we calibrate the parameter $\psi_{\mathbf{x}}$, based on the feature $\mathbf{x}$, according to three different machine learning techniques. We find $\psi_{\mathbf{x}}$ as a solution of a regression tree algorithm applied to the ratio between the death observations and the corresponding value estimated by the specified mortality model $\frac{D_{\mathbf{x}}}{d_{\mathbf{x}}^{\text{mdl}}}$:

$$\frac{D_{\mathbf{x}}}{d_{\mathbf{x}}^{\text{mdl}}} \sim \text{gender} + \text{age} + \text{year} + \text{cohort} \tag{1}$$

We denote by $\hat{\psi}_{\mathbf{x}}^{\text{mdl,ML}}$ the machine learning estimator obtained by solving Equation (1), where mdl indicates the stochastic mortality model and ML the machine learning algorithm used to improve the mortality rates given by a certain model. The estimator $\hat{\psi}_{\mathbf{x}}^{\text{mdl,ML}}$ is then applied to the central death rate of the specified mortality model, $m_{\mathbf{x}}^{\text{mdl}}$, aiming to obtain a better fit of the observed data:

$$m_{\mathbf{x}}^{\text{mdl,ML}} = \hat{\psi}_{\mathbf{x}}^{\text{mdl,ML}} \cdot m_{\mathbf{x}}^{\text{mdl}}, \quad \forall \mathbf{x} \in \mathcal{X} \tag{2}$$

As in Deprez et al. (2017), we measure the improvement in the mortality rates attained by the tree growing algorithm through the relative changes of central death rates:

$$\Delta m_{\mathbf{x}}^{\text{mdl,ML}} = \frac{m_{\mathbf{x}}^{\text{mdl,ML}} - m_{\mathbf{x}}^{\text{mdl}}}{m_{\mathbf{x}}^{\text{mdl}}} = \hat{\psi}_{\mathbf{x}}^{\text{ML}} - 1 \tag{3}$$

The work in Hainaut (2018) used neural networks to learn the logarithm of the central death rates directly from the features of the mortality data, by using age, calendar year, and gender (and region) as predictors in a neural network. We instead rely on the classical form of the Lee-Carter model that we improve ex-post using machine learning algorithms, considered complementary and not an alternative to the standard mortality modeling.

To estimate $\hat{\psi}_{\mathbf{x}}^{\text{mdl,ML}}$, we use the following tree-based machine learning (ML) techniques:

- Decision tree

- Random forest
- Gradient boosting

2.1. Decision Trees

The tree-based methods for regression and classification (Breiman et al. 1984) have become popular alternatives to linear regression. They are based on the partition of the feature space $\mathcal{X}$, through a sequence of binary splits, and the set of splitting rules used to segment the predictor space can be summarized in a tree (Hastie et al. 2016). Once the entire feature space is split into a certain number of simple regions recursively, the response for a given observation can be predicted using the mean of the training observations in the region to which that observation belongs (James et al. 2017; Alpaydin 2010).

Let $(\mathcal{X}_\tau)_{\tau \in \mathcal{T}}$ be the partition of $\mathcal{X}$; the decision tree estimator is calculated as:

$$\hat{\psi}(\mathbf{x}) = \sum_{\tau \in \mathcal{T}} \bar{\psi}_\tau \mathbb{1}_{\{\mathbf{x} \in \mathcal{X}_\tau\}} \tag{4}$$

Decision trees (DT) algorithms have advantages over other types of regression models. As pointed out by James et al. (2017): they are easy to interpret; they can easily handle qualitative predictors without the need to create dummy variables; they can catch any kind of correlation in the data. However, they suffer from some important drawbacks: they do not always have predictive accuracy levels similar to those of traditional regression and classification models; they can lack robustness: a small modification of the data can produce a tree that strongly differs from the one initially estimated.

The ML estimator is obtained using the R package `rpart` (Therneau and Atkinson 2017). The algorithm provides the estimate of $\hat{\psi}(\mathbf{x})$ given by the average of the response variable values $\psi(\mathbf{x})$ belonging to the same region identified by the regression tree. The values of the complexity parameter (cp) for the decision trees are chosen with the aim of making the number of splits considered uniform.

2.2. Random Forest

The aggregation of many decision trees can improve the predictive performance of trees. Therefore, we first apply bagging (also called bootstrap aggregation) to produce a certain number, B, of decision trees from the bootstrapped training samples, in turn obtained from the bootstrap of the original training dataset. Random forest (RF) differs from bagging in the way of considering the predictors: RF algorithms account only for a random subset of the predictors at each split in the tree, as described in detail by Breiman (2001). If there is a strong predictor in the dataset, the other predictors will have more of a chance to be chosen as split candidates from the final set of predictors (James et al. 2017). The RF estimator is calculated as follows:

$$\hat{\psi}(\mathbf{x}) = \frac{1}{B} \sum_{b=1}^{B} \hat{\psi}^{(b)}(\mathbf{x}) \tag{5}$$

The RF estimator is obtained by applying the algorithm from the R package `randomForest` (Liaw 2018). Since this procedure proved to be very costly from a computational point of view, the number of trees must be carefully chosen: it should not be too large, but at the same time able to produce an adequate percentage of variance explained and a low mean of squared residuals, MSR.

2.3. Gradient Boosting

Consider the loss in using a certain function to predict a variable on the training data; gradient boosting (GB) aims at minimizing the in-sample loss with respect to this function by a stage-wise adaptive learning algorithm that combines weak predictors.

Let $\psi(\mathbf{x})$ be the function; the gradient boosting algorithm finds an approximation $\hat{\psi}(\mathbf{x})$ to the function $\psi(\mathbf{x})$ that minimizes the expected value of the specified differentiable loss function (optimization problem). At each stage i of gradient boosting ($1 \leq i \leq N$), we suppose that there is some imperfect models $\hat{\psi}(\mathbf{x}_i)$, then the gradient boosting algorithm improves on $\hat{\psi}(\mathbf{x}_i)$ by constructing a new model that adds an estimator h to provide a better model:

$$\hat{\psi}(\mathbf{x}_i) = \hat{\psi}(\mathbf{x}_{i-1}) + \lambda_i h_i(\mathbf{x}) \tag{6}$$

where $h_i \in \mathcal{H}$ is a base learner function ($\mathcal{H}$ is the set of arbitrary differentiable functions) and λ is a multiplier obtained by solving the optimization problem. The GB estimator is obtained using the R package gbm (Ridgeway 2007). The gbm package requires choosing the number of trees (*n.trees*) and other key parameters as the number of cross-validation folds (*cv.folds*), the depth of each tree involved in the estimate (*interaction.depth*), and the learning rate parameter (*shrinkage*). The number of trees, representing the number of GB iterations, must be accurately chosen, as a high number would reduce the error on the training set, while a low number would result in overfitting. The number of cross-validation folds to perform should be chosen according to the dataset size. In general, five-fold cross-validation, which corresponds to 20% of the data involved in testing, is considered a good choice in many cases. Finally, the interaction depth represents the highest level of variable interactions allowed or the maximum nodes for each tree.

3. Mortality Models

Let us consider the generalized age period cohort (GAPC) stochastic mortality models' family (see Villegas et al. 2015 for further details). In the GAPC models, the effects of age, calendar year, and cohort are caught by a predictor, in our framework denoted by $\eta_{\mathbf{x}}$, as follows:

$$\eta_{\mathbf{x}} = \alpha_a + \sum_{i=1}^{n} \beta_a^{(i)} \kappa_t^{(i)} + \beta_a^{(0)} \gamma_{t-a}, \quad \forall \mathbf{x} = (g, a, t, c) \in \mathcal{X} \tag{7}$$

where:

- α_a: age-specific parameter providing the average age profile of mortality;
- $\beta_a^{(i)} \cdot \kappa_t^{(i)}$, $\forall i$: age-period terms describing the mortality trends ($\kappa_t^{(i)}$ is the time index, and $\beta_a^{(i)}$ modifies the effect of $\kappa_t^{(i)}$ across ages);
- $\beta_a^{(0)} \cdot \gamma_{t-a}$: represents the cohort effect, where γ_{t-a} is the cohort parameter and $\beta_a^{(0)}$ modifies its effect across ages ($c = t - a$ is the year of birth).

The mortality predictor is related to a link function g, so that: $\eta_{\mathbf{x}} = g\left(\mathbb{E}\left(\frac{D_{\mathbf{x}}}{E_{\mathbf{x}}}\right)\right)$. In this paper, we consider the log link function and assume that the numbers of deaths $D_{\mathbf{x}}$ follow a Poisson distribution.

3.1. Lee-Carter Model

Under the above-described framework, the Lee-Carter (LC) model as proposed by Brouhns et al. (2002) requires a log link function to target the central death rate. In the LC model, the logarithm of the central death rate is described by:

$$\log(m_{\mathbf{x}}) = \alpha_a + \beta_a^{(1)} \kappa_t^{(1)} \tag{8}$$

with the constraints: $\sum_{t \in \mathcal{T}} \kappa_t^{(1)} = 0$, $\sum_{a \in \mathcal{A}} \beta_a^{(1)} = 1$ to avoid identifiability problems with the parameters. In order to forecast mortality with the LC model, the time index $\kappa_t^{(1)}$ is modeled by an autoregressive integrated moving average (ARIMA) process. In general, a random walk with drift properly fits the data:

$$\kappa_t^{(1)} = \kappa_{t-1}^{(1)} + \delta + \epsilon_t, \quad \epsilon_t \sim N(0, \sigma_k^2) \tag{9}$$

where δ is the drift parameter and ϵ_t are the error terms, normally distributed with null mean and variance σ_k^2.

3.2. Renshaw-Haberman Model

The Renshaw-Haberman model (Renshaw and Haberman (2006)) extends the LC model by including a cohort effect. The model's predictor has the following expression, where the log link function is used to target the central death rate:

$$\log(m_{\mathbf{x}}) = \alpha_a + \beta_a^{(1)}\kappa_t^{(1)} + \beta_a^{(0)}\gamma_{t-a} \tag{10}$$

According to Haberman and Renshaw (2011) and Hunt and Villegas (2015), we set $\beta_a^{(0)} = 1$ $\forall a \in \mathcal{A}$, as the model is more stable with respect to the original version.

$$\log(m_{\mathbf{x}}) = \alpha_a + \beta_a^{(1)}\kappa_t^{(1)} + \gamma_{t-a} \tag{11}$$

The model is subject to the following constraints, where $c = t - a$: $\sum_{t\in\mathcal{T}} \kappa_t^{(1)} = 0$, $\sum_{a\in\mathcal{A}} \beta_a^{(1)} = 1$, and $\sum_{c\in\mathcal{C}} \gamma_c = 0$. Parameters $\kappa_t^{(1)}$ and γ_{t-a} are modeled by ARIMA processes, assuming the independence between them.

3.3. Plat Model

The Plat model Plat (2009) aims to combine M7 and LC models in order to obtain a model appropriate for the entire age range and for capturing the cohort effect, thus overcoming the disadvantages of the previous models.

$$\log(m_{\mathbf{x}}) = \alpha_a + \kappa_t^{(1)} + \kappa_t^{(2)}(\bar{a} - a) + \kappa_t^{(3)}(\bar{a} - a)^+ + \gamma_{t-a} \tag{12}$$

where $(\bar{a} - a)^+ = \max(\bar{a} - a, 0)$. This model is obtained from Equation (7) by setting $\beta_a^{(1)} = 1$, $\beta_a^{(2)} = \bar{a} - a$, $\beta_a^{(3)} = (\bar{a} - a)^+$, and $\beta_a^{(0)} = 1$ and using the log link function to target the central death rate.

The Plat model is subject to the following constraints: $\sum_t \kappa_t^{(1)} = 0$, $\sum_t \kappa_t^{(2)} = 0$, $\sum_t \kappa_t^{(3)} = 0$, $\sum_{c\in\mathcal{C}} \gamma_c = 0$, $\sum_{c\in\mathcal{C}} \gamma_c c = 0$, $\sum_{c\in\mathcal{C}} \gamma_c c^2 = 0$. As described in Villegas et al. (2015): "the first three constraints ensure that the period indexes are centered around zero, while the last three constraints ensure that the cohort effect fluctuates around zero and has no linear or quadratic trend".

4. Numerical Analysis

4.1. Model Fitting

We fit the Lee-Carter (LC), Renshaw-Haberman (RH) and Plat models on the Italian population. Data were downloaded from the Human Mortality Database (www.mortality.org), while model fitting was performed with `StMoMo` package provided by Villegas et al. (2015). The following sets of gender $\mathcal{G}$, ages $\mathcal{A}$, years $\mathcal{T}$, and cohort $\mathcal{C}$ were considered in the analysis:

$$\mathcal{G} = \{males, females\},\ \mathcal{A} = \{0, ..., 100\},\ \mathcal{T} = \{1915, ..., 2014\},\ \text{and}\ \mathcal{C} = \{1815, ..., 2014\}.$$

The model accuracy was measured by the Bayes information criterion (BIC) and the Akaike information criterion (AIC), which are measures generally used to evaluate the goodness of fit of mortality models[1]. Log-likelihood $\mathcal{L}$, AIC and BIC values are reported in Table 1, from which we observe that the RH model fits the historical data very well. It has the highest BIC and AIC values for both genders, with respect to the other models; then, in order, the LC model and the Plat model.

---

[1] The AIC and BIC statistics are both function of the log-likelihood, $\mathcal{L}$, and the number of parameters involved in the model, ν: AIC $= 2\nu - 2\mathcal{L}$, and BIC $= \nu \log N - 2\mathcal{L}$, where N is the number of observations.

Table 1. Log-likelihood, AIC and BIC statistics for LC, RH and Plat model. Ages 0–100 and years 1915–2014, Italian population.

Gender:	**Males**			**Females**		
Model:	**LC**	**RH**	**Plat**	**LC**	**RH**	**Plat**
ν	300	499	496	300	499	496
$\mathcal{L}$	−643,226	−307,985	−875,549	−176,421	−137,098	−281,518
AIC (Rank)	1,287,051 (2)	616,967 (1)	1,752,089 (3)	353,442 (2)	275,193 (1)	564,028 (3)
BIC (Rank)	1,289,218 (2)	620,570 (1)	1,755,671 (3)	355,608 (2)	278,796 (1)	567,610 (3)

The goodness of fit is also tested by the residuals analysis. From Figure 1, we can observe that the RH provided the best fit, despite the highest number of parameters. The LC model provided a good fit especially for the old-age population, while the Plat model provided the worst performance despite the high number of parameters involved.

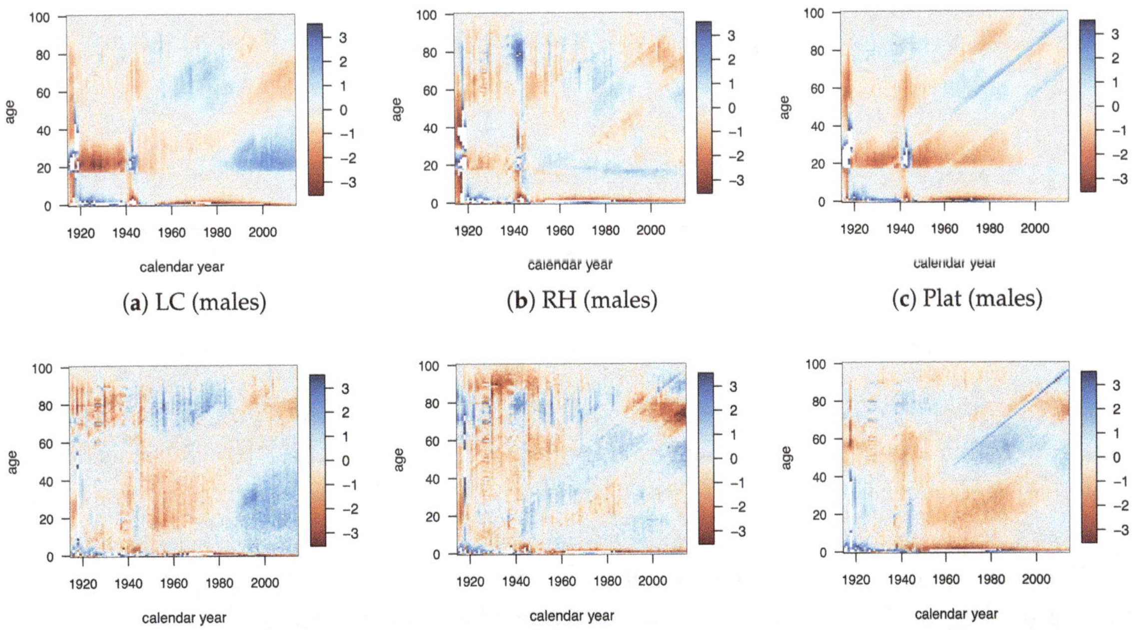

(**a**) LC (males) (**b**) RH (males) (**c**) Plat (males)
(**d**) LC (females) (**e**) RH (females) (**f**) Plat (females)

Figure 1. Heat map of standardized residuals of the mortality models. Ages 0–100 and years 1915–2014, Italian population.

4.2. Model Fitting Improved by Machine Learning

In the following, we specify the parameters used to calibrate the ML algorithms described in Section 2 using the `rpart`, `randomForest`, and `gbm` packages, respectively:

- $\hat{\psi}_{\mathbf{x}}^{\text{mdl,DT}}$ was estimated with the `rpart` package by setting: $cp = 0.003$ (complexity parameter);
- $\hat{\psi}_{\mathbf{x}}^{\text{mdl,RF}}$ was estimated with the `randomForest` package by setting: $ntrees = 200$ (number of trees). Since this procedure proved to be very costly from a computational point of view, we limited the number of trees to 200, in order to guarantee both an adequate percentage of variance explained by the model and a low mean of squared residuals, MSR (see Table 2);
- $\hat{\psi}_{\mathbf{x}}^{\text{mdl,GB}}$ is estimated with the `gbm` package by setting: $n.trees = 5000$ (number of trees); $cv.folds = 5$ (number of cross-validation folds); $interaction.depth = 6$; $shrinkage = 0.001$ (learning rate) according to the algorithm implementation speed. The parameter $cv.folds$ is used to estimate the optimal number of iterations through the function $gbm.perf$ (see Figure 2).

Table 2. Explained variance and MSR by the RF algorithm for the LC, RH, and Plat model. Ages 0–100 and years 1915–2014, Italian population.

Model	Explained Variance	MSR
LC	96.25%	0.0263
RH	86.48%	0.0057
Plat	91.14%	0.0058

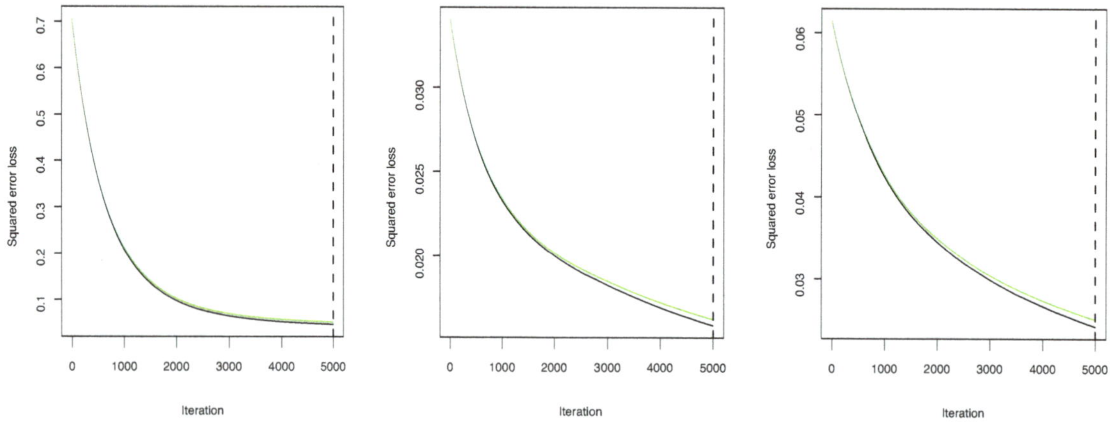

(**a**) Lee-Carter (**b**) RH (**c**) Plat

Figure 2. Estimates of the optimal number of boosting iterations for the LC, RH, and Plat model. Black line: Out-of-bag estimates; green line: cross-validation estimates.

The level of improvement in central death rates resulting from the application of ML algorithms was measured by $\Delta m_{\mathbf{x}}^{\text{mdl,ML}}$, the relative changes described in Equation (3).

Numerical results for the LC, RH, and Plat model combined with the tree-based ML algorithms are shown in Figure 3 for males. Similar results were obtained for females.

The white areas represent very small variations of $\Delta m_{\mathbf{x}}^{\text{mdl,ML}}$, approximately around zero. Larger white areas were observed for gradient boosting applied to the LC and RH model. In all cases, there were also significant changes that were less prominent for the RH model that best fit the historical data. Many regions were identified by diagonal splits (highlighting a cohort effect), strengthening our choice to insert the cohort parameter in the decision tree algorithms.

Especially for the LC model, we point out that the relative changes were mainly concentrated in the young ages. For the Plat model, we observed small values of $\Delta m_{\mathbf{x}}^{\text{PL,ML}}$ with respect to the other mortality models, with the exception of the population aged under 40 that showed quite significant changes. From these early results, DT and RT seemed to work better than the GB algorithm.

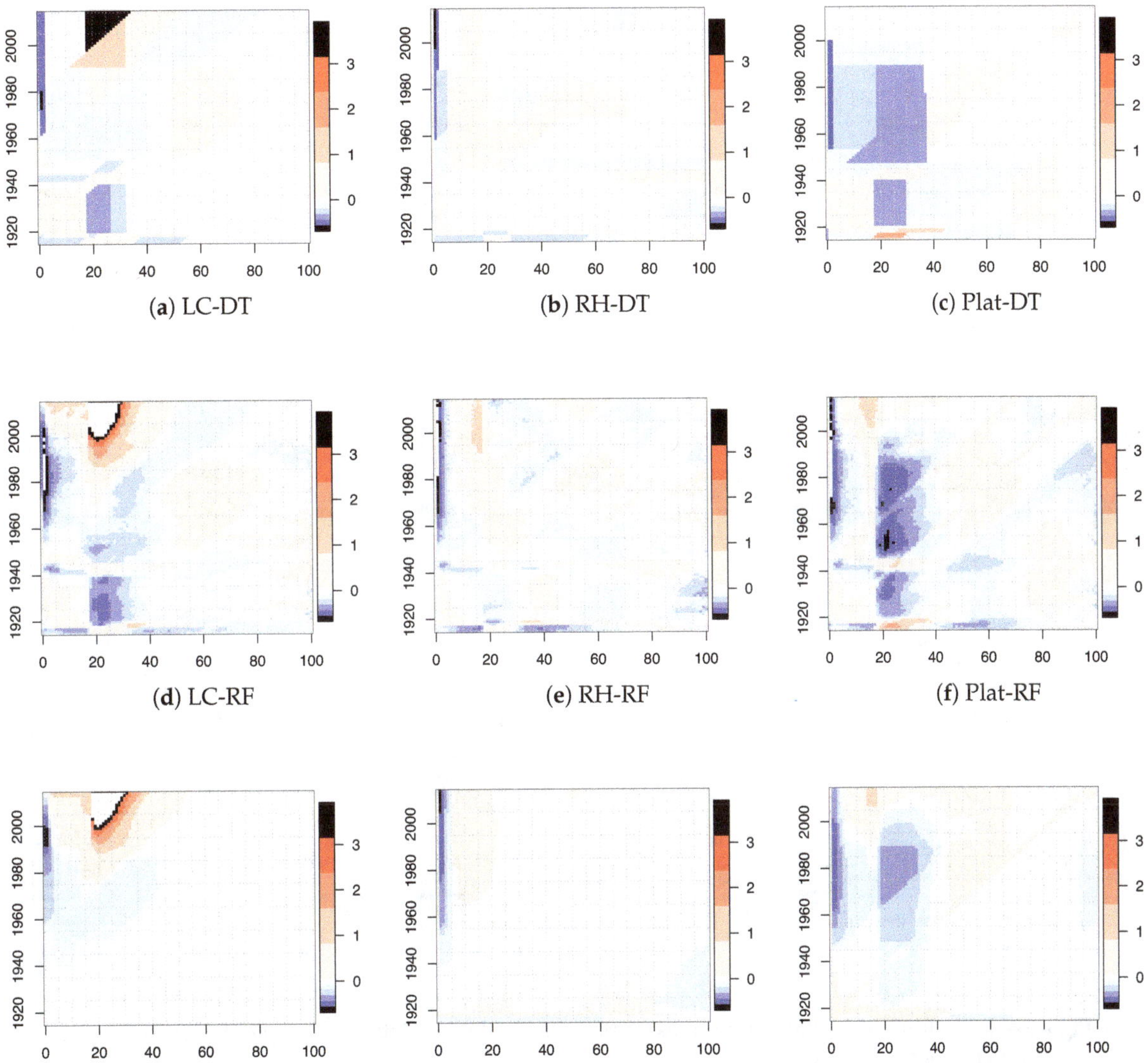

(a) LC-DT (b) RH-DT (c) Plat-DT
(d) LC-RF (e) RH-RF (f) Plat-RF
(g) LC-GB (h) RH-GB (i) Plat-GB

Figure 3. Values of $\Delta m_{\mathbf{x}}^{\mathrm{mdl,ML}}$. Italian male population. Ages 0–100 and years 1915–2014.

Since the most significant changes were concentrated in the younger ages, we show the mortality rates (in log scale) only for the age group 0–50 (Figure 4). For the sake of brevity, we show the results for the male population. Similar results were obtained for females and are reported in the Appendix (see Figure A1).

From the plots, we can argue that ML estimators led to an improvement in the quality of fit in all the mortality models considered. The plots show that the application of an ML estimator involves significant changes in the values of the mortality rate with a significant improvement in the fitting of the data. Among the stochastic mortality models considered here, the Plat model is the one that achieved the highest fit improvements from the use of ML algorithms.

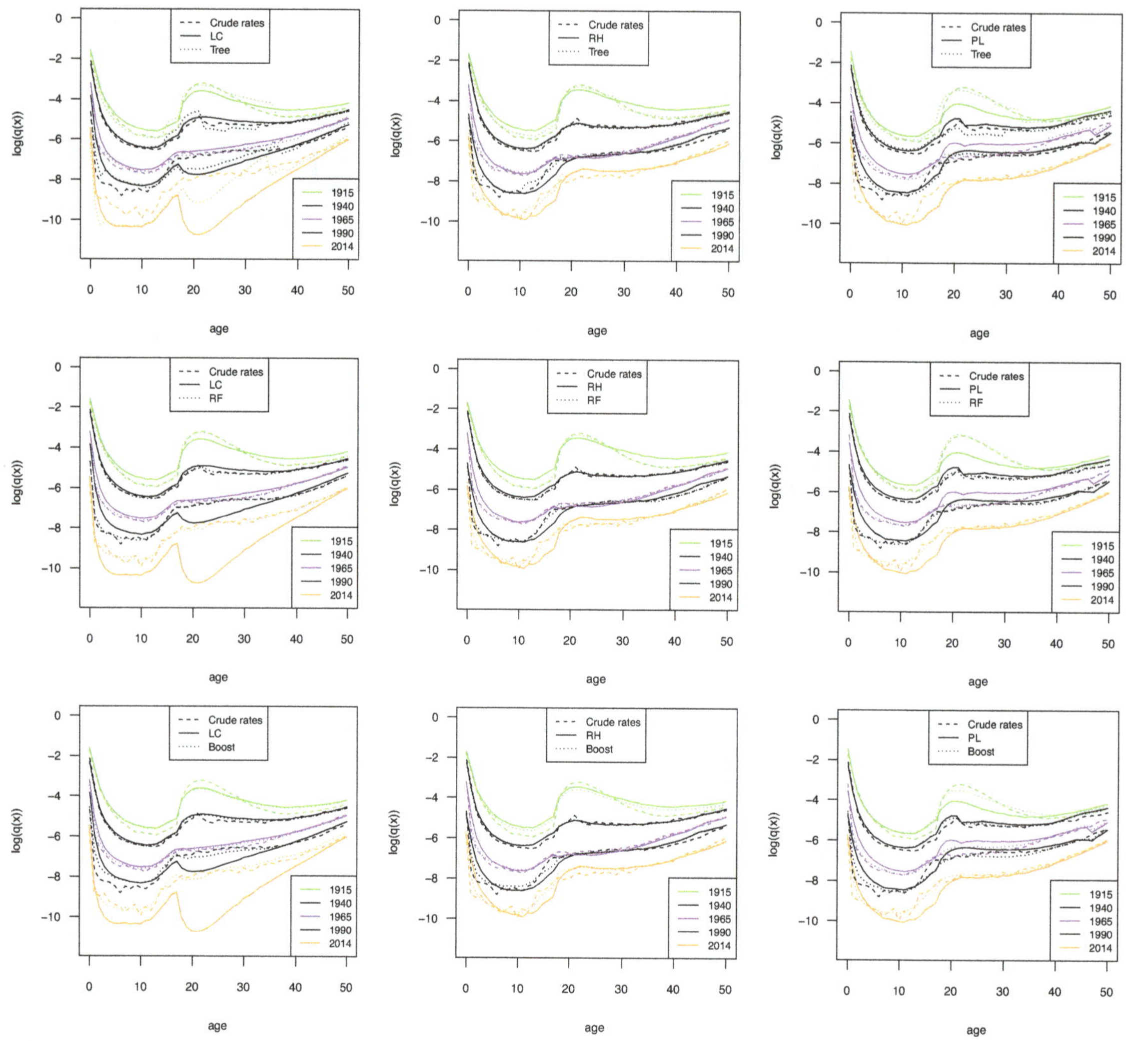

Figure 4. Logarithm of mortality rate, ages 0–50. Italian male population. Examples for cohorts born in 1915, 1940, 1965, 1990, and 2014.

Further, we measured the goodness of fit of the models with the mean absolute percent error (MAPE), defined as:

$$\text{MAPE} = \frac{100}{N}\sum_{\mathbf{x}}\left|\frac{m_{\mathbf{x}}^{\text{mdl,ML}} - \hat{m}_{\mathbf{x}}^{\text{mdl,ML}}}{m_{\mathbf{x}}^{\text{mdl,ML}}}\right| \tag{13}$$

where N is the data dimension and $m_{\mathbf{x}}^{\text{mdl,ML}}$ and $\hat{m}_{\mathbf{x}}^{\text{mdl,ML}}$ are respectively the actual and estimated values of mortality. The MAPEs are summarized in Table 3.

Table 3. MAPE of fitted with respect to observed data for the LC, RH, and Plat model, before (No ML) and after (DT, RF, GB) the application of ML algorithms. Ages 0–100 and years 1915–2014, Italian population. Values in bold indicate the specification with the smaller MAPE for each model.

Gender	Males			Females		
Model	LC	RH	Plat	LC	RH	Plat
No ML	19.48%	18.03%	25.81%	13.83%	13.96%	22.34%
DT	11.06%	11.57%	13.69%	9.42%	9.12%	11.53%
RF	**4.85%**	**4.89%**	**4.79%**	**4.61%**	**4.65%**	**4.49%**
GB	13.80%	11.35%	14.59%	8.48%	7.84%	9.77%

The highest MAPE reduction was achieved by the Plat model, with a reduction from 25.81% to 4.79% after the application of the RF algorithm (from 22.34% to 4.49% for the female population).

In summary, all the ML algorithms improved the standard stochastic mortality models herein considered, and the RF algorithm turned out to be the most effective one.

4.3. LC Model Forecasting Improved by Machine Learning

In this subsection, we describe how the ML estimator, $\hat{\psi}_{\mathrm{x}}$, can be used to obtain an improvement of the mortality forecasting given by the standard stochastic models.

Setting aside the logic of machine learning, our idea was to model and forecast $\hat{\psi}_{\mathrm{x}}$ using the same framework of the original mortality model. The forecasted values of $\hat{\psi}_{\mathrm{x}}$ were then used to improve the forecasted values of mortality rates obtained from the original model. This approach was tested on the LC model; therefore, the ML estimator $\hat{\psi}_{\mathrm{x}}^{\mathrm{LC,ML}}$ is modeled as:

$$\log(\hat{\psi}_{\mathrm{x}}^{\mathrm{LC,ML}}) = \alpha_a^{\psi} + \beta_a^{(1,\psi)}\kappa_t^{(1,\psi)} \tag{14}$$

where the sets of parameters α_a^{ψ}, $\beta_a^{(1,\psi)}$, and $\kappa_t^{(1,\psi)}$ have the same meaning of α_a, $\beta_a^{(1)}$, and $\kappa_t^{(1)}$ in Equation (8). Combining Equations (2), (8), and (14), we obtain the following LC model improved by machine learning:

$$\log(m_{\mathrm{x}}^{\mathrm{LC,ML}}) = (\alpha_a^{\psi} + \alpha_a) + \beta_a^{(1,\psi)}\kappa_t^{(1,\psi)} + \beta_a^{(1)}\kappa_t^{(1)} \tag{15}$$

To verify the model accuracy, we provide out-of-sample forecasts, where the fitting period was set to 1915–2000 and the forecasting period to 2001–2014. In the forecasting, $\kappa_t^{(1,\psi)}$ and $\kappa_t^{(1)}$ were both modeled by a random walk with drift using values for the past 41 years (1960–2000). The plots of the time-dependent parameters $\kappa_t^{(1)}$ and $\kappa_t^{(1,\psi)}$ by gender are provided in the Appendix (Figure A2).

The values of parameter $\kappa_t^{(1)}$ of the LC standard model (Figure A2a,b) have been strongly decreasing from the end of the Second World War, which resulted in a strong reduction of mortality over time, with a further acceleration after the mid-1980s. The ML algorithms reduced this effect through the parameter $\kappa_t^{(1,\psi)}$,which showed a growing trend after 1960 with greater strength since the 1980s (Figure A2c–h).

The use of the same framework of the original mortality model to fit and forecast the ML estimators $\hat{\psi}_{\mathrm{x}}$ has a dual purpose. On the one hand, it allows improving the forecasting provided by the original model and on the other hand analyzing the effect of the improvement directly on the model's parameters. As discussed in the Introduction, machine learning is recognized to be very effective at detecting unknown and unidentifiable patterns in the data, but lacks an underlying theory that may be fundamental to provide a rational explanation of the results obtained. From this point of view, our approach can contribute to filling the gap between machine learning and theory combining a data-driven approach with a model-driven one.

Goodness of Forecasting

The forecasting results given by the out-of-sample test were compared using two measures: the root mean squared logarithmic error (RMSLE) and the root mean squared error (RMSE). The first one (RMSLE) takes into account $\log m_{\mathrm{x}}$, providing a relatively large amount of weight to errors at young ages, while the second one (RMSE) is based on m_{x} and provides a relatively large amount of weight to errors at older ages.

$$\mathrm{RMSLE} = \sqrt{\frac{\sum_{\mathrm{x}} (\log(\hat{m}_{\mathrm{x}}) - \log(m_{\mathrm{x}}))^2}{N}} \tag{16}$$

$$\mathrm{RMSE} = \sqrt{\frac{\sum_{\mathrm{x}} (\hat{m}_{\mathrm{x}} - m_{\mathrm{x}})^2}{N}} \tag{17}$$

Table 4 shows the out-of-sample test results for the LC model improved by machine learning when $\hat{\psi}_x^{LC,ML}$ was forecasted using the LC framework. Values in bold indicate the model with the smaller RMSLE and RMSE. The RF algorithm provided the best performance, except for male RMSE, where GB was the best. The higher reduction of RMSLE was 77% for male and 71% for female, while when considering RMSE, it was 51% for male and 80% for females. However, we can conclude that all the ML estimators produced a significant improvement in forecasting with respect to the standard LC model.

Table 4. Out-of-sample test results: RMSLE and RMSE for the LC model without and with machine learning. ML estimator $\hat{\psi}_x^{LC,ML}$ modeled according to the LC framework. Years 2000–2014 (fitting period: 1915–2000). Values in bold indicate the model with the smaller RMSLE and RMSE.

	RMSLE		**RMSE**	
Model	**Males**	**Females**	**Males**	**Females**
LC	0.0290	0.0195	0.7282	0.7734
LC, DT	0.0139	0.0068	0.3567	0.5351
LC, RF	**0.0083**	**0.0044**	0.3624	**0.1532**
LC, GB	0.0100	0.0056	**0.3536**	0.1841

4.4. Results for a Shorter Estimation Period: 1960–2014

We now use a more recent period (starting from 1960 instead of 1915) to analyze the level of the improvement provided by ML algorithms on a smaller dataset. The aim was to check if the change of the calibration period can have an important impact on the results, since the ML algorithms work better with larger datasets. We show in Table 5 the values of MAPE used to analyze the quality of fitting. Furthermore, for a shorter calibration period, all the ML algorithms improved the standard stochastic mortality models, and the level of the improvement in the model fit remained high. The RF algorithm continued to be the best one.

Table 5. MAPE of fitted with respect to observed data for the LC, RH, and Plat model, before (No ML) and after (DT, RF, GB) the application of ML algorithms. Ages 0–100 and years 1960–2014, Italian population. Values in bold indicate the specification with the smaller MAPE for each model.

Gender		**Males**			**Females**	
Model	**LC**	**RH**	**Plat**	**LC**	**RH**	**Plat**
No ML	11.08%	8.51%	12.67%	9.20%	8.44%	12.32%
DT	5.86%	5.27%	6.25%	5.90%	5.71%	6.62%
RF	**4.07%**	**4.02%**	**3.89%**	**4.95%**	**4.79%**	**4.81%**
GB	6.04%	4.84%	6.07%	5.49%	5.16%	6.27%

The values of $\Delta m_x^{mdl,ML}$ for the LC, RH, and Plat model combined with the tree-based ML algorithms for the new calibration period are shown in Figure 5 for males. Similar results were obtained for females and are reported in the Appendix (see Figure A3).

Also in this case, there were significant changes, but there were less regions identified by diagonal splits (highlighting a cohort effect) with respect to the time period 1915–2014. Moreover, we observed that the significant changes were concentrated both in the young and old ages. The concentration in the old ages was less evident in the 1915–2014 analysis.

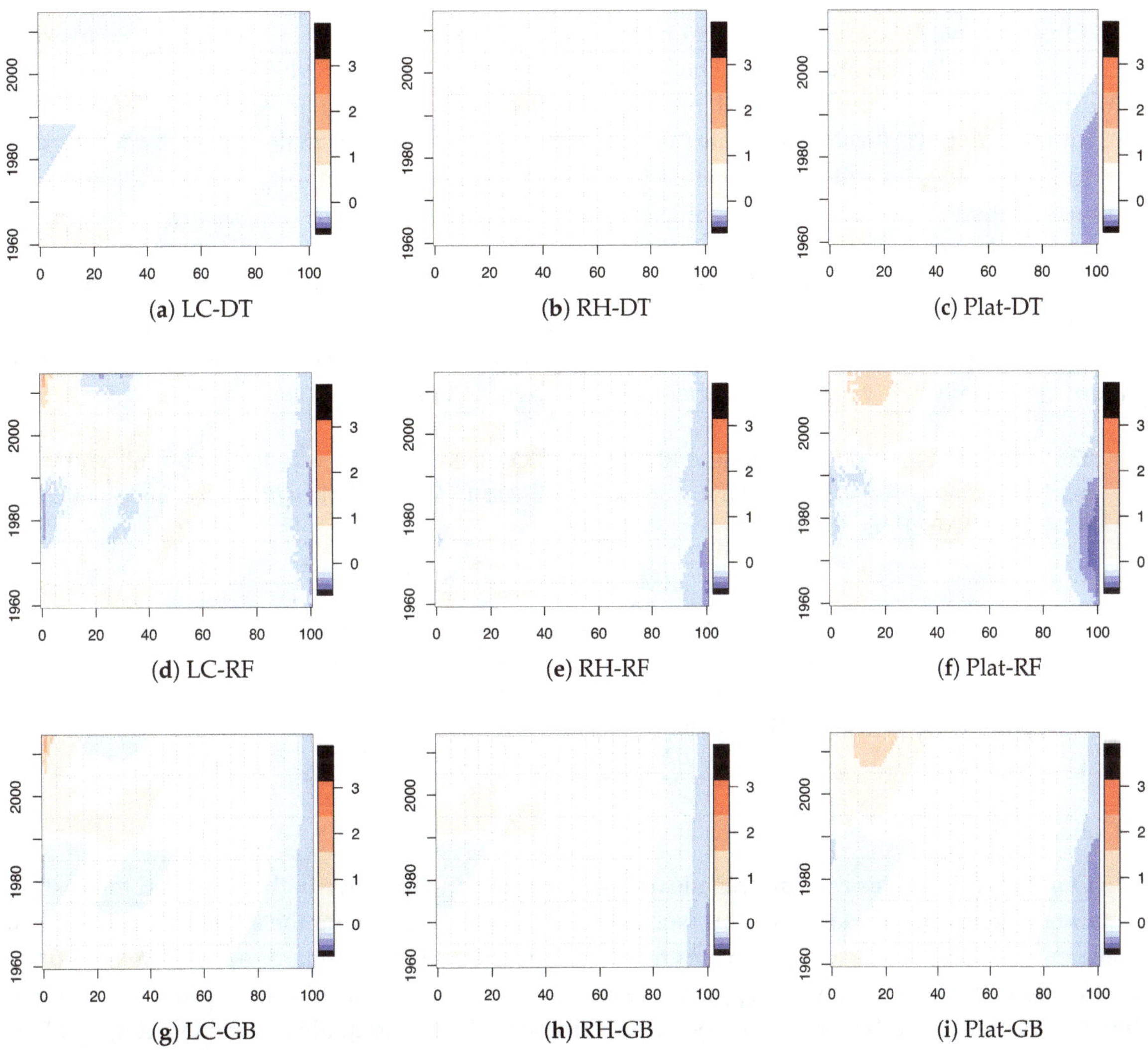

Figure 5. Values of $\Delta m_{\mathbf{x}}^{\mathrm{mdl,ML}}$. Italian male population. Ages 0–100 and years 1960–2014.

Out-of-sample tests were performed on the forecasting period 2001–2014, while the fitting period was set to 1960–2000. Also in this case, $\kappa_t^{(1,\psi)}$ and $\kappa_t^{(1)}$ were both modeled by a random walk with drift using values from 1960–2000. The plots of $\kappa_t^{(1)}$ and $\kappa_t^{(1,\psi)}$ by gender are provided in the Appendix (Figure A4). Different from the results obtained with the dataset for 1915–2000, where $\kappa_t^{(1,\psi)}$ showed a roughly monotone trend since 1960, in the case of a shorter estimation period, this trend oscillated: decreasing until the mid-1980s, increasing until 1997, then decreasing and increasing again for a few years (see Figures A2c–h and A4c–h). As a consequence, the values of future $\kappa_t^{(1,\psi)}$ were approximately constant (due to the random walk with drift behavior), while they were increasing in the case of a longer estimation period (1915–2000). We observed that the reduction of mortality over the time period 1960–2000 was less strong than that registered for the years 1915–2000[2], and this fact led to more adequate projections, requiring less adjustments from $\kappa_t^{(1,\psi)}$.

---

2 The drift of $\kappa_t^{(1)}$ for the years 1915–2000 was −2.44 for males (−3.53 for females), against −1.85 (−2.34 for females) in the years 1960–2000. Compare Figure A2a,b with Figure A4a,b.

Goodness of Forecasting

Table 6 shows the out-of-sample test results for the LC model. Values in bold indicate the model with the smaller RMSLE and RMSE. The best performance in terms of RMSLE was given by the RF algorithm, while in terms of RMSE, GB provided smaller values. The higher reduction of RMSLE was 68% for male and 64% for female, while in terms of RMSE, it was 8% for male and 6% for females.

In light of these results, we can state that, also with a smaller dataset, all the ML estimators produced a better quality of forecasting with respect to the standard LC, but the level of the improvement was less satisfactory for the older ages than the one obtained with the larger dataset (1915–2014). The reduction level obtained by RMSE for both genders was significantly lower than that achieved in the case of the 1915–2014 dataset. ML algorithms require large datasets to attain excellent performance, and using a smaller dataset makes the algorithms less effective in detecting unknown patterns, especially at old ages, where there are few observations.

Table 6. Out-of-sample test results: RMSLE and RMSE for the LC model without and with machine learning. Years 2000–2014 (fitting period: 1960–2000). Values in bold indicate the model with the smaller RMSLE and RMSE.

	RMSLE		RMSE	
Model	**Males**	**Females**	**Males**	**Females**
LC	0.0309	0.0183	0.3298	0.1840
LC, DT	0.0115	0.0074	0.3212	0.1789
LC, RF	**0.0100**	**0.0066**	0.3095	0.1761
LC, GB	0.0102	0.0070	**0.3028**	**0.1730**

5. Conclusions

Our paper illustrates how machine learning can be used to improve both fitting and forecasting of standard stochastic mortality models (such as LC, RH, and Plat), taking the advantages of artificial intelligence to better understand processes that are not identifiable by standard models. We extend the work of Deprez et al. (2017), which applied a regression tree boosting machine to improve the fitting of the LC and the RH model. We tested the improvement in the fitting quality of the LC, RH, and Plat model using not only the decision tree, but also two more powerful ML algorithms: random forest and gradient boosting. Our results, obtained from a case study structured on the Italian population, demonstrate that the random forest algorithm was more effective, though the other two algorithms produced significant improvements.

However, the main novelty of the proposed framework is the introduction of an ML estimator to improve the forecasting quality provided by standard stochastic models, where machine learning was used as a support and not as a substitute for them. Going away from the logic of machine learning, we forecasted the ML estimator using the same framework as the original mortality model. This idea was developed in the LC model framework. This approach aims to both improve the forecasted mortality rates provided by the standard LC and create a bridge between machine learning and theory to help find a rational explanation of the results. All the analysis was carried out on two different calibration periods: 1915–2014 and 1960–2014. Out-of-sample test results were encouraging, especially when considering the longer calibration period.

Author Contributions: The two authors have equally contributed to the paper.

Funding: This research received no external funding.

Acknowledgments: The authors thank the anonymous referees for helpful comments.

Conflicts of Interest: The authors declare no conflict of interest.

Appendix A

Appendix A.1 Plots for Time Period 1915–2014

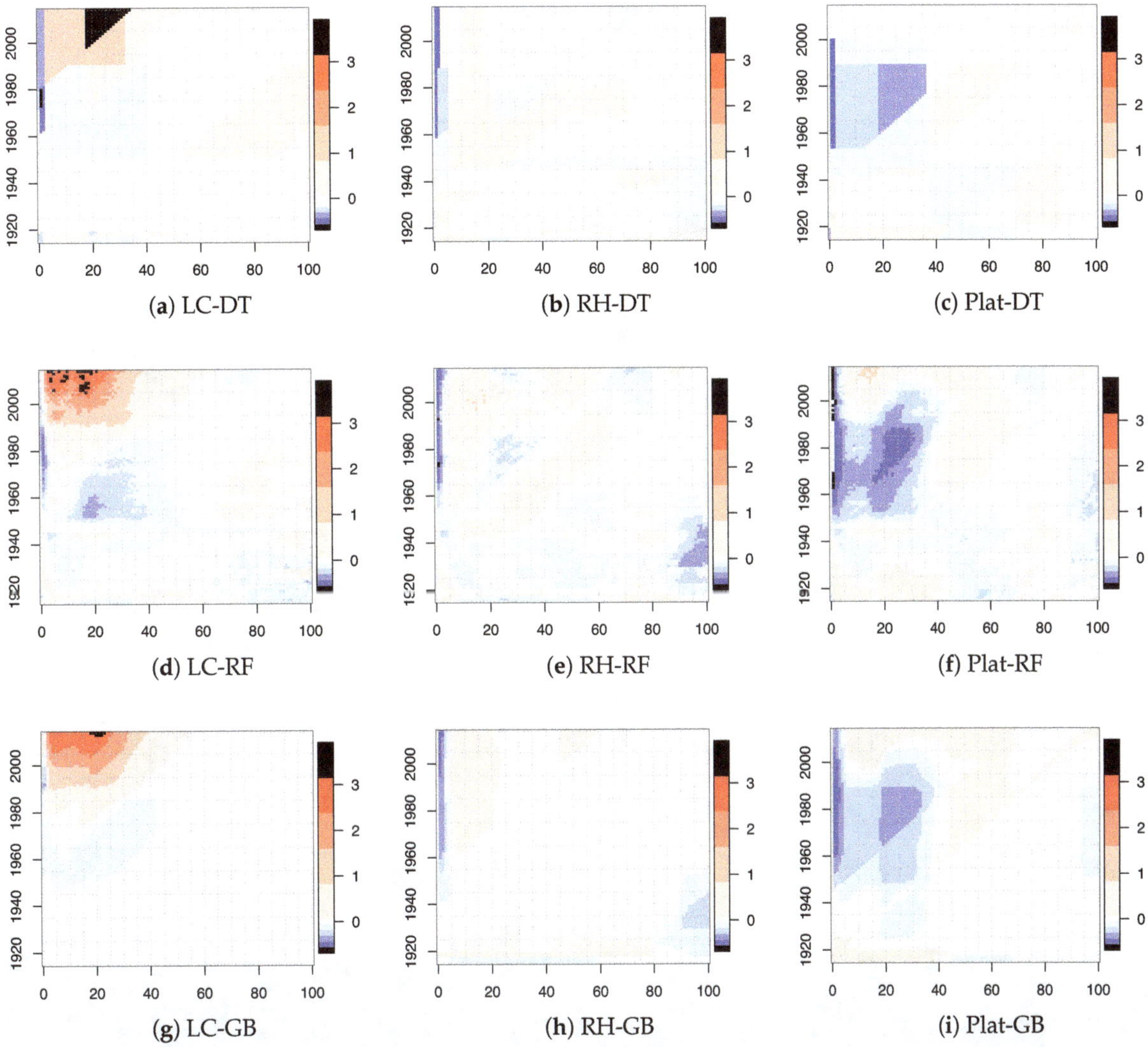

Figure A1. Values of $\Delta m_x^{\text{mdl,ML}}$. Italian female population. Ages 0–100 and years 1915–2014.

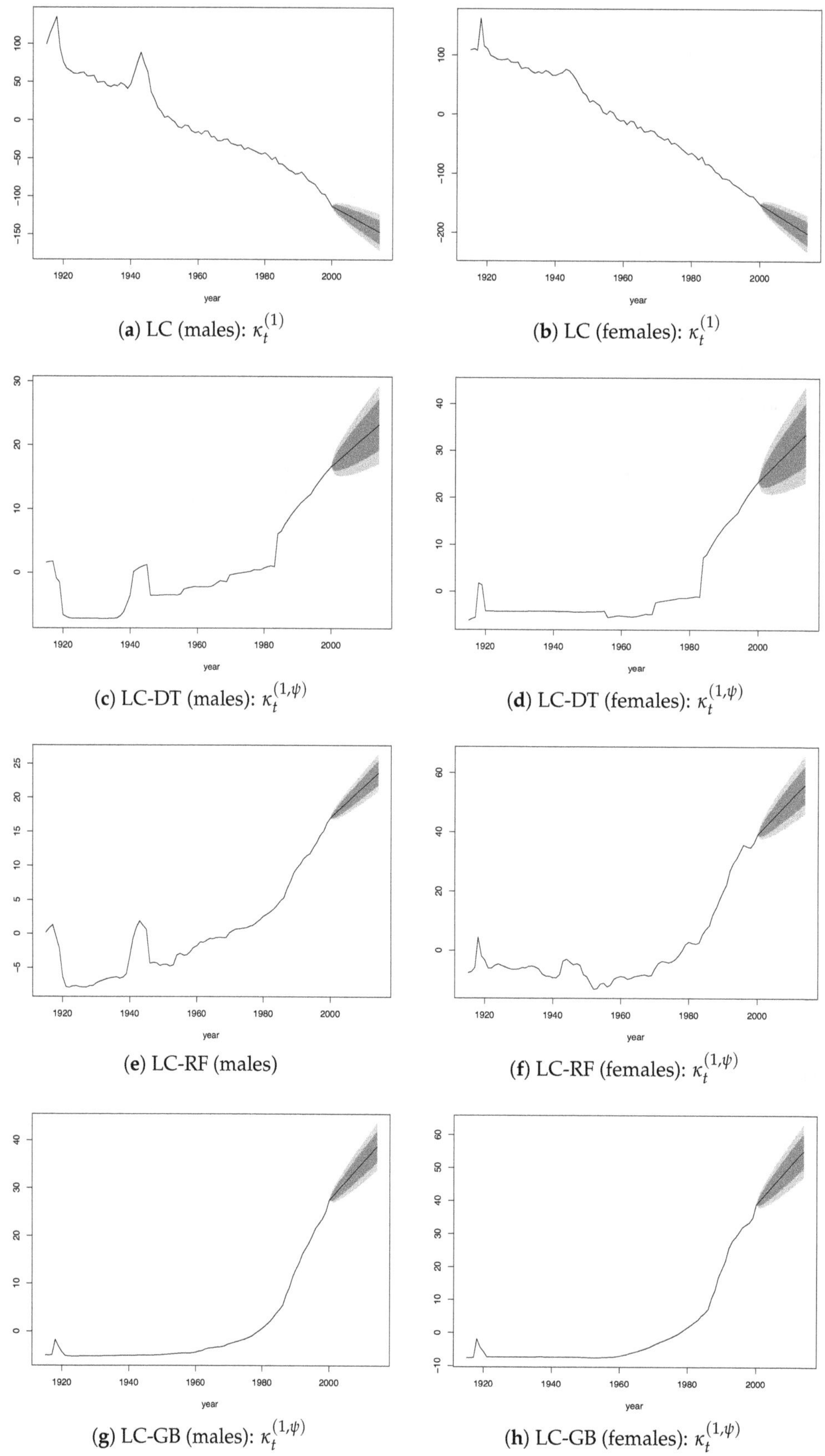

(**a**) LC (males): $\kappa_t^{(1)}$ (**b**) LC (females): $\kappa_t^{(1)}$

(**c**) LC-DT (males): $\kappa_t^{(1,\psi)}$ (**d**) LC-DT (females): $\kappa_t^{(1,\psi)}$

(**e**) LC-RF (males) (**f**) LC-RF (females): $\kappa_t^{(1,\psi)}$

(**g**) LC-GB (males): $\kappa_t^{(1,\psi)}$ (**h**) LC-GB (females): $\kappa_t^{(1,\psi)}$

Figure A2. $\kappa_t^{(1)}$ and $\kappa_t^{(1,\psi)}$: Fitted value (1915–2000) and forecasted values (2000–2014).

Appendix A.2 Plots for Time Period 1960–2014

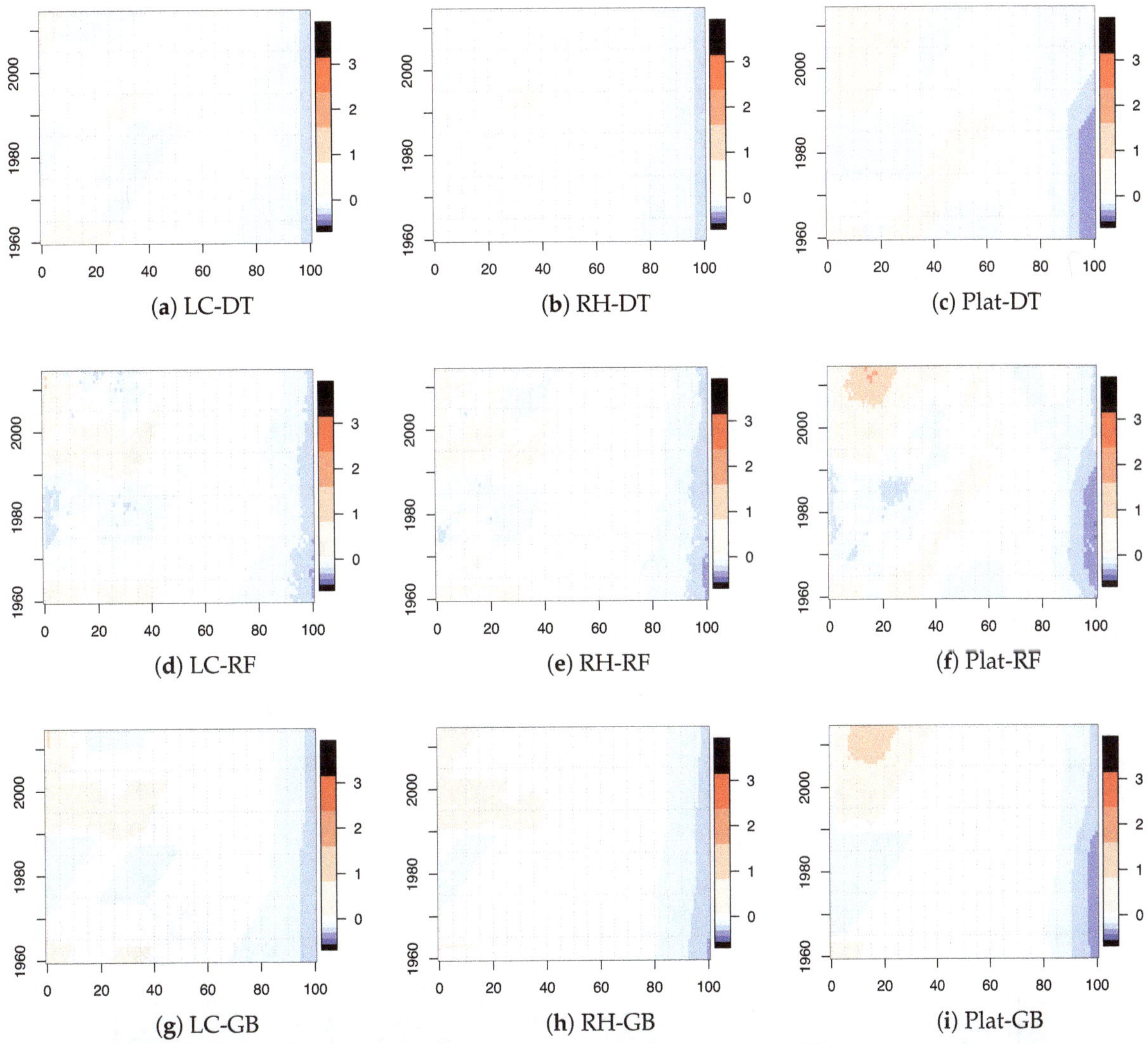

Figure A3. Values of $\Delta m_x^{\mathrm{mdl,ML}}$. Italian female population. Ages 0–100 and years 1960–2014.

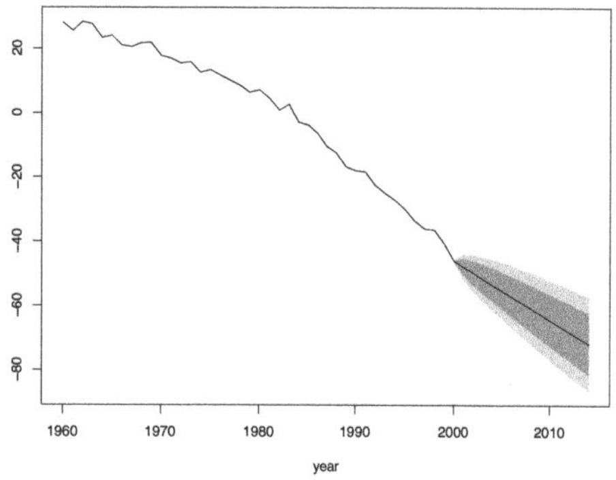

(**a**) LC (males): $\kappa_t^{(1)}$

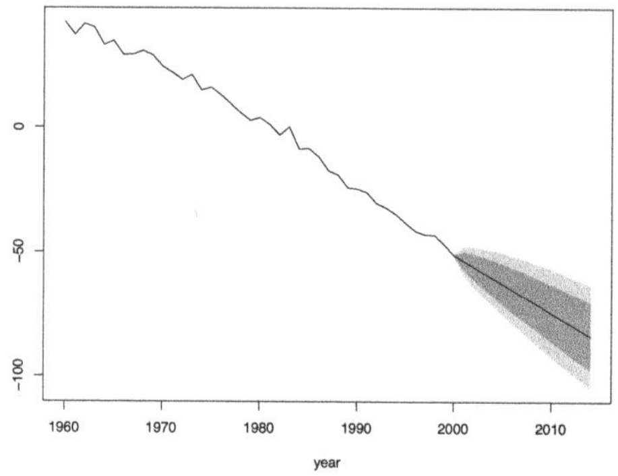

(**b**) LC (females): $\kappa_t^{(1)}$

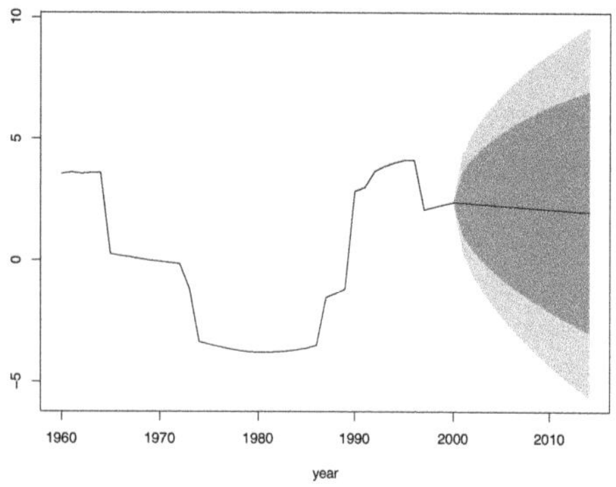

(**c**) LC-DT (males): $\kappa_t^{(1,\psi)}$

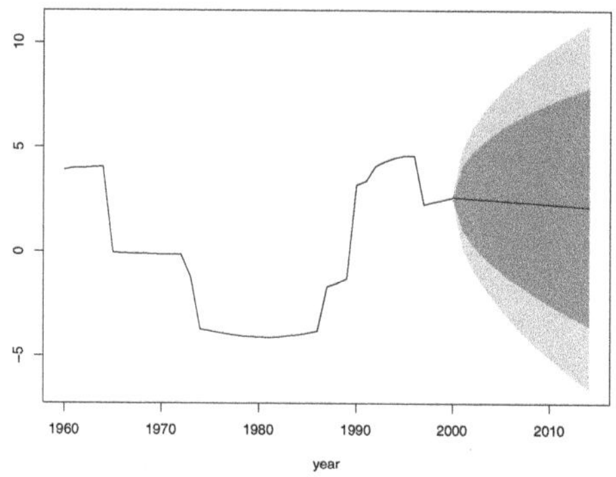

(**d**) LC-DT (females): $\kappa_t^{(1,\psi)}$

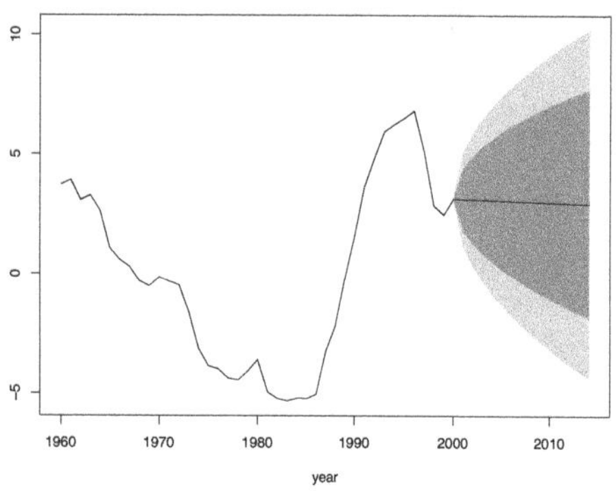

(**e**) LC-RF (males)

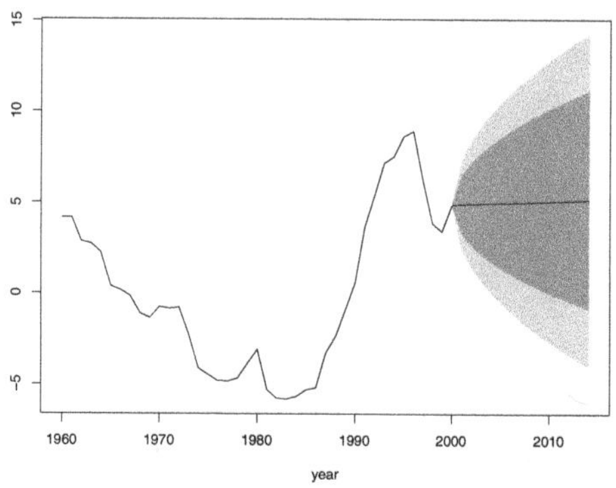

(**f**) LC-RF (females): $\kappa_t^{(1,\psi)}$

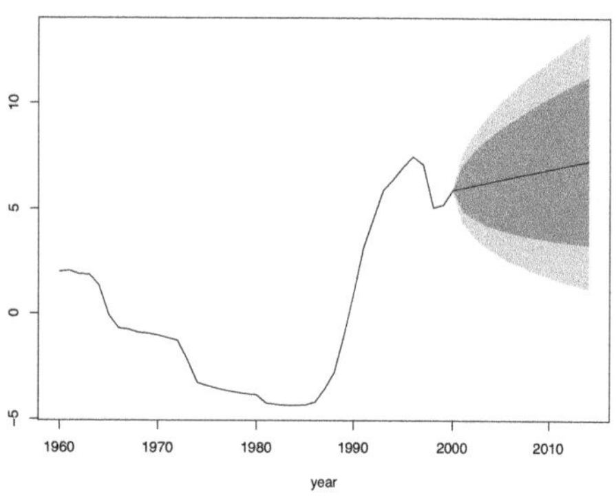

(**g**) LC-GB (males): $\kappa_t^{(1,\psi)}$

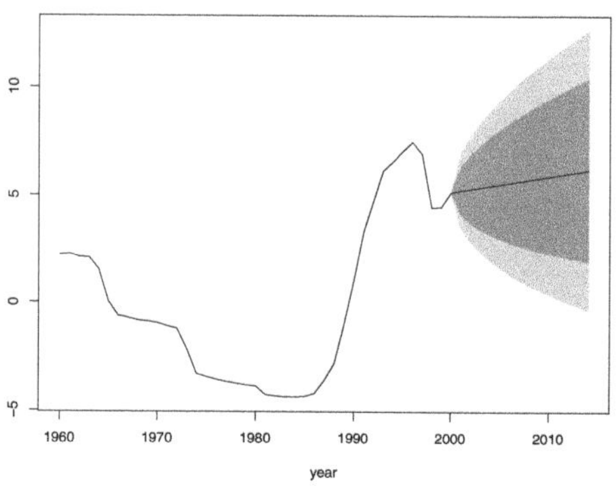

(**h**) LC-GB (females): $\kappa_t^{(1,\psi)}$

Figure A4. $\kappa_t^{(1)}$ and $\kappa_t^{(1,\psi)}$: Fitted value (1960–2000) and forecasted values (2000–2014).

References

Alpaydin, Ethem. 2010. *Introduction to Machine Learning*, 2nd ed. Cambridge: Massachusetts Institute of Technology Press, ISBN 026201243X.

Breiman, Leo, Jerome Friedman, Richard Olshen, and Charles Stone. 1984. *Classification and regression trees*. Boca Raton: CRC Press, ISBN 9780412048418. [CrossRef]

Breiman, Leo. 2001. Random forests. *Machine Learning* 45: 5–32.

Brouhns, Natacha, Michel Denuit, and Jeroen K. Vermunt. 2002. A Poisson log-bilinear regression approach to the construction of projected lifetables. *Insurance: Mathematics and Economics* 31: 373–93. [CrossRef]

Cairns, Andrew J. G., David Blake, Kevin Dowd, Guy D. Coughlan, David Epstein, Alen Ong, and Igor Balevich. 2009. A quantitative comparison of stochastic mortality models using data from England and Wales and the United States. *North American Actuarial Journal* 13: 1–35. [CrossRef]

Deprez, Philippe, Pavel V. Shevchenko, and Mario V. Wüthrich. 2017. Machine learning techniques for mortality modeling. *European Actuarial Journal* 7: 337–52. [CrossRef]

Haberman, Steven, and Arthur Renshaw. 2011. A comparative study of parametric mortality projection models. *Insurance: Mathematics and Economics* 48: 35–55. [CrossRef]

Hainaut, Donatien. 2018. A neural-network analyzer for mortality forecast. *Astin Bulletin* 48: 481–508. [CrossRef]

Hastie, Jerome, Trevor Hastie, and Robert Tibshirani. 2016. *The Elements of Statistical Learning*, 2nd ed. Data Mining, Inference, and Prediction. New York: Springer, ISBN 0387848576.

Hunt, Andrew, and Andrés M. Villegas. 2015. Robustness and convergence in the Lee-Carter model with cohorts. *Insurance: Mathematics and Economics* 64: 186–202. [CrossRef]

James, Gareth, Daniela Witten, Trevor Hastie, and Robert Tibshirani. 2017. *An Introduction to Statistical Learning: With Applications in R*. New York: Springer, ISBN 1461471370.

Lee, Ronald D., and Lawrence R. Carter. 1992. Modeling and forecasting US mortality. *Journal of the American Statistical Association* 87: 659–71.

Liaw, Andy. 2018. Package `Randomforest`. Available online: https://cran.r-project.org/web/packages/randomForest/randomForest.pdf (accessed on 21 May 2018).

Plat, Richard. 2009. On stochastic mortality modeling. *Insurance: Mathematics and Economics* 45: 393–404.

Renshaw, Arthur E., and Steven Haberman. 2006. A Cohort-Based Extension to the Lee-Carter Model for Mortality Reduction Factors. *Insurance: Mathematics and Economics* 38: 556–70. [CrossRef]

Richman, Ronald, and Mario V. Wüthrich. 2018. *A Neural Network Extension of the Lee-Carter Model to Multiple Populations*. Rochester: SSRN.

Ridgeway, Greg. 2007. Generalized Boosted Models: A Guide to the `gbm` Package. Available online: https://cran.r-project.org/web/packages/gbm/gbm.pdf (accessed on 21 May 2018).

Therneau, Terry M., and Elizabeth J. Atkinson. 2017. An Introduction to Recursive Partitioning Using the RPART Routines. Available online: https://cran.r-project.org/web/packages/rpart/vignettes/longintro.pdf (accessed on 21 May 2018).

Villegas, Andrés M., Pietro Millossovich, and Vladimir K. Kaishev. 2015. `Stmomo`: An r Package for Stochastic Mortality Modelling. Available online: https://cran.r-project.org/web/packages/StMoMo/vignettes/StMoMoVignette.pdf (accessed on 21 May 2018).

3

Optimal Bail-Out Dividend Problem with Transaction Cost and Capital Injection Constraint

Mauricio Junca [1], Harold A. Moreno-Franco [2] and José Luis Pérez [3,*]

[1] Department of Mathematics, Universidad de los Andes, Bogotá 11711, Colombia; mj.junca20@uniandes.edu.co

[2] Department of Mathematics and Statistics, Universidad del Norte, Barranquilla 080003, Colombia; hamoreno@uninorte.edu.co

[3] Department of Probability and Statistics, Centro de Investigación en Matemáticas A.C., Guanajuato 36000, Mexico

* Correspondence: jluis.garmendia@cimat.mx

Abstract: We consider the optimal bail-out dividend problem with fixed transaction cost for a Lévy risk model with a constraint on the expected present value of injected capital. To solve this problem, we first consider the optimal bail-out dividend problem with transaction cost and capital injection and show the optimality of reflected (c_1, c_2)-policies. We then find the optimal Lagrange multiplier, by showing that in the dual Lagrangian problem the complementary slackness conditions are met. Finally, we present some numerical examples to support our results.

Keywords: dividend payment; optimal control; capital injection constraint; spectrally negative Lévy processes; reflected Lévy processes; scale functions

MSC: 60G51; 91B30

---

1. Introduction

De Finetti introduced in 1957 the expected net present value (NPV) of dividends paid by an insurance company as a criterion for assessing its stability. According to this model, the maximum of the expected NPVs, if it exists, can be a proxy for the insurance company's value. In some cases (e.g., due to regulatory issues), the insurance company has to ensure the negative balance protection and therefore must be rescued by injecting capital. Hence, the company aims to maximize the total amount of expected dividend payments minus the total expected cost of capital injection while permanently keeping the surplus process non-negative.

Usually, spectrally negative Lévy processes (Lévy processes with only downward jumps) are used to model the underlying surplus process of an insurance company, which increases with premium payments and decreases with insurance payouts. The optimization problem for this model was studied by Avram et al. (2007), who proved that it is optimal to inject capital when the process is below zero and pay dividends when the process is above a suitably chosen threshold.

In this paper, we focus on the case when the insurance company pays a fixed transaction cost each time a dividend payment is made. The fixed transaction cost makes the continuous payment of dividends no longer feasible, which implies that only lump sum dividend payments are possible. In this case, a strategy is assumed to have the form of impulse control; whenever dividends are accrued, a constant transaction cost $\delta > 0$ is incurred. Unlike the barrier strategies described above, which are typically optimal for the case without transaction cost, we pursue the optimality of the reflected (c_1, c_2)-policies. In these strategies, the surplus process is brought down to c_1 whenever it exceeds the level c_2 for some $0 \leq c_1 < c_2 < \infty$, and pushes the surplus to 0 whenever it goes below 0. Previously, the version of the de Finetti's optimal dividend problem with fixed transaction cost and without bail-outs was solved for the spectrally negative case by Loeffen (2009) and for the dual model (i.e., spectrally positive Lévy processes) by Bayraktar et al. (2014b).

In this paper, we also propose a model to maximize the value of the insurance company by means of the dividend payments while keeping the expected present value of the capital injection bounded. The idea of introducing this constraint is to bound the budget needed for the company to survive and therefore to reduce the risk faced (e.g., operational risk).

Specifically, we solve the following two problems:

1. We find the solution to the optimal bail-out dividend problem with fixed transaction cost for the case of spectrally negative Lévy processes. We show that a reflected (c_1, c_2)-policy is optimal (see Theorem 1). We use scale functions to characterize the optimal thresholds as well as the value function. We prove the optimality of the proposed policy by means of a verification theorem.
2. We solve the constrained dividend maximization problem with capital injection on the set of strategies such that the expected net present value of injected capital must be bounded by a given constant. This is an offshoot of Hernández et al. (2018) for the bail-out case. Using the previous results, in Theorems 2 and 3, we present the solution when the surplus of the company is modeled by a spectrally negative Lévy process.

This paper is organized as follows. In Section 2, we introduce the problem. In Section 3, we provide a review of scale functions and some fluctuation identities of spectrally negative Lévy processes as well as their reflected versions. In Section 4, we solve the optimal bail-out dividend problem with fixed transaction cost for the case of a spectrally negative Lévy process. In Section 5, we present the solution for the constrained bail-out dividend problem. In Section 6, we illustrate our main results by giving some numerical examples.

2. Formulation of the Problem

Let $X = \{X_t : t \geq 0\}$ be a Lévy process defined on a probability space $(\Omega, \mathcal{F}, \mathbb{P})$, and let $\mathbb{F} := \{\mathcal{F}_t : t \geq 0\}$ be the completed and right-continuous filtration generated by X. Recall that a Lévy process is a process that has càdlàg paths and stationary and independent increments. For $x \in \mathbb{R}$, we denote by $\mathbb{P}_x$ the law of X, where $X_0 = x$. For convenience, we take $\mathbb{P}_0 \equiv \mathbb{P}$, when $x = 0$. The expectation operator associated with $\mathbb{P}_x$ is denoted by $\mathbb{E}_x$. We take $\mathbb{E}_0 \equiv \mathbb{E}$, where $\mathbb{E}$ is the expectation operator associated with $\mathbb{P}$.

We henceforth assume that the insurance company's surplus X is modeled by a spectrally negative process, i.e., a Lévy process that only has negative jumps. We omit the case when X has monotone trajectories to avoid trivial cases.

The Laplace exponent of X is given by

$$\psi(\theta) := \log \mathbb{E}[\theta X_1] = \gamma\theta + \frac{\sigma^2}{2}\theta^2 - \int_{(0,\infty)} (1 - \mathrm{e}^{-\theta z} - \theta z \mathbf{1}_{\{0<z\leq 1\}})\Pi(\mathrm{d}z), \quad \theta \geq 0,$$

where $\gamma \in \mathbb{R}$, $\sigma \geq 0$, and the Lévy measure of X, Π, is a measure defined on $(0, \infty)$ satisfying

$$\int_{(0,\infty)} (1 \wedge z^2)\Pi(\mathrm{d}z) < \infty.$$

As is well-known, the process X has bounded variation paths if and only if $\sigma = 0$ and $\int_{(0,1]} z\Pi(\mathrm{d}z) < \infty$. In this case, X can be written as

$$X_t = ct - \widetilde{S}_t, \qquad t \geq 0, \tag{1}$$

where $c := \gamma + \int_{(0,1]} z\Pi(\mathrm{d}z)$ and $\widetilde{S} = \{\widetilde{S}_t : t \geq 0\}$ is a drift-less subordinator. Since we omit the case when X has monotone paths, it is necessary that the constant c is greater than zero. Note that the Laplace exponent of X, with X as in Equation (1), is given as follows,

$$\psi(\theta) = c\theta - \int_{(0,\infty)} (1 - \mathrm{e}^{-\theta z})\Pi(\mathrm{d}z), \quad \theta \geq 0.$$

De Finetti's Problem with Fixed Transaction Cost and Capital Injection

Let $\pi = \{L^\pi, R^\pi\}$ be a strategy, where L^π is left-continuous $\mathbb{P}_x$-a.s., and R^π is right-continuous $\mathbb{P}_x$-a.s. Additionally, we assume that L^π and R^π are non-negative, and non-decreasing $\mathbb{P}_x$-a.s., start at zero and are adapted to the filtration $\mathbb{F}$. Then, the controlled process, X^π, associated with the strategy π, is the following

$$X_t^\pi = X_t - L_t^\pi + R_t^\pi, \quad t \geq 0.$$

For each $t \geq 0$, the quantities L_t^π and R_t^π represent the cumulative amounts that the insurance company has paid to its shareholders and has injected, respectively.

The set of admissible policies Θ consists of those policies π for which X^π is non-negative and for $x \geq 0$,

$$\mathbb{E}_x\left[\int_0^\infty \mathrm{e}^{-qt}\,\mathrm{d}R_t^\pi\right] < \infty.$$

When there is a fixed transaction cost $\delta > 0$, we only consider the class of admissible strategies $\pi = \{L^\pi, R^\pi\} \in \Theta$ such that

$$L_t^\pi = \sum_{0 \leq s \leq t} \Delta L_s^\pi, \quad t \geq 0,$$

where $\Delta L_t^\pi := L_{t+}^\pi - L_t^\pi$. We denote this class by Θ_δ and in the case $\delta = 0$, we take $\Theta_0 \equiv \Theta$.

Given an initial capital $x \geq 0$ and a policy $\pi = \{L^\pi, R^\pi\} \in \Theta_\delta$, with $\delta \geq 0$, we define the expected NPV as follows,

$$v_{\delta,\Lambda}^\pi(x) := \mathbb{E}_x\left[\int_0^\infty \mathrm{e}^{-qt}\,\mathrm{d}\left(L_t^\pi - \delta \sum_{0 \leq s \leq t} \mathbf{1}_{\{\Delta L_s^\pi > 0\}}\right) - \Lambda \int_0^\infty \mathrm{e}^{-qt}\,\mathrm{d}R_t^\pi\right], \tag{2}$$

where $q > 0$, $\delta \geq 0$, and $\Lambda > 0$ is the unit cost per capital injected.

Remark 1. *Note that in the case of proportional transaction cost the expected NPV changes to*

$$\mathbb{E}_x\left[\int_0^\infty \mathrm{e}^{-qt}\,\mathrm{d}\left(\beta L_t^\pi - \delta \sum_{0 \leq s \leq t} \mathbf{1}_{\{\Delta L_s^\pi > 0\}}\right) - \Lambda \int_0^\infty \mathrm{e}^{-qt}\,\mathrm{d}R_t^\pi\right],$$

where $0 < \beta < 1$, *so by changing* δ *and* Λ *appropriately we can recover Equation* (2).

Hence, the value function we aim to find is

$$V_{\delta,\Lambda}(x) := \sup_{\pi \in \Theta_\delta} v_{\delta,\Lambda}^\pi(x). \tag{3}$$

Remark 2. *Since we want to avoid this function taking the value* $-\infty$, *we assume that* $\psi'(0+) = \mathbb{E}[X_1] > -\infty$. *We also assume that* $\Lambda \geq 1$, *otherwise the value function will go to infinity since large amounts of dividends will be paid, given that the company will inject capital at a cheaper cost to bail out.*

Note that the problem in Equation (3) was studied by Avram et al. (2007) under the assumption $\delta = 0$ (see Section 3.2). Therefore, we focus on the optimal control problem when $\delta > 0$ (see Section 4).

3. Preliminaries

In this section, we revise the scale functions of spectrally negative Lévy processes and their properties (see, e.g., Kuznetsov et al. (2013); Kyprianou (2014)). We also recall well known results regarding optimal dividend strategies with capital injection for spectrally one-sided Lévy processes when the transaction cost is equal to 0 (i.e., $\delta = 0$).

For each $q \geq 0$, there exists a map $W^{(q)} : \mathbb{R} \longrightarrow [0, \infty)$, called q-scale function, satisfying $W^{(q)}(x) = 0$ for $x \in (-\infty, 0)$, and strictly increasing on $[0, \infty)$, which is defined by its Laplace transform:

$$\int_0^\infty e^{-\theta x} W^{(q)}(x) dx = \frac{1}{\psi(\theta) - q}, \quad \theta > \Phi(q), \tag{4}$$

where

$$\Phi(q) := \sup\{\lambda \geq 0 : \psi(\lambda) = q\}.$$

We also define, for $x \in \mathbb{R}$,

$$\overline{W}^{(q)}(x) := \int_0^x W^{(q)}(y) dy, \quad Z^{(q)}(x) := 1 + q\overline{W}^{(q)}(x),$$
$$\overline{Z}^{(q)}(x) := \int_0^x Z^{(q)}(z) dz = x + q \int_0^x \int_0^z W^{(q)}(w) dw dz.$$

Since $W^{(q)}$ is equal to zero on $(-\infty, 0)$, we have

$$\overline{W}^{(q)}(x) = 0, \quad Z^{(q)}(x) = 1 \quad \text{and} \quad \overline{Z}^{(q)}(x) = x, \quad x \leq 0.$$

Remark 3.

1. *By Equation (8.26) of Kyprianou (2014), the left- and right-hand derivatives of $W^{(q)}$ always exist on $\mathbb{R}\backslash\{0\}$. In addition, as in, e.g., (Chan et al. 2011, Theorem 3), if X is of unbounded variation or the Lévy measure is atomless, we have $W^{(q)} \in C^1(\mathbb{R}\backslash\{0\})$.*
2. *From Lemmas 3.1–3.2 of Kuznetsov et al. (2013), we know*

$$W^{(q)}(0) = \begin{cases} 0, & \text{if } X \text{ is of unbounded variation,} \\ \dfrac{1}{c}, & \text{if } X \text{ is of bounded variation,} \end{cases}$$

$$W^{(q)\prime}(0+) := \lim_{x \downarrow 0} W^{(q)\prime}(x) = \begin{cases} \dfrac{2}{\sigma^2}, & \text{if } \sigma > 0, \\ \infty, & \text{if } \sigma = 0 \text{ and } \Pi(0,\infty) = \infty, \\ \dfrac{q + \Pi(0,\infty)}{c^2}, & \text{if } \sigma = 0 \text{ and } \Pi(0,\infty) < \infty. \end{cases}$$

3. *From Lemma 3.3 of Kuznetsov et al. (2013), $W_{\Phi(q)}(x) := e^{-\Phi(q)x} W^{(q)}(x) \nearrow \psi'(\Phi(q))^{-1}$, as $x \uparrow \infty$.*

Due to Remark 3, we make the following assumption throughout the paper.

Assumption 1. *We assume that either X has unbounded variation or Π is absolutely continuous with respect to the Lebesgue measure. Under this assumption, it holds that $W^{(q)}$ is C^1 in $(0, \infty)$.*

We give the following properties related to $Z^{(q)}$ and $\overline{W}^{(q)}$ for later use.

Remark 4.

(i) *By Proposition 5.5 in Hernández et al. (2018), we have that $Z^{(q)}$ is a strictly log-convex function on $(0, \infty)$, for $q > 0$.*

(ii) *From Lemma 1 in Avram et al. (2007), it is known that $\overline{W}^{(q)}$ is a log-concave function on $(0, \infty)$.*

We define the stopping times τ_{a^-} and τ_{a^+}, respectively, as follows,

$$\tau_a^- := \inf\{t > 0 : X_t < a\} \quad \text{and} \quad \tau_a^+ := \inf\{t > 0 : X_t > a\}, \quad a \in \mathbb{R};$$

here and further on, let $\inf \varnothing = \infty$. By Theorem 8.1 in Kyprianou (2014), we have that

$$\begin{aligned} \mathbb{E}_x\left[\mathrm{e}^{-q\tau_a^+}\mathbf{1}_{\{\tau_a^+<\tau_b^-\}}\right] &= \frac{W^{(q)}(x-b)}{W^{(q)}(a-b)}, \\ \mathbb{E}_x\left[\mathrm{e}^{-q\tau_b^-}\mathbf{1}_{\{\tau_a^+>\tau_b^-\}}\right] &= Z^{(q)}(x-b) - Z^{(q)}(a-b)\frac{W^{(q)}(x-b)}{W^{(q)}(a-b)}, \end{aligned} \qquad \text{for } a > b \text{ and } x \leq a. \tag{5}$$

3.1. Reflected Lévy Processes

Let $S = \{S_t : t \geq 0\}$ and $R^0 = \{R_t^0 : t \geq 0\}$ be defined, respectively, as

$$S_t := \sup_{0\leq s\leq t}(X_s \vee 0) \quad \text{and} \quad R_t^0 := \sup_{0\leq s\leq t}(-X_s \vee 0). \tag{6}$$

We denote $\hat{Y} := S - X$ and $Y := X + R^0$, which are strong Markov processes. Observe that the process R^0 pushes X upwards whenever it attempts to down-cross the level 0; as a result the process Y only takes values on $[0, \infty)$. An introduction to the theory of Lévy processes and their reflected processes can be encountered in Bertoin (1998); Kyprianou (2014).

Let $\hat{\tau}_a$ be defined as $\hat{\tau}_a = \inf\{t > 0 : \hat{Y}_t \in (a, \infty)\}$, with $a > 0$. Then, by Proposition 2 in Pistorius (2004),

$$\mathbb{E}_{-x}\left[\mathrm{e}^{-q\hat{\tau}_a}\right] = Z^{(q)}(a-x) - qW^{(q)}(a-x)\frac{W^{(q)}(a)}{W^{(q)\prime}(a)}, \quad x \in [0, a].$$

We define for $a > 0$,

$$H(a) := \mathbb{E}_0\left[\mathrm{e}^{-q\hat{\tau}_a}\right] = Z^{(q)}(a) - q\frac{[W^{(q)}(a)]^2}{W^{(q)\prime}(a)}. \tag{7}$$

Remark 5. *Note that, by definition, the function H is strictly positive, strictly decreasing and satisfies*

$$\lim_{a\to\infty} H(a) = 0, \qquad \lim_{a\to 0} H(a) = 1 - \frac{q[W^{(q)}(0)]^2}{W^{(q)\prime}(0+)}.$$

Therefore, the function H has an inverse from $\left(0, 1 - q/\left(q + \Pi\left(0, \infty\right)\right)\right)$ onto $\left(0, \infty\right)$ when $\sigma = 0$ and $\Pi(0, \infty) < \infty$, and from $(0, 1)$ onto $(0, \infty)$ otherwise.

Similarly, taking $\kappa_b := \inf\{t > 0 : Y_t \in (b, \infty)\}$, with $b > 0$, we know from Proposition 2 in Pistorius (2004) that

$$\mathbb{E}_x\left[\mathrm{e}^{-q\kappa_b}\right] = \frac{Z^{(q)}(x)}{Z^{(q)}(b)}, \quad x \leq b. \tag{8}$$

In addition, we know from (Avram et al. 2007, page 167) that

$$\mathbb{E}_x\left[\int_{[0,\kappa_b]} \mathrm{e}^{-qt}\,\mathrm{d}R_t^0\right] = -\overline{Z}^{(q)}(x) + \Phi(q)^{-1}Z^{(q)}(x) - \frac{\psi'(0+)}{q} + \left(\overline{Z}^{(q)}(b) - \Phi(q)^{-1}Z^{(q)}(b) + \frac{\psi'(0+)}{q}\right)\frac{Z^{(q)}(x)}{Z^{(q)}(b)} = -k^{(q)}(x) + \frac{Z^{(q)}(x)}{Z^{(q)}(b)}k^{(q)}(b), \quad x \le b, \tag{9}$$

where

$$k^{(q)}(x) := \overline{Z}^{(q)}(x) + \frac{\psi'(0+)}{q}. \tag{10}$$

3.2. Optimal Dividends without Transaction Cost and with Capital Injection

When $\delta = 0$, Equation (2) becomes

$$v_\Lambda^\pi(x) := v_{0,\Lambda}^\pi(x) = \mathbb{E}_x\left[\int_0^\infty \mathrm{e}^{-qt}\,\mathrm{d}L_t^\pi - \Lambda\int_0^\infty \mathrm{e}^{-qt}\,\mathrm{d}R_t^\pi\right],$$

for any initial capital $x \ge 0$ and admissible policy $\pi = \{L^\pi, R^\pi\} \in \Theta$. Consider the strategy $\pi_{a,0} = \{L^{a,0}, R^{a,0}\}$, which consists in setting reflecting barriers at a and 0, respectively. The controlled risk process $X^{\pi_{a,0}} = X - L^{a,0} + R^{a,0}$ is a doubly reflected spectrally negative Lévy process and was studied by Avram et al. (2007). Intuitively, the process behaves similar to a Lévy process when it is inside $[0,a]$, but when it tries to cross above the level a or below the level 0 it is forced to stay inside $[0,a]$. Using Theorem 1 from Avram et al. (2007), we have that for $a > 0$ and $x \in [0,a]$,

$$\mathbb{E}_x\left[\int_0^\infty \mathrm{e}^{-qt}\,\mathrm{d}L_t^{a,0}\right] = \frac{Z^{(q)}(x)}{qW^{(q)}(a)}, \tag{11}$$

$$\mathbb{E}_x\left[\int_0^\infty \mathrm{e}^{-qt}\,\mathrm{d}R_t^{a,0}\right] = \frac{Z^{(q)}(a)}{qW^{(q)}(a)}Z^{(q)}(x) - k^{(q)}(x). \tag{12}$$

Note that the expression in Equation (12) is finite under our assumption that $\psi'(0+) > -\infty$. Using the expressions above, we can see that, for $\Lambda \ge 1$,

$$v_\Lambda^a(x) := v_\Lambda^{\pi_{a,0}}(x) = \begin{cases} Z^{(q)}(x)\zeta_\Lambda(a) + \Lambda k^{(q)}(x), & \text{if } 0 \le x \le a, \\ x - a + v_\Lambda^a(a), & \text{if } x > a, \end{cases} \tag{13}$$

where

$$\zeta_\Lambda(a) := \frac{1 - \Lambda Z^{(q)}(a)}{qW^{(q)}(a)}, \quad a > 0. \tag{14}$$

Equation (13) suggests that, to find the best barrier strategy we should maximize the function ζ_Λ. Thus, we can define the candidate for the optimal barrier by

$$a_\Lambda = \sup\{a \ge 0 : \zeta_\Lambda(a) \ge \zeta_\Lambda(x), \text{ for all } x \ge 0\}. \tag{15}$$

Remark 6. *Note that $\zeta_\Lambda : (0,\infty) \longrightarrow (-\infty, 0)$ and satisfies*

$$\lim_{a\to 0}\zeta_\Lambda(a) = -\frac{\Lambda - 1}{qW^{(q)}(0)} \quad \text{and} \quad \lim_{a\to\infty}\zeta_\Lambda(a) = -\frac{\Lambda}{\Phi(q)}.$$

Here, in case that X is of unbounded variation, the first equality is understood to be $-\infty$. The barrier level a_Λ, given in Equation (15), corresponds with the level defined in Avram et al. (2007). Using the definition of the function H, we have that

$$\frac{\mathrm{d}\zeta_\Lambda(a)}{\mathrm{d}a} = \frac{\Lambda W^{(q)\prime}(a)}{q[W^{(q)}(a)]^2}(H(a) - 1/\Lambda).$$

Since H is strictly decreasing, ζ_Λ has a unique maximum at a_Λ that is either a critical point, which is a solution of $H(a) = \frac{1}{\Lambda}$, or 0 if the right-hand derivative of ζ_Λ is negative at 0. Therefore, by Remark 5,

$$a_\Lambda = \begin{cases} 0, & \text{if } \sigma = 0,\ \Pi(0,\infty) < \infty \text{ and } \Lambda < 1 + \dfrac{q}{\Pi(0,\infty)}, \\ H^{-1}(1/\Lambda), & \text{otherwise.} \end{cases} \tag{16}$$

In addition, note that ζ_Λ is strictly increasing on $(0, a_\Lambda)$ and strictly decreasing on (a_Λ, ∞).

Hence, from Avram et al. (2007), we know that the value function in Equation (3) and the optimal strategy are given by $V_\Lambda := V_{0,\Lambda} = v_\Lambda^{a_\Lambda}$ and π_{0,a_Λ}, where $v_\Lambda^{a_\Lambda}$ and a_Λ are as in Equations (13) and (16), respectively.

Remark 7. *Note that the optimal barrier $a_\Lambda \to \infty$ as $\Lambda \to \infty$.*

4. Capital Injection and Fixed Transaction Cost

In this section, we solve the problem in Equation (3) in the presence of a fixed transaction cost $\delta > 0$. We consider strategies where the capital injection policy is R^0, given in Equation (6), and the dividend strategy is the so-called reflected (c_1, c_2)-policy, defined below.

4.1. Value Function of Reflected (c_1, c_2)-Policies

Let (c_1, c_2) be a pair such that $0 \le c_1 < c_2$. In this subsection, we define the reflected (c_1, c_2)-policy, denoted by $\pi_{(c_1,c_2),0}$, and under which we construct the controlled process. Let $Y = X + R^0$ be the Lévy process reflected from below 0, so we set

$$X_t^{(c_1,c_2),0} = Y_t, \quad \text{for } t \le T_1^{c_1,c_2},$$

where $T_1^{c_1,c_2} = \inf\{t > 0 : Y_t > c_2\}$. The process then jumps downward by $Y_{T_1^{c_1,c_2}} - c_1$ so that $X_{T_1^{c_1,c_2}}^{(c_1,c_2),0} = c_1$. Now, for $T_1^{c_1,c_2} \le t < T_2^{c_1,c_2} = \inf\{t > T_1^{c_1,c_2} : X_t^{(c_1,c_2),0} > c_2\}$, $X^{(c_1,c_2),0}$ is the reflected process from below at 0 of $X_t + (c_1 - X_{T_1^{c_1,c_2}})$, and $X_{T_2^{c_1,c_2}}^{(c_1,c_2),0} = c_1$. By repeating this procedure, we can construct the process inductively. The process $X^{(c_1,c_2),0}$ clearly admits the decomposition

$$X_t^{(c_1,c_2),0} = X_t - L_t^{(c_1,c_2),0} + R_t^{(c_1,c_2),0}, \quad t \ge 0,$$

where $L^{(c_1,c_2),0}$ and $R^{(c_1,c_2),0}$ are the cumulative amounts of dividend payments and capital injection, respectively.

Let us compute the expected NPV of dividends with transaction costs for this strategy. For this purpose, we denote

$$f_{c_1,c_2}(x) = \mathbb{E}_x\left[\int_0^\infty \mathrm{e}^{-qt}\,\mathrm{d}\left(L_t^{(c_1,c_2),0} - \delta \sum_{0 \le s \le t} \mathbf{1}_{\{\Delta L_s^{(c_1,c_2),0} > 0\}}\right)\right].$$

If $x < c_2$, by the Strong Markov Property and Equation (8), we obtain that

$$f_{c_1,c_2}(x) = \mathbb{E}_x\left[e^{-qT_1^{c_1,c_2}}\right] f_{c_1,c_2}(c_2) = \frac{Z^{(q)}(x)}{Z^{(q)}(c_2)} f_{c_1,c_2}(c_2). \tag{17}$$

When $x \geq c_2$, an amount $x - c_1$ is paid as dividends and a transaction cost δ is incurred immediately, so by using Equation (17) we obtain

$$f_{c_1,c_2}(x) = x - c_1 - \delta + f_{c_1,c_2}(c_1) = x - c_1 - \delta + \frac{Z^{(q)}(c_1)}{Z^{(q)}(c_2)} f_{c_1,c_2}(c_2).$$

Hence, taking $x = c_2$, and solving for $f_{c_1,c_2}(c_2)$ we get

$$f_{c_1,c_2}(c_2) = (c_2 - c_1 - \delta)\frac{Z^{(q)}(c_2)}{Z^{(q)}(c_2) - Z^{(q)}(c_1)}.$$

Using the aforementioned expression in Equation (17), we have for $x < c_2$,

$$f_{c_1,c_2}(x) = (c_2 - c_1 - \delta)\frac{Z^{(q)}(x)}{Z^{(q)}(c_2) - Z^{(q)}(c_1)}. \tag{18}$$

Now, let us calculate the expected NPV of the injected capital denoted by

$$g_{c_1,c_2}(x) = \mathbb{E}_x\left[\int_0^\infty e^{-qt}\, dR_t^{(c_1,c_2),0}\right].$$

Again, by the Strong Markov Property, noting that $T_1^{c_1,c_2} = \inf\{t > 0 : Y_t \in (c_2, \infty)\}$ and Equations (8)–(9), we have for $x \geq 0$

$$\begin{aligned}
g_{c_1,c_2}(x) &= \mathbb{E}_x\left[\int_{[0,T_1^{c_1,c_2}]} e^{-qt}\, dR_t^0\right] + \mathbb{E}_x\left[e^{-qT_1^{c_1,c_2}}\right] g_{c_1,c_2}(c_1) \\
&= -k^{(q)}(x) + k^{(q)}(c_2)\frac{Z^{(q)}(x)}{Z^{(q)}(c_2)} + \frac{Z^{(q)}(x)}{Z^{(q)}(c_2)} g_{c_1,c_2}(c_1).
\end{aligned}$$

Thus, setting $x = c_1$ and solving for $g_{c_1,c_2}(c_1)$, we obtain

$$\begin{aligned}
g_{c_1,c_2}(c_1) &= \left(-k^{(q)}(c_1) + k^{(q)}(c_2)\frac{Z^{(q)}(c_1)}{Z^{(q)}(c_2)}\right)\frac{Z^{(q)}(c_2)}{Z^{(q)}(c_2) - Z^{(q)}(c_1)} \\
&= \left(-\overline{Z}^{(q)}(c_1) + \overline{Z}^{(q)}(c_2)\frac{Z^{(q)}(c_1)}{Z^{(q)}(c_2)}\right)\frac{Z^{(q)}(c_2)}{Z^{(q)}(c_2) - Z^{(q)}(c_1)} - \frac{\psi'(0+)}{q}.
\end{aligned}$$

Putting the pieces together, we obtain

$$\begin{aligned}
g_{c_1,c_2}(x) &= -k^{(q)}(x) + k^{(q)}(c_2)\frac{Z^{(q)}(x)}{Z^{(q)}(c_2)} \\
&\quad + \left(\left(-\overline{Z}^{(q)}(c_1) + \overline{Z}^{(q)}(c_2)\frac{Z^{(q)}(c_1)}{Z^{(q)}(c_2)}\right)\frac{Z^{(q)}(c_2)}{Z^{(q)}(c_2) - Z^{(q)}(c_1)} - \frac{\psi'(0+)}{q}\right)\frac{Z^{(q)}(x)}{Z^{(q)}(c_2)} \\
&= -k^{(q)}(x) + \overline{Z}^{(q)}(c_2)\frac{Z^{(q)}(x)}{Z^{(q)}(c_2)} + \left(-\overline{Z}^{(q)}(c_1) + \overline{Z}^{(q)}(c_2)\frac{Z^{(q)}(c_1)}{Z^{(q)}(c_2)}\right)\frac{Z^{(q)}(x)}{Z^{(q)}(c_2) - Z^{(q)}(c_1)} \\
&= Z^{(q)}(x)\left(\frac{\overline{Z}^{(q)}(c_2) - \overline{Z}^{(q)}(c_1)}{Z^{(q)}(c_2) - Z^{(q)}(c_1)}\right) - k^{(q)}(x).
\end{aligned}$$

Hence, we have the following result.

Lemma 1. *The expected NPV associated with a reflected* (c_1, c_2)*-policy is given by*

$$v_{\delta,\Lambda}^{c_1,c_2}(x) := v_{\delta,\Lambda}^{\pi_{(c_1,c_2),0}}(x) = \begin{cases} Z^{(q)}(x)G_\Lambda(c_1,c_2) + \Lambda k^{(q)}(x), & \text{if } x \le c_2, \\ x - c_1 - \delta + v_{\delta,\Lambda}^{c_1,c_2}(c_1), & \text{if } x > c_2, \end{cases}$$

where

$$G_\Lambda(c_1,c_2) := \frac{c_2 - c_1 - \delta - \Lambda\left(\overline{Z}^{(q)}(c_2) - \overline{Z}^{(q)}(c_1)\right)}{Z^{(q)}(c_2) - Z^{(q)}(c_1)}, \quad \text{for all } c_2 > c_1 \ge 0. \tag{19}$$

Remark 8. *Note that* G_Λ *is* C^2 *on* $\mathcal{A} := \{(c_1,c_2) \in \mathbb{R}_+^2 : c_1 < c_2\}$*, and*

$$\lim_{c_2 \downarrow c_1} G_\Lambda(c_1,c_2) = -\infty, \text{ for } c_1 \ge 0 \text{ fixed,}$$

$$\lim_{|c_1|+|c_2| \to \infty} G_\Lambda(c_1,c_2) = \lim_{c_2 \to \infty} G_\Lambda(c_1,c_2) = -\frac{\Lambda}{\Phi(q)}.$$

4.2. Choice of Optimal Thresholds

To choose the optimal thresholds among reflected policies, we maximize the function G_Λ.

Proposition 1. *The function* G_Λ*, defined in Equation (19), attains its maximum on* $\mathcal{A}$*.*

Proof. Let $c_1 \ge 0$ be fixed. The first derivative of G_Λ with respect to c_2 is given by

$$\partial_{c_2} G_\Lambda(c_1,c_2) = \frac{qF_\Lambda(c_1,c_2)W^{(q)}(c_2)}{(Z^{(q)}(c_2) - Z^{(q)}(c_1))^2}, \tag{20}$$

where

$$\begin{aligned} F_\Lambda(c_1,c_2) :=& \frac{(Z^{(q)}(c_2) - Z^{(q)}(c_1))}{qW^{(q)}(c_2)}(1 - \Lambda Z^{(q)}(c_2)) - \left(c_2 - c_1 - \delta - \Lambda\left(\overline{Z}^{(q)}(c_2) - \overline{Z}^{(q)}(c_1)\right)\right) \\ =& -\Lambda\left[\frac{(Z^{(q)}(c_2))^2}{qW^{(q)}(c_2)} - \overline{Z}^{(q)}(c_2) - \left(\frac{(Z^{(q)}(c_2))}{qW^{(q)}(c_2)}Z^{(q)}(c_1) - \overline{Z}^{(q)}(c_1)\right)\right] \\ &+ \frac{Z^{(q)}(c_2) - Z^{(q)}(c_1)}{qW^{(q)}(c_2)} - (c_2 - c_1 - \delta). \end{aligned} \tag{21}$$

On the other hand, taking $a = c_2$ in Equation (12), we see

$$\frac{[Z^{(q)}(c_2)]^2}{qW^{(q)}(c_2)} - k^{(q)}(c_2) \ge 0 \quad \text{and} \quad \frac{Z^{(q)}(c_2)}{qW^{(q)}(c_2)}Z^{(q)}(c_1) - k^{(q)}(c_1) \ge 0.$$

Then, using Equation (10), we have

$$F_\Lambda(c_1,c_2) < \frac{Z^{(q)}(c_2)}{qW^{(q)}(c_2)} + \Lambda\left[\frac{Z^{(q)}(c_2)}{qW^{(q)}(c_2)}Z^{(q)}(c_1) - k^{(q)}(c_1)\right] - (c_2 - c_1 - \delta). \tag{22}$$

Therefore, since $\lim_{c_2 \to \infty} \frac{Z^{(q)}(c_2)}{qW^{(q)}(c_2)} = \frac{1}{\Phi(q)}$ (see Remark 3), the right-hand side of the aforementioned inequality goes to $-\infty$ as c_2 goes to ∞, which implies

$$\partial_{c_2} G_\Lambda(c_1,c_2) < 0, \quad \text{for } c_2 \text{ large enough.} \tag{23}$$

From here and Remark 8, we obtain that there exists $c^* \in (c_1, \infty)$ (that depends on c_1) such that

$$G_\Lambda(c_1, c_2) \le G_\Lambda(c_1, c^*), \quad \text{for all } c_2 > c_1.$$

Taking $d^*(c_1) := \sup\{c^* > c_1 : G_\Lambda(c_1, c_2) \le G_\Lambda(c_1, c^*) \text{ for all } c_2 > c_1\}$, with $c_1 \ge 0$, we see $d^*(c_1) < \infty$ for each $c_1 \ge 0$, since Equation (23) holds. From Equation (20) and the fact that $\partial_{c_2} G_\Lambda(c_1, d^*(c_1)) = 0$, it follows that $F_\Lambda(c_1, d^*(c_1)) = 0$ for $c_1 \ge 0$. Then, by the definitions of F_Λ and ζ_Λ—see Equations (21) and (14), respectively—we get

$$G_\Lambda(c_1, d^*(c_1)) = \frac{d^*(c_1) - c_1 - \delta - \Lambda(\overline{Z}^{(q)}(d^*(c_1)) - \overline{Z}^{(q)}(c_1))}{Z^{(q)}(d^*(c_1)) - Z^{(q)}(c_1)} = \zeta_\Lambda(d^*(c_1)), \quad \text{for each } c_1 \ge 0.$$

Now, let us take $\bar{c}_1 > a_\Lambda$ (where a_Λ is defined in Equation (14)). Then, using the fact that ζ_Λ is strictly decreasing in (a_Λ, ∞) (see Remark 6), we have that for any $c_2 > c_1 > d^*(\bar{c}_1)$ it holds that $d^*(\bar{c}_1) < d^*(c_1)$ and

$$G_\Lambda(c_1, c_2) \le G_\Lambda(c_1, d^*(c_1)) = \zeta_\Lambda(d^*(c_1)) < \zeta_\Lambda(d^*(\bar{c}_1)) = G_\Lambda(\bar{c}_1, d^*(\bar{c}_1)).$$

This implies that the maximum of the function G_Λ has to be achieved on the set

$$\{(c_1, c_2) \in \mathbb{R}^2_+ : c_1 < c_2 \text{ and } c_1 \in [0, \bar{c}_1]\}.$$

Finally, from Equation (22), we obtain

$$F_\Lambda(c_1, c_2) < \frac{Z^{(q)}(c_2)}{qW^{(q)}(c_2)} + \Lambda \sup_{c_1 \in [0, \bar{c}_1]} \left[\frac{Z^{(q)}(c_2)}{qW^{(q)}(c_2)} Z^{(q)}(c_1) - k^{(q)}(c_1) \right] - (c_2 - \bar{c}_1 - \delta), \quad \text{for } c_1 \in [0, \bar{c}_1].$$

Hence, for any $c_1 \in [0, \bar{c}_1]$, we can find $\bar{c}_2 > \bar{c}_1$ such that

$$\partial_{c_2} G_\Lambda(c_1, c_2)(c_1, c_2) < 0, \quad \text{for any } 0 \le c_1 \le \bar{c}_1 \text{ and } 0 \le c_2 \le \bar{c}_2.$$

Therefore, the function G_Λ attains its maximum on the set

$$\{(c_1, c_2) \in [0, \bar{c}_1] \times [0, \bar{c}_2] : c_1 < c_2\} \subset \mathcal{A}. \quad \square$$

Note that by Proposition 1 the set $\mathcal{B} \subset \mathcal{A}$ defined as

$$\mathcal{B} := \{(c_1^*, c_2^*) \in \mathcal{A} : G_\Lambda(c_1^*, c_2^*) \ge G_\Lambda(c_1, c_2) \text{ for all } (c_1, c_2) \in \mathcal{A}\},$$

is not empty. Moreover, since $G_\Lambda \in C^1(\mathcal{A})$ and using Equation (14), it follows that

$$\partial_{c_1} G_\Lambda(c_1^*, c_2^*) = \frac{qW^{(q)}(c_1^*)}{Z^{(q)}(c_2^*) - Z^{(q)}(c_1^*)} (G_\Lambda(c_1^*, c_2^*) - \zeta_\Lambda(c_1^*)) \le 0, \text{ for } (c_1^*, c_2^*) \in \mathcal{B}, \tag{24}$$

with equality if $c_1 > 0$, and

$$\partial_{c_2} G_\Lambda(c_1^*, c_2^*) = -\frac{qW^{(q)}(c_2^*)}{Z^{(q)}(c_2^*) - Z^{(q)}(c_1^*)} (G_\Lambda(c_1^*, c_2^*) - \zeta_\Lambda(c_2^*)) = 0, \quad \text{for } (c_1^*, c_2^*) \in \mathcal{B}. \tag{25}$$

Proposition 2. *There exists a unique pair* $(c_1^\Lambda, c_2^\Lambda)$ *in* $\mathcal{B}$. *Furthermore,* $0 \leq c_1^\Lambda \leq a_\Lambda < c_2^\Lambda < \infty$, *with* a_Λ *defined in Equation* (16), *and the value function associated with the* $(c_1^\Lambda, c_2^\Lambda)$*-policy is*

$$v_{\delta,\Lambda}^{c_1^\Lambda, c_2^\Lambda}(x) = \begin{cases} Z^{(q)}(x)\zeta_\Lambda(c_2^\Lambda) + \Lambda k^{(q)}(x), & \text{if } x \leq c_2^\Lambda, \\ x - c_2^\Lambda + v_{\delta,\Lambda}^{c_1^\Lambda, c_2^\Lambda}(c_2^\Lambda), & \text{if } x > c_2^\Lambda. \end{cases} \tag{26}$$

Proof. Let M be the maximum value of G_Λ in $\mathcal{B}$; therefore, for any $(c_1^*, c_2^*) \in \mathcal{B}$, we have that $\zeta_\Lambda(c_2^*) = M$ by Equation (25). From Remark 6, we know that ζ_Λ is strictly increasing on $(0, a_\Lambda)$ and strictly decreasing on (a_Λ, ∞). If $\zeta_\Lambda(0) \geq M$, ζ_Λ attains M at a unique $c_2^\Lambda > a_\Lambda$ and therefore $(0, c_2^\Lambda)$ is the only point that satisfies Equation (24). On the other hand, if $\zeta_\Lambda(0) < M$, ζ_Λ can only attain the value M at a unique $c_1^\Lambda < a_\Lambda$ and a unique $c_2^\Lambda > a_\Lambda$. Hence, $(c_1^\Lambda, c_2^\Lambda)$ is the only point that satisfies Equations (24) and (25), that is, the only existing point in $\mathcal{B}$. Now, from Lemma 1 and using that $G_\Lambda(c_1^\Lambda, c_2^\Lambda) = \zeta_\Lambda(c_2^\Lambda)$, we obtain the first part of Equation (26). For the second part, let $x > c_2^\Lambda$, then

$$v_{\delta,\Lambda}^{c_1^\Lambda, c_2^\Lambda}(x) = x - c_1^\Lambda - \delta + v_{\delta,\Lambda}^{c_1^\Lambda, c_2^\Lambda}(c_1^\Lambda) = x - c_2^\Lambda + c_2^\Lambda - c_1^\Lambda - \delta + v_{\delta,\Lambda}^{c_1^\Lambda, c_2^\Lambda}(c_1^\Lambda) = x - c_2^\Lambda + v_{\delta,\Lambda}^{c_1^\Lambda, c_2^\Lambda}(c_2^\Lambda). \quad \square$$

The following properties of $v_{\delta,\Lambda}^{c_1^\Lambda, c_2^\Lambda}$ are used below in the verification theorem.

Remark 9. *From Equations* (10) *and* (26), *we note*

$$v_{\delta,\Lambda}^{c_1^\Lambda, c_2^\Lambda}(x) \geq \frac{\Lambda\psi'(0+)}{q} + Z^{(q)}(c_2^\Lambda)\zeta(c_2^\Lambda), \quad \text{for } x > 0.$$

Remark 10 (Continuity/smoothness at zero). *Note that for* $x < 0$, $v_{\delta,\Lambda}^{c_1^\Lambda, c_2^\Lambda}(x) = v_{\delta,\Lambda}^{c_1^\Lambda, c_2^\Lambda}(0) + \Lambda x$. *Therefore,*

(i) $v_{\delta,\Lambda}^{c_1^\Lambda, c_2^\Lambda}$ *is continuous at zero.*
(ii) For the case of unbounded variation, we have that

$$v_{\delta,\Lambda}^{c_1^\Lambda, c_2^\Lambda\,\prime}(0+) = qW^{(q)}(0+)\zeta_\Lambda(c_2^\Lambda) + \Lambda = \Lambda = v_{\delta,\Lambda}^{c_1^\Lambda, c_2^\Lambda\,\prime}(0-).$$

4.3. Verification

Let us denote by $v_{\delta,\Lambda}$ the function given in Equation (26), which is the optimal value function among reflected policies. We now prove some properties of this function.

Lemma 2. *The function* $v_{\delta,\Lambda}$ *is* $C^2((0,\infty)\backslash\{c_2^\Lambda\})$ *and* $C^1(0,\infty)$.

Proof. By Assumption 1, we have that, for each $q \geq 0$, the function $W^{(q)}$ is continuously differentiable on $(0, \infty)$. This implies, by Equation (26), that $v_{\delta,\Lambda}$ is $C^2((0,\infty)\backslash\{c_2^\Lambda\})$. On the other hand, using Equation (26), we have that for $x \leq c_2^\Lambda$,

$$v_{\delta,\Lambda}'(x) = qW^{(q)}(x)\zeta_\Lambda(c_2^\Lambda) + \Lambda Z^{(q)}(x) = qW^{(q)}(x)\left(\frac{1 - \Lambda Z^{(q)}(c_2^\Lambda)}{qW^{(q)}(c_2^\Lambda)}\right) + \Lambda Z^{(q)}(x).$$

This implies that $v_{\delta,\Lambda}'(c_2^\Lambda-) = 1$. For $x > c_2^\Lambda$, we obtain by Equation (26) that

$$v_{\delta,\Lambda}'(c_2^\Lambda+) = 1 = v_{\delta,\Lambda}'(c_2^\Lambda-),$$

which implies the result. $\square$

Let $\mathcal{L}$ be the operator defined as follows,

$$\mathcal{L}F(x) := \gamma F'(x) + \frac{\sigma^2}{2}F''(x) + \int_{(0,\infty)} (F(x-z) - F(x) + F'(x)z\mathbf{1}_{\{0<z\leq 1\}})\Pi(\mathrm{d}z), \quad x > 0,$$

where $x \in \mathbb{R}$ and F is a function on $\mathbb{R}$ such that $\mathcal{L}F(x)$ is well defined.

Proposition 3.

1. $(\mathcal{L} - q)v_{\delta,\Lambda}(x) = 0$ *for* $x < c_2^{\Lambda}$.
2. $(\mathcal{L} - q)v_{\delta,\Lambda}(x) \leq 0$ *for* $x > c_2^{\Lambda}$.

Proof.

1. By the proof of Theorem 2.1 in Bayraktar et al. (2014a), we have that for $0 < x < c_2^{\Lambda}$,

$$(\mathcal{L} - q)\Big(\overline{Z}^{(q)}(x) + \frac{\psi'(0+)}{q}\Big) = 0 \quad \text{and} \quad (\mathcal{L} - q)Z^{(q)}(x) = 0.$$

This implies that for $0 < x < c_2^{\Lambda}$,

$$(\mathcal{L} - q)v_{\delta,\Lambda}(x) = 0.$$

2. We note that $v_{\delta,\Lambda}(y) = u_{\Lambda}^{c_2^{\Lambda}}(y)$ for all $y \geq 0$, where u_{Λ}^{a} is the barrier strategy at the level a for the dividend problem with capital injection given by Equation (13). Therefore,

(i) If we take $y \leq x$, and $c_2^{\Lambda} \leq x$, we obtain

$$u_{\Lambda}^{x}(y) = Z^{(q)}(y)\zeta_{\Lambda}(x) + \Lambda\Big(\overline{Z}^{(q)}(y) + \frac{\psi'(0+)}{q}\Big).$$

Recall the functions ζ_{Λ} and H are as in Equations (7) and (14), respectively. Then,

$$\begin{aligned}
\lim_{y\uparrow x} \frac{\mathrm{d}^2 u_{\Lambda}^{x}}{\mathrm{d}y^2}(y) &= \Lambda q W^{(q)}(x) + q W^{(q)\prime}(x)\zeta_{\Lambda}(x) \\
&= \frac{W^{(q)\prime}(x)}{W^{(q)}(x)}\left(1 - \Lambda\left(Z^{(q)}(x) - qW^{(q)}(x)\frac{W^{(q)}(x)}{W^{(q)\prime}(x)}\right)\right) \\
&= \frac{W^{(q)\prime}(x)}{W^{(q)}(x)}(1 - \Lambda H(x)) \\
&= -qW^{(q)}(x)\zeta_{\Lambda}'(x).
\end{aligned}$$

By Proposition 2, we know that $a_{\Lambda} < c_2^{\Lambda} \leq x$. Then, $\lim_{y\uparrow x} \frac{\mathrm{d}^2 u_{\Lambda}^{x}}{\mathrm{d}y^2}(y) \geq 0 = \frac{\mathrm{d}^2 u_{\Lambda}^{c_2^{\Lambda}}}{\mathrm{d}x^2}(x)$, since $\zeta_{\Lambda}'(x) < 0$ by Remark 6.

(ii) We have for $y \in [0, c_2^{\Lambda}]$,

$$\frac{\mathrm{d}u_{\Lambda}^{c_2^{\Lambda}}}{\mathrm{d}y}(y) = \Lambda Z^{(q)}(y) + qW^{(q)}(y)\zeta_{\Lambda}(c_2^{\Lambda}) \geq \Lambda Z^{(q)}(y) + qW^{(q)}(y)\zeta_{\Lambda}(x) = \frac{\mathrm{d}u_{\Lambda}^{x}}{\mathrm{d}y}(y),$$

which comes from the fact that for $x \geq c_2^\Lambda > a_\Lambda$, then $\zeta_\Lambda(c_2^\Lambda) \geq \zeta_\Lambda(x)$ by Remark 2. On the other hand, for $y \in (c_2^\Lambda, x]$, we have, using the fact that $\zeta_\Lambda(y) \geq \zeta_\Lambda(x)$,

$$\begin{aligned}\frac{\mathrm{d}u_\Lambda^x}{\mathrm{d}y}(y) &= \Lambda Z^{(q)}(y) + qW^{(q)}(y)\zeta_\Lambda(x) \\ &\leq \Lambda Z^{(q)}(y) + qW^{(q)}(y)\zeta_\Lambda(y) \\ &= \Lambda Z^{(q)}(y) + qW^{(q)}(y)\frac{1-\Lambda Z^{(q)}(y)}{qW^{(q)}(y)} = 1 = \frac{\mathrm{d}u_\Lambda^{c_2^\Lambda}}{\mathrm{d}y}(y).\end{aligned}$$

(iii) We note that

$$\begin{aligned}u_\Lambda^x(c_2^\Lambda) &= \Lambda\left(\overline{Z}^{(q)}(c_2^\Lambda) + \frac{\psi'(0+)}{q}\right) + Z^{(q)}(c_2^\Lambda)\zeta_\Lambda(x) \\ &\leq \Lambda\left(\overline{Z}^{(q)}(c_2^\Lambda) + \frac{\psi'(0+)}{q}\right) + Z^{(q)}(c_2^\Lambda)\zeta_\Lambda(c_2^\Lambda) = u_\Lambda^{c_2^\Lambda}(c_2^\Lambda).\end{aligned}$$

This and Point (ii) imply that $(u_\Lambda^{c_2^\Lambda} - u_\Lambda^x)(x) \geq 0$.

(iv) We have

$$\frac{\mathrm{d}u_\Lambda^{c_2^\Lambda}}{\mathrm{d}x}(x) = 1 = \lim_{y\to x}\frac{\mathrm{d}u_\Lambda^x}{\mathrm{d}y}(y).$$

Thus, by similar arguments to those in the proof of Theorem 2 in Loeffen (2008), we obtain the result. □

Lemma 3.

1. *For $x > 0$, we have that $v'_{\delta,\Lambda}(x) \leq \Lambda$.*
2. *For $x \geq y \geq 0$, we have that $v_{\delta,\Lambda}(x) - v_{\delta,\Lambda}(y) \geq x - y - \delta$.*

Proof. 1. By Equation (5) together with Equation (26), we note that for $x \leq c_2^\Lambda$,

$$\begin{aligned}v'_{\delta,\Lambda}(x) &= \Lambda\left(Z^{(q)}(x) - \frac{W^{(q)}(x)}{W^{(q)}(c_2^\Lambda)}Z^{(q)}(c_2^\Lambda)\right) + \frac{W^{(q)}(x)}{W^{(q)}(c_2^\Lambda)} \\ &= \Lambda\mathbb{E}_x\left[e^{-q\tau_0^-}\mathbf{1}_{\{\tau_0^- < \tau_{c_2^\Lambda}^+\}}\right] + \mathbb{E}_x\left[e^{-q\tau_{c_2^\Lambda}^+}\mathbf{1}_{\{\tau_{c_2^\Lambda}^+ < \tau_0^-\}}\right] \\ &\leq \Lambda\left(\mathbb{E}_x\left[e^{-q\tau_0^-}\mathbf{1}_{\{\tau_0^- < \tau_{c_2^\Lambda}^+\}}\right] + \mathbb{E}_x\left[e^{-q\tau_{c_2^\Lambda}^+}\mathbf{1}_{\{\tau_{c_2^\Lambda}^+ < \tau_0^-\}}\right]\right) \\ &\leq \Lambda\left(\mathbb{P}_x\left[\tau_0^- < \tau_{c_2^\Lambda}^+\right] + \mathbb{P}_x\left[\tau_{c_2^\Lambda}^+ < \tau_0^-\right]\right) = \Lambda.\end{aligned}$$

On the other hand, $v'_{\delta,\Lambda}(x) = 1 \leq \Lambda$ for $x > c_2^\Lambda$.

2. Let us consider $c_2^\Lambda \geq x \geq y$. We note that

$$\begin{aligned}v_{\delta,\Lambda}(x) - v_{\delta,\Lambda}(y) &= \Lambda\left(\overline{Z}^{(q)}(x) - \overline{Z}^{(q)}(y)\right) + \left(Z^{(q)}(x) - Z^{(q)}(y)\right)\zeta_\Lambda(c_2^\Lambda) \\ &= \Lambda\left(\overline{Z}^{(q)}(x) - \overline{Z}^{(q)}(y)\right) + (Z^{(q)}(x) - Z^{(q)}(y))G_\Lambda(c_1^\Lambda, c_2^\Lambda)\end{aligned}$$

$$
\begin{aligned}
&\geq \Lambda\left(\overline{Z}^{(q)}(x)-\overline{Z}^{(q)}(y)\right)+(Z^{(q)}(x)-Z^{(q)}(y))G_\Lambda(x,y)\\
&=\Lambda\left(\overline{Z}^{(q)}(x)-\overline{Z}^{(q)}(y)\right)+(Z^{(q)}(x)-Z^{(q)}(y))\frac{x-y-\delta-\Lambda\left(\overline{Z}^{(q)}(x)-\overline{Z}^{(q)}(y)\right)}{Z^{(q)}(x)-Z^{(q)}(y)}\\
&=x-y-\delta. \qquad (27)
\end{aligned}
$$

Now, suppose that $x \geq y \geq c_2^\Lambda$, then using Equation (26) we obtain

$$v_{\delta,\Lambda}(x)-v_{\delta,\Lambda}(y)=x-y\geq x-y-\delta.$$

Finally, for the case $x \geq c_2^\Lambda \geq y$, by Equation (27), we have

$$v_{\delta,\Lambda}(x)-v_{\delta,\Lambda}(y)=x-c_2^\Lambda+v_{\delta,\Lambda}(c_2^\Lambda)-v_{\delta,\Lambda}(y)\geq x-c_2^\Lambda+(c_2^\Lambda-y-\delta)=x-y-\delta. \quad \square$$

Now, we proceed to the verification theorem that proves the optimality of the $(c_1^\Lambda, c_2^\Lambda)$-policy.

Theorem 1 (Verification Theorem). *Let $V_{\delta,\Lambda}$, $v_{\delta,\Lambda}$ be as in Equations (3) and (26), respectively. Then, $v_{\delta,\Lambda}(x)=V_{\delta,\Lambda}(x)$ for all $x\geq 0$. Hence, the $(c_1^\Lambda, c_2^\Lambda)$-policy is optimal.*

Proof. By the definition of $V_{\delta,\Lambda}$, $v_{\delta,\Lambda}(x)\leq V_{\delta,\Lambda}(x)$ for all $x\geq 0$. Let us verify that $v_{\delta,\Lambda}(x)\geq v^\pi_{\delta,\Lambda}(x)$ for all admissible $\pi\in\Theta_\delta$ and for all $x\geq 0$. Recall that $v^\pi_{\delta,\Lambda}$ is defined in Equation (2). Take $\pi=\{L^\pi,R^\pi\}\in\Theta_\delta$ fixed and let $(T_n)_{n\in\mathbb{N}}$ be the sequence of stopping times where $T_n := \inf\{t>0 : X^\pi_t > n\}$. Since $X^\pi = X - L^\pi + R^\pi$, with X being a spectrally negative Lévy process, it is a semi-martingale and $v_{\delta,\Lambda}$ is sufficiently smooth on $(0,\infty)$ by Lemma 2, and continuous (respectively, continuously differentiable) at zero for the case of bounded variation (respectively, unbounded variation) by Remark 10, we can use the change of variables/Meyer-Itô's formula (cf. Theorems II.31 and II.32 of Protter (2005)) on the stopped process $(\mathrm{e}^{-q(t\wedge T_n)}v_{\delta,\Lambda}(X^\pi_{t\wedge T_n}); t\geq 0)$ to deduce under $\mathbb{P}_x$ that

$$
\begin{aligned}
\mathrm{e}^{-q(t\wedge T_n)}v_{\delta,\Lambda}(X^\pi_{t\wedge T_n})-v_{\delta,\Lambda}(x)=&\int_0^{t\wedge T_n}\mathrm{e}^{-qs}(\mathcal{L}-q)v_{\delta,\Lambda}(X^\pi_{s-})\mathrm{d}s+M_{t\wedge T_n}+J_{t\wedge T_n}\\
&+\int_{[0,t\wedge T_n]}\mathrm{e}^{-qs}v'_{\delta,\Lambda}(X^\pi_{s-})\mathrm{d}R^{\pi,c}_s, \qquad (28)
\end{aligned}
$$

where M is a local martingale with $M_0=0$, $R^{\pi,c}$ is the continuous part of R^π, and J is a jump process, which is given by

$$
\begin{aligned}
J_t=&\sum_{0\leq s\leq t}\mathrm{e}^{-qs}\left(v_{\delta,\Lambda}(X^\pi_{s-}+\Delta[X+R^\pi]_s)-v_{\delta,\Lambda}(X^\pi_{s-}+\Delta X_s)\right)1_{\{\Delta[X+R^\pi]_s\neq 0\}}\\
&+\sum_{0\leq s\leq t}\mathrm{e}^{-qs}\left(v_{\delta,\Lambda}(X^\pi_{s-}+\Delta[X+R^\pi]_s-\Delta L^\pi_s)-v_{\delta,\Lambda}(X^\pi_{s-}+\Delta[X+R^\pi]_s)\right)1_{\{\Delta L^\pi_s\neq 0\}}, \quad \text{for } t\geq 0.
\end{aligned}
$$

On the other hand, by Part (1) of Lemma 3, we obtain that

$$
\begin{aligned}
&\int_{[0,t\wedge T_n]}\mathrm{e}^{-qs}v'_{\delta,\Lambda}(X^\pi_{s-})\mathrm{d}R^{\pi,c}_s\\
&+\sum_{0\leq s\leq t\wedge T_n}\mathrm{e}^{-qs}\left[v_{\delta,\Lambda}(X^\pi_{s-}+\Delta[X+R^\pi]_s)-v_{\delta,\Lambda}(X^\pi_{s-}+\Delta X_s)\right]1_{\{\Delta[X+R^\pi]_s\neq 0\}}\\
&\leq\Lambda\int_{[0,t\wedge T_n]}\mathrm{e}^{-qs}\mathrm{d}R^{\pi,c}_s+\Lambda\sum_{0\leq s\leq t\wedge T_n}\mathrm{e}^{-qs}\Delta R^\pi_s=\Lambda\int_{[0,t\wedge T_n]}\mathrm{e}^{-qs}\mathrm{d}R^\pi_s.
\end{aligned}
$$

Similarly, by Part (2) of Lemma 3,

$$\sum_{0\le s\le t\wedge T_n} \mathrm{e}^{-qs}[v_{\delta,\Lambda}(X^\pi_{s-}+\Delta[X+R^\pi]_s-\Delta L^\pi_s)-v_{\delta,\Lambda}(X^\pi_{s-}+\Delta[X+R^\pi]_s)]1_{\{\Delta L^\pi_s\neq 0\}}$$
$$\le -\sum_{0\le s\le t\wedge T_n}\mathrm{e}^{-qs}\,\Delta L^\pi_s+\delta\sum_{0\le s\le t\wedge T_n}\mathrm{e}^{-qs}\,1_{\{\Delta L^\pi_s>0\}}$$
$$=-\int_{[0,t\wedge T_n]}\mathrm{e}^{-qs}\,\mathrm{d}\left(L^\pi_s-\delta\sum_{0\le u\le s}1_{\{\Delta L^\pi_u>0\}}\right).$$

Hence, from Equation (28), we derive that

$$v_{\delta,\Lambda}(x)\ge -\int_0^{t\wedge T_n}\mathrm{e}^{-qs}(\mathcal{L}-q)v_{\delta,\Lambda}(X^\pi_{s-})\mathrm{d}s-\Lambda\int_{[0,t\wedge T_n]}\mathrm{e}^{-qs}\,\mathrm{d}R^\pi_s$$
$$+\int_{[0,t\wedge T_n]}\mathrm{e}^{-qs}\,\mathrm{d}\left(L^\pi_s-\delta\sum_{0\le u\le s}1_{\{\Delta L^\pi_u>0\}}\right)-M_{t\wedge T_n}+\mathrm{e}^{-q(t\wedge T_n)}\,v_{\delta,\Lambda}(X^\pi_{t\wedge T_n}).$$

Using Proposition 3 along with Point 3 in the proof of Lemma 6 in Loeffen (2009), and that $X^\pi_{s-}\ge 0$ a.s. for $s\ge 0$, we observe that

$$v_{\delta,\Lambda}(x)\ge \int_{[0,t\wedge T_n]}\mathrm{e}^{-qs}\,\mathrm{d}\left(L^\pi_s-\delta\sum_{0\le u\le s}1_{\{\Delta L^\pi_u>0\}}\right)-\Lambda\int_{[0,t\wedge T_n]}\mathrm{d}R^\pi_s-M_{t\wedge T_n}+\mathrm{e}^{-q(t\wedge T_n)}\,v_{\delta,\Lambda}(X^\pi_{t\wedge T_n})$$
$$\ge \int_{[0,t\wedge T_n]}\mathrm{e}^{-qs}\,\mathrm{d}\left(L^\pi_s-\delta\sum_{0\le u\le s}1_{\{\Delta L^\pi_u>0\}}\right)-\Lambda\int_{[0,t\wedge T_n]}\mathrm{d}R^\pi_s-M_{t\wedge T_n}$$
$$+\mathrm{e}^{-q(t\wedge T_n)}\left(\frac{\Lambda\psi'(0+)}{q}+Z^{(q)}(c_2^\Lambda)\left(\zeta(c_2^\Lambda)\right)\right),\tag{29}$$

where the last inequality follows from Remark 9. In addition, by the compensation formula (see, e.g., Corollary 4.6 of Kyprianou (2014)), $(M_{t\wedge T_n}: t\ge 0)$ is a zero-mean $\mathbb{P}_x$-martingale. Now, taking expected value in Equation (29) and letting $(t\wedge T_n)\nearrow\infty$ $\mathbb{P}_x$-a.s., the monotone convergence theorem, applied separately for $\mathbb{E}_x\left[\int_{[0,t\wedge T_n]}\mathrm{e}^{-qs}\,\mathrm{d}\left(L^\pi_s-\delta\sum_{0\le u\le s}1_{\{\Delta L^\pi_u>0\}}\right)\right]$ and $\mathbb{E}_x\left(\Lambda\int_{[0,t\wedge T_n]}\mathrm{e}^{-qs}\,\mathrm{d}R^\pi_s\right)$, gives

$$v_{\delta,\Lambda}(x)\ge \mathbb{E}_x\left(\int_{[0,\infty)}\mathrm{e}^{-qs}\,\mathrm{d}\left(L^\pi_s-\delta\sum_{0\le u\le s}1_{\{\Delta L^\pi_u>0\}}\right)-\Lambda\int_{[0,\infty)}\mathrm{e}^{-qs}\,\mathrm{d}R^\pi_s\right)=v^\pi_{\delta,\Lambda}(x).$$

This completes the proof. □

5. Optimal Dividends with Capital Injection Constraint

In this section, we are interested in maximizing the expected NPV of the dividend strategy subject to a constraint in the expected present value of the injected capital. Specifically, we aim to solve

$$V_\delta(x,K):=\sup_{\pi\in\Theta_\delta}\mathbb{E}_x\left[\int_0^\infty\mathrm{e}^{-qt}\,\mathrm{d}\left(L^\pi_t-\delta\sum_{0\le s<t}\mathbf{1}_{\{\Delta L^\pi_s>0\}}\right)\right]\quad\text{s.t. }\mathbb{E}_x\left[\int_0^\infty\mathrm{e}^{-qt}\,\mathrm{d}R^\pi_t\right]\le K,\tag{30}$$

for any $x\ge 0$ and $K\ge 0$. Strategies π that do not satisfy the capital injection constraint are called infeasible. Recall that the insurance company has to inject capital to ensure the non-negativity of the risk process. Therefore, small values of K require very low dividend payments to keep the risk process non-negative, or would even make the problem infeasible. In the latter case, we define the value function as $-\infty$.

To solve this problem, we use the solution of the optimal dividend problem with capital injection found in the section above. Thus, for $\Lambda \geq 0$, we define the function

$$v^{\pi}_{\delta,\Lambda}(x,K) := v^{\pi}_{\delta,\Lambda}(x) + \Lambda K,$$

with $v^{\pi}_{\delta,\Lambda}$ as in Equation (2). It is easy to check that $V_\delta(x,K) = \sup_{\pi\in\Theta_\delta} \inf_{\Lambda\geq 0} v^{\pi}_{\delta,\Lambda}(x,K)$ since for infeasible strategies $\inf_{\Lambda\geq 0} v^{\pi}_{\delta,\Lambda}(x,K) = -\infty$. By interchanging the sup with the inf we obtain an upper bound for $V_\delta(x,K)$, the so-called weak duality. Hence, the dual problem of Equation (30) is defined as

$$V^D_\delta(x,K) := \inf_{\Lambda\geq 0} \sup_{\pi\in\Theta_\delta} v^{\pi}_{\delta,\Lambda}(x,K) = \inf_{\Lambda\geq 0}\left\{\Lambda K + \sup_{\pi\in\Theta_\delta} v^{\pi}_{\delta,\Lambda}(x)\right\} = \inf_{\Lambda\geq 1}\left\{\Lambda K + V_{\delta,\Lambda}(x)\right\}, \tag{31}$$

with $V_{\delta,\Lambda}$ given in Equation (3). The last equality in Equation (31) is true, since $V_{\delta,\Lambda}(x)$ is infinite for any $\Lambda < 1$; see Remark 2. The main goal is to prove that $V^D_\delta(x,K) \leq V_\delta(x,K)$.

5.1. No Transaction Cost

In this subsection, we consider the problem in Equation (30) without transaction cost, i.e., $\delta = 0$. For this case, we denote $V(x,K) := V_0(x,K)$ and $V^D(x,K) := V^D_0(x,K)$. From Section 3.2, recall that for each $\Lambda \geq 1$, the optimal strategy is a barrier strategy, which is determined by a_Λ defined in Equation (16), and its NPV satisfies $V_\Lambda = v^{a_\Lambda}_\Lambda$, where $v^{a_\Lambda}_\Lambda$ is as in Equation (13). Given a barrier strategy at $a > 0$ and $x \in [0,a]$, the expected NPV of the injected capital is given by the function

$$\Psi_x(a) := \mathbb{E}_x\left[\int_0^\infty e^{-qt}\,dR^{a,0}_t\right] = \frac{Z^{(q)}(a)}{qW^{(q)}(a)}Z^{(q)}(x) - k^{(q)}(x), \tag{32}$$

with $k^{(q)}$ as in Equation (10). Clearly, if $x > a$, then $\Psi_x(a) = \Psi_a(a)$. We also define

$$\underline{K}_x := \lim_{a\to\infty} \Psi_x(a). \tag{33}$$

Using Equation (12) and the properties of scale functions (see Remark 3 (3)),

$$\underline{K}_x = -k^{(q)}(x) + \frac{Z^{(q)}(x)}{\Phi(q)}.$$

Note that $\underline{K}_x$ is the expected present value of the injected capital for the pay-nothing strategy $\pi_{PN} := \{0, R^0\}$. Therefore, letting $a \to \infty$ in Equation (13), it can be verified

$$v^{\pi_{PN}}_\Lambda(x,K) = \Lambda(K - \underline{K}_x).$$

Hence, if $K \geq \underline{K}_x$, then for any $x \geq 0$,

$$V(x,K) = \sup_{\pi\in\Theta} \inf_{\Lambda\geq 0} v^{\pi}_\Lambda(x,K) \geq \inf_{\Lambda\geq 0} v^{\pi_{PN}}_\Lambda(x,K) = 0. \tag{34}$$

Conversely, if $K < \underline{K}_x$, the problem in Equation (30) is infeasible, which is verified below.

Lemma 4. *If $K < \underline{K}_x$, then $V(x,K) = -\infty$.*

Proof. First, by Remark 7 and Equation (11), it is easy to verify that

$$\lim_{\Lambda\to\infty} \mathbb{E}_x\left[\int_0^\infty e^{-qt}\,dL^{a_\Lambda,0}_t\right] = 0, \quad \text{for } x \geq 0. \tag{35}$$

Then,

$$
\begin{aligned}
V^D(x,K) &= \inf_{\Lambda\geq 1}\{\Lambda K + V_\Lambda(x)\}\\
&= \inf_{\Lambda\geq 1}\left\{\mathbb{E}_x\left[\int_0^\infty \mathrm{e}^{-qt}\,\mathrm{d}L_t^{a_\Lambda,0}\right] + \Lambda(K-\Psi_x(a_\Lambda))\right\}\\
&\leq \lim_{\Lambda\to\infty}\left\{\mathbb{E}_x\left[\int_0^\infty \mathrm{e}^{-qt}\,\mathrm{d}L_t^{a_\Lambda,0}\right] + \Lambda(K-\Psi_x(a_\Lambda))\right\} = -\infty.
\end{aligned}
$$

Now, since $V(x,K) \leq V^D(x,K)$ for any $x \geq 0, K \geq 0$, we have the result. □

The next lemma allows us to prove that, when $K = \underline{K}_x$, Equation (34) holds with equality, and it is used to prove the main result of this subsection.

Lemma 5. *Let $x \geq 0$ be fixed. The function Ψ_x is strictly decreasing on $(0,\infty)$.*

Proof. First, consider the case when $x < a$. Then, by Remark 4 (i), we have that $\dfrac{qW^{(q)}(a)}{Z^{(q)}(a)}$ is strictly increasing and the lemma is obtained. Now, when $x \geq a > 0$, a simple calculation shows that

$$
\frac{\mathrm{d}\Psi_a(a)}{\mathrm{d}a} = -\frac{Z^{(q)}(a)\left(W^{(q)\prime}(a)Z^{(q)}(a) - q[W^{(q)}(a)]^2\right)}{q[W^{(q)}(a)]^2} = -\frac{Z^{(q)}(a)W^{(q)\prime}(a)}{q[W^{(q)}(a)]^2}H(a),
$$

which is strictly negative, by Remarks 3 and 5. From here, we conclude the assertion of the lemma. □

Lemma 6. *If $K = \underline{K}_x$, then $V(x,K) = 0$ and the optimal strategy is the pay-nothing strategy π_{PN}.*

Proof. By Equation (34), we know that $V(x,K) \geq 0$. On the other hand, from Lemma 5 and Equation (33), we have that $\Lambda(K - \Psi_x(a_\Lambda)) \leq 0$ for all $\Lambda \geq 0$. Then, using Equations (33) and (35)

$$
\begin{aligned}
V^D(x,K) = \inf_{\Lambda\geq 1}\{\Lambda K + V_\Lambda(x)\} &= \inf_{\Lambda\geq 1}\left\{\mathbb{E}_x\left[\int_0^\infty \mathrm{e}^{-qt}\,\mathrm{d}L_t^{a_\Lambda,0}\right] + \Lambda(K-\Psi_x(a_\Lambda))\right\}\\
&\leq \lim_{\Lambda\to\infty}\mathbb{E}_x\left[\int_0^\infty \mathrm{e}^{-qt}\,\mathrm{d}L_t^{a_\Lambda,0}\right] = 0.
\end{aligned}
$$
□

Now, we define

$$
\overline{K} := \lim_{a\to 0}\Psi_a(a).
$$

Using Equation (12), we have that $\overline{K} = \infty$ when the risk process has unbounded variation. Otherwise, by Remark 3 (2),

$$
\overline{K} = \frac{c - \psi'(0+)}{q}, \tag{36}
$$

and $\overline{K}$ corresponds to the expected NPV of the injected capital for the strategy $\pi_{0,0}$ (see Equation (4.5) in Avram et al. (2007)).

Lemma 7. *Assume that the risk process X has bounded variation. If $K \geq \overline{K}$, then $V(x,K) = K + V_1(x)$, with $V_1(x) = x + \dfrac{\psi'(0+)}{q}$.*

Proof. If the Lévy measure is finite, by Equation (16), we have that $a_1 = 0$. The same is true for the infinite Lévy measure case since $H^{-1}(1) = 0$ by Remark 5. Using Equation (13) and Remark 6, we obtain

$$V_1(x) = v_1^0(x) = x + \frac{c}{q} - \overline{K} = x + \frac{\psi'(0+)}{q}, \quad \text{for } x \geq 0. \tag{37}$$

Now, by Equations (31), (36) and (37) and the weak duality, we get

$$V(x,K) \leq V^D(x,K) \leq K + v_1^0(x) = K + V_1(x).$$

Since $K \geq \overline{K}$, $\pi_{0,0}$ is a feasible strategy. Then, using Equation (11), it yields,

$$V(x,K) \geq \inf_{\Lambda \geq 1} \{v_\Lambda^0(x) + \Lambda K\} = x + K - \frac{c - \psi'(0+)}{q} + \frac{c}{q} = K + V_1(x).$$

Therefore, $V(x,K) = K + V_1(x)$. □

We are now ready for the main result of this subsection.

Theorem 2. *Assume $\delta = 0$ and let V and V^D as in Equation (30) and Equation (31), respectively, then $V = V^D$. Furthermore, if x and K are such that $K \in (\underline{K}_x, \overline{K})$, then*

$$V(x,K) = \Lambda^* K + V_{\Lambda^*}(x) = \mathbb{E}_x\left[\int_0^\infty \mathrm{e}^{-qt}\, \mathrm{d}L_t^{a^*,0}\right], \tag{38}$$

where $a^* = \Psi_x^{-1}(K)$, and $\Lambda^* = \dfrac{1}{H(a^*)}$.

Proof. Lemmas 4, 6 and 7 show imply that Equation (38) holds when x and K are such that $K \in [0, \underline{K}_x] \cup [\overline{K}, \infty)$. Assume now that $K \in (\underline{K}_x, \overline{K})$, then by Lemma 5 the function Ψ_x is injective, so there exists a unique $a^* > 0$ such that $\Psi_x(a^*) = K$. Note that from Equation (16), we have that there exists a unique Λ^* such that $a_{\Lambda^*} = a^*$. Then,

$$\begin{aligned} V^D(x,K) &\leq \Lambda^* K + V_{\Lambda^*}(x) \\ &= \Lambda^* K + \mathbb{E}_x\left[\int_0^\infty \mathrm{e}^{-qt}\, \mathrm{d}L_t^{a^*,0}\right] - \Lambda^* \Psi_x(a^*) \\ &= \mathbb{E}_x\left[\int_0^\infty \mathrm{e}^{-qt}\, \mathrm{d}L_t^{a^*,0}\right]. \end{aligned}$$

Meanwhile, since the strategy $\pi_{a^*,0}$ is feasible, we see

$$\begin{aligned} V(x,K) \geq \inf_{\Lambda \geq 1} \{v_\Lambda^{\pi_{a^*,0}}(x) + \Lambda K\} &= \inf_{\Lambda \geq 1} \left\{\mathbb{E}_x\left[\int_0^\infty \mathrm{e}^{-qt}\, \mathrm{d}L_t^{a^*,0}\right] + \Lambda(K - \Psi_x(a^*))\right\} \\ &= \mathbb{E}_x\left[\int_0^\infty \mathrm{e}^{-qt}\, \mathrm{d}L_t^{a^*,0}\right]. \end{aligned}$$

This implies that $V^D(x,K) \leq V(x,K)$. Finally, the weak duality gives Equation (46). □

5.2. *With Transaction Cost*

Now, we consider the problem given in Equation (30) with transaction cost $\delta > 0$. From the previous section, we know that optimal strategies are $(c_1^\Lambda, c_2^\Lambda)$-reflected strategies with $(c_1^\Lambda, c_2^\Lambda)$ given in Proposition 2.

Proposition 4. *The curve $\Lambda \mapsto (c_1^\Lambda, c_2^\Lambda)$ is continuous and unbounded, for $\Lambda \in [1, \infty)$.*

Proof. From Remark 7 and the fact that $a_\Lambda < c_2^\Lambda$ (by Proposition 2), we know that $c_2^\Lambda \to \infty$ as $\Lambda \to \infty$, so the curve is unbounded. To show the continuity of the curve, we consider two cases and use the implicit function theorem. To this end, suppose first $c_1^\Lambda = 0$. Defining $f(\Lambda, c_2) := G_\Lambda(0, c_2) - \zeta_\Lambda(c_2)$, we have $f(\Lambda, c_2^\Lambda) = 0$. Then,

$$\frac{\partial f}{\partial c_2}(\Lambda, c_2^\Lambda) = \frac{\partial G_\Lambda}{\partial c_2}(0, c_2^\Lambda) - \zeta'_\Lambda(c_2^\Lambda) = -\zeta'_\Lambda(c_2^\Lambda) > 0,$$

since $c_2^\Lambda > a_\Lambda$. From here, we see that the conditions of the implicit function theorem are satisfied. Now, if $c_1^\Lambda > 0$, define the function $f(\Lambda, c_1, c_2) = (f_1(\Lambda, c_1, c_2), f_2(\Lambda, c_1, c_2))$ by

$$\begin{aligned} f_1(\Lambda, c_1, c_2) &:= G_\Lambda(c_1, c_2) - \zeta_\Lambda(c_1), \\ f_2(\Lambda, c_1, c_2) &:= G_\Lambda(c_1, c_2) - \zeta_\Lambda(c_2). \end{aligned}$$

Then, $f(\Lambda, c_1^\Lambda, c_2^\Lambda) = (0, 0)$. Again, simple calculations show that the Jacobian determinant of this system of equations is $\zeta'_\Lambda(c_2^\Lambda)\zeta'_\Lambda(c_1^\Lambda) < 0$, since $c_1^\Lambda < a_\Lambda < c_2^\Lambda$. Therefore, the curve $\Lambda \mapsto (c_1^\Lambda, c_2^\Lambda)$ is continuous, for $\Lambda \in [1, \infty)$. $\square$

Next, we analyze the level curves of the constraint. Let $\overline{\Psi}_x(c_1, c_2)$ be the expected present value of the injected capital under a (c_1, c_2)-reflected policy. Then, the calculations given in the proof of Lemma 1 show that

$$\begin{aligned} \overline{\Psi}_x(c_1, c_2) :&= \mathbb{E}_x\left[\int_0^\infty e^{-qt}\, dR_t^{(c_1,c_2),0}\right] \\ &= \begin{cases} Z^{(q)}(x)\dfrac{\overline{Z}^{(q)}(c_2) - \overline{Z}^{(q)}(c_1)}{Z^{(q)}(c_2) - Z^{(q)}(c_1)} - k^{(q)}(x), & \text{if } 0 \le x \le c_2, \\ \dfrac{\overline{Z}^{(q)}(c_2)Z^{(q)}(c_1) - \overline{Z}^{(q)}(c_1)Z^{(q)}(c_2)}{Z^{(q)}(c_2) - Z^{(q)}(c_1)} - \dfrac{\psi'(0+)}{q}, & \text{if } x > c_2. \end{cases} \end{aligned} \tag{39}$$

Remark 11. *Note that* $\lim_{c_1 \to c_2} \overline{\Psi}_x(c_1, c_2) = \Psi_x(c_2)$, *where* Ψ_x *is as in Equation* (32).

The next lemmas describe some properties of $\overline{\Psi}_x(c_1, c_2)$.

Lemma 8. *Let* $x \ge 0$ *be fixed.*

1. *If* $c_1 \ge 0$ *is fixed, then the function* $\overline{\Psi}_x(c_1, c_2)$, *given in Equation* (39), *is strictly decreasing for all* $c_2 > c_1$, *and*
$$\lim_{c_2 \to \infty} \overline{\Psi}_x(c_1, c_2) = \underline{K}_x, \tag{40}$$
where $\underline{K}_x$ *is defined in Equation* (33).
2. *If* $c_2 > 0$ *is fixed,* $\overline{\Psi}_x(c_1, c_2)$ *is strictly decreasing for all* $c_1 \in [0, c_2)$.

Proof. Let $c_1 \ge 0$ be fixed. First, assume that $c_2 \ge x$. To show that $\overline{\Psi}_x(c_1, c_2)$ is strictly decreasing, it is sufficient to verify that

$$\frac{\overline{Z}^{(q)}(c_2) - \overline{Z}^{(q)}(c_1)}{Z^{(q)}(c_2) - Z^{(q)}(c_1)}, \tag{41}$$

is strictly decreasing, which is true if

$$\frac{\partial}{\partial c_2}\left[\frac{\overline{Z}^{(q)}(c_2) - \overline{Z}^{(q)}(c_1)}{Z^{(q)}(c_2) - Z^{(q)}(c_1)}\right] = \frac{Z^{(q)}(c_2)}{Z^{(q)}(c_2) - Z^{(q)}(c_1)} - \frac{qW^{(q)}(c_2)(\overline{Z}^{(q)}(c_2) - \overline{Z}^{(q)}(c_1))}{[Z^{(q)}(c_2) - Z^{(q)}(c_1)]^2} < 0. \tag{42}$$

Since $Z^{(q)}$ is a strictly log-convex function on $[0,\infty)$ by Remark 4 (i),

$$\frac{qW^{(q)}(\eta)}{Z^{(q)}(\eta)} < \frac{qW^{(q)}(\varsigma)}{Z^{(q)}(\varsigma)}, \text{ for } \eta \text{ and } \varsigma \text{ such that } \eta < \varsigma.$$

Taking $\varsigma = c_2$ in the inequality above and integrating between c_1 and c_2, it follows that

$$Z^{(q)}(c_2) < \frac{qW^{(q)}(c_2)[\overline{Z}^{(q)}(c_2) - \overline{Z}^{(q)}(c_1)]}{Z^{(q)}(c_2) - Z^{(q)}(c_1)}. \tag{43}$$

Then, Equation (43) yields Equation (42) and hence Equation (41) is strictly decreasing. For the case $x > c_2$, it can be verified that

$$\frac{\partial}{\partial c_2}\left[Z^{(q)}(c_2)\frac{\overline{Z}^{(q)}(c_2) - \overline{Z}^{(q)}(c_1)}{Z^{(q)}(c_2) - Z^{(q)}(c_1)} - \overline{Z}^{(q)}(c_2)\right]$$
$$= \frac{Z^{(q)}(c_1)}{Z^{(q)}(c_2) - Z^{(q)}(c_1)}\left[Z^{(q)}(c_2) - \frac{qW^{(q)}(c_2)[\overline{Z}^{(q)}(c_2) - \overline{Z}^{(q)}(c_1)]}{Z^{(q)}(c_2) - Z^{(q)}(c_1)}\right]. \tag{44}$$

Then, using Equations (43) and (44), we obtain that $\overline{\Psi}_x(c_1, c_2)$ is strictly decreasing for all $c_2 \in (c_1, x)$. Similarly, we obtain Point 2 of the lemma. Now, by L'Hôpital's rule together with Exercise 8.5 (i) in Kyprianou (2014), it is not difficult to see that Equation (40) holds for any $c_1 \geq 0$. □

Note that Equation (34) still holds if $K \geq \underline{K}_x$. On the other hand, using that $c_2^\Lambda \to \infty$ as $\Lambda \to \infty$ together with Equation (18) we have that

$$\lim_{\Lambda\to\infty} \mathbb{E}_x\left[\int_0^\infty e^{-qt}\, dL_t^{(c_1^\Lambda, c_2^\Lambda),0}\right] = \lim_{\Lambda\to\infty}(c_2^\Lambda - c_1^\Lambda - \delta)\frac{Z^{(q)}(x)}{Z^{(q)}(c_2^\Lambda) - Z^{(q)}(c_1^\Lambda)} = 0, \tag{45}$$

by Remark 3 (3).

Remark 12. *Using the same arguments as in Lemma 7, we have that* $c_1^1 = a_1 = 0 < c_2^1$ *for bounded and unbounded variation processes. Similarly, if* x *and* K *are such that* $K \geq \overline{\Psi}_x(0, c_2^1) =: \overline{K}_x$, *then* $V_\delta(x, K) = V_{\delta,1}(x) + K$. *Note also that* $\overline{K}_x < \overline{K}$.

Lemma 9. *Let* $x \geq 0$ *be fixed. Then, for each* $K \in (\underline{K}_x, \overline{K})$, *there exist* $\underline{c} \leq \overline{c}$ *such that the level curve* $L_K(\overline{\Psi}_x) := \{(c_1, c_2) : \overline{\Psi}_x(c_1, c_2) = K\}$ *is continuous, contained in the set* $[0, \underline{c}] \times [\underline{c}, \overline{c}]$ *and contains the points* $(0, \overline{c})$ *and* $(\underline{c}, \overline{c})$.

Proof. The continuity of the level curve is obtained as an immediate consequence of the continuity of $\overline{\Psi}_x$. Observe that, by Lemma 5, we know the existence of $\underline{c} > 0$ such that $\Psi_x(\underline{c}) = K$. Meanwhile, from Lemma 8, we have that there exists $\overline{c} \in [\underline{c}, \infty)$ such that $\overline{\Psi}_x(0, \overline{c}) = K$. Now, the fact that the level curve $L_K(\overline{\Psi}_x)$ is contained in $[0, \underline{c}] \times [\underline{c}, \overline{c}]$ is a consequence of Remark 11 and Lemma 8. □

Remark 13. *Lemmas 4 and 9 yield that the parametric curve* $\Lambda \mapsto (c_1^\Lambda, c_2^\Lambda)$ *and the level curve* $L_K(\overline{\Psi}_x)$ *must intersect, i.e., there exists* Λ^* *such that* $\overline{\Psi}_x(c_1^{\Lambda^*}, c_2^{\Lambda^*}) = K$, *for* $K \in (\underline{K}_x, \overline{K}_x]$.

By similar arguments as in the proof of Theorem 2, by Remarks 12 and 13, and using Equation (45), we get the following result, whose proof is omitted.

Theorem 3. *Assume* $\delta > 0$ *and let* V_δ *and* V_δ^D *as in Equations (30) and (31), respectively, then* $V_\delta = V_\delta^D$. *Furthermore, if* x, K *are such that*

1. $K < \underline{K}_x$, *then* $V_\delta(x, K) = -\infty$;

2. $K = \underline{K}_x$, *then* $V_\delta(x,K) = 0$;
3. $K \geq \overline{K}_x$, *then* $V_\delta(x,K) = V_{\delta,1}(x) + K$; *and*
4. $K \in (\underline{K}_x, \overline{K}_x)$, *then there exists* $\Lambda^* \geq 1$ *such that*

$$V_\delta(x,K) = \Lambda^* K + V_{\delta,\Lambda^*}(x) = \mathbb{E}_x\left[\int_0^\infty e^{-qt}\, d\left(L_t^{(c_1^{\Lambda^*},c_2^{\Lambda^*}),0} - \delta \sum_{0\leq s<t} \mathbf{1}_{\left\{\Delta L_s^{(c_1^{\Lambda^*},c_2^{\Lambda^*}),0}>0\right\}}\right)\right]. \quad (46)$$

6. Numerical Examples

In this section, we confirm the obtained results by a sequence of numerical examples. Here, we assume that X is of the form

$$X_t - X_0 = t + 0.5B_t - \sum_{n=1}^{N_t} Z_n, \quad 0 \leq t < \infty,$$

where $B = \{B_t : t \geq 0\}$, $N = \{N_t : t \geq 0\}$, and $Z = \{Z_n\}_{n\geq 1}$ are a standard Brownian motion, a Poisson process with arrival rate $\lambda = 0.4$, and an i.i.d. sequence of random variables with distribution Gamma (1,2), respectively, which are assumed mutually independent. Since there is no closed form for the scale function $W^{(q)}$ associated with X, we use a numerical algorithm presented in Surya (2008) in order to approximate the inverse Laplace transform of Equation (4). Similarly, we approximate the derivatives of the scale functions and use the trapezoidal rule to calculate its integrals.

We first consider the case without transaction cost presented in Section 3.2. In Figure 1 (left), we plot the function $x \mapsto V_\Lambda(x) + \Lambda K$ for various values of Λ and a fixed value of K. For $x \geq x_0$, where x_0 is such that $\underline{K}_{x_0} = K$, its minimum over the considered values of Λ provides (an approximation of) $V(x,K)$, indicated by the solid red line in the plot. Since the process has unbounded variation, then $\overline{K} = \infty$. In Figure 1 (right), we plot, for $x > x_0$, the Lagrange multiplier Λ^* given in Theorem 2. We observe that Λ^* goes to infinity as $x \downarrow x_0$ and remains always above 1.

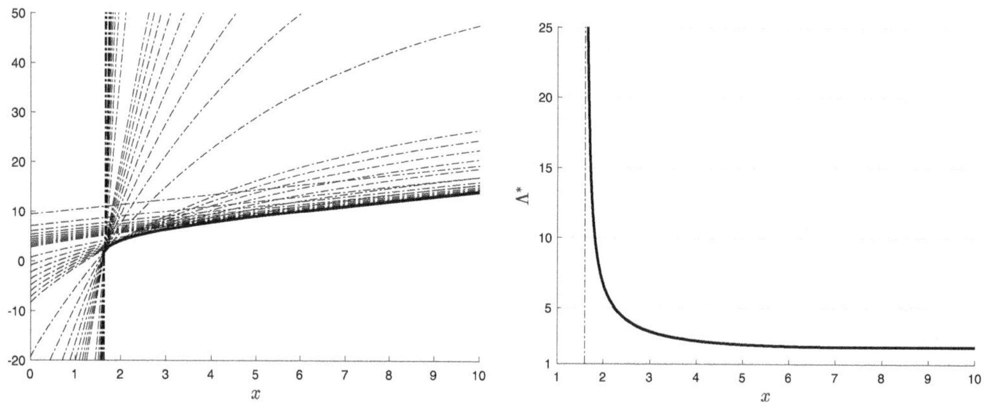

Figure 1. (**Left**) Plots of $x \mapsto V_\Lambda(x) + \Lambda K$ for $\Lambda = 1, 1.1, \ldots, 2, 3, \ldots, 10, 20, \ldots, 100, 200, \ldots, 1000, 2000, \ldots, 10{,}000, 20{,}000$ (dotted) for the case $K = 2.7$. The minimum of $V_\Lambda(x) + \Lambda K$ over Λ is shown in solid bold-face red line. (**Right**) Plot of the Lagrange multiplier Λ^* for $x > x_0$, where x_0 is such that $\underline{K}_{x_0} = K$.

In Figure 2, we show the values of $V(x,K)$ and Lagrange multiplier Λ^* as functions of (x,K). It is confirmed that $V(x,K)$ increases as x and K increase, while Λ^* increases as x and K decrease.

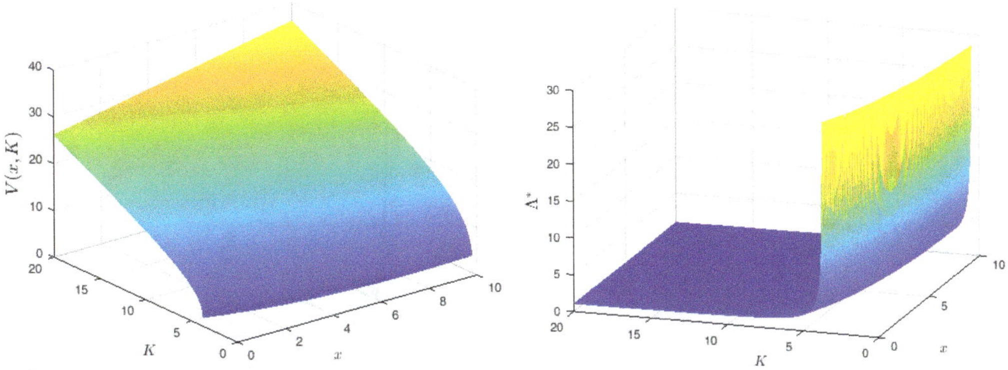

Figure 2. Plots of $V(x,K)$ (**left**); and the Lagrange multiplier Λ^* (**right**) as functions of x and K.

We now move to the case with transaction cost. First, we illustrate the results shown in Section 4. In Figure 3 (left), we plot the function $x \mapsto \zeta_\Lambda(x)$ for the values of $\Lambda = 1,\ldots,9$. We also plot its maximum value attained at a_Λ and the value attained at the corresponding optimal values $(c_1^\Lambda, c_2^\Lambda)$ with transaction cost $\delta = 0.05$. Note that, when $\Lambda = 1$, $a_\Lambda = c_1^\Lambda = 0$ and for the other values of Λ, $\zeta_\Lambda(c_1^\Lambda) = \zeta_\Lambda(c_2^\Lambda) < \zeta_\Lambda(a_\Lambda)$. In Figure 3 (right), we plot the optimal thresholds a_Λ, c_1^Λ and $, c_2^\Lambda$ as function of Λ.

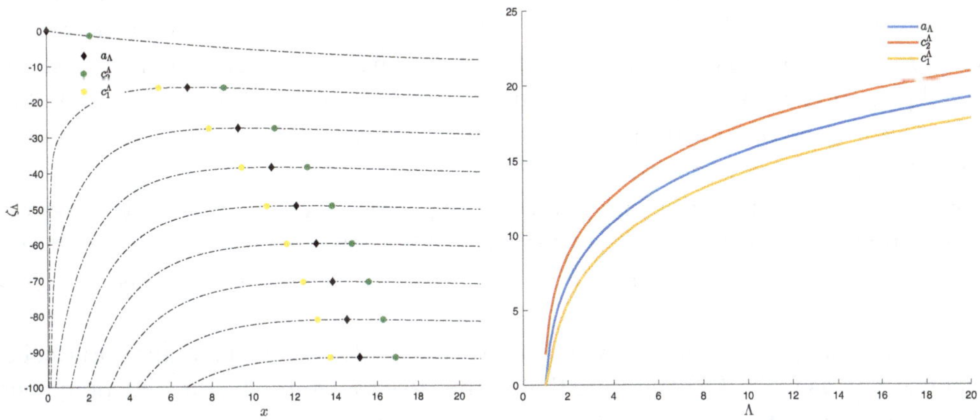

Figure 3. (**Left**) Plots of $x \mapsto \zeta_\Lambda(x)$ for $\Lambda = 1,\ldots,9$ and the corresponding values of a_Λ, c_1^Λ and $, c_2^\Lambda$ for $\delta = 0.05$. (**Right**) Plots of the functions $\Lambda \mapsto a_\Lambda, c_1^\Lambda$ and $, c_2^\Lambda$.

In Figure 4, we illustrate the findings of Section 5.2. This figure is analogous to Figure 1 but with transaction cost δ as above. It can be seen that the change in the function $V_\delta(x,K)$ is relatively very small, but the change in the optimal Lagrange multiplier Λ^* is significant, being smaller in the case of transaction cost. A similar figure as Figure 2 in the case of transaction cost is omitted since both have the same shape.

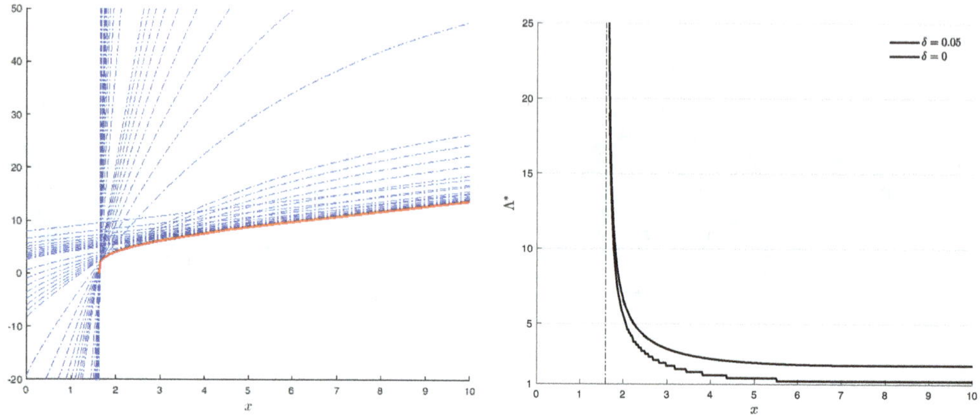

Figure 4. (**Left**) Plots of $x \mapsto V_\Lambda(x) + \Lambda K$ for $\Lambda = 1, 1.1, \ldots, 2, 3, \ldots, 10, 20, \ldots, 100, 200, \ldots, 1000, 2000, \ldots, 10,000, 20,000$ (dotted) for the case $K = 2.7$. The minimum of $V_{\delta,\Lambda}(x) + \Lambda K$ over Λ is plotted in solid bold-face red line. (**Right**) Plots of the Lagrange multipliers Λ^* for $x > x_0$, where x_0 is such that $\underline{K}_{x_0} = K$ with $\delta = 0$ and $\delta = 0.05$.

7. Concluding Remarks

In this study, we proved that the optimal strategy for the bail-out dividend problem with fixed transaction costs is given by a reflected (c_1, c_2)-policy. We also characterized the optimal thresholds and gave a semi-explicit form for the value function in terms of the scale functions. In addition, we used the previous results to solve the constrained dividend maximization problem with the restriction that the expected present value of the capital injected is bounded by a given constant. The solution of the constrained problem can provide the insurance company with a guideline to maximize the profits of the shareholders taking into account the risk of bail-out losses.

It is a legitimate and interesting question whether the optimal strategy and the associated value function with transaction costs (i.e., $\delta > 0$) converge to the corresponding optimal strategy and its value function without transaction cost as $\delta \downarrow 0$. Although we conjecture that indeed this is the case, further investigation is needed.

Another interesting generalization would involve considering fixed and proportional costs for the capital injection as well. We conjecture that in this case the optimal strategy would consist in a double band strategy, that is, a band strategy similar to the dividend payment strategy given in this paper, and a band strategy for the capital injection, which consists in pushing the process to a positive level each time the surplus process tries to cross below 0. We leave this problem as an opportunity for future research.

Author Contributions: All authors equally contributed to this paper.

Funding: This research received no external funding.

Acknowledgments: The authors would like to thank the anonymous reviewers for their comments and suggestions, which helped to improve significantly the quality of this paper. They would also like to thank Florin Avram who encouraged them to contribute to this special issue of *Risks*.

Conflicts of Interest: The authors declare no conflict of interest.

References

Avram, Florin, Zbigniew Palmowski, and Martin Pistorius. 2007. On the optimal dividend problem for a spectrally negative Lévy process. *The Annals of Applied Probability* 17: 156–80. [CrossRef]

Bayraktar, Erhan, Andreas E. Kyprianou, and Kazutoshi Yamazaki. 2014a. On optimal dividends in the dual problem. *ASTIN Bulletin* 43: 359–72. [CrossRef]

Bayraktar, Erhan, Andreas E. Kyprianou, and Kazutoshi Yamazaki. 2014b. Optimal dividends in the dual model under transaction costs. *Insurance: Mathematics and Economics* 54: 133–43. [CrossRef]

Bertoin, Jean. 1998. *Lévy Processes*. Cambridge: Cambridge University Press.

Chan, Terence, Andreas E. Kyprianou, and Mladen Savov. 2011. Smoothness of scale functions for spectrally negative Lévy processes. *Probability Theory and Related Fields* 150: 691–708. [CrossRef]

Hernández, Camilo, Mauricio Junca, and Harold Moreno-Franco. 2018. A time of ruin constrained optimal dividend problem for spectrally one-sided Lévy processes. *Insurance: Mathematics and Economics* 79: 57–68. [CrossRef]

Kuznetsov, Alexey, Andreas E. Kyprianou, and Victor Rivero. 2013. The theory of scale functions for spectrally negative Lévy processes. *Levy Matters II* 2061: 97–186.

Kyprianou, Andreas E. 2014. *Fluctuations of Lévy Processes with Applications*. Universitext. Berlin and Heidelberg: Springer.

Loeffen, Ronnie. 2008. On the optimality of the barrier strategy in de Finetti's problem for spectrally negative Lévy processes. *The Annals of Applied Probability* 18: 1669–80. [CrossRef]

Loeffen, Ronnie L. 2009. An optimal dividends problem with transaction costs for spectrally negative Lévy processes. *Insurance: Mathematics and Economics* 45: 41–48. [CrossRef]

Pistorius, Martijn R. 2004. On exit and ergodicity of the spectrally one-sided Lévy process reflected at its infimum. *Journal of Theoretical Probability* 17: 183–220. [CrossRef]

Protter, Philip. 2005. *Stochastic Integration and Differential Equations*, 2nd ed. Berlin: Springer.

Surya, Budhig A. 2008. Evaluating scale functions of spectrally negative Lévy processes. *Journal of Applied Probability* 45: 135–49. [CrossRef]

4

Pricing Options and Computing Implied Volatilities using Neural Networks

Shuaiqiang Liu [1,*], **Cornelis W. Oosterlee** [1,2] **and Sander M. Bohte** [2]

1 Delft Institute of Applied Mathematics (DIAM), Delft University of Technology, Building 28, Mourik Broekmanweg 6, 2628 XE Delft, The Netherlands; C.W.Oosterlee@cwi.nl

2 Centrum Wiskunde & Informatica, Science Park 123, 1098 XG Amsterdam, The Netherlands; S.M.Bohte@cwi.nl

* Correspondence: s.liu-4@tudelft.nl

Abstract: This paper proposes a data-driven approach, by means of an Artificial Neural Network (ANN), to value financial options and to calculate implied volatilities with the aim of accelerating the corresponding numerical methods. With ANNs being universal function approximators, this method trains an optimized ANN on a data set generated by a sophisticated financial model, and runs the trained ANN as an agent of the original solver in a fast and efficient way. We test this approach on three different types of solvers, including the analytic solution for the Black-Scholes equation, the COS method for the Heston stochastic volatility model and Brent's iterative root-finding method for the calculation of implied volatilities. The numerical results show that the ANN solver can reduce the computing time significantly.

Keywords: machine learning; neural networks; computational finance; option pricing; implied volatility; GPU; Black-Scholes; Heston

---

1. Introduction

In computational finance, numerical methods are commonly used for the valuation of financial derivatives and also in modern risk management. Generally speaking, advanced financial asset models are able to capture nonlinear features that are observed in the financial markets. However, these asset price models are often multi-dimensional, and, as a consequence, do not give rise to closed-form solutions for option values.

Different numerical methods have therefore been developed to solve the corresponding option pricing partial differential equation (PDE) problems, e.g. finite differences, Fourier methods and Monte Carlo simulation. In the context of financial derivative pricing, there is a stage in which the asset model needs to be calibrated to market data. In other words, the open parameters in the asset price model need to be fitted. This is typically *not* done by historical asset prices, but by means of *option prices*, i.e., by matching the market prices of heavily traded options to the option prices from the mathematical model, under the so-called risk-neutral probability measure. In the case of model calibration, thousands of option prices need to be determined in order to fit these asset parameters. However, due to the requirement of a highly efficient computation, certain high quality asset models are discarded. Efficient numerical computation is also increasingly important in financial risk management, especially when we deal with real-time risk management (e.g., high frequency trading) or counterparty credit risk issues, where a trade-off between efficiency and accuracy seems often inevitable.

Artificial neural networks (ANNs) with multiple hidden layers have become successful machine learning methods to extract features and detect patterns from a large data set. There are different neural network variants for particular tasks, for example, convolutional neural networks for image recognition LeCun et al. (2010) and recurrent neural networks for time series analysis Lipton (2015).

It is well-known that ANNs can approximate nonlinear functions Cybenko (1989); Hornik (1991); Hornik et al. (1990), and can thus be used to approximate solutions to PDEs Lagaris et al. (1998); Sirignano and Spiliopoulos (2018). Recent advances in data science have shown that using deep learning techniques even highly nonlinear multi-dimensional functions can be accurately represented LeCun et al. (2015). Essentially, ANNs can be used as powerful universal function approximators without assuming any mathematical form for the functional relationship between the input variables and the output. Moreover, ANNs easily allow for parallel processing to speed up evaluations, especially on Graphics Processing Units (GPUs) Oh and Jung (2004) or even Tensor Processing Units(TPUs) Jouppi et al. (2017).

We aim to take advantage of a classical ANN to speed up option valuation by learning the results of an option pricing method. From a computational point of view, the ANN does not suffer much from the dimensionality of a PDE. An "ANN solver" is typically decomposed into two separate phases, a training phase and a test (or prediction) phase. During the training phase, the ANN "learns" the PDE solver, by means of the data set generated by the sophisticated models and corresponding numerical solvers. This stage is usually time consuming, however, it can be done off-line. During the test phase, the trained model can be employed to approximate the solution on-line. The ANN solution can typically be computed as a set of matrix multiplications, which can be implemented in parallel and highly efficiently, especially with GPUs or TPUs. As a result, the trained ANN delivers financial derivative prices, or other quantities, efficiently, and the on-line time for accurate option pricing may be reduced, especially for involved asset price models. We will show in this paper that this data-driven approach is highly promising.

The proposed approach in this paper attempts to accelerate the pricing of European options under a unified data-driven ANN framework. ANNs have been used in option pricing for some decades already. There are basically two directions. One is that based on the observed market option prices and the underlying asset value, ANN-based regression techniques have been applied to fit a model-free, non-parametric pricing function, see, for example, Hutchinson et al. (1994); Yao et al. (2000); Gencay and Qi (2001); Garcia and Gençay (2000). Furthermore, the authors of Dugas et al. (2001); Yang et al. (2017) designed special kernel functions to incorporate prior financial knowledge into the neural network while forecasting option prices.

Another direction is to improve the performance of model-based pricing by means of ANNs. The interest in accelerating classical PDE solvers via ANNs is rapidly growing. The papers Han et al. (2017); Weinan et al. (2017); Beck et al. (2017) take advantage of reinforcement learning to speed up solving high-dimensional stochastic differential equations. The author of Sirignano and Spiliopoulos (2017) proposes an optimization algorithm, the so-called stochastic gradient descent in continuous time, combined with a deep neural network to price high-dimensional American options. In Fan and Mancini (2009) the pricing performance of financial models is enhanced by non-parametric learning approaches that deal with a systematic bias of pricing errors. Of course, this trend takes place not only in computational finance, but also in other engineering fields where PDEs play a key role, like computational fluid dynamics, see Hesthaven and Ubbiali (2018); Raissi and Karniadakis (2018); Sirignano and Spiliopoulos (2018); Tompson et al. (2016). The work in this paper belongs to this latter direction. Here, we use traditional solvers to generate artificial data, then we train the ANN to learn the solution for different problem parameters. Compared to Lagaris et al. (1998) or Sirignano and Spiliopoulos (2018), our data-driven approach finds, next to the solutions of the option pricing PDEs, the implicit relation between variables and a specific parameter (i.e., the implied volatility).

This paper is organized as follows. In Section 2, two fundamental option pricing models, the Black-Scholes and the Heston stochastic volatility PDEs, are briefly introduced. In addition to European option pricing, we also analyze robustness issues of root-finding methods to compute the so-called implied volatility. In Section 3, the employed ANN is presented with suitable hyper-parameters. After training the ANN to learn the results of the financial models for different problem parameters, numerical ANN results with the corresponding errors are presented in Section 4.

2. Option Pricing and Asset Models

In this section, two asset models are briefly presented, the geometric Brownian motion (GBM) asset model, which gives rise to the Black-Scholes option pricing PDE, and the Heston stochastic volatility asset model, leading to the Heston PDE. We also discuss the concept of implied volatility. We will use European option contracts as the examples, however, other types of options can be taken into consideration in a similar way.

2.1. The Black-Scholes PDE

A first model for asset prices is GBM,

$$dS_t = \mu S_t dt + \sqrt{\nu} S_t dW_t^s, \tag{1}$$

where S is the price of a non-dividend paying asset, and W^s is a Wiener process, with t being the time, μ the drift parameter, and ν the variance parameter. The volatility parameter is $\sigma = \sqrt{\nu}$. A European option contract on the underlying stock price can be valued via the Black-Scholes PDE, which can be derived from Itô's Lemma under a replicating portfolio approach or via the martingale approach. Denoting the option price by $V(t, S)$, the Black-Scholes equation reads,

$$\frac{\partial V}{\partial t} + \frac{1}{2}\sigma^2 S^2 \frac{\partial^2 V}{\partial S^2} + rS\frac{\partial V}{\partial S} - rV = 0, \tag{2}$$

with time t until to maturity T, and r the risk-free interest rate. The PDE is accompanied by a final condition representing the specific payoff, for example, the European call option payoff at time T,

$$V(t = T, S) = (S_0 - K)^+, \tag{3}$$

where K is the option's strike price. See standard textbooks for more information about the basics in financial mathematics.

An analytic solution to (2), (3) exists for European plain vanilla options, i.e.,

$$V_c(t, S) = SN(d_1) - Ke^{-r\tau} N(d_2), \tag{4a}$$

$$d_1 = \frac{\log(S/K) + (r - 0.5\sigma^2)\tau}{\sigma\sqrt{\tau}}, \quad d_2 = d_1 - \sigma\sqrt{\tau}, \tag{4b}$$

where $\tau := T - t$, $V_c(t, S)$ is the European call option value at time t for stock value S, and $N(\cdot)$ represents the normal distribution. This solution procedure (4) is denoted by $V(\cdot) = BS(\cdot)$.

Implied Volatility

Implied volatility is considered an important quantity in finance. Given an observed market option price V^{mkt}, the Black-Scholes implied volatility σ^* can be determined by solving $BS(\sigma^*; S, K, \tau, r) = V^{mkt}$. The monotonicity of the Black-Scholes equation with respect to the volatility guarantees the existence of $\sigma^* \in [0, +\infty)$. We can write the implied volatility as an implicit formula,

$$\sigma^*(K, T) = BS^{-1}(V^{mkt}; S, K, \tau, r), \tag{5}$$

where BS^{-1} denotes the inverse Black-Scholes function. Moreover, by adopting moneyness, $m = \frac{S_t}{K}$, and time to maturity, $\tau = T - t$, one can express the implied volatility as $\sigma^*(m, \tau)$, see Cont and da Fonseca (2002).

For simplicity, we denote here $\sigma^*(m, \tau)$ by σ^*. An analytic solution for Equation (5) does not exist. The value of σ^* is determined by means of a numerical iterative technique, since Equation (5) can be converted into a root-finding problem,

$$g(\sigma^*) = BS(S,\tau,K,r,\sigma^*) - V^{mkt}(S,\tau;K) = 0. \tag{6}$$

2.2. The Heston Model

One of the limitations of using the Black-Scholes model is the assumption of a constant volatility σ in (2), (4). A major modeling step away from the assumption of constant volatility in asset pricing, was made by modeling the volatility/variance as a diffusion process. The resulting models are the stochastic volatility (SV) models. The idea to model volatility as a random variable is confirmed by practical financial data which indicates the variable and unpredictable nature of the stock price's volatility. The most significant argument to consider the volatility to be stochastic is the implied volatility smile/skew, which is present in the financial market data, and can be accurately recovered by SV models, especially for options with a medium to long time to the maturity date T. With an additional stochastic process, which is correlated with the asset price process S_t, we deal with a system of SDEs, for which option valuation is more computationally expensive than for a scalar asset price process.

The most popular SV model is the Heston model Heston (1993), for which the system of stochastic equations under the risk-neural measure reads,

$$dS_t = rS_t dt + \sqrt{\nu_t} S_t dW_t^s, S_{t_0} = S_0, \tag{7a}$$
$$d\nu_t = \kappa(\bar{\nu} - \nu_t)dt + \gamma\sqrt{\nu_t} dW_t^\nu, \nu_{t_0} = \nu_0, \tag{7b}$$
$$dW_t^s dW_t^\nu = \rho dt, \tag{7c}$$

with ν_t the instantaneous variance, and W_t^s, W_t^ν are two Wiener processes with correlation coefficient ρ. The second equation in (7) models a mean reversion process for the variance, with the parameters, r the risk-free interest rate, $\bar{\nu}$ the long term variance, κ the reversion speed; γ is the volatility of the variance, determining the volatility of ν_t. There is an additional parameter ν_0, the t_0-value of the variance.

By the martingale approach, we arrive at the following multi-dimensional Heston option pricing PDE,

$$\begin{aligned}\frac{\partial V}{\partial t} &+ rS\frac{\partial V}{\partial S} + \kappa(\bar{\nu} - \nu)\frac{\partial V}{\partial \nu} + \frac{1}{2}\nu S^2\frac{\partial^2 V}{\partial S^2} \\ &+ \rho\gamma S\nu\frac{\partial^2 V}{\partial S\partial \nu} + \frac{1}{2}\gamma^2\nu\frac{\partial^2 V}{\partial \nu^2} - rV = 0.\end{aligned} \tag{8}$$

The typically observed implied volatility shapes in the market, e.g., smile or skew, can be reproduced by varying the above parameters $\{\kappa, \rho, \gamma, \nu_0, \bar{\nu}\}$. In general, the parameter γ impacts the kurtosis of the asset return distribution, and the coefficient ρ controls its asymmetry. The Heston model does not have analytic solutions, and is thus solved numerically.

Numerical methods in option pricing generally fall into three categories, finite differences (FD), Monte Carlo (MC) simulation and numerical integration methods. Finite differences for the PDE problem are often used for free boundary problems, as they occur when valuing American options, or for certain exotic options like barrier options. The derivatives of the option prices (the so-called option Greeks) are accurately computed with finite differences.

Monte Carlo simulation and numerical integration rely on the Feynman-Kac Theorem, which essentially states that (European) option values can be written as discounted expected values of the option's payoff function at the terminal time T, under the risk-neutral measure. Monte Carlo methods are often employed in this context for the valuation of path-dependent high-dimensional options, and also for the computation of all sorts of valuation adjustments in modern risk management. However, Monte Carlo methods are typically somewhat slow to converge, and particularly in the context of model calibration this can be an issue.

The numerical integration methods are also based on the Feynman-Kac Theorem. The preferred way to employ them is to first transform to the Fourier domain. The availability of the asset price's characteristic function is a pre-requisite to using Fourier techniques. One of the efficient techniques in this context is the COS method Fang and Oosterlee (2009), which utilizes Fourier-cosine series expansions to approximate the asset price's probability density function. The COS method can be used to compute European option values under the Heston model highly efficiently. However, for many different, modern asset models the characteristic function is typically not available. We will use the Heston model with the COS method here during the training of the Heston-ANN, so that training time is still relatively small.

2.3. Numerical Methods for Implied Volatility

Focussing on the implied volatility σ^*, there are several iterative numerical techniques to solve (6), for example, the Newton-Raphson method, the bisection method or the Brent method. The Newton-Raphson iteration reads,

$$\sigma^*_{k+1} = \sigma^*_k - \frac{V(\sigma^*_k) - V^{mkt}}{g'(\sigma^*_k)}, \; k = 0, \ldots. \tag{9}$$

Starting with an initial guess, σ^*_0, the approximate solutions, σ^*_{k+1}, $k = 0, \ldots$, iteratively improve, until a certain criterion is satisfied. The first derivative of Black-Scholes option value with respect to the volatility, named the option's Vega, in the denominator of (9) can be obtained analytically for European options.

However, the Newton-Raphson method may fail to converge, either when the Vega is extremely small or when the convergence stalls. The Black-Scholes equation monotonically maps an unbounded interval $\sigma \in [0, +\infty)$ to a finite range $V(t, S) \in [0, S_t - Ke^{-r\tau}]$ as illustrated in Figure 1a. As a result, the near-flat function shapes appear in certain σ-regions, especially when the option is either deep in-the-money (ITM) or deep out-the-money (OTM). For example, Figure 1b shows that the option's Vega can be very close to zero in the regions with small or large volatilities in deep ITM or OTM options, although its value is relatively large in the at-the money (ATM) region.

A possible robust root-finding algorithm for solving this problem is to employ a hybrid of the Newton-Raphson and the bisection methods. Alternatively, the author of Jäckel (2015) proposed to select a suitable initial value at the beginning of the iteration to avoid divergence. In the next subsection, we will introduce a derivative-free, robust and efficient algorithm to find the implied volatility.

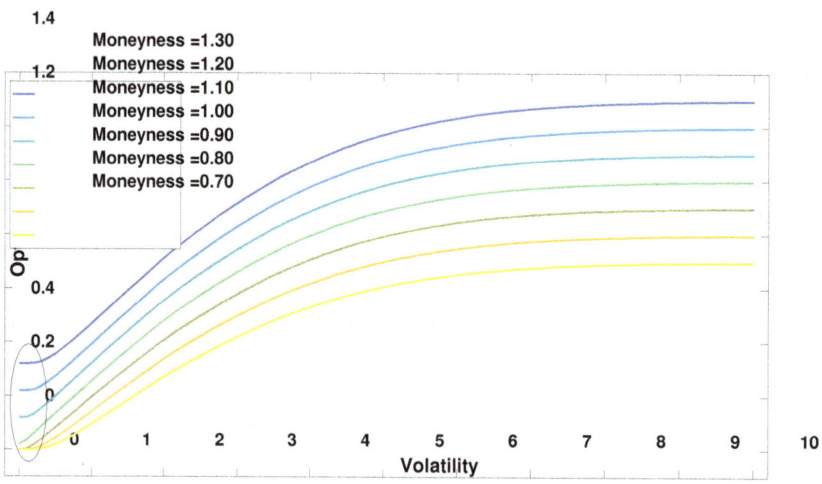

(a)

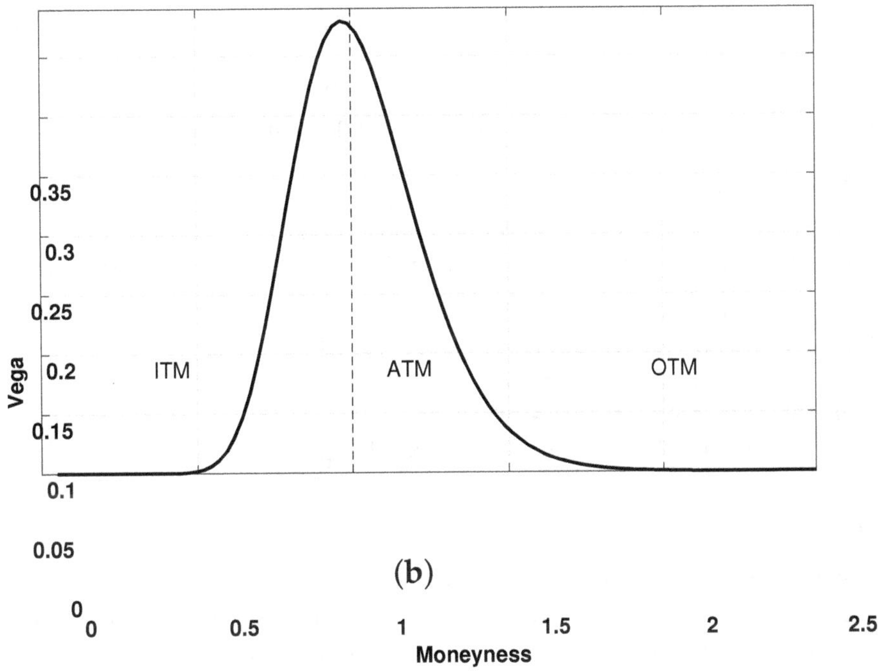

Figure 1. Vega tends to be zero in certain regions of deep ITM or OTM options. (**a**) Option price vs. volatility; (**b**) Vega vs. Moneyness.

Brent's Method for Implied Volatility

As a derivative-free, robust and efficient algorithm, Brent's method Brent (1973) combines bisection, inverse quadratic interpolation and the secant method. In order to determine the next iterant, an inverse quadratic interpolation employs three prior points (i.e., iterants) to fit an inverse quadratic function, which resembles the gradient of Newton's method, i.e.,

$$\begin{aligned}\sigma_{k+1} = &\frac{\sigma_k g(\sigma_{k-1}) g(\sigma_{k-2})}{(g(\sigma_{(k)}) - g(\sigma_{k-1}))(g(\sigma_k) - g(\sigma_{k-2}))} \\ &+ \frac{\sigma_{k-1} g(\sigma_{k-2}) g(\sigma_k)}{(g(\sigma_{k-1}) - g(\sigma_{k-2}))(g(\sigma_{k-1}) - g(\sigma_k))} \\ &+ \frac{\sigma_{k-2} g(\sigma_{k-1}) g(\sigma_k)}{(g(\sigma_{k-2}) - g(\sigma_{k-1}))(g(\sigma_{k-2}) - g(\sigma_k))}.\end{aligned} \tag{10}$$

When two consecutive approximations are identical, for example, $\sigma_k = \sigma_{k-1}$, the quadratic interpolation is replaced by an approximation based on the secant method,

$$\sigma_{k+1} = \sigma_{k-1} - g(\sigma_{k-1}) \frac{\sigma_{k-1} - \sigma_{k-2}}{g(\sigma_{k-1}) - g(\sigma_{k-2})}. \tag{11}$$

In this paper, Brent's method is used to compute the BS implied volatility related to the Heston option prices in Section 4.4.2. We will develop an ANN to approximate the implicit function relating the volatility to the option price.

3. Methodology

In this section, we present a neural network to approximate a function for financial models. The procedure comprises two main components, the generator to create the financial data for training the model and the predictor (the ANN) to approximate the option prices based on the trained model. The data-driven framework consists of the following steps (Algorithm 1),

Algorithm 1 Model framework

1: – Generate the sample data points for input parameters,
2: – Calculate the corresponding output (option price or implied volatility) to form a complete data set with inputs and outputs,
3: – Split the above data set into a training and a test part,
4: – Train the ANN on the training data set,
5: – Evaluate the ANN on the test data set,
6: – Replace the original solver by the trained ANN in applications.

3.1. Artificial Neural Network

ANNs generally constitute three levels of components, i.e., neurons, layers and the architecture from bottom to top. The architecture is determined by a combination of different layers, that are made up of numerous artificial neurons. A neuron, which involves learnable weights and biases, is the fundamental unit of ANNs. By connecting the neurons of adjacent layers, output signals of a previous layer enter a next layer as input signals. By stacking layers on top of each other, signals travel from the input layer through the hidden layers to the output layer potentially through cyclic or recurrent connections, and the ANN builds a mapping among input-output pairs.

As shown in Figure 2a, an artificial neuron basically consists of the following three consecutive operations:

1. Calculation of a summation of weighted inputs,
2. Addition of a bias to the summation,
3. Computation of the output by means of a transfer function.

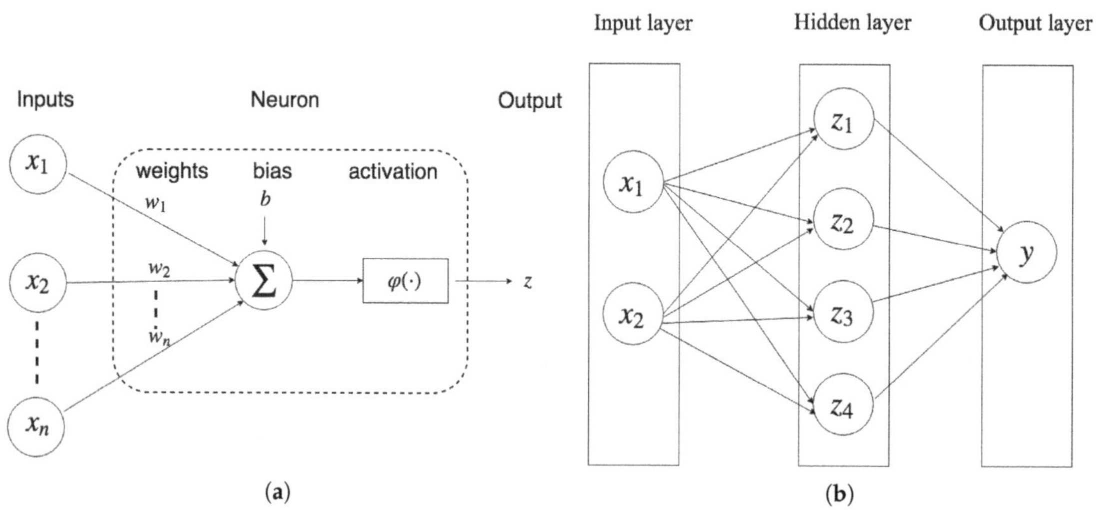

Figure 2. Illustration of a MLP configuration. (**a**) A neuron; (**b**) An example of MLP.

A multi-layer perceptron (MLP), consisting of at least one hidden layer is the simplest version of an ANN. Mathematically, MLPs are defined by the following parameters,

$$\theta = (\mathbf{W}_1, \mathbf{b}_1, \mathbf{W}_2, \mathbf{b}_2, ..., \mathbf{W}_L, \mathbf{b}_L) \tag{12}$$

where $\mathbf{W}_j$ is a weight matrix with $\mathbf{b}_j$ being a bias vector in the L-th neural layer. A function can then be expressed as follows,

$$y(\mathbf{x}) = F(\mathbf{x}|\boldsymbol{\theta}). \tag{13}$$

Let $z_j^{(l)}$ denote the value of the j-th neuron in the l-th layer, then the corresponding transfer function reads,

$$z_j^{(l)} = \varphi^{(l)}\left(\sum_i w_{ij}^{(l)} z_i^{(l-1)} + b_j^{(l)}\right), \tag{14}$$

where $z_i^{(l-1)}$ is the output value of the i-th neuron in the $(l-1)$-th layer and $\varphi(\cdot)$ is an activation function, with $w_{ij}^{(l)} \in \mathbf{W}_l$, $b_j^{(l)} \in \mathbf{b}_l$. When $l = 0$, $z^{(0)} = x$ is the input layer; When $l = L$, $z^{(L)} = y$ is the output layer; Otherwise, $z^{(l)}$ represents an intermediate variable. The activation function $\varphi(\cdot)$ adds non-linearity to the system, for example, the following activation functions may be employed,

- Sigmoid, $\varphi(x) = \frac{1}{1+e^{-x}}$,
- ReLU, $\varphi(x) = \max(x, 0)$;

see LeCun et al. (2015) for more activation functions. For example, a MLP with "one-hidden-layer" is shown in Figure 2b, and Equation (15) presents its mathematical formula,

$$\begin{cases} y = \varphi^{(2)}\left(\sum_j w_j^{(2)} z_j^{(1)} + b^{(2)}\right) \\ z_j^{(1)} = \varphi^{(1)}\left(\sum_i w_{ij}^{(1)} x_i + b_j^{(1)}\right). \end{cases} \tag{15}$$

According to the Universal Approximation Theorem Cybenko (1989), a single-hidden-layer ANN with a sufficient number of neurons can approximate any continuous function. The distance between two functions is measured by the norm of a function $||\cdot||$,

$$D(f(\mathbf{x}), F(\mathbf{x})) = ||f(\mathbf{x}) - F(\mathbf{x})||, \tag{16}$$

where $f(\mathbf{x})$ is the objective function, $F(\mathbf{x})$ is the neural network approximated function. For example, the p-norm reads,

$$||f(\mathbf{x}) - F(\mathbf{x}|\boldsymbol{\theta})||_p = \sqrt[p]{\int_{\mathbf{X}} |f(\mathbf{x}) - F(\mathbf{x}|\boldsymbol{\theta})|^p d\mu(\mathbf{x})},$$

where $1 \leq p < \infty$ and $\mu(\mathbf{x})$ is a measure over the space $\mathbf{X}$. We choose $p = 2$ to evaluate the averaged accuracy, which corresponds to the mean squared error (MSE). Within supervised learning, the loss function is equivalent to the above distance,

$$L(\boldsymbol{\theta}) := D(f(\mathbf{x}), F(\mathbf{x}|\boldsymbol{\theta})). \tag{17}$$

The training process aims to learn the optimal weights and biases in Equation (13) to make the loss function as small as possible. The process can be formulated as an optimization problem,

$$arg \min_{\boldsymbol{\theta}} L(\boldsymbol{\theta}|(\mathbf{x}, \mathbf{y})), \tag{18}$$

given the known input-output pairs $(\mathbf{x}, \mathbf{y})$ and a loss function $L(\boldsymbol{\theta})$.

Several back-propagation gradient descent methods Ruder (2016) have been successfully applied to solve Equation (18), for instance, Stochastic Gradient Descent (SGD) and its variants Adam and RMSprop. These optimization algorithms start with initial values and move in the direction in which the loss function decreases. The formula for updating the parameters reads,

$$\begin{cases} \mathbf{W} \leftarrow \mathbf{W} - \eta(i)\frac{\partial L}{\partial \mathbf{W}}, \\ \mathbf{b} \leftarrow \mathbf{b} - \eta(i)\frac{\partial L}{\partial \mathbf{b}}, \\ i = 0, 1, 2, ..., \end{cases} \tag{19}$$

where η is a learning rate, which may vary during the iterations. The learning rate plays an important role during the training, as a "large" learning rate value causes the ANN's convergence to oscillate, whereas a small one results in ANNs learning slowly, and even getting trapped in local optima regions. An adaptive learning rate is often preferred, and more detail will be given in Section 3.3.

3.2. Hyper-Parameters Optimization

Training deep neural networks involves numerous choices for the commonly called "hyper-parameters". These include the number of layers, neurons, and the specific activation function, etc. First, determining the depth (the number of hidden layers) and the width (the number of neurons) of the ANN is a challenging problem. We experimentally find that a MLP architecture with four hidden layers has an optimal capacity of approximating option pricing formulas of our current interest.

Built on a four hidden layer architecture, the other hyper-parameters are optimized using automatic machine learning Bergstra et al. (2011). There are different techniques to implement the automatic search. In a grid search technique, all candidate parameters are systematically parameterized on a pre-defined grid, and all possible candidates are explored in a brute-force way. The authors of Bergstra and Bengio (2012) concluded that random search is more efficient for hyper-parameters optimization. Recently, Bayesian hyper-parameter optimization Snoek et al. (2012) has been developed to efficiently reduce the computational cost by navigating through the hyper-parameters space. However, it is still difficult to outperform random search in combination with certain expert knowledge at the current stage.

Neural networks may not necessarily converge to a global minimum. However, using a proper *random initialization* may help the model with suitable initial values. *Batch normalization* scales the output of a layer by subtracting the batch mean and dividing by the batch standard deviation. This can speed up the training of the neural network. The batch size indicates the number of samples that enter the model to update the learnable parameters within one iteration. A *dropout operation* selects a random set of neurons and deactivates them, which forces the network to learn more robust features. The dropout rate refers to the proportion of the deactivated neurons in a layer.

There are two stages to complete the hyper-parameter optimization. During this model selection process, over-fitting can be reduced by adopting the k-fold cross validation as follows (Algorithm 2).

Algorithm 2 k-fold cross validation

–Split the training data set into k different subsets,
–Select one set as the validation data set,
–Train the model on the remaining k-1 subsets,
–Calculate the metric by evaluating the trained model on the validation part,
–Continue the above steps by exploring all subsets,
–Calculate the final metric which is averaged over k cases,
–Explore the next set of hyper-parameters,
–Rank the candidates according to their averaged metric.

In the first stage, we employ random search combined with a 3-fold cross validation to find initial hyper-parameter configurations for the neural network. As shown in Table 1, each model is trained 200 epochs using MSE as the loss metric. An epoch is the moment when the model has processed the whole training data set. It is found that the prediction accuracy increases with the training data set size growing (more related details will be discussed in Section 4.1). Therefore, the random search is implemented on a small data set, which is then followed by training the selected ANN on larger data sets in application.

Table 1. The setting of random search for hyper-parameters optimization.

Parameters	Options or Range
Activation	ReLU, Tanh, Sigmoid, ELU
Dropout rate	[0.0, 0.2]
Neurons	[200, 600]
Initialization	uniform, Glorot_uniform, He_uniform
Batch normalization	yes, no
Optimizer	SGD, RMSprop, Adam
Batch size	[256, 3000]

Table 2. The selected model after the random search.

Parameters	Options
Hidden layers	4
Neurons(each layer)	400
Activation	ReLU
Dropout rate	0.0
Batch-normalization	No
Initialization	Glorot_uniform
Optimizer	Adam
Batch size	1024

In the second stage, we further enhance the top 5 network configurations by averaging the different values, to yield the final ANN model, as listed in Table 2. As Table 2 shows, the optimal parameter values, i.e., neurons and batch size, do not lie at the boundaries of the search space (except for the drop out rate). Compared to Sigmoid, ReLU is more likely to cause a better convergence (e.g., overcome the gradient vanishing in a deep neural network). As an extension to SGD, Adam can handle an optimization problem more adaptively. However, batch normalization and drop-out do not improve the model accuracy in this regression problem, and one possible reason is that the output value is sensitive to the input parameters, which is different from sparse features in an image (where these operations usually work very well). Subsequently, we train the selected network on the whole (training and validation) data set, to obtain the final weights. This procedure can result in an ANN with sufficient accuracy to approximate the financial option values.

3.3. *Learning Rates*

The learning rate, one of the key hyper-parameters, represents the rate at which the weights are updated each iteration. A large learning rate leads to fluctuations around a local minimum, and sometimes even to divergence. Small learning rates may cause an inefficiently slow training stage. It is common practice to start with a large learning rate and then gradually decrease it until a well-trained model has resulted. There are different ways to vary the learning rate during training, e.g. by step-wise annealing, exponential decay, cosine annealing, see Smith (2015) for a cyclical learning rate (CLR) and Loshchilov and Hutter (2016) for the stochastic descent gradient restart (SDGR). The basic idea of CLR and SDGR is that at certain points of the training stage, a relatively large learning rate may move the weights from their current values, by which ANNs may leave a local optimum and converge to a better one.

We employ the method proposed in Smith (2015) to determine the lower and upper bound of learning rates. The method is based on the insight of how the averaged training loss varies over different learning rates, by starting with a small learning rate and increasing it progressively in the first few iterations. By monitoring the loss function against the learning rate, it is shown in Figure 3 that the loss stabilizes when the learning rate is small, then drops rapidly and finally oscillates and diverges when the learning rate is too large. The optimal learning rate lies here between 10^{-5} and 10^{-3}, where the slope is the steepest and the training loss reduces quickly. Therefore, the learning rate is reduced from 10^{-3} to 10^{-5} in our experiments.

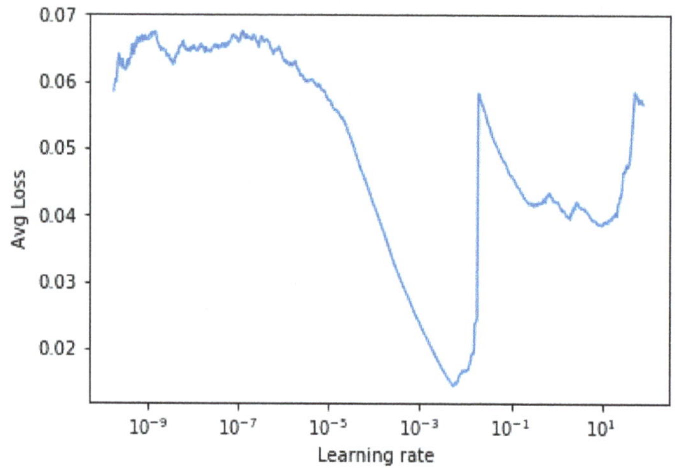

Figure 3. Average training loss against varying learning rates.

We present, as an example, the results of the training stage of the ANN solver for the Heston model option prices to compare three different learning rate schedules. Figure 4 demonstrates that the training error and the validation error agree well and that over-fitting does not occur when using these schedules. As shown in Figure 5, in this case a decay rate-based schedule outperforms the CLR with the same learning rate bounds, although with the CLR the difference between training and validation losses are smaller. This is contrary to the conclusion in Smith (2015), but their network included batch normalization and L2 regularization. For the tests in this paper, we will employ the CLR to find the optimal range of learning rates, which is then applied in the DecayLR schedule to train the ANNs.

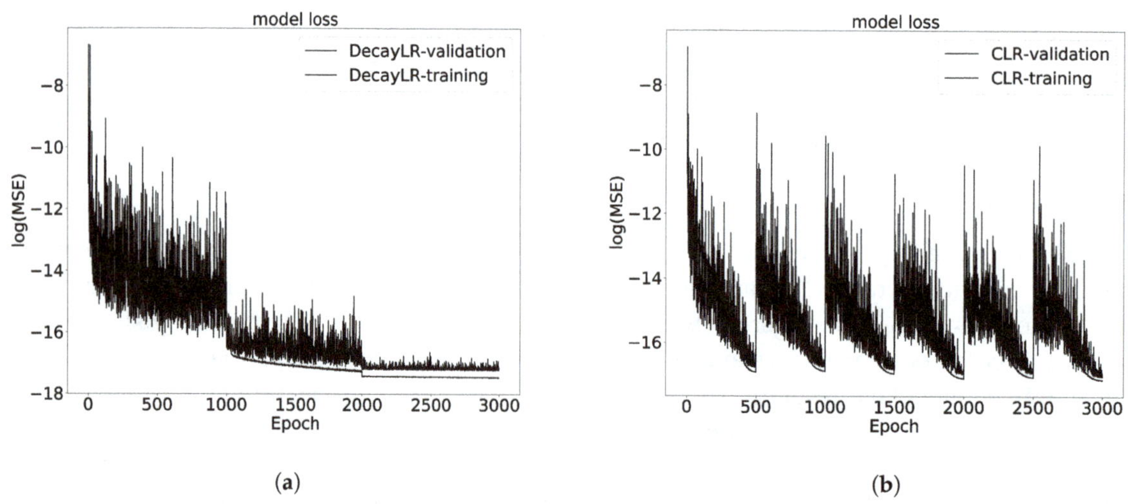

Figure 4. The history of training and validation losses for the Heston model. (**a**) Losses with decaying learning rates; (**b**) Losses with cyclical learning rates.

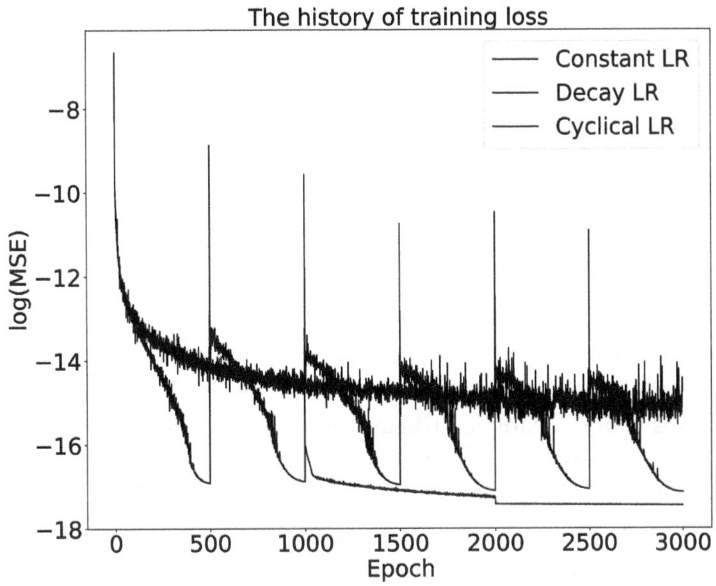

Figure 5. Different learning rate schedules for training ANNs on Heston model.

4. Numerical Results

We show the performance of the ANNs for solving the financial models, based on the following accuracy metrics (which forms the basis for the training),

$$\text{MSE} = \frac{1}{n}\sum(y_i - \hat{y}_i)^2, \tag{20}$$

where y_i is the actual value and $\hat{y}_i$ is the ANN predicted value. For completeness, however, we also report the other well-known metrics,

$$\text{RMSE} = \sqrt{\text{MSE}}, \tag{21a}$$

$$\text{MAE} = \frac{1}{n}\sum|y_i - \hat{y}_i|, \tag{21b}$$

$$\text{MAPE} = \frac{1}{n}\sum\frac{|y_i - \hat{y}_i|}{y_i}. \tag{21c}$$

The MSE is used as the training metric to update the weights, and all above metrics are employed to evaluate the selected ANN.

We start with the Black-Scholes model which gives us closed-form option prices, that are learned by the ANN. We also train the ANN to learn the implied volatility, based on the iterative root-finding Brent method. Finally, the ANN learns the results obtained by the COS method to solve the Heston model with several different parameters.

4.1. Details of the Data Set

As a data-driven approach, the quality of a data set has an impact on the performance of the resulting model. Theoretically, an arbitrary number of samples can be generated since the mathematical model is known. In reality, a sampling technique with good space-filling properties should be preferable. Latin hypercube sampling (LHS) McKay et al. (1979) is able to generate random samples of the parameter values from a multidimensional distribution, resulting in a better representation of the parameter space. When the sample data set for the input parameters is available, we select the appropriate numerical methods to generate the training results. For the Black-Scholes model, the option prices are obtained by the closed-form formula. For the Heston model, the prices are calculated by the COS method with a robust version. With the Heston prices determined, Brent's method will be used to find the corresponding implied volatility. The whole data set is randomly divided into two groups, 90% will be the training and 10% the test set.

Table 3. The different sizes of training data set when training the ANN.

Case	0	1	2	3	4	5	6
Training size (×24300)	1/8	1/4	1/2	1	2	4	8

In order to investigate the relation between the prediction accuracy and the size of the training set, we increase the number of training samples from $\frac{1}{8}$ to 8 times the baseline set, as shown in Table 3. Meanwhile, the test data is kept unchanged. The example here is learning the implied volatility. We first train the ANN on each data set separately by using a decaying learning rate, as described in Section 3.3, and repeat the training stage for each case 5 times with different random seeds and average the model performance. As shown in Figure 6, with an increasing data size, the prediction accuracy increases and the corresponding variance, indicated by the error bar, decreases. So, we employ random search for the hyper-parameters on a small-sized data set, and train the selected ANN on a large data set. The schedule of decaying learning rates is as discussed in Section 3.3. The training and validation losses remain close, which indicates that there is no over-fitting.

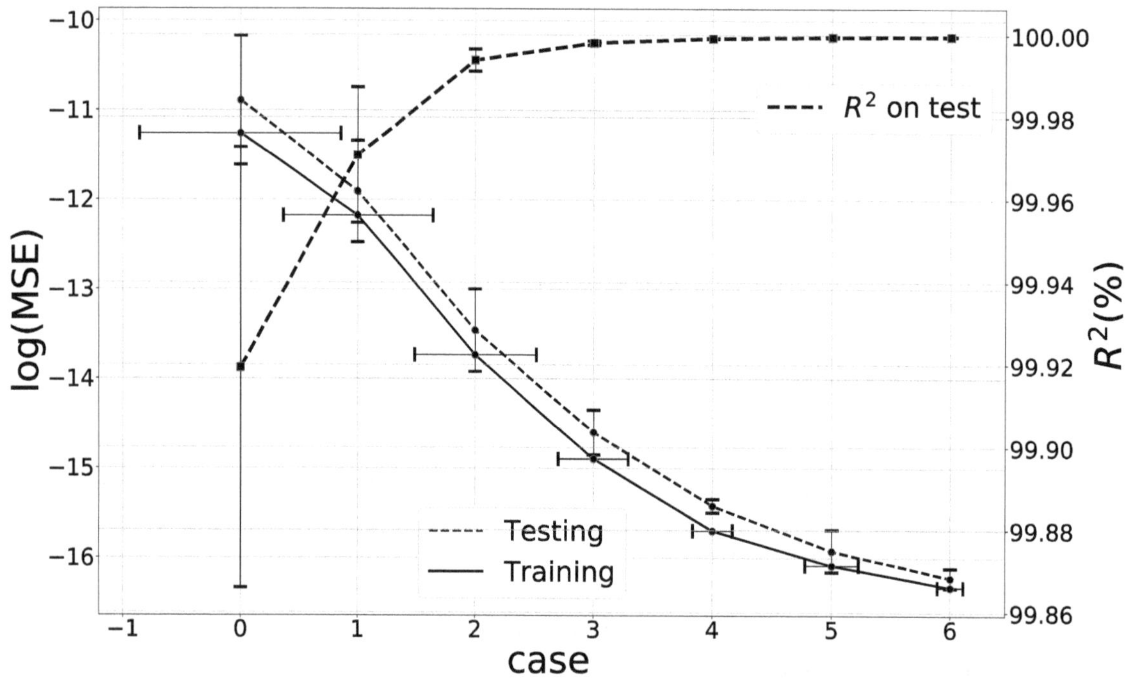

Figure 6. R^2 and MSE vs. size of the training set. The figure shows improvement in the loss, which is an indicator of the model performance.

4.2. Black-Scholes Model

Focussing on European call options, we generate 1,000,000 random samples for the input parameters, see Table 4. We calculate the corresponding European option prices $V(S,t)$ of Equation (2) with the solution in (4). As a result, each sample contains five variables $\{S_0/K, \tau, r, \sigma, V/K\}$. The training samples are fed into the ANN, where the input includes $\{S_0/K, \tau, r, \sigma\}$, and the output is the scaled option price V/K.

Table 4. Wide and narrow Black-Scholes parameter ranges.

BS-ANN	Parameters	Wide Range	Narrow Range	Unit
Input	Stock price (S_0/K)	[0.4, 1.6]	[0.5, 1.5]	-
	Time to Maturity (τ)	[0.2, 1.1]	[0.3, 0.95]	year
	Risk free rate (r)	[0.02, 0.1]	[0.03, 0.08]	-
	Volatility (σ)	[0.01, 1.0]	[0.02, 0.9]	-
Output	Call price (V/K)	(0.0, 0.9)	(0.0, 0.73)	-

We distinguish during the evaluation of the ANN, two different test data sets, i.e., a wide test set and a slightly more narrow test set. The reason is that we observe that often the ANN approximations in the areas very close to parameter domain boundaries may give rise to somewhat larger approximation errors, and the predicted values in the middle part are of higher accuracy. We wish to alleviate this boundary-related issue.

The wide test data set is based on the same parameter ranges as the training data set. As shown in Table 5, the root averaged mean-squared error (RMSE) is around 9×10^{-5}, which is an indication that the average pricing error is 0.009% of the strike price. Figure 7a shows the histogram of prediction errors, where it can be seen that the error approximately exhibits a normal distribution, and the maximum absolute error is around 0.06%.

The narrow test set is based on a somewhat more narrow parameter range than the training data set. As Table 5 shows, when the range of parameters in the test set is smaller than the training data set, ANN's test performance slightly improves. Figure 7 shows that the largest deviation becomes smaller, being less than 0.04%. The goodness of fit R^2-criterion measures the distance between the actual values and the predicted ones. There is no significant difference in R^2 in both cases with R^2 being close to 1.0.

Overall, it seems a good practice to train the ANN on a (slightly too) wide data set, when the parameter range of interest is somewhat smaller. In the next sections, however, we list the performance of the ANN on the wide test data set.

Table 5. BS-ANN performance on the test data set.

BS-ANN	MSE	RMSE	MAE	MAPE
Training-wide	8.04×10^{-9}	8.97×10^{-5}	6.73×10^{-5}	3.75×10^{-4}
Testing-wide	8.21×10^{-9}	9.06×10^{-5}	6.79×10^{-5}	3.79×10^{-4}
Testing-narrow	7.00×10^{-9}	8.37×10^{-5}	6.49×10^{-5}	3.75×10^{-4}

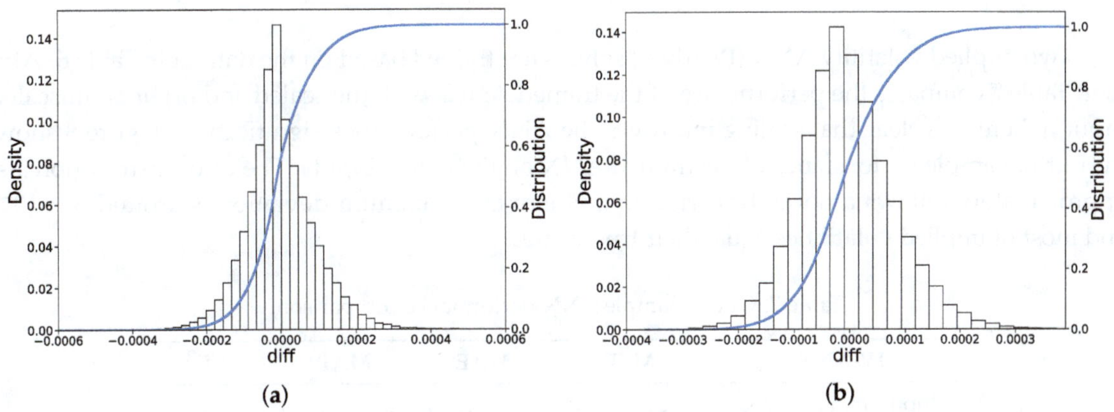

Figure 7. BS-ANN performance. (**a**) Error distribution on the wide test data set; (**b**) Error distribution on the narrow test data set.

4.3. Implied Volatility

The aim here is to learn the implicit relationship between implied volatilities and option prices, which is guided by Equation (5). The option Vega can become arbitrarily small, which also may give rise to a steep gradient problem in the ANN context. It is well-known that an ANN may generate significant prediction errors in regions with large gradients. We therefore propose a gradient-squash approach to handle this issue.

First of all, each option price can be split into a so-called *intrinsic value* and a *time value*, and we subtract the intrinsic value, as follows,

$$\tilde{V} = V_t - \max(S_t - Ke^{-r\tau}, 0),$$

where $\tilde{V}$ is the option time value. Please note that this change only applies to ITM options, since the OTM intrinsic option value is equal to zero. The proposed approach to overcome approximation issues is to reduce the gradient's steepness by furthermore working under a log-transformation of the option value. The resulting input is then given by $\{\log(\tilde{V}/K), S_0/K, r, \tau\}$. The adapted gradient approach increases the prediction accuracy significantly.

4.3.1. Model Performance

In this case, the data samples can be created in a forward stage, i.e., we will work with the Black-Scholes solution (instead of the root-finding method) to generate the training data set. Given σ, τ, K, r and S, the generator, i.e., the Black-Scholes formula, gives us the option price $V(t_0, S_0) = BS(S_0, K, \tau, r, \sigma)$. For the data collection $\{V, S_0, K, \tau, r, \sigma\}$, we then take the input σ as the implied volatility $\sigma^* \equiv \sigma$ and place it as the output of the ANN. Meanwhile, the other variables $\{V, S_0, K, \tau, r\}$ will become the input of the ANN, followed by the log-transformation $\log(\tilde{V}/K)$. In addition, we do not take into consideration the samples whose time values are extremely small, like those for which $\tilde{V} < 10^{-7}$.

Table 6. Parameter range of data set.

IV-ANN	Parameters	Range	Unit
Input	Stock price (S_0/K)	[0.5, 1.4]	-
	Time to maturity (τ)	[0.05, 1.0]	year
	Risk-free rate (r)	[0.0, 0.1]	-
	Scaled time value ($\log(\tilde{V}/K)$)	[−16.12, −0.94]	-
Output	Volatility (σ)	(0.05, 1.0)	-

Two implied volatility ANN (IV-ANN) solvers are trained based on the dataset in Table 6. After that, Table 7 compares the performance of the trained ANNs with the scaled and original (unscaled) input, where it is clear that scaling improves the ANN performance significantly. Figure 8 shows the out-of-sample performance of the trained ANN on the scaled inputs. The error distribution also approximately follows a normal distribution, where the maximum deviation is around 6×10^{-4}, and most of implied volatilities equal their true values.

Table 7. Out-of-Sample ANN performance comparison.

IV-ANN	MSE	MAE	MAPE	R^2
Input: $m, \tau, r, V/K$ Output: σ^*	6.36×10^{-4}	1.24×10^{-2}	7.67×10^{-2}	0.97510
Input: $m, \tau, r, log(\tilde{V}/K)$ Output: σ^*	1.55×10^{-8}	9.73×10^{-5}	2.11×10^{-3}	0.9999998

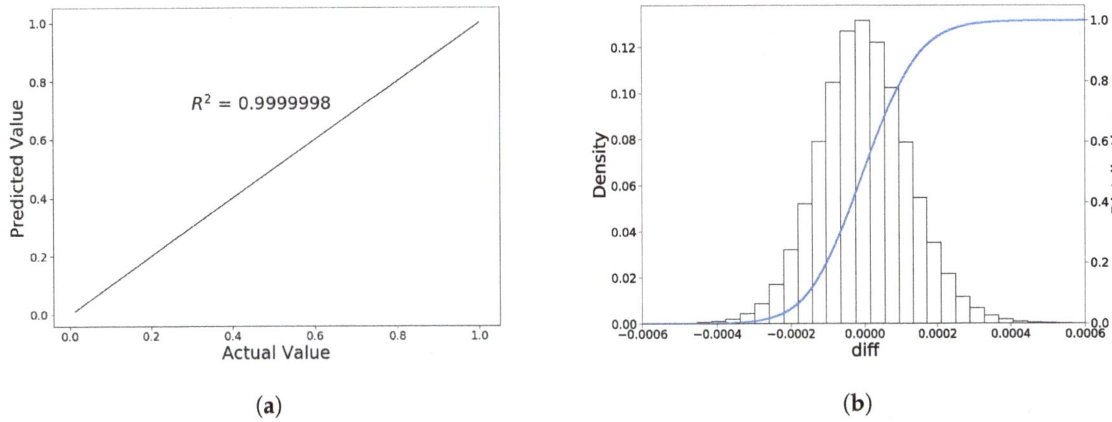

Figure 8. Out-of-Sample IV-ANN performance on the scaled input. (**a**) Comparison of implied volatilities; (**b**) The error distribution.

4.3.2. Comparison of Root-Finding Methods

We compare the performance of five different implied-volatility-finding methods, including IV-ANN, Newton-Raphson, Brent, the secant and the bisection method, in terms of run-time on a CPU and on a GPU. For this purpose, we compute 20,000 European call options for which all numerical methods can find the implied volatility. The σ-value range for bisection and for Brent's method is set to $[0, 1.1]$, and the initial guess for the Newton-Raphson and secant method is chosen $\sigma_0^* = 0.5$. The true volatility varies in the range $[0.01, 0.99]$, with the parameters, $r = 0$, $T = 0.5$, $K = 1.0$, $S_0 = 1.0$.

Table 8 shows that Brent's method is the fastest *among the robust* iterative methods (without requiring domain knowledge to select a suitable initial value). From a statistical point-of-view, the ANN solver gives rise to an acceptable averaged error MAE $\approx 10^{-4}$, and, importantly, its computation is faster by a factor 100 on a GPU and 10 on a CPU, as compared to the Newton-Raphson iteration. By the GPU architecture, the ANN processes the input 'in batch mode', calculating several implied volatilities simultaneously, which is the reason for the much higher speed. Besides, the acceleration on the CPU is also obvious, as only matrix multiplications or inner products are required.

Table 8. Performance comparison: CPU (Intel i5, 3.33GHz with cache size 4MB) and GPU(NVIDIA Tesla P100).

Method	GPU (seconds)	CPU (seconds)	Robustness
Newton-Raphson	19.68	23.06	No
Brent	52.08	60.67	Yes
Secant	88.73	103.76	No
Bi-section	337.94	390.91	Yes
IV-ANN	0.20	1.90	Yes

4.4. *The Heston Stochastic Volatility Model*

This section presents the quality of the ANN predictions of the Heston option prices and the corresponding implied volatilities. The performance of the Heston-ANN solver is also evaluated.

4.4.1. Heston Model for Option Prices

The Heston option prices are computed by means of the COS method in this section. The solution to the Heston model also can be obtained by other numerical techniques, like PDEs discretization or Monte Carlo methods. The COS method has been proved to guarantee a high accuracy with less computational expense.

According to the given ranges of Heston parameters in Table 9, for the COS method, the integration interval is based on $L_{COS} = 50$, with the number of Fourier cosine terms in the expansion being $N_{COS} = 1500$. The prices of deep OTM European call options are calculated using the put-call parity, as the COS method call prices that are close to zero may be inaccurate due to truncation errors. In Table 9, we list the range of the six Heston input parameters $(r, \rho, \kappa, \bar{v}, \gamma, v_0)$ as well as the two option contract-related parameters (τ, m), with a fixed strike price, $K = 1$. We generate around one million data points by means of the Latin hypercube sampling, using 10% as testing, 10% as validation and 80% as the training data set. After 3000 epochs with a decaying learning rate schedule, as shown in Table 10, the Heston-ANN solver has been well trained, avoiding over-fitting and approximating the prices accurately. Although the number of input parameters is doubled as compared to the Black-Scholes model, the Heston-ANN accuracy is also highly satisfactory and the error pattern is similar to that of the BS-ANN solver, see Figure 9.

Table 9. The Heston parameter ranges for traing the ANN.

ANN	Parameters	Range	Method
Input	Moneyness, $m = S_0/K$	(0.6, 1.4)	LHS
	Time to maturity, τ	(0.1, 1.4)(year)	LHS
	Risk free rate, r	(0.0%, 10%)	LHS
	Correlation, ρ	(−0.95, 0.0)	LHS
	Reversion speed, κ	(0.0, 2.0)	LHS
	Long average variance, $\bar{v}$	(0.0, 0.5)	LHS
	Volatility of volatility, γ	(0.0, 0.5)	LHS
	Initial variance, v_0	(0.05, 0.5)	LHS
Output	European call price, V	(0, 0.67)	COS

Table 10. The trained Heston-ANN performance.

Heston-ANN	MSE	MAE	MAPE	R^2
Training	1.34×10^{-8}	8.92×10^{-5}	5.66×10^{-4}	0.9999994
Testing	1.65×10^{-8}	9.51×10^{-5}	6.27×10^{-4}	0.9999993

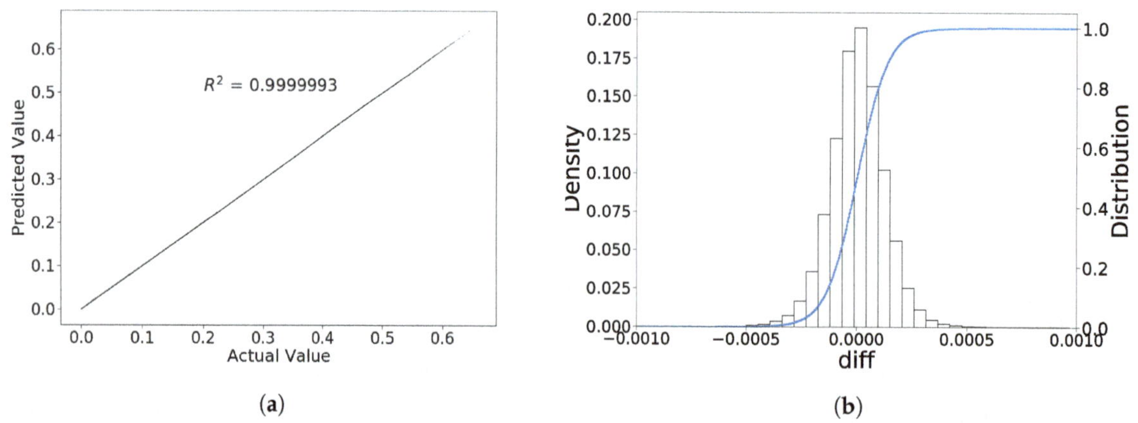

Figure 9. Out-of-sample Heston-ANN performance. (**a**) COS vs. Heston-ANN prices; (**b**) The error distribution.

4.4.2. Heston Model and Implied Volatility

We design two experiments to illustrate the ANN's ability of computing the implied volatility based on the Heston option prices. In the first experiment, the ground truth for the implied volatility is generated by means of two steps. Given the Heston input parameters, we first use the COS method to compute the option prices, after which we use Brent's method to compute the Black-Scholes implied volatility σ^*. The machine learning approach is also based on two steps, as shown in Figure 10. First of all, the Heston-ANN is used to compute the option prices, and, subsequently, we use IV-ANN to compute the corresponding implied volatilities. We compare these two approaches as follows.

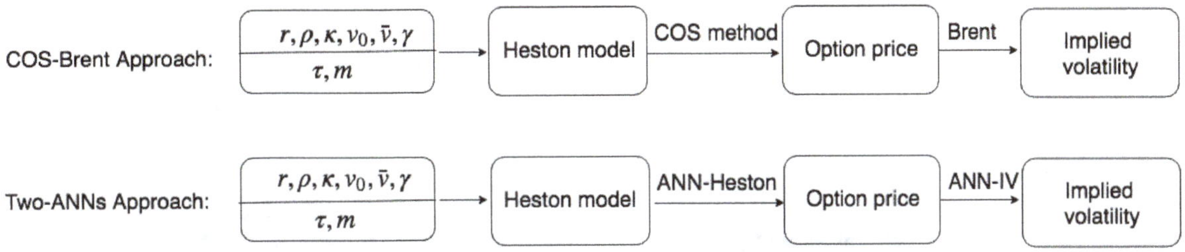

Figure 10. Two approaches of computing implied volatility for Heston model.

Please note that the ANN solver performs best in the middle of all parameter ranges, and tends to become worse at the domain boundaries. We therefore first choose the range of moneyness $m \in [0.7, 1.3]$ and the time to maturity $\tau \in [0.3, 1.1]$. Table 11 shows the overall performance of the ANN. As the IV-ANN takes the output of the Heston-ANN as the input, the accumulated error reduces the overall accuracy slightly. However, the root averaged mean error is still small, RMSE $\approx 7 \times 10^{-4}$. Then we reduce the range of the parameters, as listed in the third row of Table 11, and find that the prediction accuracy increases with the parameter ranges shrinking. Comparing the results in Figure 11 and Table 11, the goodness of fit as well as the error distribution improve with the slightly smaller parameter range, which is similar to our findings for the BS-ANN solver.

Table 11. Out-of-sample performance of the Heston-ANN plus the IV-ANN.

Heston-ANN & IV-ANN	RMSE	MAE	MAPE	R^2
Case 1: $\tau \in [0.3, 1.1], m \in [0.7, 1.3]$	7.12×10^{-4}	4.19×10^{-4}	1.46×10^{-3}	0.999966
Case 2: $\tau \in [0.4, 1.0], m \in [0.75, 1.25]$	5.53×10^{-4}	3.89×10^{-4}	1.14×10^{-3}	0.999980

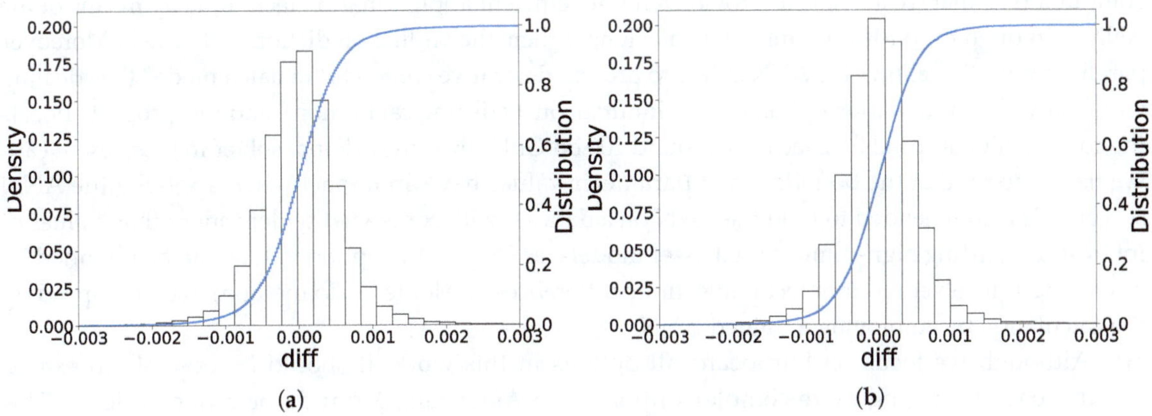

Figure 11. The error distribution of the implied volatility: The combined Heston-ANN and IV-ANN techniques for implied volatility. (**a**) Case 1: The error distribution; (**b**) Case 2: The error distribution.

Another experiment is to show that the IV-ANN can generate a complete implied volatility surface for the Heston model. With the following Heston parameters (an example to produce a smile surface), $\rho = -0.05$, $\kappa = 1.5$, $\gamma = 0.3$, $\bar{v} = 0.1$, $v_0 = 0.1$ and $r = 0.02$, we calculate the option prices by the COS method for the moneyness $m \in [0.7, 1.3]$ and time to maturity $\tau \in [0.5, 1.0]$. The implied volatility surface approximated by means of the IV-ANN is shown in Figure 12a, and Figure 12b shows that the maximum deviation between the ground-truth and the predicted values is no more than 4×10^{-4}.

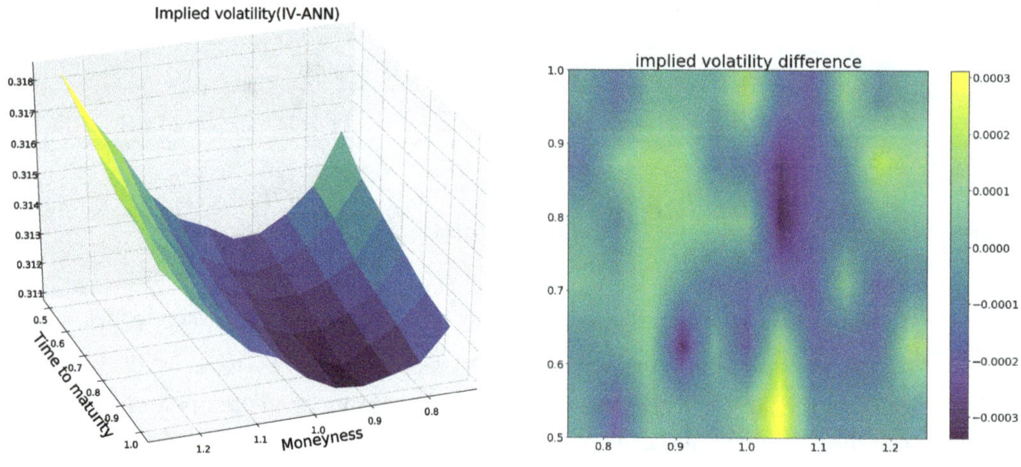

(a) (b)

Figure 12. (**a**) Heston implied volatility surface generated by IV-ANN. (**b**) Heston implied volatility difference between Brent's method and IV-ANN.

Concluding, the ANN can approximate the Heston option prices as well as the implied volatilities accurately. The characteristic function of the financial model is not required during the test phase of the ANN.

5. Conclusions and Discussion

In this paper we have proposed an ANN approach to reduce the computing time of pricing financial options, especially for high-dimensional financial models. We test the ANN approach on three different solvers, including the closed-form solution for the Black-Scholes equation, the COS method for the Heston model and Brent's root-finding method for the implied volatilities. Our numerical results show that the ANN can compute option prices and implied volatilities efficiently and accurately in a robust way. This means, particularly for asset price processes leading to much more time-consuming computations, that we are able to provide a highly efficient approximation technique by means of the ANN. Although the off-line training will take longer then, the on-line prediction will be fast. Moreover, parallel computing allows the ANN solver to process derivative contracts "in batch mode" (i.e., dealing with many observed market option prices simultaneously during calibration), and this property boosts the computational speed by a factor of around 100 on GPUs over the original solver in the present case. We have shown that the boundaries of parameter values have an impact when applying the ANN solver. It is recommended to train the ANN on a data set with somewhat wider ranges than values of interest. Regarding high-dimensional asset models, as long as the option values can be obtained by any numerical solver (Fourier technique, finite differences or Monte Carlo method), we may speed up the calculation by employing a trained ANN.

Although we focus on European call options in this work, it should be possible to extend the approach to pricing more complex options, like American, Bermuda or exotic options. This work initially demonstrates the feasibility of learning a data-driven solver to speed up solving parametric financial models. The model accuracy can be further improved, for example, by using deeper neural networks, more complex NN architectures. The solver's speed may also improve, for example, by designing a more shallow neural network, extracting insight from the complex network Hinton et al. (2015).

Furthermore, the option Greeks, representing the sensitivity of option prices with respect to the market or model parameters, are important in practice (i.e., for hedging purposes). As ANNs approximate the solution to the financial PDEs, the related derivatives can also be recovered from the trained ANN. There are several ways to calculate Greeks from the ANN solver. A straightforward way is to extract the gradient information directly from the ANN, since the approximation function in Equation (19) is known analytically. Alternatively, a trained ANN may be interpreted as an implicit function, where Auto-Differentiation Baydin et al. (2015) can help to calculate the derivatives accurately. Merging two neural networks, the Heston-ANN and the IV-ANN, into a single network should make it more efficient when computing the implied volatility surface for the Heston model.

Author Contributions: Supervision, C.W.O. and S.M.B.; Writing—original draft, S.L.

Funding: This research received no external funding.

Acknowledgments: The authors would like to thank the China Scholarship Council (CSC) for the financial support. This research was conducted using the supercomputer Little Green Machine II in the Netherlands.

Conflicts of Interest: The authors declare no conflict of interest.

References

Baydin, Atilim Gunes, Barak A. Pearlmutter, and Alexey Andreyevich Radul. 2015. Automatic Differentiation in Machine Learning: A survey. Available online: https://arxiv.org/abs/1502.05767 (accessed on 25 January 2018).

Beck, Christian, E. Weinan, and Arnulf Jentzen. 2017. Machine Learning Approximation Algorithms for High-Dimensional Fully Nonlinear Partial Differential Equations and Second-Order Backward Stochastic Differential Equations. Available online: https://arxiv.org/abs/1709.05963 (accessed on 2 February 2018).

Bergstra, James S., Rémi Bardenet, Yoshua Bengio, and Balázs Kégl. 2011. Algorithms for Hyper-Parameter Optimization. Paper presented at the 24th International Conference on Neural Information Processing Systems, Granada, Spain, December 12–15.

Bergstra, James, and Yoshua Bengio. 2012. Random Search for Hyper-Parameter Optimization. *Journal of Machine Learning Research* 13: 281–305.

Brent, Richard Peirce. 1973. An Algorithm with Guaranteed Convergence for Finding a Zero of a Function. In *Algorithms for Minimization without Derivatives*. New York: Dover.

Cont, Rama, and José da Fonseca. 2002. Dynamics of implied volatility surfaces. *Quantitative Finance* 2: 45–60. [CrossRef]

Cybenko, George. 1989. Approximation by superpositions of a sigmoidal function. *Mathematics of Control, Signals and Systems* 2: 303–14. [CrossRef]

Dugas, Charles, Yoshua Bengio, François Bélisle, Claude Nadeau, and René Garcia. 2001. Incorporating second-order functional knowledge for better option pricing. In *Proceedings of the 13th International Conference on Neural Information Processing Systems*. Cambridge: MIT Press, pp. 451–7.

Fan, Jianqing, and Loriano Mancini. 2009. Option Pricing With Model-Guided Nonparametric Methods. *Journal of the American Statistical Association* 104: 1351–72. [CrossRef]

Fang, Fang, and Cornelis W. Oosterlee. 2009. A Novel Pricing Method for European Options Based on Fourier-Cosine Series Expansions. *SIAM Journal on Scientific Computing* 31: 826–48. [CrossRef]

Garcia, René, and Ramazan Gençay. 2000. Pricing and hedging derivative securities with neural networks and a homogeneity hint. *Journal of Econometrics* 94: 93–115. [CrossRef]

Gencay, Ramazan, and Min Qi. 2001. Pricing and hedging derivative securities with neural networks: Bayesian regularization, early stopping, and bagging. *IEEE Transactions on Neural Networks* 12: 726–34. [CrossRef] [PubMed]

Han, Jiequn, Arnulf Jentzen, and E Weinan. 2017. Solving High-Dimensional Partial Differential Equations Using Deep Learning. Available online: https://arxiv.org/abs/1707.02568 (accessed on 10 December 2017).

Hesthaven, Jan S., and Stefano Ubbiali. 2018. Non-intrusive reduced order modeling of nonlinear problems using neural networks. *Journal of Computational Physics* 363: 55–78. [CrossRef]

Heston, Steven L. 1993. A Closed-Form Solution for Options with Stochastic Volatility with Applications to Bond and Currency Options. *Review of Financial Studies* 6: 327–43. [CrossRef]

Hinton, Geoffrey, Oriol Vinyals, and Jeff Dean. 2015. Distilling the Knowledge in a Neural Network. *arXiv* arXiv:1503.02531.

Hornik, Kurt. 1991. Approximation capabilities of multilayer feedforward networks. *Neural Networks* 4: 251–7. [CrossRef]

Hornik, Kurt, Maxwell Stinchcombe, and Halbert White. 1990. Universal approximation of an unknown mapping and its derivatives using multilayer feedforward networks. *Neural Networks* 3: 551–60. [CrossRef]

Hutchinson, James M., Andrew W. Lo, and Tomaso Poggio. 1994. A Nonparametric Approach to Pricing and Hedging Derivative Securities Via Learning Networks. *The Journal of Finance* 49: 851–89. [CrossRef]

Jäckel, Peter. 2015. Let's Be Rational. *Wilmott* 2015: 40–53. [CrossRef]

Jouppi, Norman P., Cliff Young, Nishant Patil, David Patterson, Gaurav Agrawal, Raminder Bajwa, Sarah Bates, Nan Boden, Al Borchers, Rick Boyle, et al. 2017. In-datacenter performance analysis of a tensor processing unit. Paper presented at 44th Annual International Symposium on Computer Architecture, Toronto, ON, Canada, June 24–28, pp. 1–12. [CrossRef]

Lagaris, Isaac E., Aristidis Likas, and Dimitrios I. Fotiadis. 1998. Artificial neural networks for solving ordinary and partial differential equations. *IEEE Transactions on Neural Networks* 9: 987–1000. [CrossRef] [PubMed]

LeCun, Yann, Yoshua Bengio, and Geoffrey Hinton. 2015. Deep learning. *Nature* 521: 436–44. [CrossRef] [PubMed]

LeCun, Yan, Koray Kavukcuoglu, and Clement Farabet. 2010. Convolutional networks and applications in vision. Paper presented at 2010 IEEE International Symposium on Circuits and Systems, Paris, France, May 30–June 2. [CrossRef]

Lipton, Zachary Chase. 2015. A Critical Review of Recurrent Neural Networks for Sequence Learning. Available online: https://arxiv.org/abs/1506.00019 (accessed on 12 November 2017).

Loshchilov, Ilya, and Frank Hutter. 2016. SGDR: Stochastic Gradient Descent with Restarts. Available online: https://arxiv.org/abs/1608.03983 (accessed on 10 October 2017).

McKay, Michael D., Richard J. Beckman, and William J. Conover. 1979. A Comparison of Three Methods for Selecting Values of Input Variables in the Analysis of Output from a Computer Code. *Technometrics* 21: 239. [CrossRef]

Oh, Kyoung-Su, and Keechul Jung. 2004. Gpu implementation of neural networks. *Pattern Recognition* 37: 1311–14. [CrossRef]

Raissi, Maziar, and George Em Karniadakis. 2018. Hidden physics models: Machine learning of nonlinear partial differential equations. *Journal of Computational Physics* 357: 125–41. [CrossRef]

Ruder, Sebastian. 2016. An Overview of Gradient Descent Optimization Algorithms. Available online: https://arxiv.org/abs/1609.04747 (accessed on 18 October 2017).

Sirignano, Justin, and Konstantinos Spiliopoulos. 2017. Stochastic gradient descent in continuous time. *SIAM Journal on Financial Mathematics* 8: 933–61. [CrossRef]

Sirignano, Justin, and Konstantinos Spiliopoulos. 2018. Dgm: A deep learning algorithm for solving partial differential equations. *Journal of Computational Physics*. [CrossRef]

Smith, Leslie N. 2015. Cyclical lEarning Rates for Training Neural Networks. Available online: https://arxiv.org/abs/1506.01186 (accessed on 15 April 2018).

Snoek, Jasper, Hugo Larochelle, and Ryan P. Adams. 2012. Practical bayesian optimization of machine learning algorithms. Paper presented at the 25th International Conference on Neural Information Processing Systems, Lake Tahoe, NV, USA, December 3–6, pp. 2951–2959.

Tompson, Jonathan, Kristofer Schlachter, Pablo Sprechmann, and Ken Perlin. 2016. Accelerating Eulerian Fluid Simulation with Convolutional Networks. Available online: https://arxiv.org/abs/1607.03597 (accessed on 18 November 2017).

Weinan, E., Jiequn Han, and Arnulf Jentzen. 2017. Deep learning-based numerical methods for high-dimensional parabolic partial differential equations and backward stochastic differential equations. *Communications in Mathematics and Statistics* 5: 349–80. doi:10.1007/s40304-017-0117-6. [CrossRef]

Yang, Yongxin, Yu Zheng, and Timothy Hospedales. 2017. Gated neural networks for option pricing: Rationality by design. Paper presented at The Thirty-First AAAI Conference on Artificial Intelligence, San Francisco, CA, USA, February 4–9.

Yao, Jingtao, Yili Li, and Chew Lim Tan. 2000. Option price forecasting using neural networks. *Omega* 28: 455–66. [CrossRef]

5

Determining Distribution for the Product of Random Variables by Using Copulas

Sel Ly [1], Kim-Hung Pho [1,*], Sal Ly [1] and Wing-Keung Wong [2,3,4]

1 Faculty of Mathematics and Statistics, Ton Duc Thang University, Ho Chi Minh City 756636, Vietnam; lysel@tdtu.edu.vn (S.L.); shanlee5611@gmail.com (S.L.)
2 Department of Finance, Fintech Center, and Big Data Research Center, Asia University, Tai Chung 41354, Taiwan; wong@asia.edu.tw
3 Department of Medical Research, China Medical University Hospital, Taichung 40402, Taiwan
4 Department of Economics and Finance, Hang Seng University of Hong Kong, Shatin 999077, Hong Kong
* Correspondence: phokimhung@tdtu.edu.vn

Abstract: Determining distributions of the functions of random variables is one of the most important problems in statistics and applied mathematics because distributions of functions have wide range of applications in numerous areas in economics, finance, risk management, science, and others. However, most studies only focus on the distribution of independent variables or focus on some common distributions such as multivariate normal joint distributions for the functions of dependent random variables. To bridge the gap in the literature, in this paper, we first derive the general formulas to determine both density and distribution of the product for two or more random variables via copulas to capture the dependence structures among the variables. We then propose an approach combining Monte Carlo algorithm, graphical approach, and numerical analysis to efficiently estimate both density and distribution. We illustrate our approach by examining the shapes and behaviors of both density and distribution of the product for two log-normal random variables on several different copulas, including Gaussian, Student-t, Clayton, Gumbel, Frank, and Joe Copulas, and estimate some common measures including Kendall's coefficient, mean, median, standard deviation, skewness, and kurtosis for the distributions. We found that different types of copulas affect the behavior of distributions differently. In addition, we also discuss the behaviors via all copulas above with the same Kendall's coefficient. Our results are the foundation of any further study that relies on the density and cumulative probability functions of product for two or more random variables. Thus, the theory developed in this paper is useful for academics, practitioners, and policy makers.

Keywords: copulas; dependence structures; product of random variables; density functions; distribution functions

---

1. Introduction

The problem of determining the distributions of different functions of random variables is one of the most important problems in statistics and mathematics because the distributions of different functions have wide range of applications in numerous areas in economics, finance, risk management, science, and many other areas (see, for example Donahue (1964); Galambos and Simonelli (2004); Springer (1979)). However, thus far, most studies only focus on independence structure with some common distributions of the functions of random variables (see, for instance Dettmann and Georgiou (2009); Garg et al. (2016); Springer and Thompson (1966, 1970); Yang and Wang (2013)). There are few studies on determining distributions for statistical models involving dependence structures of some common distributions for several functions of random variables (see, for example Ly et al. (2016, 2019); Joe (1997)).

Thus far, the distributions of product of random variables are based on the assumption of statistical independence or on stochastic dependence through multivariate normal joint distribution by using the techniques of the change-of-variable integration or applying the technique of Mellin's transformation (see Dettmann and Georgiou (2009); Donahue (1964); Galambos and Simonelli (2004); Garg et al. (2016); Glen et al. (2004); Lomnicki (1967); Maller (1981); Salo et al. (2006); Springer and Thompson (1966, 1970); Bohrnstedt and Goldberger (1969); Springer and Thompson (1970)), albeit it still always becomes dependent through non-normal distributions or unwieldy integration problems. Thus, developing the framework for modeling dependence structures for the distributions of product of dependent random variables is still an open problem in risk management.

Copula, proposed by Abe Sklar in 1959, is a very important theory in mathematics and statistics. The theory has been gaining attention in the past few decades because it has many applications in many areas including economics, finance, and risk management, especially in modeling financial risk and derivatives (see, for example Cherubini et al. (2004); Frey et al. (2001); Joe (1997); Tang (2014); Tran et al. (2015, 2017) and references therein). Using copula could enable academics to develop a framework for modeling dependence structures for the distributions of product of dependent random variables. Thus, to bridge the gap in the literature, in this paper, we first apply copula to develop a theory to study both density and distribution functions of the product of two and more dependent and independent random variables via copulas to capture the structures among the variables.

In addition, in this paper, we propose an approach combining Monte Carlo algorithm, graphical approach, and numerical analysis to efficiently estimate both density and distribution when parameters vary because the formula of both density and distribution of the product of dependent random variables are very complicated, and it is very difficult, if not impossible, to obtain their exact forms. Thereafter, we illustrate our approach by examining the shapes of both density and distribution of the product of two log-normal random variables on several different copulas, including Gaussian, Student-t, Clayton, Gumbel, Frank, and Joe Copulas. We find that different types of copulas affect the behavior of the distributions differently. For example, the distributions of the product using Gaussian and Student-t copulas behave similarly while the distributions using Clayton, Gumbel, Frank, and Joe copulas also behave similarly with impacts of different degrees. Our findings are useful to academics, practitioners, and policy makers if they need to study the shapes of both density and distribution functions and some common measures for the product of dependent or independent random variables by using different copulas.

The rest of the paper is organized as follows. Section 2 discusses the background theory for both density and distribution of the product of the random variables while Section 3 first briefly discusses some simple copula results on bivariate copula and then discusses the results on the high dimensions copula. In Section 4, we develop the theory for both density and distribution of the product of two or more random variables. In Section 5, we examine the behavior of the product of two log-normal random variables by using different copulas. The last section concludes.

2. Background Theory

We first discuss some work on copula methods that is related to the problem studied in this paper. Readers may refer to Ly et al. (2016) for more information. For a weighted sum of two dependent random variables with special emphasis on the applications in estimating distortion risk measures and diversification, we assume that a portfolio Y that is a linear combination of two assets X_1 and X_2 with respect to their weights w_1 and w_2 is expressed as follows:

$$Y = w_1 X_1 + w_2 X_2 \quad \text{with} \quad w_1 + w_2 = 1. \tag{1}$$

Let F_{X_1}, F_{X_2}, and F_Y denote the cumulative distribution functions (CDFs) of X_1, X_2, and Y, respectively. Suppose that investors are interested in estimating risks of the portfolio Y under distortion risk measure (see Ly et al. (2016)), given by

$$R_g[Y] = \int_0^\infty g(\overline{F}_Y(y))dy + \int_{-\infty}^0 [g(\overline{F}_Y(y)) - 1]dy,$$

where g is a *distortion function* and $\overline{F}_Y(y) = 1 - F_Y(y)$ is a survival function of Y. In this model setting, some academics and practitioners are interested in deriving the distribution of Y. Recall that, if $Y = X_1 + X_2$ and X_1, X_2 are independent, then it is well-known that one can use convolution product of two density functions f_{X_1} and f_{X_2} to find the density of Y, given by

$$f_Y(y) = f_{X_1} * f_{X_2}(y) = \int_{-\infty}^\infty f_{X_1}(x) f_{X_2}(y - x)dx. \tag{2}$$

Cherubini et al. (2011) relaxed the independence assumption and used copulas to define a C-convolution for the dependence case as expressed in the following:

$$\begin{aligned} F_{X_1+X_2}(y) &= F_{X_1} \overset{C}{*} F_{X_2}(y) \\ &= \int_0^1 \frac{\partial}{\partial u} C\left(u, F_{X_2}\left(y - F_{X_1}^{-1}(u)\right)\right) du. \end{aligned} \tag{3}$$

Ly et al. (2016) further extended the theory by deriving a more general sum of variables, as stated in the following formula:

$$F_{w_1X_1+w_2X_2}(y) = \mathbf{1}_{\{w_2<0\}} + \text{sgn}(w_2) \int_0^1 \frac{\partial}{\partial u} C\left(u, F_{X_2}\left(\frac{y - w_1 F_{X_1}^{-1}(u)}{w_2}\right)\right) du, \tag{4}$$

where C is a copula Nelsen (2007) which captures the dependence structure of X_1 and X_2. Furthermore, to deal with credit models, Frey et al. (2001) expressed the total loss in terms of the aggregation of products of risk factors. Thus, it is necessary to develop formulas for multiplication case. To do this, this study first uses copula to find the density and distribution of the absolutely continuous random variable Y that is defined by

$$Y = X_1 X_2, \tag{5}$$

or the n-product $Y_n = X_1 X_2 \ldots X_n$ for $n \geq 2$. We discuss the latter in the next section.

3. Copulas

In this section, we first briefly discuss the simple theory of bivariate copula, and then discuss the theory of high-dimensional copula Joe (1997); Nelsen (2007). Letting $\mathbb{I} = [0, 1]$ be the closed unit interval and $\mathbb{I}^2 = [0, 1] \times [0, 1]$ be the closed unit square interval, we define the bivariate copula as follows:

Definition 1. ***(Copula)*** *A two-dimensional copula is a function $C\colon \mathbb{I}^2 \to \mathbb{I}$ satisfying the following conditions:*

(i) $C(u, 0) = C(0, v) = 0$ *for any u and $v \in \mathbb{I}$.*
(ii) $C(u, 1) = u$ *and* $C(1, v) = v$ *for any u and $v \in \mathbb{I}$.*
(iii) for any u_1, u_2, v_1, and $v_2 \in \mathbb{I}$ such that $u_1 \leq u_2$ and $v_1 \leq v_2$,. We have

$$C(u_2, v_2) + C(u_1, v_1) - C(u_2, v_1) - C(u_1, v_2) \geq 0.$$

The most crucial role in the copula theory is Sklar's Theorem (1959). Specifically, given that X_1 and X_2 are random variables with absolutely continuous marginal distribution functions F_{X_1} and F_{X_2}, respectively, by Sklar's Theorem (see Joe (1997); Nelsen (2007)), there exists a unique copula C such that

$$\begin{aligned} H(x_1,x_2) &= C\left(F_{X_1}(x_1),F_{X_2}(x_2)\right), \\ h(x_1,x_2) &= H''(x_1,x_2) = c\left(F_{X_1}(x_1),F_{X_2}(x_2)f_{X_1}(x_1)f_{X_2}(x_2)\right), \end{aligned} \tag{6}$$

where $c(u,v) := \frac{\partial^2}{\partial u \partial v}C(u,v)$ denotes density of copula C, f_{X_i} is probability density function (PDF) of X_i for $i=1,2$, and $H''(x_1,x_2) = \frac{\partial^2}{\partial x_1 \partial x_2}H(x_1,x_2) = h(x_1,x_2)$ is the joint density function of X_1 and X_2. The copula C is used to capture the dependence structure of X_1 and X_2. For example, X_1 and X_2 are independent if and only if $C(u,v)=uv$; X_1 and X_2 are comonotonic (that is, $X_2 = f(X_1)$, where f is strictly increasing) if and only if $C(u,v) = \min(u,v)$; and X_1 and X_2 are countermonotonic (that is, $X_2 = f(X_1)$ a.s., where f is strictly decreasing) if and only if $C(u,v) = \max(u+v-1,0)$. Copulas can be used not only to model the dependence structures of the variables, but also to capture the correlation between the variables. Thus, Kendall's coefficient τ can be expressed in terms of copulas as shown in the following:

$$\tau(X_1,X_2) = \tau(C) = 4\int\int_{\mathbb{I}^2} C(u,v)dC(u,v) - 1. \tag{7}$$

Readers may refer to Cherubini et al. (2004); Joe (1997); Nelsen (2007) for more details on different families of copulas, the concept of dependence structures and measures of dependence with applications. We now define the copula for higher dimension in the following:

Definition 2. *A n-copula is a function $C : \mathbb{I}^n \to \mathbb{I}$ satisfying:*

(i) C is grounded; that is, $C(u_1,u_2,\ldots,u_n) = 0$ where $(u_1,u_2,\ldots,u_n) \in \mathbb{I}^n$ such that at least one $u_i = 0$ for $i = 1,2,\ldots,n$.

(ii) $C(1,\ldots,1,u_i,1,\ldots,1) = u_i,\ \forall u_i \in \mathbb{I},\ i = 1,2,\ldots,n.$

(iii) C is an n-increasing function; that is, $\forall B = B_1 \times B_2 \cdots \times B_n$ where $B_i = [a_i,b_i] \subset [0,1]$ for $i = 1,2,\ldots,n$. Then, we have:

$$V_C(B) = \int_B dC(u_1,\ldots,u_n) = \sum_{v\in B} sign(v)C(v) \geq 0,$$

where the sum is taken over all vertices $v = (v_1,v_2,\ldots,v_n)$ of the hyperrectangle B, i.e. $v_i = a_i$ or $v_i = b_i$ and

$$sign(v) = \begin{cases} 1, & if \quad v_k = a_k, \quad \text{for an even number of } k\text{'s; and} \\ -1, & if \quad v_k = a_k, \quad \text{for an odd number of } k\text{'s.} \end{cases}$$

We illustrate here how to compute $V_C(B)$. This information is useful in deriving Equation (20). Letting

$$\Delta_{a_k}^{b_k}C(v) := C\left(v_1,\ldots,v_{k-1},b_k,v_{k+1},\ldots,v_n\right) - C\left(v_1,\ldots,v_{k-1},a_k,v_{k+1},\ldots,v_n\right),$$

we get

$$V_C(B) = \Delta_a^b C(v) = \Delta_{a_n}^{b_n}\ldots\Delta_{a_2}^{b_2}\Delta_{a_1}^{b_1}C(v_1,\ldots,v_n) \geq 0.$$

In the special case in two dimensions such that $C(v) = C(v_1,v_2)$, we have $B = [a_1,b_1]\times[a_2,b_2]$, and thus,

$$V_C(B) = \Delta_a^b C(v) = \Delta_{a_2}^{b_2}\Delta_{a_1}^{b_1} C(v_1, v_2) = \Delta_{a_2}^{b_2}\left[C(b_1, v_2) - c(a_1, v_2)\right]$$
$$= \Delta_{a_2}^{b_2} C(b_1, v_2) - \Delta_{a_2}^{b_2} C(a_1, v_2) = C(b_1, b_2) - C(b_1, a_2) - C(a_1, b_2) + C(a_1, a_2).$$

In the three-dimensional case with $C(v) = C(v_1, v_2, v_3)$, we have $B = [a_1, b_1] \times [a_2, b_2] \times [a_3, b_3]$, and thus,

$$\begin{aligned}
V_C(B) &= \Delta_a^b C(v) = \Delta_{a_3}^{b_3}\Delta_{a_2}^{b_2}\Delta_{a_1}^{b_1} C(v_1, v_2, v_3) \\
&= \Delta_{a_3}^{b_3}\Delta_{a_2}^{b_2}\left[C(b_1, v_2, v_3) - c(a_1, v_2, v_3)\right] \\
&= \Delta_{a_3}^{b_3}\Delta_{a_2}^{b_2} C(b_1, v_2, v_3) - \Delta_{a_3}^{b_3}\Delta_{a_2}^{b_2} c(a_1, v_2, v_3) \\
&= \Delta_{a_3}^{b_3}\left[C(b_1, b_2, v_3) - C(b_1, a_2, v_3)\right] - \Delta_{a_3}^{b_3}\left[C(a_1, b_2, v_3) - C(a_1, a_2, v_3)\right] \\
&= C(b_1, b_2, b_3) - C(b_1, b_2, a_3) - C(b_1, a_2, b_3) + C(b_1, a_2, a_3) \\
&\quad - C(a_1, b_2, b_3) + C(a_1, b_2, a_3) + C(a_1, a_2, b_3) - C(a_1, a_2, a_3).
\end{aligned}$$

4. Theory

In this section, we develop the theorems on the probability distribution of the product of dependent random variables by using copulas. We first study the bivariate case.

4.1. Bivariate Model

We first establish the formulas for both density and distribution functions of the two-dimensional case as shown in the following theorem:

Theorem 1. *Suppose that (X_1, X_2) is a vector of two absolutely continuous random variables with marginal distributions F_1 and F_2, respectively. Let C be an absolutely continuous copula modeling the dependence structure of the random vector (X_1, X_2) and define Y as*

$$Y = X_1 X_2, \tag{8}$$

then the density and distribution functions of Y are

$$f_Y(y) = \int_0^1 \frac{1}{|F_1^{-1}(u)|} c\left(u, F_2\left(\frac{y}{F_1^{-1}(u)}\right)\right) f_2\left(\frac{y}{F_1^{-1}(u)}\right) du, \tag{9}$$

$$F_Y(y) = F_1(0) + \int_0^1 \operatorname{sgn}\left(F_1^{-1}(u)\right) \frac{\partial}{\partial u} C\left(u, F_2\left(\frac{y}{F_1^{-1}(u)}\right)\right) du, \tag{10}$$

respectively, where F_1^{-1} is an inverse function of F_1, c denotes the density of copula C, and $\operatorname{sgn}(\cdot)$ is a sign function such that

$$\operatorname{sgn}(x) = \begin{cases} 1, & \text{if } x > 0, \\ -1, & \text{if } x < 0. \end{cases}$$

Proof. We start by setting

$$\begin{cases} Y_1 = X_1 X_2, \\ Y_2 = X_1. \end{cases}$$

Then, the inverse transformation is given by

$$\begin{cases} X_1 = Y_2 \\ X_2 = \dfrac{Y_1}{Y_2}, \end{cases}$$

and the Jacobian is

$$J = \begin{vmatrix} 0 & 1 \\ \frac{1}{Y_2} & -\frac{Y_1}{Y_2^2} \end{vmatrix} = -\frac{1}{Y_2}, \quad Y_2 \neq 0, \ a.s.$$

We note that, since X_1 and X_2 are both continuous random variables, $P(X_1 = 0) = P(Y_2 = 0) = 0$; that is, $Y_2 \neq 0$ almost surely. Hence, the inverse transformation $X_2 = \frac{Y_1}{Y_2}$ always exists with probability 1, and thus, we obtain the following joint density of Y_1 and Y_2:

$$\begin{aligned} h(y_1, y_2) &= f(y_2, \frac{y_1}{y_2}) \left| \frac{1}{y_2} \right| \\ &= \left| \frac{1}{y_2} \right| c\left(F_1(y_2), F_2\left(\frac{y_1}{y_2}\right) \right) f_1(y_2) f_2\left(\frac{y_1}{y_2}\right), \end{aligned} \tag{11}$$

and the density of Y_1

$$f_{Y_1}(y_1) = \int_{-\infty}^{\infty} \left| \frac{1}{y_2} \right| c\left(F_1(y_2), F_2\left(\frac{y_1}{y_2}\right) \right) f_1(y_2) f_2\left(\frac{y_1}{y_2}\right) dy_2 \tag{12}$$

$$= \int_0^1 \frac{1}{\left| F_1^{-1}(u) \right|} c\left(u, F_2\left(\frac{y_1}{F_1^{-1}(u)}\right) \right) f_2\left(\frac{y_1}{F_1^{-1}(u)}\right) du. \tag{13}$$

The CDF of Y_1 can then be determined by

$$F_{Y_1}(t) = \int_0^1 \int_{-\infty}^{t} \frac{1}{\left| F_1^{-1}(u) \right|} c\left(u, F_2\left(\frac{y_1}{F_1^{-1}(u)}\right) \right) f_2\left(\frac{y_1}{F_1^{-1}(u)}\right) dy_1 du. \tag{14}$$

Taking $v = F_2\left(\frac{y_1}{F_1^{-1}(u)}\right) \Longrightarrow dv = f_2\left(\frac{y_1}{F_1^{-1}(u)}\right) \frac{1}{F_1^{-1}(u)} dy_1$ and since

$$F_1^{-1}(u) \geq 0 \Longleftrightarrow u \geq F_1(0), \text{ and } F_1^{-1}(u) \leq 0 \Longleftrightarrow u \leq F_1(0),$$

we have

$$\begin{aligned} F_{Y_1}(t) &= -\int_0^{F_1(0)} \int_1^{F_2\left(\frac{t}{F_1^{-1}(u)}\right)} \frac{\partial^2}{\partial u \partial v} C(u,v)\, dv du + \int_{F_1(0)}^1 \int_0^{F_2\left(\frac{t}{F_1^{-1}(u)}\right)} \frac{\partial^2}{\partial u \partial v} C(u,v)\, dv du \\ &= -\int_0^{F_1(0)} \left[\frac{\partial}{\partial u} C\left(u, F_2\left(\frac{t}{F_1^{-1}(u)}\right) \right) - \frac{\partial}{\partial u} C(u,1) \right] du + \int_{F_1(0)}^1 \left[\frac{\partial}{\partial u} C\left(u, F_2\left(\frac{t}{F_1^{-1}(u)}\right) \right) - \frac{\partial}{\partial u} C(u,0) \right] du \\ &= F_1(0) - \int_0^{F_1(0)} \frac{\partial}{\partial u} C\left(u, F_2\left(\frac{t}{F_1^{-1}(u)}\right) \right) du + \int_{F_1(0)}^1 \frac{\partial}{\partial u} C\left(u, F_2\left(\frac{t}{F_1^{-1}(u)}\right) \right) du \\ &= F_1(0) + \int_0^1 \operatorname{sgn}\left(F_1^{-1}(u) \right) \frac{\partial}{\partial u} C\left(u, F_2\left(\frac{t}{F_1^{-1}(u)}\right) \right) du. \end{aligned} \tag{15}$$

In addition, because the role of X_1 and X_2 can be exchangeable, the density and CDF of Y_1 can be obtained as shown in the following:

$$f_Y(y) = \int_0^1 \frac{1}{|F_2^{-1}(v)|} c\left(F_1\left(\frac{y}{F_2^{-1}(v)}\right), v \right) f_1\left(\frac{y}{F_2^{-1}(v)}\right) dv, \tag{16}$$

$$F_Y(y) = F_2(0) + \int_0^1 \operatorname{sgn}\left(F_2^{-1}(v) \right) \frac{\partial}{\partial v} C\left(F_1\left(\frac{y}{F_2^{-1}(v)}\right), v \right) dv. \tag{17}$$

Thus, the assertions of Theorem 1 hold. □

In a special case in which X_1 and X_2 are independent, applying Equation (9), we obtain the following corollary:

Corollary 1. *When X_1 and X_2 are independent, the copula $C(u,v) = uv$ has the density $c(u,v) = 1 \, \forall u, v \in \mathbb{I}$ and the density of the product of two independent random variables become*

$$f_Y(y) = \int_{-\infty}^{\infty} f_1(x) f_2\left(\frac{y}{x}\right) \frac{1}{|x|} dx.$$

This result is well known in the literature.

4.2. Multivariate Model

We now turn to extend Theorem 1 to a vector of more than two random variables as stated in the following theorem:

Theorem 2. *Supposing that $(X_1, X_2, \ldots, X_n)$ is a vector of absolutely continuous random variables with the marginal distributions $F_1, F_2, \ldots, F_n$, respectively, C is an absolutely continuous copula modeling dependence structure of $(X_1, X_2, \ldots, X_n)$, and Y satisfies*

$$Y = X_1 X_2 \ldots X_n, \qquad n \geq 2. \tag{18}$$

Then, the density and the distribution function of Y are

$$f_Y(y) = \underbrace{\int_0^1 \cdots \int_0^1}_{n-1 \text{ times}} \frac{1}{\left|\prod_{i=1}^{n-1} F_i^{-1}(u_i)\right|} c\left(u_1, \ldots, u_{n-1}, F_n\left(y'\right)\right) f_n\left(y'\right) du_1 \ldots du_{n-1}, \tag{19}$$

$$F_Y(y) = V_{C_{n-1}(A)} + \underbrace{\int_0^1 \cdots \int_0^1}_{n-1 \text{ times}} \operatorname{sgn}\left(\prod_{i=1}^{n-1} F_i^{-1}(u_i)\right) \frac{\partial^{n-1}}{\partial u_1 \ldots \partial u_{n-1}} C\left(u_1, \ldots, u_{n-1}, F_n\left(y'\right)\right) du_1 \ldots du_{n-1}, \tag{20}$$

respectively, in which $A := \{(u_1, \ldots, u_{n-1}) \in [0,1]^{n-1} : \prod_{i=1}^{n-1} F_i^{-1}(u_i) \leq 0\}$; $V_{C_{n-1}(A)}$ denotes C_{n-1}-Volume of the set A defined by

$$V_{C_{n-1}}(A) = \int_A \frac{\partial^{n-1}}{\partial u_1 \ldots \partial u_{n-1}} C\left(u_1, \ldots, u_{n-1}, 1\right) du_1 du_2 \ldots du_{n-1} = \int_A dC(u_1, \ldots, u_{n-1}, 1);$$

c denotes the density of copula C with $\operatorname{sgn}(\cdot)$ being a sign function such that

$$\operatorname{sgn}(x) = \begin{cases} 1, & \text{if } x > 0, \\ -1, & \text{if } x < 0, \end{cases}$$

and

$$y' = \frac{y}{\prod_{i=1}^{n-1} F_i^{-1}(u_i)}.$$

Proof. We set

$$\begin{cases} Y_1 = X_1 X_2 \ldots X_n \\ Y_2 = X_1 \\ Y_3 = X_2 \\ \ldots \\ Y_n = X_{n-1}. \end{cases}$$

Then, the inverse transformation is

$$\begin{cases} X_1 = Y_2 \\ X_2 = Y_3 \\ \dots \\ X_{n-1} = Y_n \\ X_n = \dfrac{Y_1}{Y_2 Y_3 \dots Y_n}, \end{cases} \tag{21}$$

with Jacobian

$$J = \begin{vmatrix} \frac{\partial X_1}{\partial Y_1} & \frac{\partial X_1}{\partial Y_2} & \dots & \frac{\partial X_1}{\partial Y_n} \\ \frac{\partial X_2}{\partial Y_1} & \frac{\partial X_2}{\partial Y_2} & \dots & \frac{\partial X_2}{\partial Y_n} \\ \dots & \dots & \dots & \dots \\ \frac{\partial X_{n-1}}{\partial Y_1} & \frac{\partial X_{n-1}}{\partial Y_2} & \dots & \frac{\partial X_{n-1}}{\partial Y_n} \\ \frac{\partial X_n}{\partial Y_1} & \frac{\partial X_n}{\partial Y_2} & \dots & \frac{\partial X_n}{\partial Y_n} \end{vmatrix} = \begin{vmatrix} 0 & 1 & 0 & \dots & 0 \\ 0 & 0 & 1 & \dots & 0 \\ \dots & \dots & \dots & \dots & \dots \\ 0 & 0 & 0 & \dots & 1 \\ \frac{1}{Y_2 Y_3 \dots Y_n} & \frac{-Y_1}{Y_2^2 Y_3 \dots Y_n} & \frac{-Y_1}{Y_2 Y_3^2 \dots Y_n} & \dots & \frac{-Y_1}{Y_2 Y_3 \dots Y_n^2} \end{vmatrix} = \frac{(-1)^{n+1}}{Y_2 Y_3 \dots Y_n},$$

in which $Y_2 Y_3 \cdots Y_n \neq 0$, almost surely because all $Y_2, Y_3, \cdots, Y_n$ are continuous random variables with $P(Y_2 Y_3 \dots Y_n = 0) = 0$. Hence, the joint density of $Y_1, Y_2, \cdots, Y_n$ becomes

$$\begin{aligned} h(y_1, y_2, \dots, y_n) &= f\left(y_2, \dots, y_n, \frac{y_1}{y_2 y_3 \dots y_n}\right) |J| \\ &= \frac{1}{|y_2 y_3 \dots y_n|} c\left(F_1(y_2), \dots, F_{n-1}(y_n), F_n\left(\frac{y_1}{y_2 y_3 \dots y_n}\right)\right) \\ &\quad \times f_1(y_2) \dots f_{n-1}(y_n) f_n\left(\frac{y_1}{y_2 y_3 \dots y_n}\right), \end{aligned}$$

and, thus, the density of Y_1 can be derived as

$$\begin{aligned} f_{Y_1}(y_1) &= \underbrace{\int_{-\infty}^{\infty} \cdots \int_{-\infty}^{\infty}}_{n-1 \text{ times}} h(y_1, y_2, \dots, y_n) dy_2 \dots dy_n \\ &= \underbrace{\int_{-\infty}^{\infty} \cdots \int_{-\infty}^{\infty}}_{n-1 \text{ times}} \frac{1}{|y_2 y_3 \dots y_n|} c\left(F_1(y_2), \dots, F_{n-1}(y_n), F_n\left(\frac{y_1}{y_2 y_3 \dots y_n}\right)\right) \\ &\quad \times f_1(y_2) \dots f_{n-1}(y_n) f_n\left(\frac{y_1}{y_2 y_3 \dots y_n}\right) dy_2 \dots dy_n. \end{aligned}$$

Thereafter, we let $u_i := F_i(y_{i+1})$ for $i = 1, 2, \dots, n-1$ and $y_1' := \dfrac{y_1}{y_2 y_3 \dots y_n}$. Then, we obtain $y_2 y_3 \dots y_n = \prod_{i=1}^{n-1} F_i^{-1}(u_i)$, $y_1' = \dfrac{y_1}{\prod_{i=1}^{n-1} F_i^{-1}(u_i)}$, and

$$f_{Y_1}(y_1) = \underbrace{\int_0^1 \cdots \int_0^1}_{n-1 \text{ times}} \frac{1}{\left|\prod_{i=1}^{n-1} F_i^{-1}(u_i)\right|} c\left(u_1, \dots, u_{n-1}, F_n(y_1')\right) f_n(y_1')\, du_1 du_2 \dots du_{n-1}.$$

The CDF of Y_1 can then be obtained as follows:

$$F_{Y_1}(t) = \int_{-\infty}^{t} f_{Y_1}(y_1)dy_1$$
$$= \underbrace{\int_0^1 \cdots \int_0^1}_{n-1 \text{ times}} \int_{-\infty}^{t} \frac{1}{|\prod_{i=1}^{n-1} F_i^{-1}(u_i)|} c\left(u_1, \ldots, u_{n-1}, F_n\left(y_1'\right)\right) f_n\left(y_1'\right) dy_1 du_1 du_2 \ldots du_{n-1}.$$

Taking $u_n := F_n(y_1')$, letting $A := \left\{(u_1, .., u_{n-1}) \in [0,1]^{n-1} : \prod_{i=1}^{n-1} F_i^{-1}(u_i) \leq 0\right\}$, and denoting its compliment set by $\overline{A}$, we get

$$F_{Y_1}(t) = \int_{\overline{A}} \int_0^{F_n\left(\frac{t}{\prod_{i=1}^{n-1} F_i^{-1}(u_i)}\right)} c\left(u_1, \ldots, u_{n-1}, u_n\right) du_n du_1 du_2 \ldots du_{n-1}$$
$$- \int_A \int_1^{F_n\left(\frac{t}{\prod_{i=1}^{n-1} F_i^{-1}(u_i)}\right)} c\left(u_1, \ldots, u_{n-1}, u_n\right) du_n du_1 du_2 \ldots du_{n-1}$$
$$= \int_{\overline{A}} \frac{\partial^{n-1}}{\partial u_1 \ldots \partial u_{n-1}} C\left(u_1, \ldots, u_{n-1}, F_n\left(\frac{t}{\prod_{i=1}^{n-1} F_i^{-1}(u_i)}\right)\right) du_1 du_2 \ldots du_{n-1}$$
$$- \int_A \frac{\partial^{n-1}}{\partial u_1 \ldots \partial u_{n-1}} C\left(u_1, \ldots, u_{n-1}, F_n\left(\frac{t}{\prod_{i=1}^{n-1} F_i^{-1}(u_i)}\right)\right) du_1 du_2 \ldots du_{n-1} + V_{C_{n-1}}(A),$$

where

$$V_{C_{n-1}}(A) = \int_A \frac{\partial^{n-1}}{\partial u_1 \ldots \partial u_{n-1}} C\left(u_1, \ldots, u_{n-1}, 1\right) du_1 du_2 \ldots du_{n-1}$$
$$= \int_A dC(u_1, \ldots, u_{n-1}, 1)$$

denotes C_{n-1}-volume of the set A calculated via $(n-1)-$dimensional copula C. Using the sign function $sgn(\cdot)$, we obtain the following result:

$$F_{Y_1}(t) = V_{C_{n-1}(A)} +$$
$$+ \underbrace{\int_0^1 \cdots \int_0^1}_{n-1 \text{ times}} \operatorname{sgn}\left(\prod_{i=1}^{n-1} F_i^{-1}(u_i)\right) \frac{\partial^{n-1}}{\partial u_1 \ldots \partial u_{n-1}} C\Big(u_1, \ldots, u_{n-1}, F_n\Big(\frac{t}{\prod_{i=1}^{n-1} F_i^{-1}(u_i)}\Big)\Big) du_1 \ldots du_{n-1}.$$

Thus, the assertions in Theorem 2 hold. □

From Equation (20), one could notice that it contains the quantity $V_{C_{n-1}}(A)$. Using this result, we obtain the following corollary:

Corollary 2. *For* $n = 2$, *we have* $A := \{u_1 \in [0,1] : F_1^{-1}(u_1) \leq 0\} = [0, F_1(0)]$ *and* $V_{C_1}(A) = V_{C(u_1,1)}(A) = F_1(0)$.

This result can be used for the bivariate model and one could easily apply Corollary 2 to obtain Theorem 1. In addition, we obtain the following corollary:

Corollary 3. *For* $n = 3$,

$$A := \{(u_1, u_2) \in [0,1]^2 : F_1^{-1}(u_1) F_2^{-1}(u_2) \leq 0\} = [0, F_1(0)] \times [F_2(0), 1] \cup [F_1(0), 1] \times [0, F_2(0)]$$

and

$$V_{C_2}(A) = V_{C(u_1,u_2,1)(A)} = C(F_1(0),1,1) + C(0,F_2(0),1) - C(0,1,1) - C(F_1(0),F_2(0),1) + C(1,F_2(0),1) + C(F_1(0),0,1) - C(1,0,1) - C(F_1(0),F_2(0),1) = F_1(0) + F_2(0) - 2C(F_1(0),F_2(0),1).$$

This result can be used for the trivariate model and one could apply Corollary 3 to obtain the density and distribution functions of $Y = X_1X_2X_3$.

When $X_1, \ldots, X_n$ are independent, applying Theorem 2, we obtain the following corollary:

Corollary 4. *When $X_1, \ldots, X_n$ are independent,*

$$f_Y(y) = \underbrace{\int_0^1 \cdots \int_0^1}_{n-1 \text{ times}} \frac{1}{\left|\prod_{i=1}^{n-1} F_i^{-1}(u_i)\right|} f_n\left(\frac{y}{\prod_{i=1}^{n-1} F_i^{-1}(u_i)}\right) du_1 \ldots du_{n-1},$$

$$= \underbrace{\int_{-\infty}^{\infty} \cdots \int_{-\infty}^{\infty}}_{n-1 \text{ times}} \frac{1}{|x_1x_2\ldots x_{n-1}|} f_1(x_1)\ldots f_{n-1}(x_{n-1}) f_n\left(\frac{y}{x_1x_1\ldots x_{n-1}}\right) dx_1 \ldots dx_{n-1}.$$

Since Equations (9), (10), (19), and (20) may not have any close form, in this paper, we propose to use the Monte Carlo (MC) simulation method to obtain the solutions of Equations (9), (10), (19), and (20). We discuss the issue in the next section.

5. Simulation Study

Because the density and the CDF formula of the product $Y = X_1X_2$ expressed in both (9) and (10) that are in terms of integrals are very complicated, we cannot obtain the exact forms of their density and CDF. To circumvent the difficulty, in this paper, we propose to use numerical analysis and graphical approach to examine the behavior of both density and distribution and the changes of their shapes when parameters are changing.

Let X_1 and X_2 be log-normal random variables denoted by $X_i \sim LN(\mu_i, \sigma_i^2)$ with the following PDF:

$$f_{X_i}(x) = \frac{1}{x\sqrt{2\pi}\sigma_i}\exp\left(-\frac{(\ln(x)-\mu_i)^2}{2\sigma_i^2}\right),$$

for $i = 1,2$. Without loss of generality, we assume $\mu_1 = \mu_2 = 0$ and $\sigma_1 = \sigma_2 = 1$. We note that, if X_1 and X_2 are independent, then $Y \sim LN(\mu = 0, \sigma^2 = 2)$. In this paper, we consider several dependence structures of X_1 and X_2 through different copula functions and study the shapes of the corresponding PDF and CDF of Y. For each copula $C_\theta(u,v)$, the PDF and CDF of Y can be plotted on the interval $[0,4]$ by using the following steps:

(i) For each y belonging to the sequence $\{0, 0.01, 0.02, 0.03, \ldots, 4\}$, generate the uniform random variable U on the unit interval; that is, $U \sim Uniform(0,1)$ with the sample size N, say N =10,000.

(ii) Estimate the values for $f_Y(y)$ and $F_Y(y)$ by using

$$\widehat{f_Y}(y) \approx \frac{1}{N}\sum_{i=1}^{N} \frac{1}{|F_1^{-1}(u_i)|} c_\theta\left(u_i, F_2\left(\frac{y}{F_1^{-1}(u_i)}\right)\right) f_2\left(\frac{y}{F_1^{-1}(u_i)}\right), \quad (22)$$

$$\widehat{F_Y}(y) \approx F_1(0) + \frac{1}{N}\sum_{i=1}^{N} \operatorname{sgn}\left(F_1^{-1}(u_i)\right) \frac{\partial}{\partial u} C_\theta\left(u_i, F_2\left(\frac{y}{F_1^{-1}(u_i)}\right)\right), \quad (23)$$

in which the density copula $c_\theta(u_i, v_i)$ and the derivative $\frac{\partial}{\partial u}C_\theta(u_i, v_i)$ can be obtained by using the packages of *VineCopula* in *R* language.

(iii) Plot $\widehat{f}_Y(y)$ and $\widehat{F}_Y(y)$, with $y \in \{0, 0.01, 0.02, 0.03, \cdots, 4\}$.

To estimate the mean, median, standard deviation (sd), skewness, and kurtosis of Y, we first construct the joint distribution of (X_1, X_2) by using Sklar's Theorem, as shown in the following. For each copula $C_\theta(u, v)$, we first obtain the joint CDF of (X_1, X_2)

$$H_\theta(x_1, x_2) = C_\theta\Big(F_1(x_1), F_2(x_2)\Big).$$

We then perform 5000 repetitions, $k = 1, 2, \ldots, 5000$ to use the following steps for the computation:

(1) For each repetition $k = 1, 2, \ldots, 5000$:

(i) Generate (X_1, X_2) from $H_\theta(x_1, x_2)$ of sample size 10^4 by using the package *copula* in *R* language and define

$$y_i^{(k)} = x_{1i}^{(k)} x_{2i}^{(k)}, \quad i = 1, 2, \cdots, 10^4.$$

(ii) Estimate the mean $\bar{y}^{(k)}$, median $\tilde{y}^{(k)}$, standard deviation $s^{(k)}$, skewness $skew(y)^{(k)}$ and kurtosis $kur(y)^{(k)}$ of Y by using the following formula

$$\begin{aligned}
\bar{y}^{(k)} &= \frac{1}{10^4}\sum_{i=1}^{10^4} y_i^{(k)}, \\
\tilde{y}^{(k)} &= \frac{y_{(5000)}^{(k)} + y_{(5001)}^{(k)}}{2}, \text{ where } y_{(j)}^{(k)} \text{ denotes order statistic of } y^{(k)}, \\
s^{(k)} &= \sqrt{\frac{1}{10^4 - 1}\sum_{i=1}^{10^4}\left(y_i^{(k)} - \bar{y}^{(k)}\right)^2}, \\
skew(y)^{(k)} &= \frac{\frac{1}{10^4}\sum_{i=1}^{10^4}\left(y_i^{(k)} - \bar{y}^{(k)}\right)^3}{\left[\frac{1}{10^4}\sum_{i=1}^{10^4}\left(y_i^{(k)} - \bar{y}^{(k)}\right)^2\right]^{3/2}}, \\
kur(y)^{(k)} &= \frac{\frac{1}{10^4}\sum_{i=1}^{10^4}\left(y_i^{(k)} - \bar{y}^{(k)}\right)^4}{\left[\frac{1}{10^4}\sum_{i=1}^{10^4}\left(y_i^{(k)} - \bar{y}^{(k)}\right)^2\right]^2}.
\end{aligned}$$

(2) Finally, take the mean for each of the above quantities by using the following formula:

$$\begin{aligned}
\bar{y} &= \frac{1}{5000}\sum_{k=1}^{5000} \bar{y}^{(k)}, \\
\tilde{y} &= \frac{1}{5000}\sum_{k=1}^{5000} \tilde{y}^{(k)}, \\
s &= \frac{1}{5000}\sum_{k=1}^{5000} s^{(k)}, \\
skew(y) &= \frac{1}{5000}\sum_{k=1}^{5000} skew(y)^{(k)}, \\
kur(y) &= \frac{1}{5000}\sum_{k=1}^{5000} kur(y)^{(k)},
\end{aligned}$$

to obtain the estimates of the mean, median, standard deviation (sd), skewness, and kurtosis for Y.

We first use the above-mentioned algorithm to examine Gaussian Copula and discuss our analysis in the next subsection.

5.1. Gaussian Copula

We first investigate the dependence structure of X_1 and X_2 through the following Gaussian Copula $C_r(u,v)$ and observe the shapes of the corresponding distribution for Y:

$$C_r(u,v) = \frac{1}{2\pi\sqrt{1-r^2}} \int_{-\infty}^{\Phi^{-1}(u)} \int_{-\infty}^{\Phi^{-1}(v)} \exp\left(-\frac{s^2 - 2rst + t^2}{2(1-r^2)}\right) dsdt,$$

where $\Phi^{-1}(x)$ is the inverse of standard normal CDF and r is Pearson correlation coefficient between X_1 and X_2 with $|r| < 1$. Considering $r = -0.9, -0.5, 0, 0.5$, and 0.9, we plot both PDFs and CDFs of Y in Figure 1 and display some descriptive statistics for $Y = X_1X_2$ in Table 1, including the dependence measure Kendall τ, mean, median, standard deviation (sd), skewness, and kurtosis. The special case of $r = 0$ corresponds to the situation in which X_1 and X_2 are independent. As can be seen from the graph and table, for parameter $r \in [0,1]$ (positive correlation), PDFs of Y tends to be more right skewed than those from $r \in [-1,0)$ (negative correlation). When the parameter r varies from negative values to positive values, one can easily notice that the mean, sd, and kurtosis are all significantly increasing while the median is unchanged.

Table 1. Descriptive Statistics for $Y = X_1X_2$ when (X_1, X_2) follows Gaussian copulas.

r	$\tau(C_r)$	Mean	Median	sd	Skewness	Kurtosis
−0.9	−0.71	1.11	1	0.52	1.51	7.30
−0.5	−0.33	1.65	1	2.16	5.84	85.43
0	0	2.72	1	6.77	14.27	466.41
0.5	0.33	4.48	1	18.21	23.23	1045.26
0.9	0.71	6.68	1	38.59	30.15	1585.27

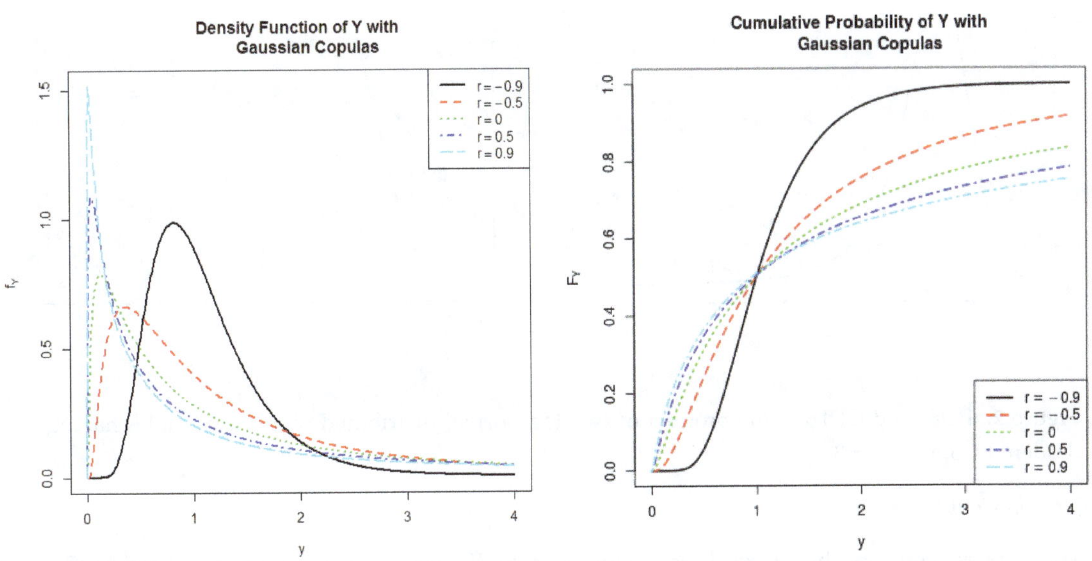

Figure 1. PDFs and CDFs of the product of two log-normal distributed random variables having Gaussian Copulas.

5.2. Student-t Copula

We turn to study the dependence structures of X_1 and X_2 through the following Student-t Copula $C_{r,v}(u,v)$:

$$C_{r,\nu}(u,v) = \frac{1}{2\pi\sqrt{1-r^2}} \int_{-\infty}^{t_\nu^{-1}(u)} \int_{-\infty}^{t_\nu^{-1}(v)} \left(1 + \frac{s^2 - 2rst + t^2}{v(1-r^2)}\right)^{(v+2)/2} dsdt,$$

and investigate the shape of the distribution for $Y = X_1X_2$ where $t_\nu^{-1}(x)$ is the inverse of Student CDF with ν degrees of freedom and r is the Pearson correlation coefficient between X_1 and X_2 with $|r| < 1$ and the degree of freedom $\nu > 2$.

We illustrate our proposed approach by examining $r = -0.9, -0.5, 0, 0.5$, and 0.9 with $\nu = 3$. To do so, we first plot both PDFs and CDFs of Y in Figure 2 and exhibit some descriptive statistics for $Y = X_1X_2$ in Table 2. Similar to the case of Gaussian copula, $r = 0$ is for the case in which there is no linear correlation. We find that the more positive r is, the higher the mean and higher the variance of Y tend to be. However, different from the Gaussian case, Student t-copula can capture the tail dependence between X_1 and X_2 that yields larger kurtosis and larger skewness for Y than for the case of Gaussian copula.

Table 2. Descriptive Statistics for $Y = X_1X_2$ when (X_1, X_2) follows Student-t copulas, $\nu = 3$.

r	$\tau(C_r)$	Mean	Median	sd	Skewness	Kurtosis
−0.9	−0.71	1.13	1	1.42	3.62	2221.42
−0.5	−0.33	1.92	1	9.26	40.75	2562.20
0	0	3.30	1	20.44	37.01	2182.05
0.5	0.33	5.51	1	32.58	34.03	1903.21
0.9	0.71	6.89	1	44.09	32.31	1766.27

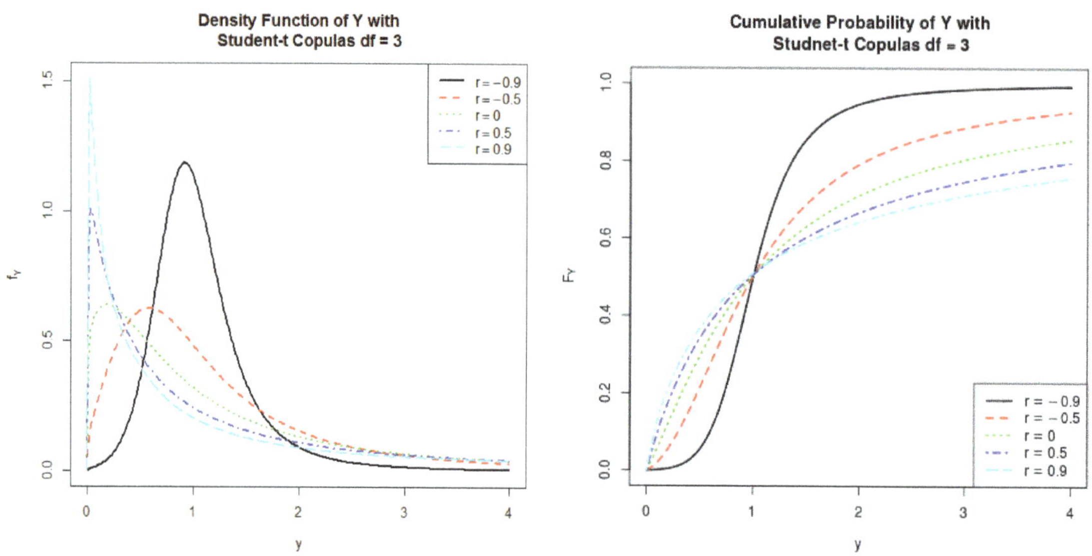

Figure 2. PDFs and CDFs of the product of two log-normal distributed random variables having Student t-Copulas $\nu = 3$.

5.3. Clayton Copula

We now investigate the dependence structures of X_1 and X_2 through the following Clayton Copula $C_\theta(u,v)$:

$$C_\theta(u,v) = \max\left\{u^{-\theta} + v^{-\theta} - 1, 0\right\}^{-\frac{1}{\theta}}, \ \theta \in [-1; +\infty) \setminus 0, \tag{24}$$

and examine the shape of the distribution for Y.

We follow the common practice to use $\theta > 0$ that leads to the following formula

$$C_\theta(u,v) = \left(u^{-\theta} + v^{-\theta} - 1\right)^{-\frac{1}{\theta}}, \ \theta > 0.$$

For $\theta = 1, 2, 3$, and 4, we plot both PDFs and CDFs of Y in Figure 3. From the results in the figure, we confirm that Clayton copula can be used to model left tail dependence; that is, dependency at small values. We also find that, when parameter $\theta \to \infty$, it becomes more positive dependence and yields higher mean and higher standard deviation for Y but makes both the right skewness and the fatness of tail (kurtosis) smaller for Y (see Table 3).

Table 3. Descriptive Statistics for $Y = X_1X_2$ when (X_1, X_2) follows Clayton copulas.

θ	$\tau(C_\theta)$	Mean	Median	sd	Skewness	Kurtosis
1	0.33	3.53	1.12	8.93	13.12	403.90
2	0.5	4.01	1.13	10.43	12.81	389.76
3	0.60	4.34	1.11	11.55	12.65	379.99
4	0.67	4.59	1.08	12.41	12.36	359.40

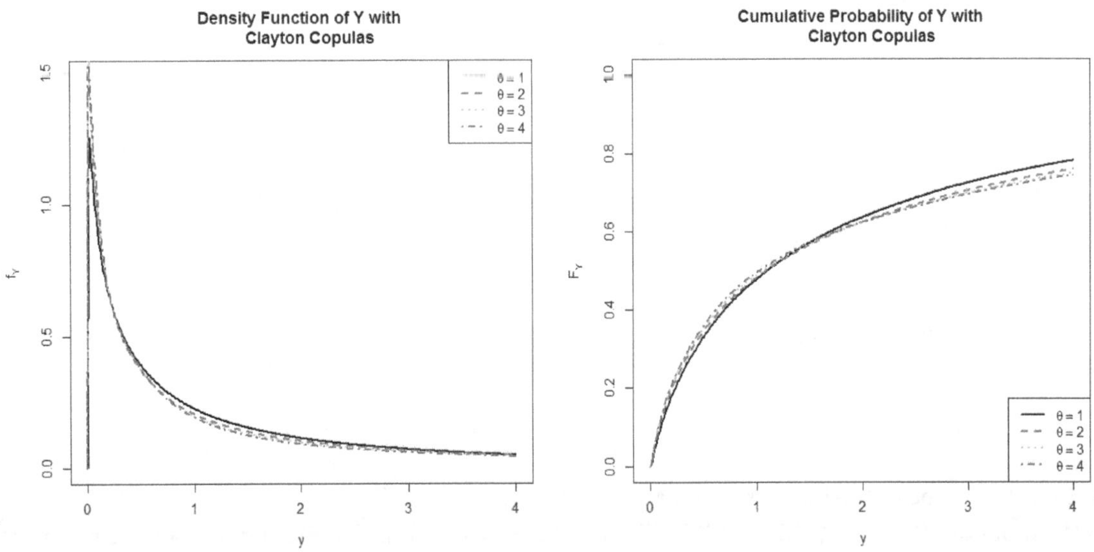

Figure 3. PDFs and CDFs of the product of two log-normal distributed random variables having Clayton Copulas.

5.4. Gumbel Copula

We turn to study the dependence structure of X_1 and X_2 through the following Gumbel Copula $C_\theta(u,v)$:

$$C_\theta(u,v) = \exp\left(-\left[(-\ln u)^\theta + (-\ln v)^\theta\right]^{\frac{1}{\theta}}\right), \ \theta > 0,$$

and investigate the shape of the distributions for Y.

We plot both PDFs and CDFs of Y in Figure 4 for $\theta = 1, 2, 3$, and 4. For Gumbel copula, $\theta = 1$ is for the case in which X_1 and X_2 are independent. In contrast to Clayton, Gumbel copula is used to capture dependency at large values (right tail dependence). Hence, it makes Y to get bigger mean, higher variance, more right skewness, and heavier tail (kurtosis). However, in this case, the median is clearly smaller than that in the case of Clayton copula (see Table 4).

Table 4. Descriptive Statistics for $Y = X_1X_2$ when (X_1, X_2) follows Gumbel copulas.

θ	$\tau(C_\theta)$	Mean	Median	sd	Skewness	Kurtosis
1	0	2.72	1	6.78	14.41	477.10
2	0.5	6.47	0.95	41.52	32.34	1756.88
3	0.67	7.01	0.97	44.46	31.88	1719.80
4	0.75	7.19	0.98	44.83	31.66	1696.71

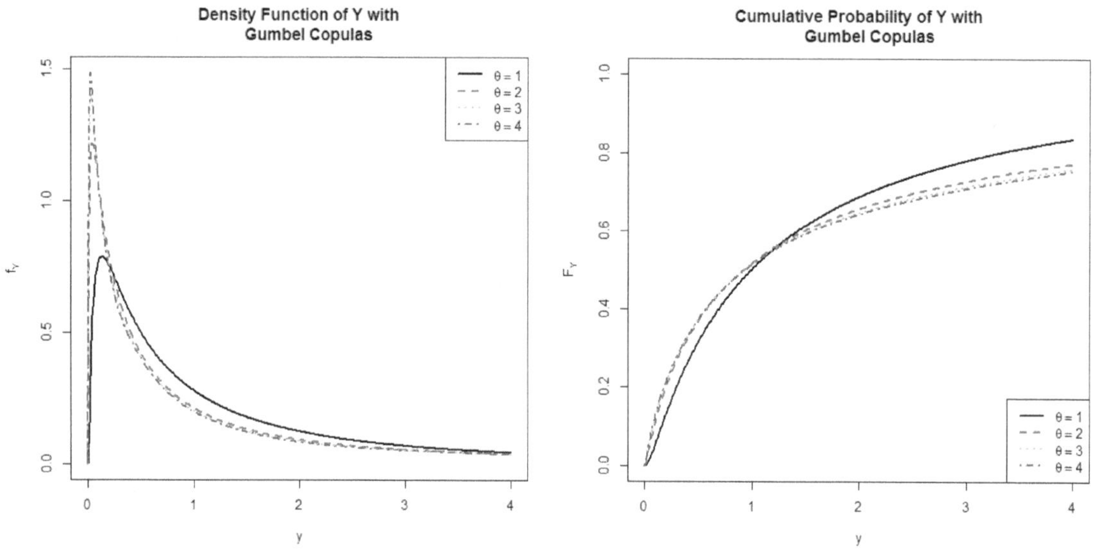

Figure 4. PDFs and CDFs of the product of two log-normal distributed random variables having Gumbel Copulas.

5.5. Frank Copula

We next examine the dependence structure of X_1 and X_2 through the following Frank Copula $C_\theta(u, v)$:

$$C_\theta(u,v) = -\frac{1}{\theta} \ln \left(1 + \frac{\left(e^{-\theta u} - 1\right)\left(e^{-\theta v} - 1\right)}{e^{-\theta} - 1} \right), \quad \theta \in \mathbb{R} \backslash \{0\};$$

and study the shape of the distribution for Y.

We plot both PDFs and CDFs of Y in Figure 5 for $\theta = 1, 2, 3$, and 4 and display some descriptive statistics in Table 5. For Frank copula, the parameter $\theta \to 0$ is for the case in which the two variables are independent. In addition, the structure becomes more monotonic when $\theta \to \infty$ and becomes counter monotonicity when $\theta \to -\infty$. Comparing with both Clayton and Gumbel, Frank copula cannot capture left or right tail dependence. It does not affect the median as in the case of both Gaussian and Student-t copulas. However, the mean and the standard deviation are higher and both skewness and fatness are smaller when the value of the parameter increases.

Table 5. Descriptive Statistics for $Y = X_1X_2$ when (X_1, X_2) follows Frank copulas.

θ	$\tau(C_\theta)$	Mean	Median	sd	Skewness	Kurtosis
1	0.11	3.10	1	8.06	13.84	440.25
2	0.21	3.47	1	9.26	13.49	419.00
3	0.31	3.81	1	10.35	13.07	394.79
4	0.39	4.11	1	11.34	12.88	384.20

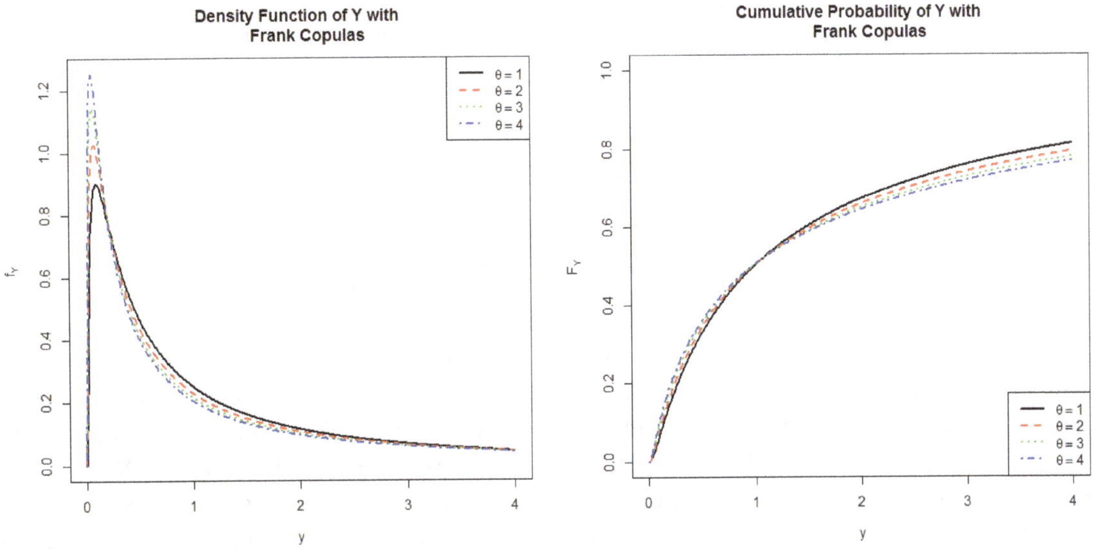

Figure 5. PDFs and CDFs of the product of two log-normal distributed random variables having Frank Copulas.

5.6. *Joe Copula*

Finally, we study the dependence structure of X_1 and X_2 through the following Joe Copula $C_\theta(u,v)$:

$$C_\theta(u,v) = 1 - [(1-u)^\theta + (1-v)^\theta - (1-u)^\theta(1-v)^\theta]^{1/\theta}, \quad \theta \in [1,\infty),$$

and examine the shape of the distribution for Y.

We plot both PDFs and CDFs of Y in Figure 6 for $\theta = 1, 2, 3,$ and 4 and display some descriptive statistics in Table 6. From the results in the figure and table, we find that the dependency captured by Joe Copula is similar to that captured by Gumbel Copula in the way that the variables are independence for $\theta = 1$ and becomes more monotonic when $\theta \to \infty$. We also find that the variations of all other measures are changing in a similar manner.

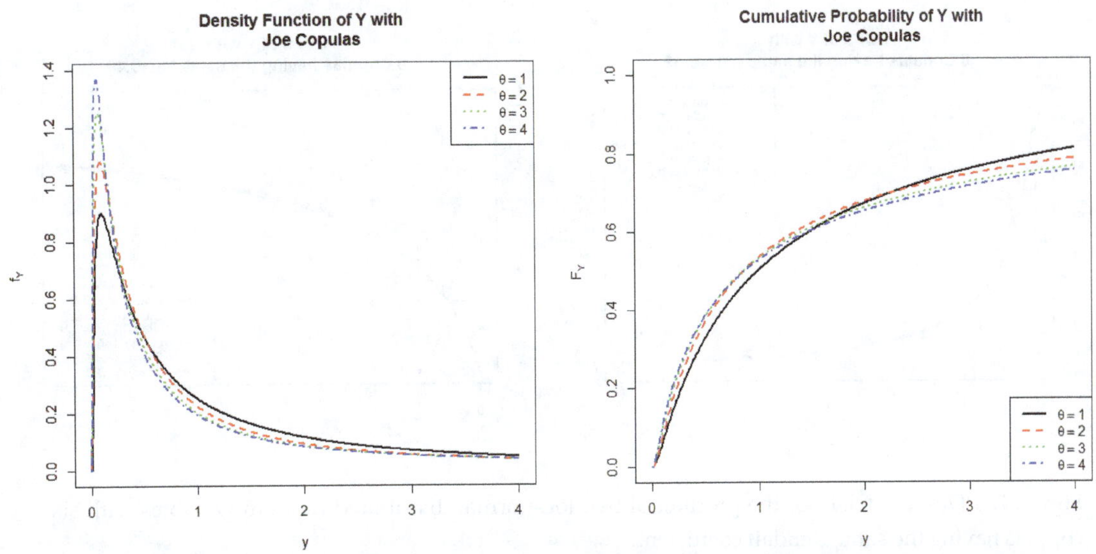

Figure 6. PDFs and CDFs of the product of two log-normal distributed random variables having Joe Copulas.

Table 6. Descriptive Statistics for $Y = X_1X_2$ when (X_1, X_2) follows Joe copulas.

θ	$\tau(C_\theta)$	Mean	Median	sd	Skewness	Kurtosis
1	0	2.72	1.00	6.76	14.28	466.67
2	0.36	6.30	0.87	42.01	32.67	1789.96
3	0.52	6.91	0.88	44.31	31.65	1692.84
4	0.61	7.11	0.90	45.01	31.79	1720.81

5.7. Comparison of Copulas for the Same Measure of Dependence

In this section, we investigate the effects of the six copulas families as discussed above on the shapes of different distributions for the random variable $Y := X_1X_2$ when they have the same measure of dependence—the Kendall's coefficient τ. Here, the parameters are chosen to each copula to correspond to Kendall $\tau = 0.49$. We exhibit the corresponding CDFs and PDFs of Y in Figure 7, estimate the mean, median, standard deviation, skewness, and kurtosis, and display the values in Table 7. As can be seen on the table and figure, Y attains the largest mean (6.84) and standard deviation (44.67) but the smallest median (0.87) when it follows Joe copula. In contrast, Clayton copula produces the smallest mean (0.39) and standard deviation (10.27) but attains the largest median (1.13). Using Student-t copula gets the largest skewness (33.58) and fatness (1876.99), followed by using Gumbel and Joe copulas. On the other hand, using Frank copula gets the lowest skewness (12.59) and the lowest fatness (362.17) for Y and Gaussian copula is ranked the fourth by mean, sd, skewness, and kurtosis.

Table 7. Descriptive Statistics for $Y = X_1X_2$ in which (X_1, X_2) is modeled with six copulas having the same Kendall coefficient $\tau = 0.49$.

Copulas	Parameters	$\tau(C)$	Mean	Median	sd	Skewness	Kurtosis
Gaussian	0.7	0.49	5.47	1.00	26.98	27.42	1375.98
Student-t	$0.7, \nu = 3$	0.49	5.95	1.00	38.33	33.58	1876.99
Clayton	1.90	0.49	3.97	1.13	10.27	12.74	382.27
Gumbel	1.95	0.49	6.42	0.95	41.54	32.41	1764.93
Frank	5.5	0.49	4.47	1.00	12.58	12.59	362.17
Joe	2.8	0.49	6.84	0.87	44.67	32.37	1766.43

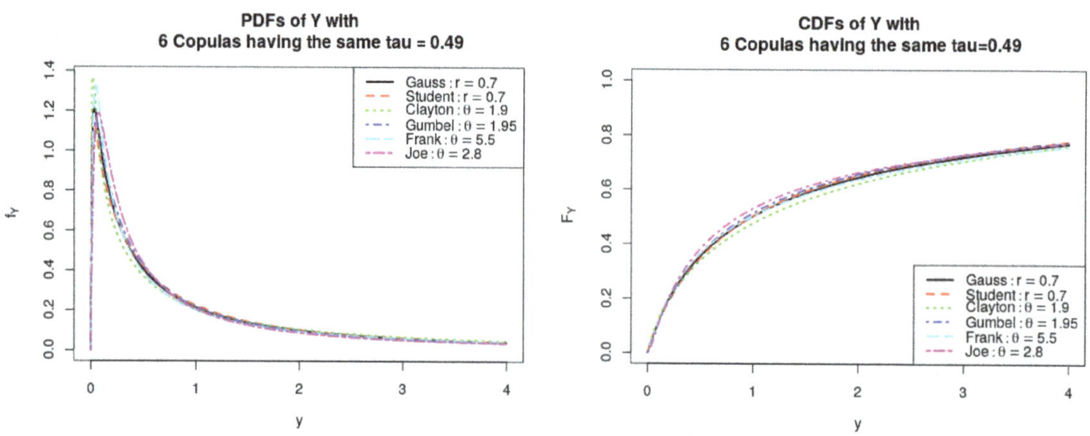

Figure 7. PDFs and CDFs of the product of two log-normal distributed random variables with six copulas having the same Kendall coefficient.

6. Conclusions

Determining distributions of the functions of random variables is one of the most important problems in statistics and applied mathematics because it has wide range of applications in numerous areas including economics, finance, risk management, science, and many other areas, especially in modeling financial risk and derivatives. However, most studies only focus on structure for independent variables with some common distributions of the functions for the variables. There are few studies on determining distributions for statistical models involving dependence structure. Nonetheless, to the best of our knowledge, the problem of determining distribution function of product for two or more dependent random variables using copulas has not been studied. Thus, to bridge the gap in the literature, in this paper, we develop the theory to establish the formulas of both density and distribution functions for the product of two and more dependent and independent random variables via copulas to capture the structure among the variables.

Because the density and distribution of the product for dependent random variables are in terms of integrals, the forms of both density and distribution are very complicated, and, thus, it is very difficult, if not impossible, to obtain the exact forms of the density and distribution. To circumvent the problem, in this paper, we propose using Monte Carlo algorithm, graphical approach, and numerical analysis to efficiently compute their complicated integrals and examine the behaviors of both density and distribution and the changes of their shapes when parameters vary.

We illustrated our proposed approaches by using simulation and graphical approaches to study the behavior of the distribution for the product of two log normal random variables on several different copulas, including Gaussian, Student-t, Clayton, Gumbel, Frank, and Joe Copulas. We found that different types of copulas have different impact on the behaviors of distributions. For example, since both Gaussian and Student-t copulas belong to elliptical family, their distributions of the product behave similarly. On the other hand, because Clayton, Gumbel, Frank, and Joe copulas belong to Archimedean family, their distributions of the product behave similarly but with impacts of different degrees. Furthermore, we found that there are some differences on location, variance, skewness, fatness of tail, and others when the values of the parameters vary.

In this paper, we derive formulas for both density and cumulative probability functions of the product of n random variables for $n \geq 2$. We also propose a Monte Carlo algorithm to compute both density and cumulative probability functions. The Monte Carlo algorithm we proposed enables academics and practitioners to obtain both density and cumulative probability functions easily. Furthermore, we drawn some useful information on the product of two lognormal-distributed random variables. Our results are the foundations of any further study that relies on the density and cumulative probability functions of the product of n random variables. We note that, although the theory we developed in our paper is not difficult to derive, as far as we know, our findings are new and there is no study obtaining similar results as our findings. Readers may read Cherubini et al. (2004); Nelsen (2007) for all related theories. Thus, the theory we developed in this paper is new, useful, and the contribution of our paper is important in the literature.

Our findings are useful to academics if studying the shapes and basic measures of both density and distributions of the product of dependent or independent random variables by using different copulas is their interest. Because the product of dependent or independent random variables by using different copulas are widely used in many empirical applications in economics, finance, and many other areas, our findings are useful to practitioners and policy makers in economics, finance, and many other areas if they need to study the shapes of both density and distribution functions for the product of dependent or independent random variables by using different copulas.

Author Contributions: Writing–original draft preparation, S.L. (Sel Ly) and K.H.P.; writing–review and editing, W.K.W.; visualization, S.L. (Sel Ly) and S.L. (Sal Ly).

Funding: This research has been supported by Ton Duc Thang University, Asia University, China Medical University Hospital, Hang Seng University of Hong Kong, Research Grants Council (RGC) of Hong Kong (project number 12500915), and Ministry of Science and Technology (MOST, Project Numbers 106-2410-H-468-002 and 107-2410-H-468 -002-MY3), Taiwan.

Acknowledgments: The authors are grateful to Chia-Lin Chang and Michael McAleer, the Guest Editors, and anonymous referees for substantive comments that have significantly improved this manuscript. The fourth author would like to thank Robert B. Miller and Howard E. Thompson for their continuous guidance and encouragement.

Conflicts of Interest: The authors declare no conflict of interest.

References

Bohrnstedt, George W., and Arthur S. Goldberger. 1969. On the exact covariance of products of random variables. *Journal of the American Statistical Association* 64: 1439–42. [CrossRef]

Cherubini, Umberto, Elisa Luciano, and Walter Vecchiato. 2004. *Copula Methods in Finance*. Hoboken: John Wiley & Sons.

Cherubini, Umberto, Sabrina Mulinacci, and Silvia Romagnoli. 2011. A copula-based model of speculative price dynamics in discrete time. *Journal of Multivariate Analysis* 102: 1047–63. [CrossRef]

Dettmann, Carl P., and Orestis Georgiou. 2009. Product of n independent uniform random variables. *Statistics & Probability Letters* 79: 2501–3.

Donahue, James D. 1964. *Products and Quotients of Random Variables and Their Applications*. Technical Report. Fort Collins: MARTIN CO DENVER CO.

Frey, Rüdiger, Alexander J. McNeil, and Mark Nyfeler. 2001. Copulas and credit models. *Risk* 10: 111–4.

Galambos, Janos, and Italo Simonelli. 2004. *Products of Random Variables: Applications to Problems of Physics and to Arithmetical Functions*. Boca Raton: CRC Press.

Garg, Mridula, Ajay Sharma, and Pratibha Manohar. 2016. The distribution of the product of two independent generalized trapezoidal random variables. *Communications in Statistics-Theory and Methods* 45: 6369–84. [CrossRef]

Glen, Andrew G., Lawrence M. Leemis, and John H. Drew. 2004. Computing the distribution of the product of two continuous random variables. *Computational Statistics & Data Analysis* 44: 451–64.

Joe, Harry. 1997. *Multivariate Models and Multivariate Dependence Concepts*. Boca Raton: Chapman and Hall/CRC.

Lomnicki, Z. A. 1967. On the distribution of products of random variables. *Journal of the Royal Statistical Society Series B (Methodological)* 29: 513–24. [CrossRef]

Ly, Sel, Hoang-Uyen Pham, and Radim Briš. 2016. On the distortion risk measure using copulas. In *Applied Mathematics in Engineering and Reliability*. Boca Raton: CRC Press, p. 309.

Ly, Sel, Kim-Hung Pho, Sal Ly, and Wing-Keung Wong. 2019. Distribution of quotient of dependent and independent random variables using copulas. *Journal of Risk and Financial Management*. First revision.

Maller, Ross A. 1981. A theorem on products of random variables, with application to regression. *Australian Journal of Statistics* 23: 177–85. [CrossRef]

Nelsen, Roger B. 2007. *An Introduction to Copulas*. Berlin: Springer Science & Business Media.

Salo, Jari, Hassan M. El-Sallabi, and Pertti Vainikainen. 2006. The distribution of the product of independent Rayleigh random variables. *IEEE Transactions on Antennas and Propagation* 54: 639–43. [CrossRef]

Springer, Melvin Dale, and W. E. Thompson. 1966. The distribution of products of independent random variables. *SIAM Journal on Applied Mathematics* 14: 511–26. [CrossRef]

Springer, Melvin Dale, and W. E. Thompson. 1970. The distribution of products of beta, gamma and Gaussian random variables. *SIAM Journal on Applied Mathematics* 18: 721–37. [CrossRef]

Springer, Melvin Dale. 1979. *The Algebra of Random Variables*, 1st ed. Hoboken: Wiley.

Tang, Jiechen, Songsak Sriboonchitta, Vicente Ramos, and Wing-Keung Wong. 2014. Modelling dependence between tourism demand and exchange rate using copula-based GARCH model. *Current Issues in Method and Practice* 19: 1–19. [CrossRef]

Tran, Duy-Hien, Hoang-Uyen Pham, Sel Ly, and Trung Vo-Duy. 2015. A new measure of monotone dependence by using Sobolev norms for copula. In *International Symposium on Integrated Uncertainty in Knowledge Modelling and Decision Making*. Belin: Springer, pp. 126–37.

Tran, Duy-Hien, Hoang-Uyen Pham, Sel Ly, and Trung Vo-Duy. 2017. Extraction dependence structure of distorted copulas via a measure of dependence. *Annals of Operations Research* 256: 221–36. [CrossRef]

Yang, Yang, and Yuebao Wang. 2013. Tail behavior of the product of two dependent random variables with applications to risk theory. *Extremes* 16: 55–74. [CrossRef]

6

Risk Model Validation: An Intraday VaR and ES Approach Using the Multiplicative Component GARCH

Ravi Summinga-Sonagadu and Jason Narsoo *

Department of Economics and Statistics, University of Mauritius, Réduit 80837, Mauritius; ravisonagadu@gmail.com
* Correspondence: j.narsoo@uom.ac.mu

Abstract: In this paper, we employ 99% intraday value-at-risk (VaR) and intraday expected shortfall (ES) as risk metrics to assess the competency of the Multiplicative Component Generalised Autoregressive Heteroskedasticity (MC-GARCH) models based on the 1-min EUR/USD exchange rate returns. Five distributional assumptions for the innovation process are used to analyse their effects on the modelling and forecasting performance. The high-frequency volatility models were validated in terms of in-sample fit based on various statistical and graphical tests. A more rigorous validation procedure involves testing the predictive power of the models. Therefore, three backtesting procedures were used for the VaR, namely, the Kupiec's test, a duration-based backtest, and an asymmetric VaR loss function. Similarly, three backtests were employed for the ES: a regression-based backtesting procedure, the Exceedance Residual backtest and the V-Tests. The validation results show that non-normal distributions are best suited for both model fitting and forecasting. The MC-GARCH(1,1) model under the Generalised Error Distribution (GED) innovation assumption gave the best fit to the intraday data and gave the best results for the ES forecasts. However, the asymmetric Skewed Student's-t distribution for the innovation process provided the best results for the VaR forecasts. This paper presents the results of the first empirical study (to the best of the authors' knowledge) in: (1) forecasting the intraday Expected Shortfall (ES) under different distributional assumptions for the MC-GARCH model; (2) assessing the MC-GARCH model under the Generalised Error Distribution (GED) innovation; (3) evaluating and ranking the VaR predictability of the MC-GARCH models using an asymmetric loss function.

Keywords: model validation; high-frequency; Multiplicative Component Generalised Autoregressive Heteroskedasticity (MC-GARCH); error distributions; intraday value-at-risk (VaR); intraday expected shortfall (ES); backtests

---

1. Introduction

Since the financial crisis of 2008, there has been an ever-growing need for financial entities to accurately assess their exposure to financial risks. Risk being commonly characterised by increasing volatility in the financial market, the modelling and forecasting of the volatility have become a very important research area among academics and practitioners in the last decade. According to Poon and Granger (2001), volatility can be viewed as a 'barometer for the vulnerability of financial markets and the economy'. It is, therefore, important to forecast volatility accurately. Volatility is also an essential tool in the computation of other risk metrics such as Value-at-Risk (VaR) and Expected Shortfall (ES).

Value-at-Risk (VaR) is a mandatory risk management tool in the insurance and banking industry as per the regulatory norms of the Solvency II framework (Solvency II European Directive (2009/138/EC))

and the Basel committee (BCBS 2010), respectively. However, it was observed that under the stress conditions of the global financial crisis, VaR forecasts were exceeded multiple times. In the Basel Committee on Banking Supervision BCBS (2016) report, it was concluded that during times of significant financial market stress, ES will ensure that tail risk and capital adequacy are captured in a more prudent manner. Interest in ES grew alarmingly ever since the Basel Committee on Banking Supervision (BCBS) brought forward their intention to replace VaR with ES, BCBS (2012).

For a long time, researchers and academics have made use of low-frequency data in financial time series analysis to forecast risk metrics such as volatility, Value-at-Risk (VaR) and Expected Shortfall (ES). However, low-frequency data misses out on precious information and as addressed by Engle and Russell (2004): "Like the view from the airplane above, classic asset pricing research assumes only that prices eventually reach their equilibrium value, the route taken and speed of achieving equilibrium is not specified". Low-frequency data lacks important details on the price adjustment compared to analysing high-frequency data. High-frequency data is defined as observations made over a short period of time, usually a day or less.

As mentioned by Zivot (2005), the unique characteristics of high-frequency data render the process of econometric and statistical analysis even more complicated. This in turn makes the forecasting of intraday VaR and ES quite challenging. For instance, econometric models or the modelling process should be able to take into account the intraday periodicity and the high excess kurtosis of the data to provide reliable forecast of the risk metrics. Moreover, the number of observations in high-frequency financial datasets can be overwhelming at times, and these observations may also be irregularly time-spaced.

Although forecasting VaR and ES using high-frequency data is challenging, it is also meaningful at the same time. As frequently mentioned in the literature, the volatility model is a fundamental ingredient which influences the measurement of both VaR and ES. It has been shown that the use of high-frequency data provides much more accurate estimates of volatility, Giot (2000). Due to the intense trading system nowadays, firms are forced to constantly build and devise strategies with the aim to beat the market. As mentioned by Müller (2000), it is no longer adequate to analyse these risk metrics based on daily data only. Today, more and more intraday price movements can be observed. Therefore, intraday VaR and ES estimates might be very beneficial to short-term traders involved in algorithmic and high-frequency trading, since the real-time market risk is quantified.

Despite the growing amount of research in the field of high-frequency financial data analysis, few studies have focused on model validation and high-frequency risk measures. This study contributes to the literature in the following ways:

(1) A rigorous model validation, both in terms of in-sample fit and out-sample performance for the Multiplicative Component Generalised Autoregressive Heteroskedasticity (MC-GARCH) model under five error distributions is provided. Statistical and graphical tests are conducted to validate the models.

(2) One component of the MC-GARCH model is the daily variance forecast. For this purpose, the GARCH(1,1) and EGARCH(1,1) under the five error distributions are compared and the best model among the 10 GARCH models is used to forecast the daily variance.

(3) The modelling and forecasting performance of the MC-GARCH model under different distributional assumptions is assessed in this study.

(4) The 99% intraday VaR is forecasted and three backtesting procedures are used. This is the first study to assess the VaR predictive ability of the MC-GARCH models by using an asymmetric VaR loss function.

(5) This is the first study to forecast the intraday expected shortfall under different distributional assumptions for the MC-GARCH model. Again, three backtests are used including the recently proposed ES regression backtest of Bayer and Dimitriadis (2018).

Due to the high importance of risk management, the results of this study may contribute in many fields. This study is highly relevant to the banking industry since banks are required to calculate risk metrics on a daily basis for internal control purposes and for determining their capital requirements. Risk measurement is also essential to the insurance industry from the pricing of insurance contracts to determining the Solvency Capital Requirement (SCR), and therefore, the results of this study might be useful. Any other organisation with exposure to some kind of financial risk might benefit from this study. For instance, as mentioned by Culp et al. (1998), an airline company might use these intraday risk metrics to assess their exposure to jet fuel prices.

The rest of this paper is organized as follows. Section 2 provides a brief literature review on the MC-GARCH model, followed by Section 3, which details the various methodologies employed in this study. Section 4 presents the application of the MC-GARCH models and the various backtesting results. Finally, Section 5 will seal off the research with a summing up of the entire research outcome and will also provide recommendations for further study.

2. Past Studies on MC-GARCH Model

The literature on Autoregressive Conditional Heteroscedasticity (ARCH) models and Generalised Autoregressive Conditional Heteroscedasticity (GARCH) has grown impressively since they were first introduced by Engle (1982) and Bollerslev (1987), respectively. As noted in Andersen and Bollerslev (1997), since GARCH models are associated with a geometric decay in their autocorrelation structure of returns, they cannot take into account the pronounced intraday seasonal pattern present in the high-frequency financial returns. Over the years, to circumvent this limitation, researchers have come up with different solutions by augmenting the basic GARCH family of models. For instance, Andersen and Bollerslev (1997, 1998) and Andersen et al. (1999) took a novel approach by first deseasonalising the absolute returns prior to model fitting. The year 2011 saw the introduction of the MC-GARCH model of Engle and Sokalska (2011), which is a more sophisticated model designed specifically for high-frequency financial time series data. Basically, in this model, the variance part is decomposed into three multiplicative components: a daily component, a diurnal component and a stochastic volatility component. What makes the MC-GARCH model different from other typical GARCH models is that it includes a component which independently takes into account the intraday seasonality.

Previous studies have shown that, indeed, the MC-GARCH model is well capable of forecasting intraday volatility and risk metrics. The MC-GARCH model was applied to three equally spaced intervals of 1 min, 5 min and 10 min intraday data of Australia's S&P/ASX-50 stock market by Singh et al. (2013). The model yielded satisfactory results for intraday VaR forecast. Their results were supported by another study by Diao and Tong (2015), who found that the MC-GARCH model performed well in forecasting the intraday VaR in Chinese stock market. The dataset used was 5-min intraday returns of CSI7-300 index. In both studies, the innovation process of the variance equation was assumed to have a Gaussian distribution.

Narsoo (2016) applied the MC-GARCH model under four innovation distributions namely the Gaussian, the symmetric Student's-t, the skewed Student's-t and the reparametrised Johnson SU (JSU) distribution on the intraday 1-min EUR/USD exchange rates data to forecast the 99% VaR. Based on the Kupiec's test, it was concluded that the Skewed Student's-t MC-GARCH model delivered the best VaR forecast.

However, there are still a lot of open research areas on the MC-GARCH model. For instance, there is no study dealing with the model validation of the MC-GARCH model under various distributional assumptions and assessing the performance, both in terms of model fitting and forecasting. Also, there is no study on the expected shortfall (ES) forecasting performance of the MC-GARCH model under different error distributions. This paper therefore contributes to the high-frequency trading and backtesting literature by forecasting the intraday Value-at-Risk (VaR) and intraday Expected Shortfall (ES) at 99% confidence level using the MC-GARCH model under five distributional assumptions, which are the Normal, the Student's-t, the Skewed Student's-t distribution, the reparametrised Johnson SU

(JSU) and the Generalized Error Distribution (GED). After model fitting, the models will be validated in terms of in-sample fit based on a series of statistical and graphical tests. Due to the low statistical power of the Kupiec's test, two other backtests are also employed to rigorously assess the competency of the MC-GARCH models in predicting the intraday VaR. Three backtesting procedures will also be used to test the ES forecasting ability of the models.

3. Methodology

This study focuses on forecasting the intraday Value-at-Risk (VaR) and intraday Expected Shortfall (ES) at 99% confidence level using the MC-GARCH model under five distributional assumptions. This section explains the various models used to model both daily and intraday data. The backtesting procedures to assess the intraday VaR and ES forecasts are also presented.

3.1. Model Specification

3.1.1. Models for the Daily Variance Component

GARCH(1,1)

The standard GARCH(1,1) model can be specified by the following set of equations:

$$r_t = m_t + \varepsilon_t$$

$$h_t = \omega + \alpha_1 \varepsilon_{t-1}^2 + \beta_1 h_{t-1}$$

where m_t is the conditional mean process made up of both autoregressive (AR) and moving averages (MA) terms and r_t represents the daily log returns. We assume ε_t is the error term which can be decomposed as $\varepsilon_t = \sqrt{h_t z_t}$. The second equation is the variance equation and h_t is the volatility process to be estimated. The innovation term, z_t are i.i.d. variables.

In the variance equation, $\omega > 0$, $\alpha_1 > 0$, $\beta_1 > 0$ and $\alpha_1 + \beta_1 < 1$ to satisfy wide-sense stationarity.

EGARCH(1,1) Model

The Exponential GARCH model (EGARCH) of Nelson (1991) is also employed. It captures the asymmetric effects between positive and negative asset returns and models the logarithm of the conditional variance h_t. The EGARCH(1,1) specification has the following form:

$$\ln(h_t) = \omega + \frac{\alpha_1 \varepsilon_{t-1} + \gamma_1 |\varepsilon_{t-1}|}{h_{t-1}} + \beta_1 \ln(h_{t-1})$$

To ensure non-negative variance, the model is an AR(1) on $\ln(h_t)$ instead of h_t.

3.1.2. Model for Intraday Returns

MC-GARCH(1,1) Model

The Multiplicative Component GARCH model (MC-GARCH) is a variant of the GARCH model which is specifically designed to model and forecast the intraday returns of financial assets. Basically, in this model, the conditional variance equation is specified by a multiplicative product of a daily volatility component, a diurnal volatility component and also a stochastic/intraday volatility component. For the sake of clarity, let $R_{t,i}$ be the conditional compounded return series for a particular financial asset A, where t is representing any particular day and i is the regularly spaced intraday time period. In the MC-GARCH model, the intraday return process of $R_{t,i}$ may be represented as follows:

$$R_{t,i} = \sqrt{h_t s_i q_{t,i} \varepsilon_{t,i}}$$

where $\varepsilon_{t,i} \sim N(0,1)$ and

- h_t denotes the daily variance component
- s_i denotes the diurnal/calendar variance component in each intraday period
- $q_{t,i}$ denotes the intraday variance component
- $\varepsilon_{t,i}$ is an error term following a specified distribution

This study employs GARCH and EGARCH to forecast the daily variance component h_t, based on the paper by Andersen and Bollerslev (1997). The choice of the model is based on the best-performing one among the GARCH and EGARCH models under five error distributions, which are the normal distribution, the Student's-t distribution, the Generalised Error Distribution (GED), the skewed Student's-t and the Johnson SU (JSU) distribution.

The diurnal volatility component s_i, is estimated as the variance of intraday returns in each regularly spaced intraday time period as represented below:

$$\frac{R_{t,i}^2}{h_t} = s_i q_{t,i} \varepsilon_{t,i}^2$$

$$s_i = \frac{1}{T} \sum_{t=1}^{T} \frac{R_{t,i}^2}{h_t}$$

By using the daily variance and the diurnal variance, the returns are normalized in the following way:

$$\begin{aligned} z_{t,i} &= \frac{R_{t,i}}{\sqrt{h_i s_i}} \\ &= \sqrt{q_{t,i}} \varepsilon_{t,i} \end{aligned}$$

After the normalization of the returns by both the daily and diurnal variance, the next step consists of modelling the stochastic intraday variance component $q_{t,i}$ as a GARCH(1,1) process, which is given as follows:

$$q_{t,i} = \omega^* + \alpha_1^* \left(\frac{R_{t,i-1}}{\sqrt{h_t s_{i-1}}}\right)^2 + \beta_1^* q_{t,i-1}$$

where $\omega^* > 0, \alpha_1^* \geq 0, \beta_1^* \geq 0$.

3.2. Parameter Estimation

In this paper, all the parameters of the various GARCH models employed will be estimated using maximum likelihood estimation (MLE), since it is the most popular method for estimating GARCH type models. Moreover, this method yields asymptotically efficient parameter estimates for the GARCH models.

3.3. Value-at-Risk and Expected Shortfall Evaluation

Value-at-Risk Evaluation:

According to McNeil et al. (2005), the Value-at-Risk (VaR) of a portfolio at time t for a given confidence level $q \in (0,1)$ is given by the smallest number x_q such that the loss at time $t+1$, which is denoted by X_{t+1}, will be less than x_q with probability q:

$$\begin{aligned} VaR_q^t &= \inf\{x_q \in \Re : P(X_{t+1} \leq x_q) \geq q\} \\ &= \inf\{x_q \in \Re : P(X_{t+1} > x_q) \leq 1 - q\} \end{aligned}$$

The one-step-ahead VaR is computed as follows:

$$VaR_{t+1}^{\alpha} = \mu_{t+1} + \sigma_{t+1} F^{-1}(\alpha)$$

where the probability distribution function F of the return innovations z_t, is strictly monotone or has a generalised inverse of the cumulative distribution function. In this paper, z_t is assumed to follow five probability distributions namely the Normal, Student's-t, Skewed Student's-t, JSU and GED.

Expected Shortfall Evaluation:

The Expected Shortfall (ES) at a given level α is defined as being the expected value at time t of X_{t+1}, which is the loss in the next period conditional on the loss exceeding VaR_{α}^{t}:

$$ES_{\alpha}^{t} = E_t[X_{t+1}|X_{t+1} < VaR_{\alpha}]$$

$$ES_{\alpha} = \frac{1}{1-\alpha}\int_{\alpha}^{1} VaR_x \, dx$$

According to García Jorcano (2018), the one-step-ahead ES can be further simplified using the properties of the expectation operator:

$$ES_{t+1}^{\alpha} = \mu_{t+1} + \sigma_{t+1}\mathbb{E}_{t+1}[z_{t+1}|z_{t+1} < F^{-1}(\alpha)]$$

where:

- $z_{t+1} = \frac{X_{t+1}-\mu_{t+1}}{\sigma_{t+1}}$
- $F^{-1}(\alpha) = \frac{VaR_{t+1}^{\alpha}-\mu_{t+1}}{\sigma_{t+1}}$

3.4. Backtesting

After forecasting the risk metrics VaR and ES, a backtesting procedure is employed to assess the accuracy of the forecasts. In the backtesting procedure, actual profits and losses are compared to the estimates of VaR and ES in a systematic manner.

3.4.1. Value-at-Risk Backtesting

Kupiec's Unconditional Coverage Test

The Kupiec's test was developed by Kupiec (1995) and is the most famous VaR test that is based on failure rates. It is also known as the proportion of failures (POF) test. The null hypothesis of the test assumes that the number of exceptions follows a binomial distribution.

The null hypothesis for the test is as follows:

$$H_0 = p = \hat{p} = \frac{x}{T}$$

where T is the number of observations and x is the number of exceptions.

The test is in fact a likelihood ratio test where the test statistics are as follows:

$$LR_{POF} = -2\ln\left(\frac{(1-p)^{T-x}p^{x}}{[1-(x/T)]^{T-x}(x/T)^{x}}\right)$$

Under the null hypothesis, the LR_{POF} is asymptotically chi-square distributed with one degree of freedom.

A Duration-Based Approach to VaR Backtesting

According to Christoffersen and Pelletier (2003), a more robust test to determine the adequacy of a risk model is by considering the duration between VaR violations. Ideally, the duration between the VaR violations should be independent of one another and should not cluster. The null hypothesis of this test is that under a correctly specified risk model, the VaR violations should be memoryless and should therefore follow an exponential distribution as follows:

$$g(d_v;\alpha) = \alpha \exp\left(-\alpha d_v\right)$$

Under the alternative hypothesis, a Weibull distribution is used for the duration variable, since it embeds the exponential distribution as a restricted case:

$$h(d_v;a,b) = a^b b d_v^{b-1} \exp[-(a d_v)^b]$$

Also, $H_{0,IND} : b = 1$ and $H_{0,CC} : b = 1, a = \alpha$, where IND denotes independence and CC denotes Conditional Coverage.

Asymmetric VaR Loss Function

Even though the two VaR backtesting procedures discussed above are highly relevant for testing the model adequacy, they do, however, fail to judge the model based on its predictive accuracy. In other words, they do not provide statistical evidence as to whether there is any difference in the forecasting performance between the different models employed. Therefore, González-Rivera et al. (2004) proposed an asymmetric VaR loss function to compare the performance of the different model on the basis of the loss function. The loss function is defined as:

$$\updownarrow(r_{t+1}, VaR^{\tau}_{j,t+1|t}) = T_0^{-1}\rho_{\tau}(r_{t+1} - VaR^{\tau}_{j,t+1|t}), t = 1,2,\ldots,T_0$$

where T_0 is the length of the backtesting period, j is the model indicator, r_{t+1} denotes the return at time $t+1$, $VaR^{\tau}_{j,t+1|t}$ denotes the VaR at $t+1$ given the information set up to time t. Moreover, $\rho_{\tau} = z(\tau - I_{-\infty,0}(z))$ denotes the τth quantile loss function. Since it is an asymmetric loss function, it penalises observations below the τth quantile level more heavily as compared to observations above it. The best model is the one which minimises this loss function.

Model Confidence Set Procedure

Hansen et al. (2011) proposed the model confidence set (MCS) procedure, whereby a sequence of statistical tests are carried out with the objective of building a "Superior Set of Models" (SSM). Basically, the equal predictive ability (EPA) test statistic is calculated for an arbitrary loss function satisfying the general weak stationarity conditions. In this procedure, the loss function employed is the asymmetric VaR loss function of González-Rivera et al. (2004). For a chosen level of confidence, the null hypothesis stating EPA is not rejected. This procedure is implemented to rank the models, in ascending order, according to their VaR forecasting power.

3.4.2. Expected Shortfall Backtesting

The Bivariate ES Regression Backtest

The first ES backtest that will be considered is the very recently proposed Bivariate ES Regression Backtest of Bayer and Dimitriadis (2018). They proved that this backtest has far more power than other ES backtests. It is also more convenient for regulators since it is the only backtest method in the literature which uses only the ES forecasts for the backtesting of the risk metric.

The Bivariate ES Regression Backtest simply tests if a series of ES forecasts denoted by $\{\hat{e}_t, t = 1, \ldots T\}$ from a forecasting model is specified correctly with respect to the series of realized returns denoted by $\{Y_t = 1, \ldots, T\}$. Basically, in this backtest, the returns Y_t are regressed on the ES forecasts $\hat{e}_t$ including an intercept term which is designed particularly for the functional ES.

$$Y_t = \alpha + \beta \hat{e}_t + u_t^e \tag{1}$$

where $ES_\tau(u_t^e|\mathcal{F}_{t-1}) = 0$. Moreover, the condition on the error term can be specified in another way since $\hat{e}_t$ is generated using the same filtration set $\mathcal{F}_{t-1}$:

$$ES_\tau(Y_t|\mathcal{F}_{t-1}) = \alpha + \beta\hat{e}_t$$

The null hypothesis H_0 is tested against the alternative hypothesis H_1 where:

$$H_0 : (\alpha, \beta) = (0, 1)$$

$$H_1 : (\alpha, \beta) \neq (0, 1)$$

The null hypothesis H_0 states that the ES forecasts are specified correctly since $\hat{e}_t = ES_\tau(Y_t|\mathcal{F}_{t-1})$. This backtest is called a bivariate backtest, since the parameters α and β are tested simultaneously based on the regression framework.

The estimation of Equation (1) is carried out by the semiparametric estimation of the joint system:

$$Y_t = \gamma + \delta\hat{e}_t + u_t^q$$

$$Y_t = \alpha + \beta\hat{e}_t + u_t^e$$

where $\mathcal{Q}_\tau(u_t^q|\mathcal{F}_{t-1}) = 0$ and $ES_\tau(u_t^e|\mathcal{F}_{t-1}) = 0$. Thus, Y_t is the response variable and $(1, \hat{e}_t)$ are the explanatory variables in the regression. A Wald statistic is computed incorporating the parameters (α, β) to test the null hypothesis as follows:

$$T_{ESR} = \left((\hat{\alpha}, \hat{\beta})' - (0,1)'\right)' \hat{\Sigma}_{ES}^{-1} \left((\hat{\alpha}, \hat{\beta})' - (0,1)'\right)'$$

where $\hat{\Sigma}_{ES}$ is an estimator for the covariance matrix of the M-estimator for the parameters α and β. The test statistic follows a chi-square distribution with two degrees of freedom.

Bayer and Dimitriadis (2018) also showed that the backtest procedure has even greater power when combined with bootstrapping. The backtest will therefore also be carried out using bootstrapping where B = 1000 bootstrap Wald statistics will be computed. The bootstrap p-value will simply be the share of the 1000 bootstrap test statistics greater or equal to the test statistic for the original sample.

Exceedance Residual (ER) Backtest

McNeil and Frey (2000) was among the first to propose an expected shortfall backtesting procedure. This procedure analyses the difference between the next period's return X_{t+1} and $ES_q^t(X_{t+1})$ which is the expected shortfall at time t, conditional on the fact that X_{t+1} exceeds the VaR at time t, $VaR_q^t(X_{t+1})$.

$$r_{t+1} = \frac{x_{t+1} - \hat{E}S_q^t(X_{t+1})}{\hat{\sigma}_{t+1}}$$

Under the null hypothesis (H_0), they postulated that the modified series r_t should be i.i.d with mean 0 and variance 1. To test H_0, the non-parametric bootstrapping method is employed on the n observations in r_t against the alternative hypothesis which states that the mean of excess violation of VaR is greater than 0. The bootstrap methodology was devised by Efron and Tibshirani (1994).

V-Test for the Expected Shortfall

Different methods to evaluate the performance of the ES estimates were proposed by McNeil et al. (2005). These methods were based on the relative size of test statistics. These test statistics are regarded more as a diagnostic tool than a formal statistical test, since there is no null hypothesis testing involved.

The first statistic, V_1, takes the average between the forecasted ES and the actual return whenever a VaR violation occurs. A correctly specified model should yield a value close to 0 for V_1. For a given probability q, V_1 is defined as:

$$V_1 = \frac{\sum_{t=1}^{T}(x_{t+1} - \hat{ES}_q^t(X_{t+1}))1_{\{X_{t+1} > \hat{x}_q^t\}}}{\sum_{t=1}^{T} 1_{\{X_{t+1} > \hat{x}_q^t\}}}$$

where T denotes the total number of ES estimates.

However, the main drawback of V_1 is that it is too dependent on the VaR estimates. Therefore, McNeil et al. (2005) proposed a second test statistic V_2, which is defined as follows:

$$V_2 = \frac{\sum_{t=1}^{T}(x_{t+1} - \hat{ES}_q^t(X_{t+1}))1_{\{D_t > D_q\}}}{\sum_{t=1}^{T} 1_{\{D_t > D_q\}}}$$

$D_t = (x_{t+1} - \hat{ES}_q^t(X_{t+1}))$ and D_q is the empirical q-quantile of $\{D_t, t = 1, 2, \ldots, T\}$.

A third measure was also brought forward which combines V_1 and V_2 to strike a balance between the test statistic V_1, which relies too heavily on theory, and the test statistic V_2, which is more practically oriented. This measure is denoted by V, and it is defined as:

$$V = \frac{|V_1| + |V_2|}{2}$$

A good model would therefore bring the test statistics V_2 and V close to 0.

4. Estimation Results

4.1. Data Description

The intraday 1-min EUR/USD exchange rate price dataset consists of 28,290 observations for the month of February 2016 equivalent to 21 days intraday logarithmic returns. Moreover, the daily returns of the EUR/USD exchange rate are also used since a GARCH model will be employed to forecast the daily variance component in the MC-GARCH model. The daily data of the EUR/USD exchange rate prices span from 2 December 2003 to 29 February 2016 and consists of 3160 observations. The intraday dataset is split into two samples, where a sample of 20 days is used for estimating the models and a sample of 1 day is used to assess the forecasting ability of the models.

The daily log return r_t can be calculated as below. The same principle applies to the intraday log return process $R_{t,i}$.

$$r_t = \ln\left(\frac{P_t}{P_{t-1}}\right)$$

In the above equation, P_t is the exchange rate price at time t and P_{t-1} is the exchange rate price at time $t - 1$. Calculating the log returns actually transforms the financial time series into a stationary series. The Augmented Dickey-Fuller (ADF) test results presented in Appendix A actually confirm the stationary property of both the 1-min and daily exchange rate log-returns.

4.2. Heteroskedasticity and Normality Tests of the Return Series

Figure 1 shows the return series plot for the 1-min EUR/USD exchange rate returns. Figure 2 is the correlogram of the absolute returns for the 1-min EUR/USD returns for the month of February 2016. Clearly, a strong pattern repeating approximately every 1500 observations, corresponding to a day, can be observed. Volatility is high at the opening and closing hours. This depicts the strong intraday seasonality revealed in the high-frequency literature.

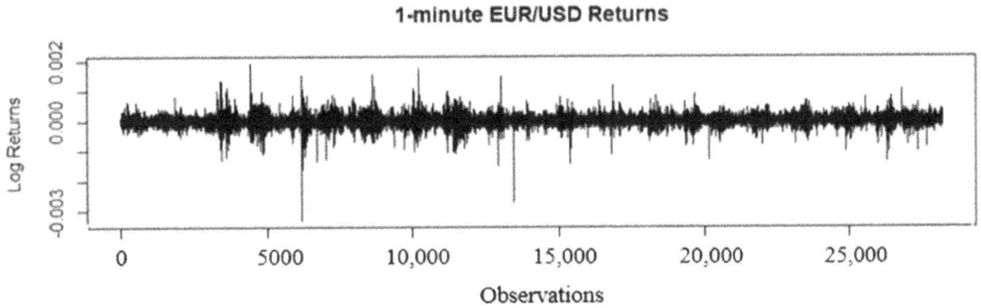

Figure 1. Return series plot for the 1-min EUR/USD exchange rate returns.

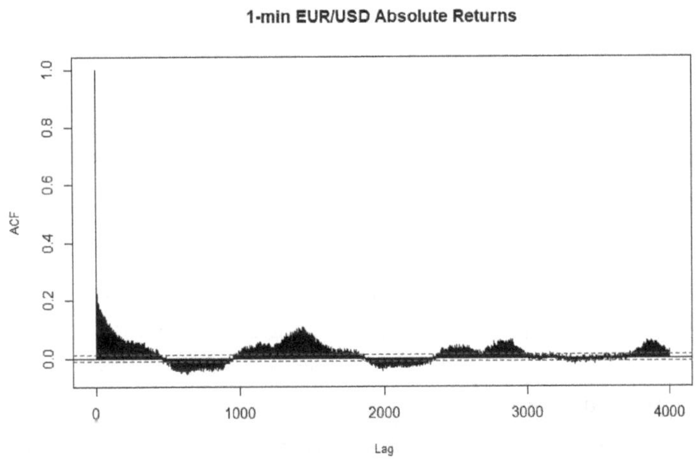

Figure 2. Correlogram of the absolute returns for the 1-min EUR/USD returns. ACF: Auto Correlation Function.

The descriptive statistics and normality tests of the EUR/USD exchange rate returns for the high-frequency 1-min returns and for the daily returns are presented in Appendix A.

4.3. *Identifying the Conditional Mean Equation*

The first step to the implementation of GARCH-type models for the conditional variance, involves identifying a suitable model for the conditional mean of the data. Literature suggests the implementation of an Auto Regressive Integrated Moving Average (ARIMA) model for modelling the conditional mean. Since both return series are stationary, the order of the parameter d in the ARIMA(p, d, q) model is equal to 0.

The next step consists of determining the order of the parameters p and q for the two return datasets. A graphical analysis of the Auto Correlation Function (ACF) and Partial Auto Correlation Function (PACF) of the two returns series is first carried out to visually determine the orders of their Auto Regressive Moving Average or ARMA(p,q) model. The ACF for both returns series are plotted in Figure 3 along with their respective PACF.

While analysing the ACF and PACF plots, it seems that an ARMA(0,0) model is appropriate for both the 1 min returns and for the daily returns. To further confirm the order of the mean equation, several ARMA(p,q) models are estimated, and the best model was chosen based on two criteria: the minimum Akaike information criterion (AIC) value and the maximum log-likelihood value. As stated by Mondal et al. (2014), the Box-Jenkins methodology states that the value of p and q for an ARIMA(p, d, q) model should be equal to or less than 2, or the total number of parameters should be no more than 3. Therefore, the AIC and log-likelihood values are checked only for those ARMA model with parameters p and q having a value of 2 or less. The ARMA(0,0) model provided the lowest AIC value and the maximum log-likelihood value for both the 1-min return and for the daily returns series and therefore outperforms the other ARMA specifications for the conditional mean.

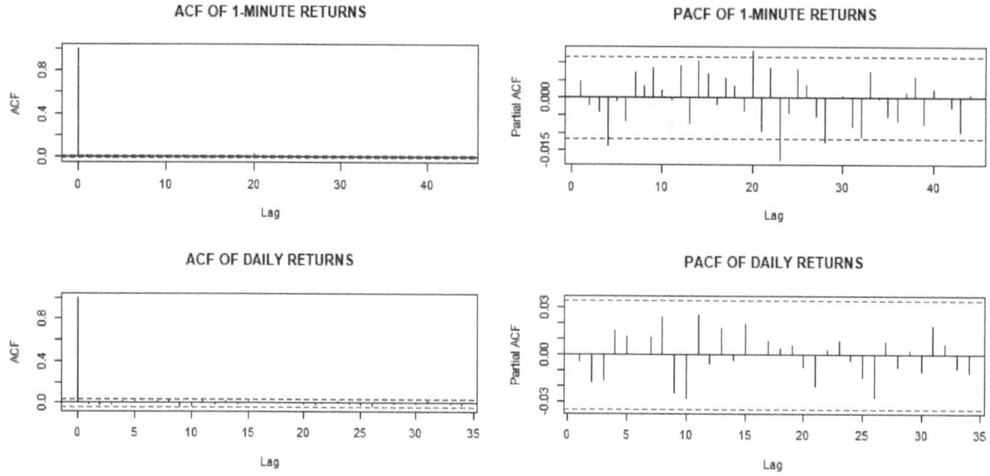

Figure 3. ACF and PACF plots for intraday and daily return series. PACF: Partial Auto Correlation Function.

4.4. Model Checking for the Mean Equation

According to Tsay (2005), there is a need to eliminate any significant correlations in the return series prior to fitting any GARCH-type model. The residuals of the mean equation are therefore tested for the presence of autocorrelations using the Ljung-Box Q test. All the p values were greater than 5% at 10 and 20 degrees of freedom, implying that the residuals of the mean equation are not serially autocorrelated for the two return datasets.

At this stage, since the two return datasets exhibit stylized features such as excess kurtosis and clustering of volatility and given the adequacy of the ARMA specifications for the mean equations, the specification of GARCH models to the returns datasets is analysed.

4.5. Estimation of Daily Variance Forecast

As stated by Engle and Sokalska (2011), the implementation of the MC-GARCH model first necessitates a model for the daily variance component. The GARCH(1,1) and the EGARCH(1,1) models are implemented under the five error distributions, and the best model is retained for the daily variance component. The parameter estimates of the GARCH-type models for the daily variance forecast are statistically significant. Since the parameter γ_1, which is the indicator for asymmetric volatility, was significant across all innovations for the EGARCH(1,1) model, this is indicative that an asymmetric GARCH might be preferred over a symmetric GARCH model. The parameter γ_1 being positive irrespective of the error distribution used, imply that shocks including both good news and bad news which may impact the daily EUR/USD returns will affect volatility for a long period of time in the future.

To choose the best model for the daily variance component, three criteria will be used: the AIC value, the Bayesian information criterion (BIC) value, and the log-likelihood value. The best model will be the one minimising both the AIC and BIC score while maximising the log-likelihood value. The results are presented in Tables 1 and 2.

Table 1. Daily variance forecast: GARCH(1,1) model.

	GARCH(1,1)				
	Normal	**Student's-t**	**Skewed Student's-t**	**JSU**	**GED**
AIC	−7.4566	−7.4665	−7.4659	−7.4662	−7.4704
BIC	−7.449	−7.4569	−7.4543	−7.4547	−7.4608
Log-likelihood	11,781.8	11,798.33	11,798.32	11,798.9	11,804.5

Table 2. Daily variance forecast: EGARCH(1,1) model.

	EGARCH(1,1)				
	Normal	**Student's-t**	**Skewed Student's-t**	**JSU**	**GED**
AIC	−7.4602	−7.4695	−7.4689	−7.4693	−7.4734
BIC	−7.4506	−7.458	−7.4555	−7.4559	−7.4619
Log-likelihood	11,788.4	11,804.14	11,804.15	11,804.8	11,810.2

It can be observed that the asymmetric EGARCH(1,1) model outperforms the GARCH(1,1) model under all error distributions since the former model yields the minimum AIC and BIC scores and yields higher log-likelihood values. This can be explained by the fact that the EGARCH(1,1) models are able to capture the leverage effect feature of the daily return series. However, the best-performing model is clearly the EGARCH model under the GED innovation assumption (EGARCH-GED) since this model yields the minimum AIC and BIC value while maximising log-likelihood. Hence, this model specification will be used for the daily variance forecast.

4.6. Fitting Performance

The MC-GARCH models is now fitted to the complete dataset of 28,289 1-min EUR/USD observations. Table 3 displays the results of the MC-GARCH parameter estimation. The corresponding p-values provided within parentheses.

Table 3. MC-GARCH(1,1) parameter estimates.

	MC-GARCH(1,1)				
	Normal	**Student's-t**	**Skewed Student's-t**	**JSU**	**GED**
μ	0 (0.62316)	0 (0.94151)	0 (0.53047)	0 (0.59145)	0 (0.98539)
ω	0.011999 (0)	0.008613 (0)	0.008651 (0)	0.008727 (0)	0.009911 (0)
α_1	0.037484 (0)	0.043874 (0)	0.043774 (0)	0.043762 (0)	0.041275 (0)
β_1	0.950441 (0)	0.949255 (0)	0.949335 (0)	0.949197 (0)	0.949529 (0)
shape, ν	-	6.893944 (0)	6.894106 (0)	1.878735 (0)	1.340094 (0)
skewness	-	-	1.012434 (0)	0.037765 (0)	-

All the parameter estimates are statistically significant at 5% level except for the conditional mean, which is insignificant at 5% level across all innovations for the MC-GARCH model, and also, the skewness parameter is insignificant for the JSU innovation. Almost all the parameter estimates being statistically significant gives an indication that the MC-GARCH models are correctly specified.

The statistical significance of the ARCH parameter α_1 and GARCH parameter β_1 for all innovations of the MC-GARCH model suggests that lagged conditional variance and lagged squared disturbance have an impact on the current conditional variance. This simply implies that news about volatility from the previous periods have an explanatory power on the current volatility. Moreover, the high significance of the parameter α_1 validates the presence of volatility clustering in the dataset.

The shape, ν, parameter being highly statistically significant and greater than 4 for the Student's-t and skewed Student's-t error distributions and less than 2 for the GED innovation confirms the presence of thick tails as was shown by the excess kurtosis in the return dataset of the 1-min EUR/USD returns.

Moreover, the skewness parameter for the skewed Student's-t innovation being highly statistically significant also confirms the presence of skewness in the return series as was shown by the negative skewness of the dataset. These results suggest that a non-normal innovation might be a more suitable candidate for the MC-GARCH model.

To determine the best fitting model, three criteria will be used namely the AIC value, BIC value and the Log-Likelihood. These results are displayed in Table 4, below.

Table 4. Model selection for the MC-GARCH(1,1) model.

	MC-GARCH(1,1)				
	Normal	**Student's-t**	**Skewed Student's-t**	**JSU**	**GED**
AIC	−15.021	−15.046	−15.046	−15.048	−15.057
BIC	−15.019	−15.045	−15.044	−15.046	−15.055
Log-Likelihood	212,463	212,826	212,827.4	212,849.3	212,976.5
Rank	5	4	3	2	1

From Table 4, it can be observed that the model yielding the worst results is the MC-GARCH model under the normal innovation. This can be explained by the fact that being a symmetric distribution and having a kurtosis of 3, the MC-GARCH model under the normal error distribution fails to capture features such as the leptokurtic nature of the 1-min EUR/USD returns.

The best model is clearly the MC-GARCH model under the GED innovation, since it yields the highest log-likelihood value of 212,976.5 while simultaneously yielding the lowest AIC value of −15.057 and BIC value of −15.055.

Model Validation: In-Sample Fit:

In this section, the chosen GARCH model is validated. The estimated, standardised residuals of the MC-GARCH model under the GED innovation should be independent and identically distributed and for this purpose, the ACF of the standardised residuals is analysed. It can be observed from Figure 4 that there are no significant lags, and therefore the residuals are not serially correlated and behave as a white noise process.

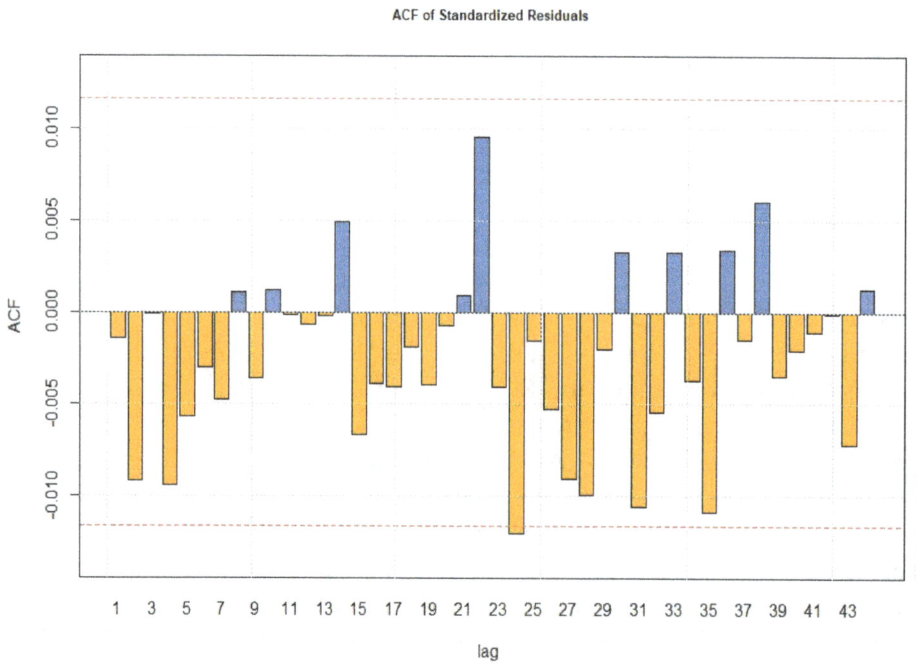

Figure 4. ACF of the standardised residuals.

The ARCH LM test was performed on the residuals of the MC-GARCH models at various lag lengths, and it was found that the null hypothesis stating that there is no ARCH effects cannot be rejected. This suggests that the conditional heteroskedasticity that was present in the raw series was successfully removed, thereby validating the MC-GARCH model. This result was backed by the Ljung-Box Test on the residuals.

The empirical density of the standardised residuals is plotted below to check whether the GED distribution gives the best fit.

Indeed, from Figure 5, it can be seen that the GED assumption fits well to the residuals, as compared to the other distributions.

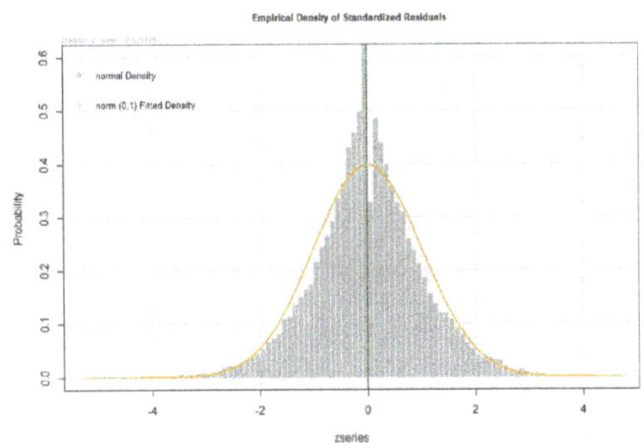

(**a**) Normal density vs. norm(0,1) fitted density

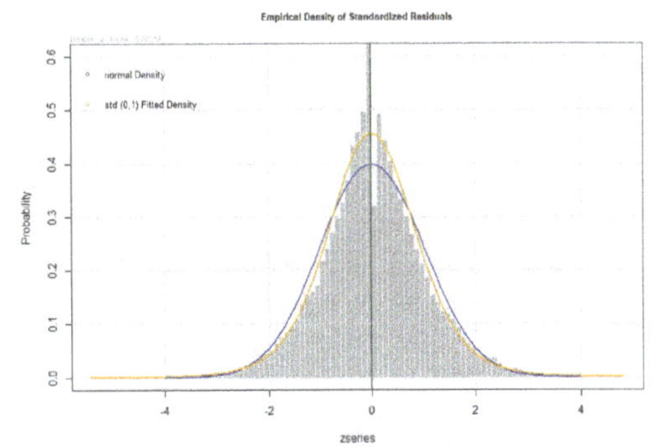

(**b**) Normal density vs. std(0,1) fitted density

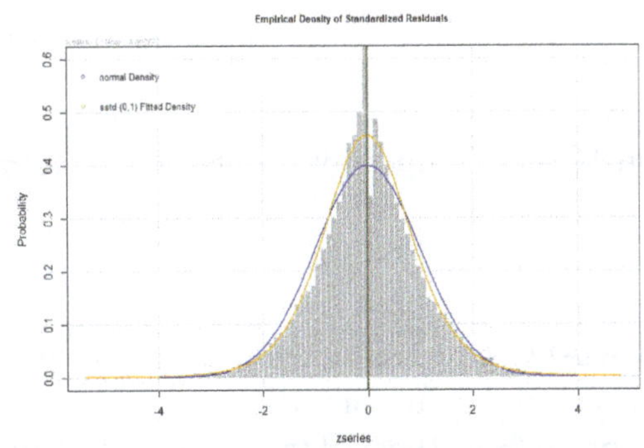

(**c**) Normal density vs. sstd(0,1) fitted density

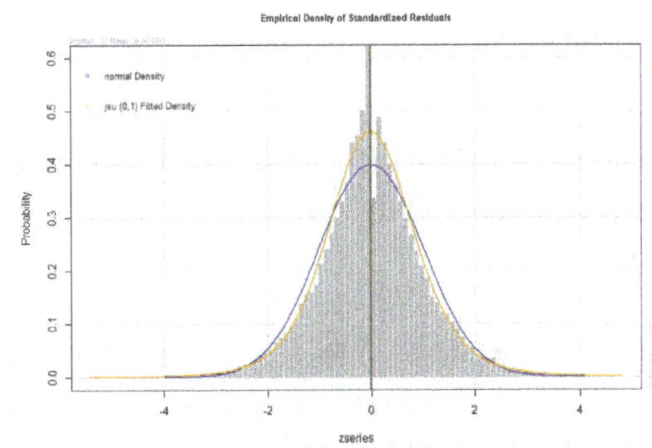

(**d**) Normal density vs. jsu(0,1) fitted density

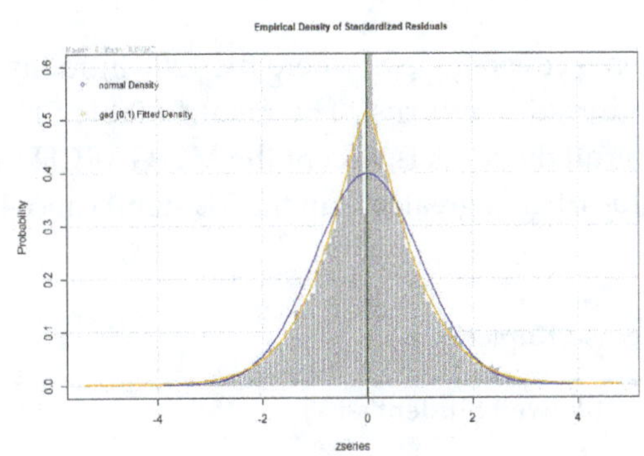

(**e**) Normal density vs. ged(0,1) fitted density

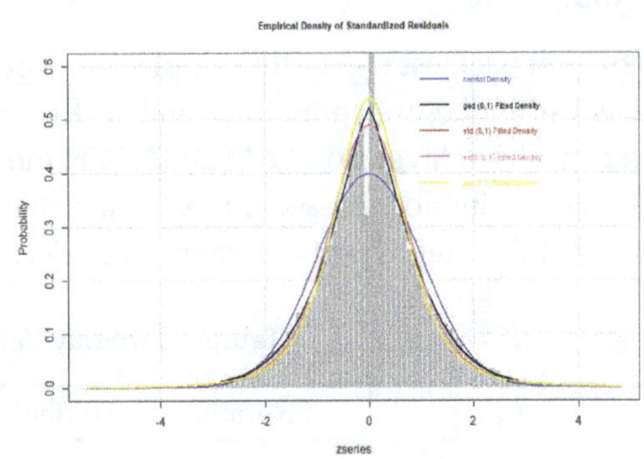

(**f**) Comparison of fitted densities

Figure 5. Empirical density of the standardised residuals.

The figure below (Figure 6) displays the volatility decomposition into the different components for the MC-GARCH model under GED innovation: the diurnal component, the daily volatility component, the intradaily volatility component, and the total composite volatility for the intraday 1-min data, which is obtained by combining the three volatility components.

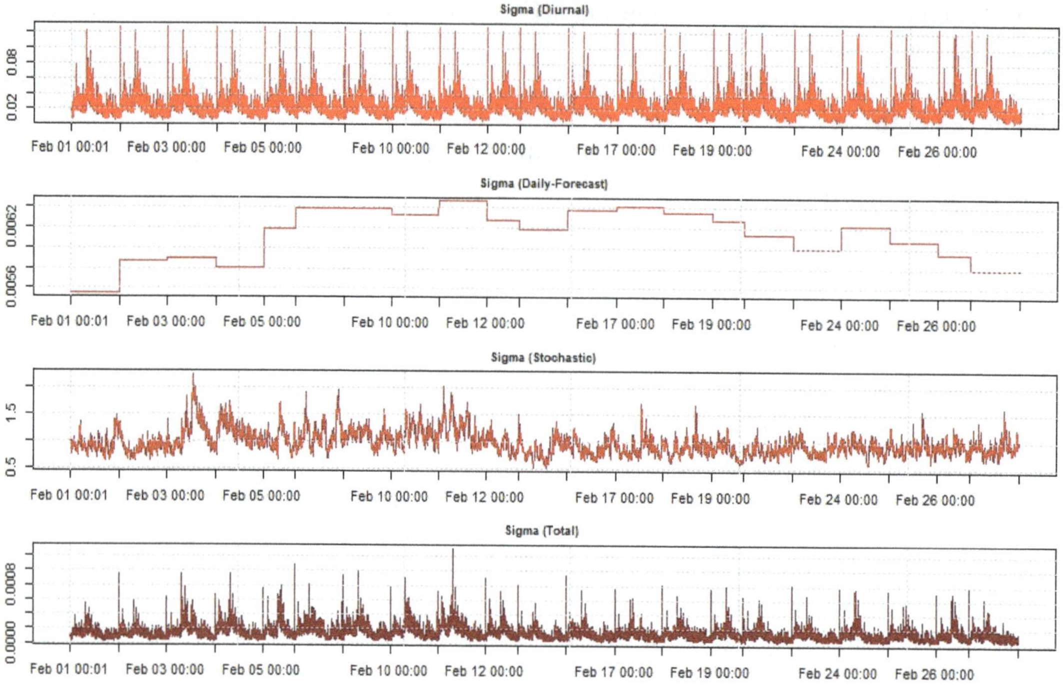

Figure 6. Diurnal component, daily volatility component, intradaily volatility component, and total composite volatility.

The MC-GARCH model is also valid, since it includes a component to cater for the intraday seasonality (sigma (Diurnal)).

4.7. Intraday VaR Forecast

The 99% intraday VaR is forecasted using the MC-GARCH models on the 1-min intraday return series. A rolling backtest procedure is then undertaken on the out-sample period and a moving window of 1 day will be used in the VaR backtesting procedure. The backtesting period is one day, which relates to 1500 1-min datapoints.

4.7.1. Kupiec's Test

The first backtest used is the Kupiec's unconditional coverage test, where the 1500 intraday VaR forecasts estimated are compared against the actual intraday returns. The results (Table 5) of the backtest speaks in favour of the MC-GARCH model, as all the models, except the MC-GARCH under the normal distribution, passed this test since the p-values, being greater than the 5% significance level, indicate that the null hypothesis cannot be rejected.

Table 5. Intraday VaR forecast: Kupiec's test.

	Normal	Student's-t	Skewed Student's-t	JSU	GED
Expected VaR Exceedances	15	15	15	15	15
Actual VaR Exceedances	27	21	22	21	20
Actual %	1.80%	1.40%	1.50%	1.40%	1.30%
p-value	0.005	0.142	0.089	0.142	0.217

4.7.2. VaR Duration Test

The results of the VaR duration test are displayed in Table 6.

Table 6. Intraday VaR forecast: duration-based approach VaR backtesting results.

Model	*b*	*p*-Value
MC-GARCH_norm	0.877439	0.397975
MC-GARCH_std	0.85151	0.392917
MC-GARCH_sstd	0.85151	0.392917
MC-GARCH_jsu	0.85151	0.392917
MC-GARCH_ged	0.85151	0.392917

The second column '*b*' is the estimated Weibull parameter for the different models. Since the *p*-values for all models are greater than the significance level of 5%, this gives evidence that the duration of time between the VaR violations possess no memory and that they do not cluster. All the models passed the VaR duration-based backtest.

4.7.3. Backtesting VaR Using an Asymmetric Loss Function

A more rigorous backtesting procedure is carried out. As stated in Bernardi et al. (2014), though the Kupiec's test is able to compare VaR violations of several competing models, it fails, however, to rank the models according to their predictive accuracy of the VaRs. Moreover, many models satisfy the unconditional coverage test, as it is observed in this study. The risk manager therefore cannot select a unique method. Lopez (1998) suggested to measure the accuracy of VaR forecasts based on a loss function and the models are ranked accordingly.

To present results which are less sensitive to the low number of theoretical violations and to deal with the problem of the Kupiec's test, the Model Confidence Set (MCS) procedure proposed by Hansen et al. (2011) is applied together with the asymmetric VaR function of González-Rivera et al. (2004). The results for the MCS procedure are presented in Table 7. Only those models which passed the Kupiec's test and the VaR duration test are considered. The best-performing model according to this procedure is the MC-GARCH under the skewed Student's-t distribution, since it minimises the loss function.

Table 7. Intraday VaR forecast: MCS results and ranking.

Superior Set of Model		
Model	**Rank**	**Loss ($\times 10^{-6}$)**
MC-GARCH_std	2	4.61995
MC-GARCH_sstd	1	4.615442
MC-GARCH_jsu	4	4.744222
MC-GARCH_ged	3	4.639826

The sigma forecast plot and the VaR backtesting plot for the MC-GARCH(1,1) model under the skewed Student's-t distribution are displayed below in Figures 7 and 8 respectively.

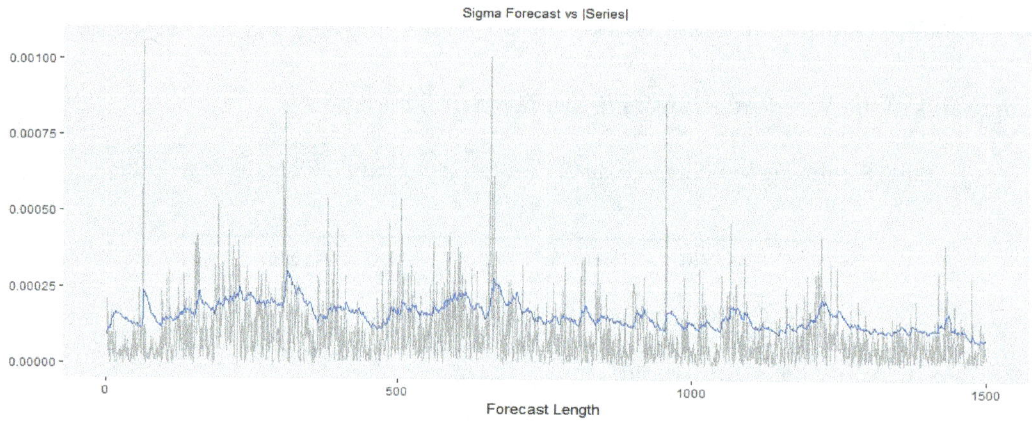

Figure 7. Sigma forecast plot.

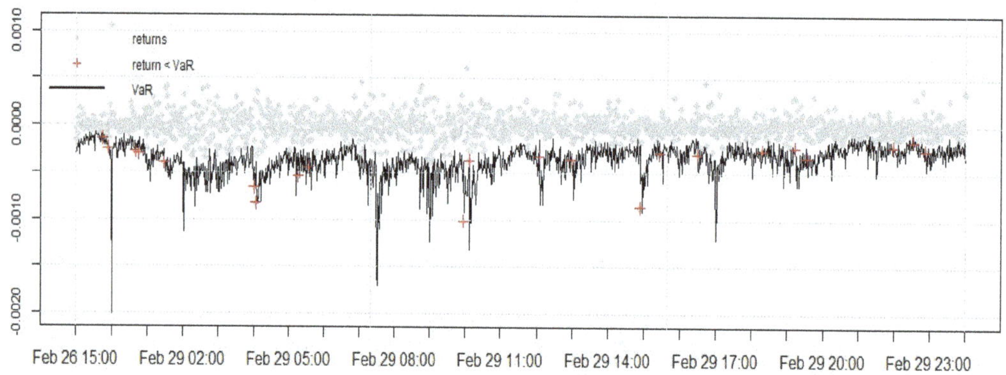

Figure 8. VaR backtest graph.

As noted in Singh et al. (2013), the spikes in the VaR forecasts as shown in the backtest plot in Figure 8 is due to the seasonal component during the opening of each trading day.

4.8. Intraday ES Forecast

The backtesting of the Expected Shortfall (ES) is now conducted, and three backtests are implemented to determine the accuracy of the ES forecast.

4.8.1. A Regression-Based ES Backtesting Procedure: the Bivariate ES Regression Backtest

The results for this backtest, both with and without bootstrapping, are shown in Table 8, below. All *p*-values are greater than the 5% significance level. The null hypothesis, which states that the 'ES forecasts are correctly specified' is not rejected. Moreover, the bootstrap *p*-values are also highly significant. Therefore, it can be concluded that the MC-GARCH models are able to forecast accurately the risk measure ES.

Table 8. Intraday ES forecast: bivariate ESR backtest results.

Model	*p*-Value	Boot *p*-Value
MC-GARCH_std	0.806	0.580
MC-GARCH_sstd	0.763	0.527
MC-GARCH_jsu	0.755	0.492
MC-GARCH_ged	0.868	0.664

Two classical ES backtests are employed to determine which model delivers the best ES estimates.

4.8.2. Exceedance Residual (ER) Backtest

The Exceedance Residual (ER) backtest of McNeil and Frey (2000) is also employed in this paper. The corresponding results are displayed in Table 9, below.

Table 9. Intraday ES forecast: Exceedance Residual (ER) backtest.

Model	Expected Exceedances	Actual Exceedances	p-Value
MC-GARCH_std	15	21	0.1845
MC-GARCH_sstd	15	22	0.1322
MC-GARCH_jsu	15	21	0.1302
MC-GARCH_ged	15	20	0.1077

The null hypothesis, which states that "Mean of Excess Violations of VaR is Equal to zero", is not rejected, since all p-values are greater than 5% confidence level. Based on this backtesting procedure, it can therefore be ascertained that the MC-GARCH models succeed in accurately predicting the ES estimates. Although the actual ES exceedances are comparable across the four MC-GARCH specifications, it can be observed that the MC-GARCH model under the GED error ditribution yields the least exceedances.

4.8.3. V-Tests

The V-Test statistics backtesting procedure can be regarded more as a diagnostic tool than a formal statistical testing procedure, since there is no null hypothesis involved.

Table 10 displays the results for the V_1, V_2 and V_3 test statistics. The first observation is that the sign of the V_1, V_2 and V_3 test statistics are positive, thus implying that all the models are, on average, overestimating the ES risk measure. Moreover, since the magnitude of the values of the test statistics are very close to zero, it implies that the models are only slightly overestimating the ES. These results speak in favour of the MC-GARCH models since risk managers are less concerned about overestimation of the risk metric as compared to an underestimation.

Table 10. Intraday ES Forecast: V-tests Backtesting Results.

Model	V_1	V_2	V
MC-GARCH_std	0.0004419	0.0015778	0.0010099
MC-GARCH_sstd	0.0004391	0.0015690	0.0010041
MC-GARCH_jsu	0.0004383	0.0015667	0.0010025
MC-GARCH_ged	0.0004243	0.0015206	0.0009724

Furthermore, it can be observed that the magnitude of the V_1 test statistic is smaller for the MC-GARCH model under GED innovation assumption as compared to the other innovation assumptions thereby indicating that it performs relatively better. The same observation can be made for the other two test statistics, V_2 and V_3. Therefore, the MC-GARCH model under the GED error ditribution is the best model for ES under this backtest.

Figure 9 displays the ES forecasts for the MC-GARCH model under the GED innovation process. Once more it can be seen that the MC-GARCH models are able to adequately forecast ES.

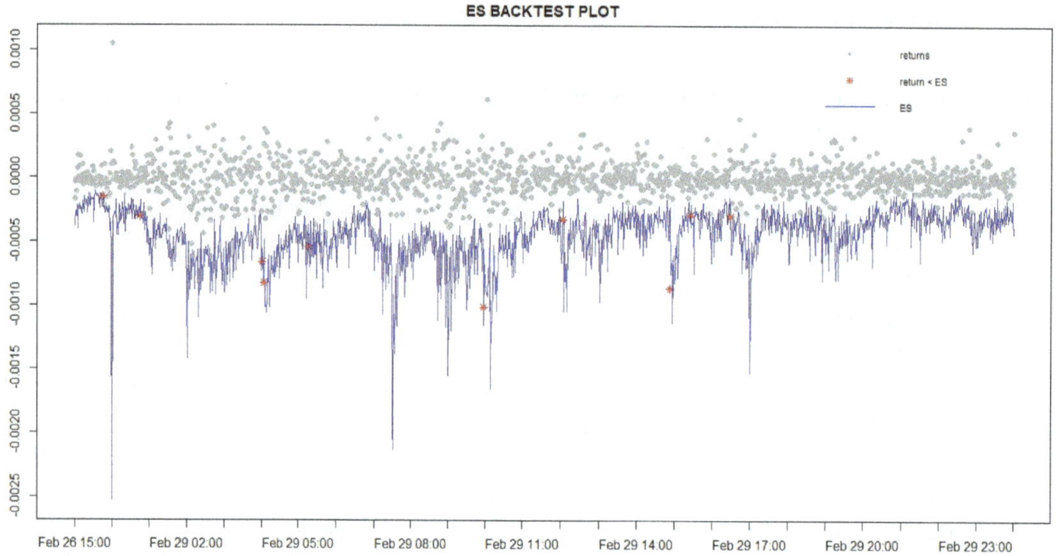

Figure 9. ES backtest graph for MC-GARCH_GED.

Figure 10 displays the forecast for both VaR and ES at 99% for the MC-GARCH_GED model.

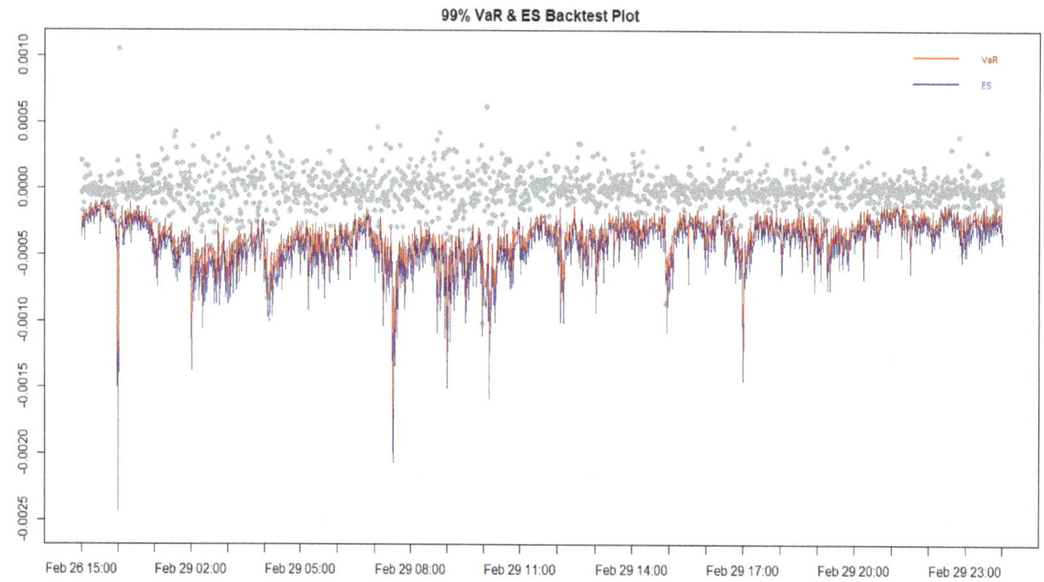

Figure 10. Backtest graph for MC-GARCH_GED.

5. Conclusions

A typical question that sparks a lot of interest in the high-frequency trading literature concerns which GARCH model tends to be the best when it comes to forecasting intradaily risk metrics such as Value-at-Risk (VaR) and Expected Shortfall (ES). This paper therefore focuses on the performance analysis of the MC-GARCH model in forecasting 1-min VaR and 1-min ES.

The first objective of this study was to determine which GARCH-type model gives the best in-sample fit to the daily EUR/USD returns for the daily variance forecast for the MC-GARCH model. It was found that overall the EGARCH(1,1) models were preferred over the GARCH(1,1) models. The EGARCH model under the GED innovation assumption however yielded the best results.

The second aim of the study was to analyse the effects of different distributional assumption for the innovation process of the GARCH models for both model fitting and forecasting. Overall, it was found that non-normal distributional assumptions gave better results for model fitting as well as forecasting. This is due to the fact that non-normal distributions are able to take into account features such as excess kurtosis and asymmetry of the high-frequency EUR/USD returns. Furthermore, they are able to replicate these features when forecasting volatility. The MC-GARCH(1,1) model under the GED innovation assumption actually gave the best fit to the intraday data as per the ranking procedure carried out based on AIC, BIC and log-likelihood criteria.

The one-day ahead 99% intraday VaR values were forecasted using the MC-GARCH models. Three VaR backtesting procedures were carried out namely the Kupiec's test, the VaR duration-based backtest and a backtest based on an asymmetric VaR loss function. Based on the number of VaR violations, the MC-GARCH(1,1) model under the GED distribution gave the best results. When the asymmetric VaR loss function, which is a more robust backtesting procedure, was implemented, the MC-GARCH(1,1) model under the skewed Student's-t distribution minimised the loss function with the smallest value and proved to be the best model.

The one-day ahead 99% intraday ES was also forecasted using these models. Three backtesting procedures were employed for the ES, namely, the Bivariate ES regression backtest, the Exceedance Residuals backtest and the V-tests. It was found that the MC-GARCH models under the non-normal distribution assumptions are able to produce accurate intraday ES forecasts. The MC-GARCH(1,1) model under the GED distribution however yields the best results.

5.1. *Recommendations for Practitioners*

It is recommended to avoid the use of normal innovation distribution for MC-GARCH modelling, as it significantly overestimates risk. Such risk overestimation in the insurance and banking industries may actually lead to an excess of capital requirements, which may be unnecessary and hence loss-making for the institution. The MC-GARCH, under other innovation distributions such as Student's-t, the Skewed Student's-t distribution (sstd), the reparametrised Johnson SU (JSU) and the Generalised Error Distribution (GED), also overestimates the risk metrics, but yields empirical sizes closer to the expected size for both the VaR and ES. It is, however, recommended to employ the MC-GARCH(1,1) model under the GED distribution as it yields least overestimation results, which minimise the excess of capital requirement.

5.2. *Further Studies*

There still exist a multitude of areas for further research using the MC-GARCH models. Other distributional assumptions for the innovation process such as the skewed GED, Normal Inverse Gaussian (NIG) can be implemented. Moreover, the performance of the MC-GARCH models in predicting the risk metrics VaR and ES at higher confidence levels such as 99.5% or even 99.9% can also be assessed. The combination of Extreme Value Theory (EVT) with the MC-GARCH model can be analysed in forecasting intraday VaR and ES. A comparison between the MC-GARCH-EVT and the MC-GARCH models in predicting VaR and ES at different sampling frequency such as 1-min, 5-min and 10 min returns would be a particularly interesting study.

Author Contributions: Conceptualization, J.N.; Formal analysis, R.S.S.; Methodology, R.S.S. and J.N.; Software, R.S.S.; Supervision, J.N.; Validation, R.S.S.; Writing—original draft, R.S.S.; Writing—review & editing, J.N.

Funding: This research received no external funding.

Acknowledgments: The authors thank the reviewers for their valuable suggestions.

Conflicts of Interest: The authors declare no conflict of interest.

Appendix A

The preliminary analysis is laid out in this section.

It can be seen in Table A1 that the mean for both series hovers around 0 which in fact coincides with past studies on high-frequency financial returns. Moreover, the skewness values for both return series are negative which may imply that these series experience more negative shocks than positive shocks and that there is a higher probability of obtaining a negative return. All kurtosis values being greater than 3, which is the kurtosis of any univariate normal distribution, imply that return distributions have thicker tails and sharper peaks at the centre as compared to a normal distribution. When comparing the degree of kurtosis and skewness for the 1-min returns (18.31108, −0.38839) with that of the daily returns (4.90965, −0.08208), it can be established that the kurtosis and the skewness values are much higher for the 1-min returns. This suggests that both the kurtosis and the degree of skewness increase with the frequency at which the data is recorded, thus confirming the findings of Andersen and Bollerslev (1998). The high kurtosis value for the 1-min returns is yet another stylised fact of high-frequency financial returns. The minimum value for the daily return occurred during the global financial crisis.

Table A1. EUR/USD Returns descriptive statistics.

	1-min Returns	Daily Returns
Mean	1.23×10^{-7}	4.62×10^{-5}
Standard deviation	0.00017	0.00633
Maximum	0.00193	0.02781
Minimum	−0.00332	−0.03733
Skewness	−0.38839	−0.08208
Kurtosis	18.31108	4.90965
Observations	28,289	3159

These will aid to further confirm the presence of different stylised facts present in the return series.

To further demonstrate that both returns series deviate from normality, the Jarque-Bera (JB) test is carried out and their kernel estimates of the density are inspected. The results are presented in Table A2.

Table A2. Jarque Bera test.

	Test Statistic	p-Value	Decision
1-min returns	277,030	0	Reject H_0
Daily returns	483.55	0	Reject H_0

The p-value for the 1-min returns and for the daily returns series being equal to 0 for the JB normality test allows us to safely conclude, at a 5% significance level, that indeed these distributions do not follow a normal distribution. The same conclusion can be derived when analyzing the kernel density estimates in Figure A1 for both the 1 min returns (left) and the daily returns (right) since they clearly display leptokurticity.

To determine whether the series is stationary, the Augmented Dickey-Fuller (ADF) test is carried out on both return series. If the ADF test detects the presence of a unit root in the series, it can be deduced that the series is non-stationary and need differencing. Table A3 shows the results for the ADF test:

Table A3. ADF test.

	Test Statistic	Lag Order	p-Value
1-min returns	−30.596	30	0.01
Daily returns	−14.03	14	0.01

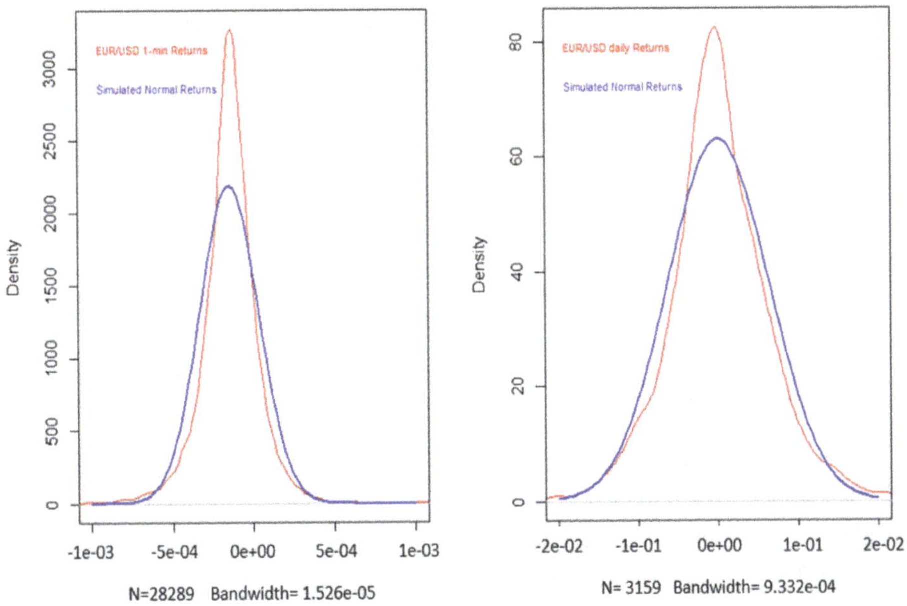

Figure A1. Kernel density estimates for 1 min returns (**left**) and daily returns (**right**).

The p-values for both returns series are less than 5% and this allows the rejection of the null hypothesis that a unit root is present in the series. Therefore, both return series are stationary and the order of the parameter d in the ARIMA(p, d, q) model for both series is equal to 0.

References

Andersen, Torben G., and Tim Bollerslev. 1997. Intraday periodicity and volatility persistence in financial markets. *Journal of Empirical Finance* 4: 115–58. [CrossRef]

Andersen, Torben G., and Tim Bollerslev. 1998. Answering the Skeptics: Yes, Standard Volatility Models do Provide Accurate Forecasts. *International Economic Review* 39: 885. [CrossRef]

Andersen, Torben G., Tim Bollerslev, and Steve Lange. 1999. Forecasting financial market volatility: Sample frequency vis-à-vis forecast horizon. *Journal of Empirical Finance* 6: 457–77. [CrossRef]

Bayer, Sebastian, and Timo Dimitriadis. 2018. Regression Based Expected Shortfall Backtesting. *arXiv*, arXiv:1801.04112.

Basel Committee on Banking Supervision. 2010. *Basel III: A Global Regulatory Framework for More Resilient Banks and Banking Systems*. Basel: Bank for International Settlements.

Basel Committee on Banking Supervision. 2012. *Fundamental Review of the Trading Book*. Basel: Bank for International Settlements.

Basel Committee on Banking Supervision. 2016. *Minimum Capital Requirements for Market Risk*. Basel: Bank for International Settlements.

Bernardi, Mauro, Leopoldo Catania, and Lea Petrella. 2014. Are news important to predict large losses? *arXiv*, arXiv:1410.6898.

Bollerslev, Tim. 1987. A Conditionally Heteroskedastic Time Series Model for Speculative Prices and Rates of Return. *The Review of Economics and Statistics* 69: 542. [CrossRef]

Christoffersen, Peter, and Denis Pelletier. 2003. Backtesting Value-at-Risk: A Duration-Based Approach. *SSRN Electronic Journal*. [CrossRef]

Culp, Christopher L., Merton H. Miller, and Andrea M. P. Neves. 1998. Value at Risk: Uses and Abuses. *Journal of Applied Corporate Finance* 10: 26–38. [CrossRef]

Diao, Xundi, and Bin Tong. 2015. Forecasting intraday volatility and VaR using multiplicative component GARCH model. *Applied Economics Letters* 22: 1457–64. [CrossRef]

Efron, Bradley, and Robert J. Tibshirani. 1994. *An Introduction to the Bootstrap*. Boca Raton: Chapman & Hall/CRC.

Engle, Robert F. 1982. A general approach to lagrange multiplier model diagnostics. *Journal of Econometrics* 20: 83–104. [CrossRef]

Engle, Robert Fry, and Jeffrey Russell. 2004. Analysis of High Frequency Financial Data. In *Handbook of Financial Econometrics*. Edited by Yacine Ait-Sahalia and Lars Hansen. Amsterdam: North Holland Press.

Engle, Robert F., and Magdalena E. Sokalska. 2011. Forecasting intraday volatility in the US equity market. Multiplicative component GARCH. *Journal of Financial Econometrics* 10: 54–83. [CrossRef]

García Jorcano, Laura. 2018. Sample Size, Skewness and Leverage Effects in Value at Risk and Expected Shortfall Estimation. Ph.D. Dissertation, Universidad Complutense de Madrid, Madrid, Spain.

Giot, Pierre. 2000. Time transformations, intraday data, and volatility models. *The Journal of Computational Finance* 4: 31–62. [CrossRef]

González-Rivera, Gloria, Tae-Hwy Lee, and Santosh Mishra. 2004. Forecasting volatility: A reality check based on option pricing, utility function, value-at-risk, and predictive likelihood. *International Journal of Forecasting* 20: 629–45. [CrossRef]

Hansen, Peter R., Asger Lunde, and James M. Nason. 2011. The Model Confidence Set. *Econometrica* 79: 453–97. [CrossRef]

Kupiec, Paul. 1995. Techniques for Verifying the Accuracy of Risk Measurement Models. *The Journal of Derivatives* 3: 73–84. [CrossRef]

Lopez, Jose A. 1998. Methods for Evaluating Value-at-Risk Estimates. *SSRN Electronic Journal*. [CrossRef]

McNeil, Alexander J., and Rüdiger Frey. 2000. Estimation of tail-related risk measures for heteroscedastic financial time series: An extreme value approach. *Journal of Empirical Finance* 7: 271–300. [CrossRef]

McNeil, Alexander J., Rüdiger Frey, and Paul Embrechts. 2005. *Quantitative Risk Management: Concepts, Techniques and Tools*. Princeton: Princeton University Press.

Mondal, Prapanna, Labani Shit, and Saptarsi Goswami. 2014. Study of Effectiveness of Time Series Modeling (Arima) in Forecasting Stock Prices. *International Journal of Computer Science, Engineering and Applications* 4: 13–29. [CrossRef]

Müller, Ulrich A. 2000. Volatility Computed by Time Series Operators at High Frequency. *SSRN Electronic Journal*. [CrossRef]

Narsoo, Jason. 2016. High Frequency Exchange Rate Volatility Modelling Using the Multiplicative Component GARCH. *International Journal of Statistics and Applications* 6: 8–14.

Nelson, Daniel B. 1991. Conditional Heteroskedasticity in Asset Returns: A New Approach. *Econometrica* 59: 347. [CrossRef]

Poon, Ser-Huang, and C. Granger. 2001. Forecasting Financial Market Volatility: A Review. *SSRN Electronic Journal*. [CrossRef]

Singh, Abhay Kumar, David E. Allen, and Robert J. Powell. 2013. Intraday Volatility Forecast in Australian Equity Market. *SSRN Electronic Journal*. [CrossRef]

Tsay, Ruey S. 2005. *Analysis of Financial Time Series*. New York: Wiley.

Zivot, Eric. 2005. Analysis of High Frequency Financial Data: Models, Methods and Software. Part I: Descriptive Analysis of High Frequency Financial Data with S-PLUS. Available online: https://faculty.washington.edu/ezivot/research/hflectures.pdf (accessed on 15 January 2019).

7

Credible Regression Approaches to Forecast Mortality for Populations with Limited Data

Apostolos Bozikas and Georgios Pitselis *

Department of Statistics and Insurance Science, University of Piraeus, 18534 Piraeus, Greece; bozikas@unipi.gr
* Correspondence: pitselis@unipi.gr

Abstract: In this paper, we propose a credible regression approach with random coefficients to model and forecast the mortality dynamics of a given population with limited data. Age-specific mortality rates are modelled and extrapolation methods are utilized to estimate future mortality rates. The results on Greek mortality data indicate that credibility regression contributed to more accurate forecasts than those produced from the Lee–Carter and Cairns–Blake–Dowd models. An application on pricing insurance-related products is also provided.

Keywords: credible regression approach; random coefficients; Lee–Carter model; CBD model

---

1. Introduction

During the last decades, mortality has significantly declined in most developed countries around the world, mainly due to the continuous improvement of living conditions and the evolution of medical science and technology. This decline in mortality results in a steady increase of life expectancy, which creates higher financial responsibilities for governments and annuity providers. Consequently, finding ways to manage the mortality dynamics of a population is a very important step in building a sustainable health and pension system. In this spirit, actuaries and demographers have focused on the development of novel methods to model and forecast the mortality rates of a population.

Lee and Carter (1992) proposed a pioneer modelling method to forecast the mortality of the total population of the United States, by decomposing the mortality rates into two age and one period parameters. A remarkable variant of the Lee–Carter method, particularly designed for higher ages, was proposed by Cairns et al. (2006), who incorporated two period parameters. In the literature, we can find many extensions to these methods. Renshaw and Haberman (2006) extended the Lee–Carter model by including a cohort effect, while Cairns et al. (2009) added a cohort parameter to the Cairns et al. (2006) model. In addition, Plat (2009) proposed a model which combines preferable characteristics of the Lee and Carter (1992) and Cairns et al. (2006) models.

An issue that sometimes appears in mortality modelling is that, for some countries, there are too few data to fit. This issue affects the existing modelling methods, which inevitably base their forecasts on population datasets of a limited historical period of observations. In the literature, there are extensions of the Lee–Carter method that can be utilized when dealing with limited datasets. For instance, Li et al. (2004) extended the Lee–Carter model to be applied for Chinese and South Korean mortality data, which are available at only a few points in time and at unevenly spaced intervals. Zhao (2012) modified the Lee–Carter model by incorporating linearized cubic splines and other additive functions to approximate the model parameters and forecast mortality for short-base-period Chinese data and Huang and Browne (2017) presented a stochastic modification of the CMI (Continuous Mortality Investigation) model to project mortality improvement rates for limited Chinese data using clustering analysis techniques.

Recently, some alternative modelling approaches have also been proposed as a tool in mortality forecasting. Differently from the above Lee–Carter variants and extensions, these approaches are based on credibility theory, aiming to model the period patterns of limited mortality data for a specific age, using useful information from a wider age span. Bühlmann (1967) established the theoretical foundation of modern credibility theory (also known as greatest accuracy credibility theory), which is widely used in non-life insurance and Hachemeister (1975) introduced a credibility regression model to estimate auto-mobile bodily injury claims for various states in the USA.

Credibility regression has a long history in credibility literature, with applications mainly in non-life insurance: De Vylder (1978) proposed estimators for the structural parameters in a more general regression model; Norberg (1980) proposed empirical credibility estimators under various model assumptions and established asymptotic optimality; Ledolter et al. (1991) derived a credibility method that allows for time-varying parameters in the process; and Pitselis (2004) presented the relationship between claim amounts and a set of explanatory variables into a credibility regression model with cross-section and time effects, with applications for general insurance data. For an extensive review on credibility theory for non-life insurance, we also refer to the works of Goovaerts et al. (1990), Bühlmann and Gisler (2005) and Klugman et al. (2012).

Regarding some life insurance applications of credibility theory, Hardy and Panjer (1998) used empirical Bayes credibility theory to provide a theoretical basis for the calculation of risk measures associated with mortality risk for insurance companies. Salhi et al. (2016) proposed a credibility approach, which consists on reviewing the fitting parameters of a Makeham mortality curve, as new observations arrive. Schinzinger et al. (2016) presented a multivariate evolutionary credibility model for mortality improvement rates to describe the joint dynamics of mortality through time in several populations. Moreover, Li and Lu (2018) proposed a Bayesian non-parametric model for the mortality of a small population, when a benchmark mortality table of a larger population is also available and serves as part of the prior information. By using an adaptive smoothing procedure based on the local likelihood, Salhi and Thérond (2018) proposed a methodology to adjust the graduated mortality table based on credibility techniques. In addition, Gong et al. (2018) highlighted the importance of using credibility procedures in individual life and annuity business.

Two recent contributions to modelling mortality under a credibility framework were also made by Tsai and Lin (2017a, 2017b). In the first paper, they applied Bühlmann credibility to mortality data of Japan, the United Kingdom and the United States, while, in the second one, they incorporated Bühlmann credibility into the Lee and Carter (1992) model, the Cairns–Blake–Dowd model (Cairns et al. 2006) and the linear relational model of Tsai and Yang (2015) to improve forecasting performance for the United Kingdom dataset. However, it has been observed that the age-specific mortality rates show a clear downward trend over time. Moreover, when we have limited mortality data experience for a specific age, but extensive data experience for the entire age range, the use of credibility regression techniques should be preferred to capture mortality trends. Our work aims to exploit the advantages of credibility regression compared with the most widely used mortality models, as an alternative to Bühlmann credibility, to forecast the mortality rates, especially for populations with limited data.

The rest of this paper is organized as follows. Section 2 briefly reviews the Lee–Carter, the Cairns–Blake–Dowd and the random coefficients regression models. Section 3 proposes a credibility regression approach with randomly varying coefficients and a special case with fixed coefficients to model mortality rates. Section 4 presents the extrapolation methods used to estimate future mortality rates under the credibility regression approaches. An empirical illustration using Greek male and female data is presented in Section 5.1, in which forecasting performances of credibility regression, and the Lee–Carter and Cairns–Blake–Dowd methods are evaluated with the *MAFE* and *RMSFE* measures. A comparison between Bühlmann credibility and credibility regression forecasting methods is also presented in Section 5.2 and an application on pricing insurance-related products follows in Section 5.3. Finally, concluding remarks are discussed in Section 6.

2. Mortality Modelling: A Review of Methods

In this section, we briefly review the Lee–Carter model, the Cairns–Blake–Dowd model and the random coefficients regression models that will be utilized in next sections.

2.1. The Lee–Carter Model

In its original form, the Lee–Carter (LC) model links the natural logarithm of the observed mortality rates $Y_{t,x} = \log m(t,x)$ for age $x = x_0, \ldots, x_{k-1}$ and year $t = t_0, \ldots, t_{n-1}$ with the following model predictor:

$$Y_{t,x} = \alpha_x^{(1)} + \alpha_x^{(2)} \kappa_t + \epsilon_{t,x}, \tag{1}$$

where $\alpha_x^{(1)}$ is an age parameter that reflects the average mortality at age x, κ_t is a period parameter which indicates the general level of mortality in year t and $\alpha_x^{(2)}$ is an age parameter that indicates the deviation from the average mortality at age x, as the general level of mortality changes. The errors $\epsilon_{t,x}$ are expected to be normally distributed, with zero mean and constant variance, reflecting specific period and age effects not captured by the model. Thus, after assuming that errors are independent and homoscedastic with zero mean, Lee and Carter (1992) suggested a close approximation to the SVD (Singular Value Decomposition) method, under the constraints $\sum_{x=x_0}^{x_{k-1}} \alpha_x^{(2)} = 1$ and $\sum_{t=t_0}^{t_{n-1}} \kappa_t = 0$, to obtain the following parameter estimates:

$$\widehat{\alpha}_x^{(1)} = \frac{1}{t_{n-1} - t_0 + 1} \sum_{t=t_0}^{t_{n-1}} \log m(t,x) \,,$$

$$\widehat{\kappa}_t = \sum_{x=x_0}^{x_{k-1}} [\log m(t,x) - \widehat{\alpha}_x^{(1)}] \,,$$

$$\widehat{\alpha}_x^{(2)} = \frac{\sum_{t=t_0}^{t_{n-1}} [\log m(t,x) - \widehat{\alpha}_x^{(1)}] \widehat{\kappa}_t}{\sum_{t=t_0}^{t_{n-1}} \widehat{\kappa}_t^2} \,.$$

Later on, to allow for heteroscedasticity in error variance, Brouhns et al. (2002) assumed that $D(t,x)$ follows a Poisson distribution with mean $m(t,x) \cdot E(t,x)$. Under this approach, age and period parameters are estimated by maximising the log-likelihood function of (1).

After choosing one of the above estimation approaches, period estimates are extrapolated using time series methods. Lee and Carter (1992) suggested a random walk with a drift parameter $\widehat{\theta}$ to project period parameter for $h = 1, 2, \ldots, H$ years ahead, according to $\widehat{\kappa}_{t_{n-1}+h} = \widehat{\kappa}_{t_{n-1}} + \widehat{\theta} h$. Then, projected κ_ts are utilized along with the estimates of age parameters $\alpha_x^{(1)}$ and $\alpha_x^{(2)}$ to obtain the following mortality forecasts:

$$\widehat{Y}_{t_{n-1}+h,x} = \widehat{\alpha}_x^{(1)} + \widehat{\alpha}_x^{(2)} \widehat{\kappa}_{t_{n-1}+h} = \widehat{Y}_{t_{n-1},x} + (\widehat{\alpha}_x^{(2)} \widehat{\theta}) h, \text{ for } h = 1, 2, \ldots, H. \tag{2}$$

2.2. The Cairns–Blake–Dowd Model

The Cairns–Blake–Dowd (CBD) model links the logit transformation of one-year probabilities of death $Y_{t,x} = \operatorname{logit} q(t,x)$ with the following model predictor:

$$Y_{t,x} = \operatorname{logit} q(t,x) = \kappa_t^{(1)} + (x - \bar{x}) \kappa_t^{(2)} + \epsilon_{t,x}, \tag{3}$$

where $\kappa_t^{(1)}$ is a period parameter which indicates the general level of mortality in year t and $\kappa_t^{(2)}$ is a period parameter that shows how mortality affects each age, while $\bar{x}$ is the mean age of the considered fitting age interval and $\epsilon_{t,x}$ reflects specific effects not captured by the model and is expected to be normally distributed, with zero mean and constant variance. Again, we briefly present the estimates of the model parameters, which can be obtained by regressing logit $q(t,x)$ on $(x-\bar{x})$ for each t:

$$\widehat{\kappa}_t^{(1)} = \frac{1}{x_{k-1} - x_0 + 1} \sum_{x=x_0}^{x_{k-1}} \operatorname{logit} q(t,x) \text{ and } \widehat{\kappa}_t^{(2)} = \frac{\sum_{x=x_0}^{x_{k-1}} [\operatorname{logit} q(t,x)(x-\bar{x})]}{\sum_{x=x_0}^{x_{k-1}} (x-\bar{x})^2} .$$

Alternatively, Cairns et al. (2009) assumed that deaths follow a Poisson distribution with mean $m(t,x) \cdot E(t,x)$, where $m(t,x) = -\log[1-q(t,x)]$. Then, the CBD model parameters are obtained by maximizing the log-likelihood function of (3). Assuming that period estimates are independent, each one of them is extrapolated using a random walk with a drift parameter ($\widehat{\theta}_i$, $i=1,2$) and then mortality forecasts for $h = 1,2,\ldots,H$ are obtained by

$$\widehat{Y}_{t_{n-1}+h,x} = (\widehat{\kappa}_{t_{n-1}}^{(1)} + \widehat{\theta}_1 h) + (x-\bar{x})(\widehat{\kappa}_{t_{n-1}}^{(2)} + \widehat{\theta}_2 h) = \widehat{Y}_{t_{n-1},x} + [\widehat{\theta}_1 + (x-\bar{x})\widehat{\theta}_2]h . \tag{4}$$

Remark 1. *We can easily observe that expressions in Equations* (2) *and* (4) *are both linear functions of the forecasting horizon h, where their intercepts are equal to the fitted rates of the last observed year and their slopes are the products of the estimated age parameters with the drift terms.*

2.3. The Random Coefficients Regression Model

Empirical data indicate that mortality in each age $x = x_0,\ldots,x_{k-1}$ decreases linearly over time. Especially in higher ages, mortality rates have been significantly improving over the last few years. We are interested in a model structure able to capture the improvement trends and describe the mortality evolution through time. For this reason, we consider a regression structure with random coefficients, aiming to capture the underlying mortality effects that are not included in the explanatory variables.

For each age x, the regression model with random coefficients is defined by $Y_{t,x} = \beta_{1t,x} + \sum_{k=2}^{p} \beta_{kt,x} Z_{kt,x} + \epsilon_{0t,x}$, for $t = t_0, t_1, \ldots, t_{n-1}$, where $Y_{t,x}$ is the response variable, $\beta_{kt,x}$, $k = 1,2,\ldots,p$ are the randomly varying coefficients and $Z_{kt,x}$ are the explanatory variables. Then, each coefficient element can be decomposed in $\beta_{kt,x} = \beta_{k,x} + \epsilon_{kt,x}$, for all t and k, with β_k, x and $\epsilon_{kt,x}$ being the fixed and random parts, respectively, assuming that $E(\epsilon_{kt,x}) = 0$, $\operatorname{Var}(\epsilon_{kt,x}) = \sigma_{k,x}^2$ for all t and $\operatorname{Cov}(\epsilon_{kt,x}, \epsilon_{k't',x}) = 0$ for $k \neq k'$ and $t \neq t'$. For more details on regression models with random coefficients, we refer to the works of Hildreth and Houck (1968), Hsiao (1986) and Greene (2012).

The above formulation means that the unknown regression coefficients can take different values over an observed period. Actually, mortality dynamics for a specific age can vary over time, due to unknown or exogenous[1] factors.

Nevertheless, the random coefficients regression model may be reduced to a fixed coefficients model with heteroscedastic variances, defined as

$$Y_{t,x} = \beta_{1,x} + \sum_{k=2}^{p} \beta_{k,x} Z_{kt,x} + v_{t,x}, \text{ with } v_{t,x} = (\epsilon_{0t,x} + \epsilon_{1t,x}) + \sum_{k=2}^{p} Z_{kt,x}\epsilon_{kt,x}, \tag{5}$$

where

$$E(v_{t,x}) = 0,\ \operatorname{Var}(v_{t,x}) = E(v_{t,x}^2) = (\sigma_{0,x}^2 + \sigma_{1,x}^2) + \sum_{k=2}^{p} \sigma_{k,x}^2 Z_{kt,x}^2 \text{ and } \operatorname{Cov}(v_{t,x}, v_{t',x}) = 0, \tag{6}$$

for all x and t, with $t \neq t'$.

---

1 Medical, biological, environmental or other factors that affect mortality evolution of each corresponding age over consecutive years are treated as unknown or exogenous due to the lack of specific data.

We have to point out that error variances $\sigma^2_{0,x}$ and $\sigma^2_{1,x}$ cannot be identified separately, while the sum $(\sigma^2_{0,x} + \sigma^2_{1,x})$ can. Therefore, without loss of generality, $\sigma^2_{0,x}$ is dropped and the above variance is simplified to $\text{Var}(v_{t,x}) = \sigma^2_{1,x} + \sum_{k=2}^{p} \sigma^2_{k,x} Z^2_{kt,x}$. Note that variance heteroscedasticity is still present even if $\sigma^2_{k,x} = \sigma^2_x$ for $k = 1, 2, \ldots, p$, due to the existence of squared explanatory variables $Z^2_{kt,x}$.

3. Credible Regression Mortality Models

In this section, we propose a mortality modelling approach embedded, for the first time, in a credibility regression framework with varying coefficients. The parameter estimation procedure is described and a special case with fixed coefficients is also provided.

3.1. A Credibility Regression Approach with Randomly Varying Coefficients

Denote $D(t,x)$ as the observed number of deaths at age x in year t and $E(t,x)$ as the average population aged x during year t (also called as population exposure to risk). Then, age-specific mortality rates $m(t,x)$ are obtained by the ratio $D(t,x)/E(t,x)$ and one-year probabilities of death can be derived from the identity $q(t,x) = 1 - \exp[-m(t,x)]$, which is implied by the assumption of a constant force of mortality over each year of integer age and over each calendar year.

We assume that response variable $Y_{t,x}$ refers to an appropriate transform (log or logit) of a mortality measure $\left[m(t,x) \text{ or } q(t,x)\right]$ for age $x = x_0, \ldots, x_{k-1}$ of year $t = t_0, \ldots, t_{n-1}$, where variable x corresponds to consecutive integer ages (k in total) and t corresponds to consecutive calendar years (n in total). We also consider A_x as an age-related random risk parameter, $\mathbf{Y}_x = (Y_{t_0,x}, Y_{t_1,x}, \ldots, Y_{t_{n-1},x})'$ as a mortality vector and $\mathbf{Z}_x$ as the design matrix of explanatory variables. We note that, in general, the design matrix could consist of various explanatory variables that reflect mortality characteristics. For instance, in a medical study, mortality may depend on various factors, such as the genetic background of an individual aged x, the life style, the nutrition, the toxicity of the environment, a possible infectious cause (bacteria, parasites, or fungi) or other socio-demographic factors that should affect mortality dynamics. Therefore, the pair that describes mortality evolution in age x is $(A_x, \mathbf{Y}_x)$, under the following assumptions:

(i) The pairs $(A_{x_0}, \mathbf{Y}_{x_0})$, $(A_{x_1}, \mathbf{Y}_{x_1})$, $\ldots$, $(A_{x_{k-1}}, \mathbf{Y}_{x_{k-1}})$ are independent and $A_{x_0}, \ldots, A_{x_{k-1}}$ are independent and identically distributed.

(ii) $E(\mathbf{Y}_x|A_x) = \mathbf{Z}_x \boldsymbol{\beta}(A_x)$, where $\mathbf{Z}_x$ is a fixed $n \times p$ design matrix of full rank p $(< n)$ and $\boldsymbol{\beta}(A_x)$ is an unknown regression vector of length p.

(iii) $\text{Cov}(\mathbf{Y}_x|A_x) = \text{diag}\left[d_{t_0t_0}(A_x), \ldots, d_{t_{n-1}t_{n-1}}(A_x)\right]$,
where $d_{tt}(A_x) = \sigma_1^2(A_x) + \sum\limits_{k=2}^{p} \sigma_k^2(A_x)\, Z^2_{kt,x}$, with $\sigma_1^2(A_x) = \sigma_{01}^2(A_x) + \sigma_{11}^2(A_x)$,
or in matrix formulation:

$$\text{Cov}(\mathbf{Y}_x|A_x) = \begin{pmatrix} \sigma_1^2(A_x) + \sum\limits_{k=2}^{p} \sigma_k^2(A_x)\, Z^2_{kt_0,x} & & 0 \\ & \ddots & \\ 0 & & \sigma_1^2(A_x) + \sum\limits_{k=2}^{p} \sigma_k^2(A_x)\, Z^2_{kt_{n-1},x} \end{pmatrix}.$$

The structural parameters are defined as follows:

$$\begin{gathered} \boldsymbol{b} = E(\boldsymbol{\beta}(A_x)),\ \boldsymbol{\Phi} = \text{Cov}[\boldsymbol{\beta}(A_x)],\ \boldsymbol{s}^2 = E[\boldsymbol{\sigma}^2(A_x)] = E\left[(\sigma_1^2(A_x), \ldots, \sigma_p^2(A_x))'\right] \text{ and} \\ \boldsymbol{\Delta}_x = E[\text{Cov}(\mathbf{Y}_x|A_x)]. \end{gathered} \tag{7}$$

In such a regression setting, $\boldsymbol{\Delta}_x$ has to be estimated. Consequently, instead of the ordinary least squares method, regression coefficients are estimated with the generalised least squares method (*GLS*). Then, an individual estimator of $\boldsymbol{\beta}(A_x)$ can be obtained by

$$\widehat{\boldsymbol{\beta}}_x = (\mathbf{Z}_x'\boldsymbol{\Delta}_x^{-1}\mathbf{Z}_x)^{-1}\mathbf{Z}_x'\boldsymbol{\Delta}_x^{-1}\mathbf{Y}_x \text{ and } \mathrm{Cov}(\widehat{\boldsymbol{\beta}}_x|A_x) = (\mathbf{Z}_x'\boldsymbol{\Delta}_x^{-1}\mathbf{Z}_x)^{-1}. \tag{8}$$

Proposition 1. *Under the above assumptions, the credibility estimator of $\boldsymbol{\beta}(A_x)$ is given by*

$$\boldsymbol{B}_x^{RC} = \boldsymbol{C}_x\,\widehat{\boldsymbol{\beta}}_x + (\boldsymbol{I} - \boldsymbol{C}_x)\,\boldsymbol{b}, \tag{9}$$

with

$$\boldsymbol{C}_x = \boldsymbol{\Phi}(\boldsymbol{\Xi}_x + \boldsymbol{\Phi})^{-1}, \tag{10}$$

where $\widehat{\boldsymbol{\beta}}_x$ is given in (8), *$\boldsymbol{b}$ and $\boldsymbol{\Phi}$ are defined in* (7), *$\boldsymbol{\Xi}_x = E[Cov(\widehat{\boldsymbol{\beta}}_x|A_x)]$ and $\boldsymbol{I}$ is the $p \times p$ identity matrix.*

Proof. The mean square error of (9) can be defined in terms of the norm $||.||_E^2$ as

$$\begin{aligned} Q &= \|\boldsymbol{\beta}(A_x) - \boldsymbol{B}_x^{RC}\|_E^2 \\ &= E\{[\boldsymbol{\beta}(A_x) - \boldsymbol{B}_x^{RC}]'[\boldsymbol{\beta}(A_x) - \boldsymbol{B}_x^{RC}]\} \\ &= E\Big[[\boldsymbol{\beta}^0(A_x)]'\boldsymbol{\beta}^0(A_x) + (\boldsymbol{\beta}_x^0)'\boldsymbol{C}_x'\,\boldsymbol{C}_x\,\boldsymbol{\beta}_x^0 - [\boldsymbol{\beta}^0(A_x)]'\,\boldsymbol{C}_x\,\boldsymbol{\beta}_x^0 - (\boldsymbol{C}_x\,\boldsymbol{\beta}_x^0)'\boldsymbol{\beta}^0(A_x)\Big], \end{aligned} \tag{11}$$

where $\boldsymbol{\beta}^0(A_x) = \boldsymbol{\beta}(A_x) - \boldsymbol{b}$ and $\boldsymbol{\beta}_x^0 = \boldsymbol{\beta}_x - \boldsymbol{b}$. Using the product rule and differentiating with respect to matrix $\boldsymbol{C}_x$, we have

$$\frac{\partial Q}{\partial(\boldsymbol{C}_x)} = -2E\big[\boldsymbol{\beta}^0(A_x)(\boldsymbol{\beta}_x^0)' - \boldsymbol{C}_x\,\boldsymbol{\beta}_x^0\,(\boldsymbol{\beta}_x^0)'\big]. \tag{12}$$

By substituting the values of $\boldsymbol{\beta}^0(A_x)$ and $\boldsymbol{\beta}_x^0$ and setting (12) equal to zero, we obtain

$$\begin{aligned} \boldsymbol{C}_x &= E\Big\{[\boldsymbol{\beta}(A_x) - \boldsymbol{b}]\,[\boldsymbol{\beta}_x - \boldsymbol{b}]'\Big\}\Big\{E\Big[(\boldsymbol{\beta}_x - \boldsymbol{b})(\boldsymbol{\beta}_x - \boldsymbol{b})'\Big]\Big\}^{-1} \\ &= \mathrm{Cov}[\boldsymbol{\beta}(A_x), \boldsymbol{\beta}_x]\,[\mathrm{Cov}(\boldsymbol{\beta}_x)]^{-1} \\ &= \{E\,\{\mathrm{Cov}[\boldsymbol{\beta}(A_x), \boldsymbol{\beta}_x|A_x]\} + \mathrm{Cov}\{E[\boldsymbol{\beta}(A_x)|A_x], E[\boldsymbol{\beta}_x|A_x]\}\}\,[\mathrm{Cov}(\boldsymbol{\beta}_x)]^{-1} \\ &= \{0 + \mathrm{Cov}[\boldsymbol{\beta}(A_x)]\}\,\{E[\mathrm{Cov}(\boldsymbol{\beta}_x|A_x) + \mathrm{Cov}[E(\boldsymbol{\beta}_x|A_x)]\}^{-1}, \end{aligned} \tag{13}$$

which yields (10). □

Then, the credibility estimator of future mortality rates $Y_{t_{n-1}+h,x}$, $h = 1, 2, \ldots, H$ may be compactly written as

$$\boldsymbol{Y}_x^{n+h} = \boldsymbol{Z}_x^{n+h}\,\boldsymbol{B}_x^{RC},$$

where $\boldsymbol{Z}_x^{n+h}$ denotes the design matrix of future periods.

3.2. Estimation of Structural Parameters

To estimate the structural parameters of the random coefficients credibility regression model, we can proceed similarly as in Hildreth and Houck (1968). Let $\boldsymbol{r}_x = (r_{t_0,x}, \ldots, r_{t_{n-1},x})'$ be the vector of the least squares residuals from the regression of $\boldsymbol{Y}_x$ on $\boldsymbol{Z}_x$ given A_x, which is obtained by

$$\boldsymbol{r}_x = \boldsymbol{Y}_x - \boldsymbol{Z}_x\widehat{\boldsymbol{\beta}}_x = \boldsymbol{M}_x\boldsymbol{v}_x, \tag{14}$$

where $\widehat{\beta}_x = (Z_x' Z_x)^{-1} Z_x' Y_x$ is the least squares estimator of coefficients in ordinary regression, $M_x = I - Z_x(Z_x'Z_x)^{-1}Z_x'$ is a symmetric and idempotent matrix of order $n \times n$ and $v_x = Y_x - Z_x\, \beta(A_x)$ is the error term. Then, given A_x, the variance matrix of r_x, via (6), becomes

$$E(r_x r_x' | A_x) = E(M_x v_x v_x' M_x | A_x), \tag{15}$$

from which we can get

$$E(\dot{r}_x | A_x) = \dot{M}_x \dot{Z}_x \sigma^2(A_x), \tag{16}$$

where $\dot{r}_x = (r^2_{t_0,x}, \dots, r^2_{t_{n-1},x})'$, $\dot{M}_x = \{m^2_{ts,x}\}_{t,s=t_0,\dots,t_{n-1}}$ and $\dot{Z}_x = \{Z^2_{kt,x}\}_{k=1,\dots,p,\; t=t_0,\dots,t_{n-1}}$ are the Hadamard products of matrices r_x, M_x and Z_x, respectively, while $\sigma^2(A_x)$ is as defined in (7). In addition, (16) implies that, for given A_x, least squares residuals $\dot{r}_x$ are regressed on $\sigma^2(A_x)$, which yields

$$\dot{r}_x = \dot{M}_x \dot{Z}_x \sigma^2(A_x) + e_x = G_x \sigma^2(A_x) + e_x, \tag{17}$$

where $G_x = \dot{M}_x \dot{Z}_x$ and e_x is a $n \times 1$ disturbance vector, such that $E(e_x|A_x) = 0$. Hence, its variance-covariance matrix is given by

$$\begin{aligned} \mathrm{Cov}(e_x|A_x) &= E\{[\dot{r}_x - E(\dot{r}_x|A_x)][\dot{r}_x - E(\dot{r}_x|A_x)]' |A_x\} \\ &= E(\dot{r}_x|A_x)[E(\dot{r}_x|A_x)]' + 2E(r_x r_x'|A_x) * E(r_x r_x'|A_x) - E(\dot{r}_x|A_x)[E(\dot{r}_x|A_x)]' \\ &= 2\dot{\Psi}_x, \end{aligned} \tag{18}$$

where $\dot{\Psi}_x$ represents the Hadamard product of matrix Ψ_x by itself, with

$$\Psi_x = E(r_x r_x'|A_x) = E(M_x v_x (M_x v_x)'|A_x) = M_x E(v_x v_x'|A_x) M_x = M_x \Delta_x M_x.$$

Then, if σ_k^2s are known, the *GLS* estimator of $\sigma^2(A_x)$ in (17) is obtained by minimising the criterion function $[\dot{r}_x - G_x\sigma^2(A_x)]'(2\dot{\Psi}_x)^{-1}[\dot{r}_x - G_x\sigma^2(A_x)]$, which gives

$$\widehat{\sigma}^2_x = (G_x' \dot{\Psi}_x^{-1} G_x)^{-1} G_x' \dot{\Psi}_x^{-1} \dot{r}_x\,. \tag{19}$$

However, estimators of $\beta(A_x)$ in (8) and $\sigma^2(A_x)$ in (19) are non-operational, because the variance-covariance matrices Δ_x and $2\dot{\Psi}_x$ are functions of unknown variances. Therefore, operational estimators of $\beta(A_x)$ and $\sigma^2(A_x)$ can be obtained by replacing unknown matrices with estimators $\widehat{\Delta}_x$ and $\widehat{2\dot{\Psi}}_x$, respectively. A least squares estimator of the unknown variances $\sigma^2(A_x)$ is directly obtained from (17) as follows:

$$\begin{aligned} \widehat{\sigma}^2_x &= (G_x' G_x)^{-1} G_x' \dot{r}_x \\ &= [(\dot{M}_x \dot{Z}_x)'(\dot{M}_x \dot{Z}_x)]^{-1} (\dot{M}_x \dot{Z}_x)' \dot{r}_x \\ &= (\dot{Z}_x' \dot{M}_x^2 \dot{Z}_x)^{-1} \dot{Z}_x' \dot{M}_x \dot{r}_x\,, \end{aligned} \tag{20}$$

where equality $\dot{M}_x' = \dot{M}_x$ holds true, since $(M_x * M_x)' = M_x * M_x$ for a symmetric matrix M_x.

Remark 2. *In the actuarial literature, there are many other types of estimators for variance in* (17). *For instance, Hildreth and Houck (1968) suggested the unbiased estimator* $\widehat{\sigma}^{2\,(alt1)}_x = (\dot{Z}_x' \dot{M}_x \dot{Z}_x)^{-1} \dot{Z}_x' \dot{r}_x$, *while Rao (1973) proposed the so-called "Minimum Norm Quadratic Unbiased Estimator" (MINQUE), given by* $\widehat{\sigma}^{2\,(alt2)}_x = (\dot{Z}_x' \dot{M}_x \dot{Z}_x)^{-1} \dot{Z}_x' \dot{M}_x \dot{r}_x$.

The random coefficients (*RC*) credibility estimator of $\beta(A_x)$, denoted as $\widehat{B}^{RC}_x = (\widehat{B}^{RC}_{1x}, \dots, \widehat{B}^{RC}_{px})'$, is given by

$$\widehat{B}^{RC}_x = \widehat{C}_x\, \widehat{\widehat{\beta}}_x + (I - \widehat{C}_x)\, \widehat{b}\,, \tag{21}$$

where

$$\widehat{\widehat{\beta}}_x = (Z_x'\widehat{\Delta}_x^{-1}Z_x)^{-1}Z_x'\widehat{\Delta}_x^{-1}Y_x$$

and $\widehat{\Delta}_x = \text{diag}\left(\widehat{\delta}^x_{t_0t_0}, ..., \widehat{\delta}^x_{t_{n-1},t_{n-1}}\right)$, with $\widehat{\delta}^x_{tt} = \widehat{s}_1^2 + \sum_{k=2}^{p} \widehat{s}_k^2 Z_{kt,x}^2$, $t = t_0, ..., t_{n-1}$, obtained according to (7), by using the mean of the estimated variances in (20). Future mortality estimates follow from

$$\widehat{Y}_x^{n+h} = Z_x^{n+h}\widehat{B}_x^{RC} = Z_x^{n+h}\widehat{C}_x\,\widehat{\widehat{\beta}}_x + Z_x^{n+h}(I - \widehat{C}_x)\,\widehat{b}, \quad h = 1, 2, \ldots, H, \tag{22}$$

where $\widehat{C}_x = \widehat{\Phi}(\widehat{\Xi}_x + \widehat{\Phi})^{-1}$, $x = x_0, \ldots, x_{k-1}$, is the corresponding credibility factor. We suggest the following estimators for parameters b, Ξ_x and Φ to obtain De Vylder's (1978) optimality (minimum variance within the class of unbiased estimators):

$$\widehat{b} = (\sum_{x=x_0}^{x_{k-1}} \widehat{C}_x)^{-1} \sum_{x=x_0}^{x_{k-1}} \widehat{C}_x\,\widehat{\widehat{\beta}}_x\,, \tag{23}$$

$$\widehat{\Xi}_x = \frac{1}{x_{k-1} - x_0 + 1} \sum_{x'=x_0}^{x_{k-1}} (Z_x'\widehat{\Delta}_{x'}^{-1}Z_x)^{-1} \tag{24}$$

and

$$\widehat{\Phi} = \frac{1}{x_{k-1} - x_0} \sum_{x=x_0}^{x_{k-1}} \widehat{C}_x(\widehat{\widehat{\beta}}_x - \widehat{b})(\widehat{\widehat{\beta}}_x - \widehat{b})'\,. \tag{25}$$

Note that the estimators of $\widehat{\Phi}$ and $\widehat{b}$ are implicit functions of the parameter to be estimated and should be calculated iteratively, by imposing $(\widehat{\Phi} + \widehat{\Phi}')/2 = 0$ to retain symmetry after each iteration.

3.3. *Credibility Regression with Fixed Coefficients and Weights: A Special Case*

In the case of fixed regression's coefficients, the previous model reduces to a special case of Hachemeister's (1975) model with no weighs, i.e., $W_x = I$. In particular, some weights may appear in each regression line of A_x. For instance, population exposures $E(t, x)$, for $t = t_0, \ldots, t_{n-1}$ can be used as weights. In this case, we have the standard regression case of Hachemeister's model. To proceed, we follow the same Assumptions (i) and (ii) as in the random coefficients case, but covariance matrix in Assumption (iii) is simplified to $\text{Cov}(Y_x|A_x) = \sigma^2(A_x)W_x$, where W_x is a fixed $n \times n$ positive definite diagonal matrix, with weights $W_x = \text{diag}\,[E(t_0, x), \ldots, E(t_{n-1}, x)]$. The structural parameters are now defined as

$$b = E[\beta(A_x)],\ U = \text{Cov}[\beta(A_x)] \text{ and } s^2 = E[\sigma^2(A_x)] \tag{26}$$

and the ordinary least squares estimator of the coefficients vector $\beta(A_x)$ is given by

$$\widehat{\beta}_x = (Z_x'W_x^{-1}Z_x)^{-1}Z_x'W_x^{-1}Y_x \tag{27}$$

and the variance-covariance matrix is obtained by $\text{Cov}(\widehat{\beta}_x|A_x) = \sigma^2(A_x)(Z_x'W_x^{-1}Z_x)^{-1}$, while its expected value is given by $E[\text{Cov}(\widehat{\beta}_x|A_x)] = E[\sigma^2(A_x)(Z_x'W_x^{-1}Z_x)^{-1}] = s^2(Z_x'W_x^{-1}Z_x)^{-1}$.

Based on the above assumptions, the credibility estimator $\widehat{B}_x^{FC} = (\widehat{B}_{1x}^{FC}, \ldots, \widehat{B}_{px}^{FC})'$ of $\beta(A_x)$ for the fixed coefficients (*FC*) model is given by

$$\widehat{B}_x^{FC} = \widehat{K}_x\,\widehat{\beta}_x + (I - \widehat{K}_x)\,\widehat{b}\,, \tag{28}$$

where $\widehat{K}_x = \widehat{U}[\widehat{s}^2(Z_x'W_x^{-1}Z_x)^{-1} + \widehat{U}]^{-1}$ is the estimated credibility factor. Similarly, for the derivation of (28), we refer to Bühlmann and Gisler (2005). To recapture De Vylder's (1978) optimality, we use the following estimators:

$$\widehat{s}^2 = \frac{1}{(x_{k-1} - x_0 + 1)(t_{n-1} - t_0 + 1 - p)} \sum_{x=x_0}^{x_{k-1}} (\boldsymbol{Y}_x - \boldsymbol{Z}_x\widehat{\boldsymbol{\beta}}_x)' \boldsymbol{W}_x^{-1} (\boldsymbol{Y}_x - \boldsymbol{Z}_x\widehat{\boldsymbol{\beta}}_x) , \tag{29}$$

$$\widehat{\boldsymbol{U}} = \frac{1}{x_{k-1} - x_0} \sum_{x=x_0}^{x_{k-1}} \widehat{\boldsymbol{K}}_x (\widehat{\boldsymbol{\beta}}_x - \widehat{\boldsymbol{b}})(\widehat{\boldsymbol{\beta}}_x - \widehat{\boldsymbol{b}})' , \tag{30}$$

$$\widehat{\boldsymbol{b}} = (\sum_{x=x_0}^{x_{k-1}} \widehat{\boldsymbol{K}}_x)^{-1} \sum_{x=x_0}^{x_{k-1}} \widehat{\boldsymbol{K}}_x \, \widehat{\boldsymbol{\beta}}_x . \tag{31}$$

Again, the estimators of $\widehat{\boldsymbol{U}}$ and $\widehat{\boldsymbol{b}}$ should be calculated iteratively, imposing $(\widehat{\boldsymbol{U}} + \widehat{\boldsymbol{U}}')/2 = 0$ after each iteration.

4. Extrapolation Methods for Estimating Future Mortality Rates

In this section, we fit the random coefficients (RC) and the fixed coefficients (FC) credibility regression models to mortality rates for age $x = x_0, \ldots, x_{k-1}$ of year $t = t_0, \ldots, t_{n-1}$. For both models, the fitted rates up to year t_{n-1} can be compactly written as $\widehat{\boldsymbol{Y}}_x = \boldsymbol{Z}_x\widehat{\boldsymbol{\beta}}_x$. As we noted before, design matrix $\boldsymbol{Z}_x$ could consist of various independent variables that reflect risk factors for any given age x, but due to lack of specific data, we assume that $\boldsymbol{Y}_x$s for each given age x, depend only on the period effects of each calendar year, i.e., $\boldsymbol{Z}_x = \boldsymbol{Z}$. However, if specific data are available, for instance in case of life insurance datasets, then more explanatory variables can be incorporated in the regression model.

Henceforth, we consider the same design matrix $\boldsymbol{Z} = \begin{pmatrix} 1 & 1 & \ldots & 1 \\ 1 & 2 & \ldots & n \end{pmatrix}'$ for all $\boldsymbol{Y}_x$s.

4.1. *Standard Extrapolation Method* (SEM)

Based on current fitting data of the response variable $\widehat{\boldsymbol{Y}_x} = (Y_{t_0,x}, Y_{t_1,x}, \ldots, Y_{t_{n-1},x})'$, mortality rates for one-year ahead are estimated by

$$\widehat{Y}_{t_{n-1}+1,x} = \widehat{B}^c_{1x} + \widehat{B}^c_{2x}\,(t_{n-1} - t_0 + 2), \text{where } c = \text{RC or FC}. \tag{32}$$

Similarly, estimates of future mortality rates for age $x = x_0, \ldots, x_{k-1}$ are given by extrapolating one-year ahead estimates in (32) to $\widehat{Y}_{t_{n-1}+h,x} = \widehat{B}^c_{1x} + \widehat{B}^c_{2x}\,(t_{n-1} - t_0 + 1 + h)$, for $h = 2, 3, \ldots, H$, where the credibility estimators $\widehat{\boldsymbol{B}}^c_x = (\widehat{B}^c_{1x}, \widehat{B}^c_{2x})'$ are obtained by (21) for the RC or (28) for the FC model. Hence, under this method, future estimates are based on the mortality data of the initial fitting span $[t_0, t_{n-1}]$.

4.2. *Other Extrapolation Methods*

In practice, two additional methods can also be used to extrapolate mortality rates over a given forecasting horizon $h = 1, 2, \ldots, H$. Thus, for each one of the RC and FC models, one-year ahead estimates $\widehat{Y}_{t_{n-1}+1,x}$ can be embedded to the existing fitting span, with $Y_{t_0,x}$ simultaneously excluded from it, so that the fitting year span is moved forward by one year each time to $[t_1, t_{n-1}+1]$, $[t_2, t_{n-1}+2]$, $[t_3, t_{n-1}+3]$, ... Then, after repeating the estimation procedure, we can consecutively obtain $\widehat{Y}_{t_{n-1}+2,x}, \widehat{Y}_{t_{n-1}+3,x}, \widehat{Y}_{t_{n-1}+4,x}, \ldots, \widehat{Y}_{t_{n-1}+H,x}$. Under this "moving extrapolation method (MEM)", future estimates are based on more recent mortality trends.

Alternatively, one-year ahead estimates $\widehat{Y}_{t_{n-1}+1,x}$ can be embedded to the existing fitting span, without removing $Y_{t_0,x}$, so that the fitting year span is extended by one year each time to $[t_0, t_{n-1}+1]$, $[t_0, t_{n-1}+2]$, $[t_0, t_{n-1}+3]$, ... Hence, in each estimation step, credibility regression models are fitted on a continuously extended response variable, to obtain $\widehat{Y}_{t_{n-1}+2,x}, \widehat{Y}_{t_{n-1}+3,x}, \widehat{Y}_{t_{n-1}+4,x}, \ldots, \widehat{Y}_{t_{n-1}+H,x}$. Under this "extended extrapolation method (EEM)", future mortality trends are based on both the initial mortality rates and the recent ones that have been obtained after each estimation step.

Similar practical approaches have also been adopted by Luan (2015). The numerical results in the following section justify that all methods can be efficiently applied in actuarial practice.

Remark 3. *Similar extrapolation methods may be used in other regression or time series contexts, but here are customized to be used with the credibility regression models presented in Section 3.*

5. Empirical Illustration

In this section, the Lee–Carter (LC), the Cairns–Blake–Dowd (CBD) and the credibility regression models are fitted on Greek mortality data. Then, forecasting results are evaluated using the mean absolute forecast error (*MAFE*) and the root mean of squared forecast error (*RMSFE*) measures. Greek data have a limited number of historical mortality observations (1981–2013), which are available on the Human Mortality Database (2017), structured by year, age and gender. Furthermore, in life insurance datasets similar limitations frequently exist. Credibility regression can efficiently capture the underlying data trends, especially in cases where there is limited mortality experience for a specific age, but extensive experience for the entire age range (the case of Greek data). Of course, credibility regression methods can also be used for larger datasets.

Mortality evolution for the period 1981–2010 in Greece is illustrated in Figures 1 and 2 for $\log m(t,x)$ and $\text{logit}\, q(t,x)$, respectively. Both mortality measures show a linearity for discrete ages $x = 40$, 60, 80 of males (left panels of Figures 1 and 2) and females (middle panels of Figures 1 and 2). In addition, for both genders, average mortality decline shows a clear downward trend over time (right panels of Figures 1 and 2).

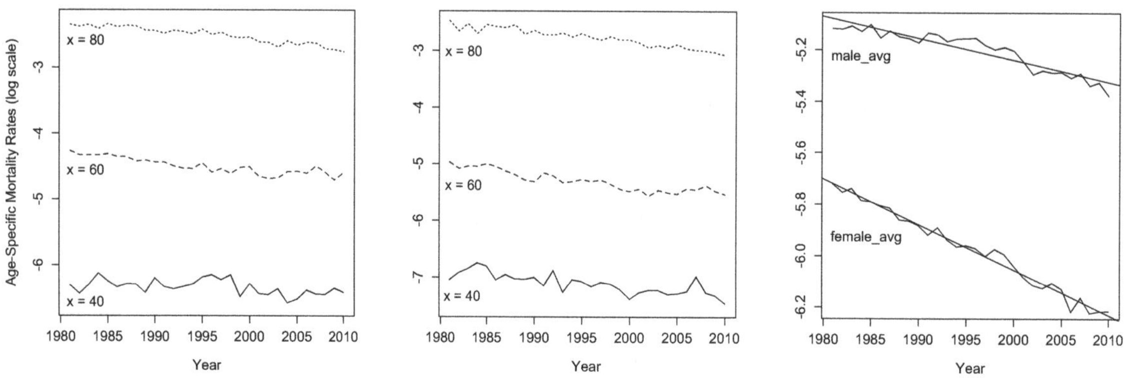

Figure 1. Observed $\log m(t,x)$ of the period 1981–2010 in Greece, for males (**left**) and females (**middle**) at the age of 40, 60 and 80. Average male and female $\log m(t,x)$ values over ages 15–84 are illustrated in (**right**), where straight lines show the corresponding trends in mortality decline.

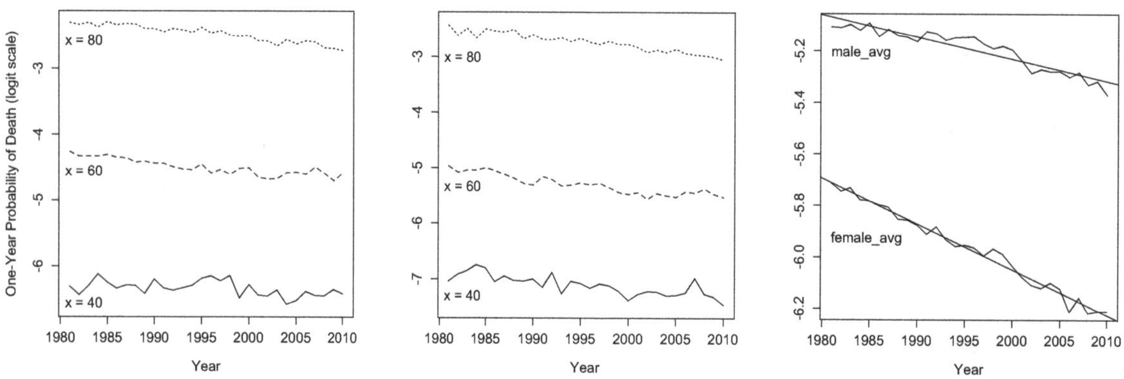

Figure 2. Observed $\text{logit}\, q(t,x)$ of the period 1981–2010 in Greece, for males (**left**) and females (**middle**) at the age of 40, 60 and 80. Average male and female $\text{logit}\, q(t,x)$ values over ages 15–84 are illustrated in (**right**), where straight lines show the corresponding trends in mortality decline.

5.1. Forecasting Results

For the numerical illustration that follows, we used the empirical age-specific mortality rates $m(t,x)$ from 1981 to 2010, for males and females at the ages of 15 to 84. This age span choice is in accordance with similar studies (Tsai and Lin 2017a, 2017b) as it corresponds to the age of a young adult up to the overall level of life expectancy in developed countries. To ensure robustness, relative to changes in the fitting range of data, we used two age and three period spans to extract forecasts for a 10-year ($H = 10$) forecasting horizon, presented in Table 1. In particular, for the FC model, we used $\boldsymbol{W}_x = \boldsymbol{I}$ as weights. The credibility regression methods, as well as the LC and the CBD mortality models, were implemented in R (R Core Team 2017). In particular, for the Poisson LC and CBD fitting methods, we used the "LifeMetrics" R package[2].

Table 1. Selected fitting and forecasting periods.

Fitting Ages	Fitting Period	Forecasting Period
$[x_0, x_{k-1}]$	$[t_0, t_{n-1}]$	$[t_{n-1}+1, t_{n-1}+H]$
[15,84]	[1981,2000]	[2001,2010]
[15,84]	[1986,2000]	[2001,2010]
[15,84]	[1991,2000]	[2001,2010]
[55,84]	[1981,2000]	[2001,2010]
[55,84]	[1986,2000]	[2001,2010]
[55,84]	[1991,2000]	[2001,2010]

To retain linearity over each corresponding fitting period, the logarithmic transform $Y_{t,x} = \log m(t,x)$ was used for the age-specific mortality rates and the logit transform $Y_{t,x} = \operatorname{logit} q(t,x) = \log \frac{q(t,x)}{1-q(t,x)}$ for the one-year probabilities of death. Forecast errors were then evaluated over the 10-year forecasting horizon using *MAFE* and *RMSFE* measures[3], where smaller values indicate a better forecasting performance. Averaged (avg) *MAFE* and *RMSFE* values are obtained by using

$$MAFE_{avg} = \frac{1}{H \times (x_{k-1} - x_0 + 1)} \sum_{h=1}^{H} \sum_{x=x_0}^{x_{k-1}} |\widehat{m}(t_{n-1}+h, x) - m(t_{n-1}+h, x)| \times 100 \tag{33}$$

and

$$RMSFE_{avg} = \sqrt{\frac{1}{H \times (x_{k-1} - x_0 + 1)} \sum_{h=1}^{H} \sum_{x=x_0}^{x_{k-1}} [\widehat{m}(t_{n-1}+h, x) - m(t_{n-1}+h, x)]^2 \times 100}\,. \tag{34}$$

Similarly, in the case of using $Y_{t,x} = \operatorname{logit} q(t,x)$ as response variable, $m(t,x)$ should be replaced by $q(t,x)$ in above formulas. Forecast accuracy results at percentage (%) scales are evaluated over the period [2001, 2010]. *MAFE* and *RMSFE* values for fitting ages [15, 84], using $Y_{t,x} = \log m(t,x)$ are illustrated in Table 2 (a) and (b), respectively, while the corresponding values for ages [55, 84] with $Y_{t,x} = \operatorname{logit} q(t,x)$ are presented in Table 3 (a) and (b), respectively. Note that CBD model is included only for comparisons in fitting ages [55, 84], as it has been particularly designed for higher ages.

2 The software, which is not part of CRAN, is available from http://www.macs.hw.ac.uk/~andrewc/lifemetrics/.

3 For instance, use of *MAFE* is demonstrated in the modelling comparison study of Shang et al. (2011), while *RMSFE* in Hansen (2013) and Van Berkum et al. (2016).

For both genders, accuracy results in Table 2 (a), (b) for fitting ages [15, 84] and Table 3 (a), (b) for ages [55, 84] indicate that, for each fitting period, credibility regression models outperform LC and CBD models for both error measures. Average values over the whole period are given in the last rows of each measure's subtable. More precisely, for ages [15, 84], the FC-MEM and FC-SEM produce the smallest average *MAFE* and *RMSFE*, while for ages [55, 84], RC-MEM performs better in average under both measures, which indicates that forecasts for higher ages are based on more recent mortality trends. Moreover, we observe that errors are getting evidently larger, when shortening the age fitting span to [55, 84]. This is due to the fact that both $|\widehat{m}(t_{n-1}+h,x) - m(t_{n-1}+h,x)|$ in (33) and $[\widehat{m}(t_{n-1}+h,x) - m(t_{n-1}+h,x)]^2$ in (34) are generally increasing with age x. Therefore, $MAFE_{avg}$ and $RMSFE_{avg}$ for ages [55, 84] are larger than those for [15, 84].

We note that, for our comparison, we used the Lee–Carter (1992) and Cairns–Blake–Dowd (2006) models, which incorporate only age and period effects. Models with cohort parameters were intentionally excluded from our analysis to be consistent with the age-period structure of the proposed credibility regression methods that model the period dynamics of mortality across the ages. For a modelling comparison study on Greek data that allows for models with cohort effects, we refer to the work of Bozikas and Pitselis (2018).

Table 2. *MAFE* and *RMSFE* values of forecast errors over the period [2001, 2010] for ages [15, 84].

(a) *MAFE* Values									
$MAFE_{[15,84]}$		**Lee–Carter**		**Random Coefficients (RC)**			**Fixed Coefficients (FC)**		
Fitting Period	**Gender**	**LC**	**LC-Poisson**	***SEM***	***MEM***	***EEM***	***SEM***	***MEM***	***EEM***
[1981, 2000]	Male	0.1513	0.1569	0.1338	0.1205	0.1322	0.1352	0.1256	0.1361
	Female	0.0831	0.0861	0.0702	0.0740	0.0711	0.0691	0.0657	0.0690
[1986, 2000]	Male	0.1684	0.1514	0.1175	0.1196	0.1158	0.1203	0.1221	0.1206
	Female	0.0625	0.0799	0.0650	0.0696	0.0758	0.0608	0.0651	0.0613
[1991, 2000]	Male	0.1468	0.1681	0.1275	0.1257	0.1280	0.1288	0.1289	0.1289
	Female	0.0763	0.0959	0.0705	0.0678	0.0750	0.0622	0.0663	0.0669
Average		0.1147(7)	0.1231(8)	0.0974(5)	0.0962(3)	0.0997(6)	0.0961(2)	0.0956(1)	0.0971(4)
(b) RMSFE Values									
$RMSFE_{[15,84]}$		**Lee–Carter**		**Random Coefficients (RC)**			**Fixed Coefficients (FC)**		
Fitting Period	**Gender**	**LC**	**LC-Poisson**	***SEM***	***MEM***	***EEM***	***SEM***	***MEM***	***EEM***
[1981, 2000]	Male	0.3165	0.3220	0.2661	0.2349	0.2629	0.2716	0.2511	0.2745
	Female	0.1791	0.1825	0.1398	0.1594	0.1457	0.1376	0.1365	0.1374
[1986, 2000]	Male	0.3543	0.3200	0.2257	0.2265	0.2204	0.2362	0.2364	0.2375
	Female	0.1307	0.1742	0.1410	0.1509	0.1700	0.1264	0.1385	0.1288
[1991, 2000]	Male	0.3180	0.4010	0.2478	0.2457	0.2470	0.2570	0.2551	0.2516
	Female	0.1694	0.2415	0.1580	0.1511	0.1707	0.1302	0.1438	0.1476
Average		0.2447(7)	0.2735(8)	0.1964(4)	0.1948(3)	0.2028(6)	0.1932(1)	0.1936(2)	0.1962(5)

Table 3. *MAFE* and *RMSFE* values of forecast errors over the period [2001, 2010] for ages [55, 84].

(a) *MAFE* Values

$MAFE_{[55,84]}$		Mortality Models				Random Coefficients (RC)			Fixed Coefficients (FC)		
Fitting Period	Gender	LC	LC-Poisson	CBD	CBD-Poisson	*SEM*	*MEM*	*EEM*	*SEM*	*MEM*	*EEM*
[1981, 2000]	Male	0.3191	0.3322	0.2924	0.3247	0.2885	0.2642	0.2846	0.2871	0.2673	0.2870
	Female	0.1884	0.1933	0.1694	0.1884	0.1624	0.1458	0.1611	0.1629	0.1448	0.1627
[1986, 2000]	Male	0.2928	0.3186	0.2682	0.2988	0.2506	0.2547	0.2494	0.2544	0.2581	0.2541
	Female	0.1577	0.1769	0.1618	0.1708	0.1287	0.1377	0.1344	0.1289	0.1351	0.1288
[1991, 2000]	Male	0.3091	0.3622	0.2790	0.3348	0.2483	0.2461	0.2464	0.2538	0.2493	0.2525
	Female	0.1723	0.2126	0.1659	0.1868	0.1324	0.1350	0.1363	0.1363	0.1382	0.1361
Average		0.2399(8)	0.2660(10)	0.2228(7)	0.2507(9)	0.2018(3)	0.1973(1)	0.2020(4)	0.2039(6)	0.1988(2)	0.2035(5)

(b) *RMSFE* Values

$RMSFE_{[55,84]}$		Mortality Models				Random Coefficients (RC)			Fixed Coefficients (FC)		
Fitting Period	Gender	LC	LC-Poisson	CBD	CBD-Poisson	*SEM*	*MEM*	*EEM*	*SEM*	*MEM*	*EEM*
[1981, 2000]	Male	0.4616	0.4848	0.3904	0.4467	0.4041	0.3644	0.3963	0.4065	0.3786	0.4061
	Female	0.2795	0.2842	0.2221	0.2512	0.2260	0.1996	0.2213	0.2304	0.2010	0.2299
[1986, 2000]	Male	0.4320	0.4872	0.3551	0.4073	0.3506	0.3522	0.3419	0.3631	0.3653	0.3618
	Female	0.2340	0.2699	0.2165	0.2244	0.1805	0.1940	0.1895	0.1803	0.1897	0.1800
[1991, 2000]	Male	0.4671	0.6129	0.3698	0.4625	0.3484	0.3423	0.3389	0.3660	0.3501	0.3616
	Female	0.2652	0.3721	0.2202	0.2510	0.1866	0.1888	0.1912	0.1961	0.1930	0.1954
Average		0.3566(9)	0.4185(10)	0.2957(7)	0.3405(8)	0.2827(4)	0.2736(1)	0.2799(3)	0.2904(6)	0.2796(2)	0.2891(5)

Credibility Effects on Mortality Modelling

In the preceding section, we used the proposed credibility regression methods to estimate the actual mortality trend for a specific age, by weighting the mortality trend for this age and the mean trend over a wider group of ages that encompasses much more information. Figure 3 illustrates the linear trend of the actual (observed) logit $q(t,x)$ for Greek males (left panel) and females (right panel), aged 55, 65 and 75 over the period 1981–2010. The intuition behind using credibility regression is that the proposed methods could potentially lead us to more accurate estimates for the intercept and the slope of the mortality curve for a given age $x = x_0, \ldots, x_{k-1}$. To assure this, we used the absolute forecast errors by age (AFE_x) to compare the linear trend (intercept and the slope) of the logit $q(2000+h,x)$, $h = 1, \ldots, 10$ between the actual rates and the rates produced from the best performing models for both genders over years [2001, 2010], with and without credibility, for pension ages [65, 84], fitted for [1981, 2000]. For each model, AFE_x can be obtained by

$$AFE_x = |\text{logit}\,\widehat{q}(2000+h,x) - \text{logit}\,q(2000+h,x)| \times 100\,. \tag{35}$$

Figure 4 displays the AFE_x comparison results, which indicate that, almost for all ages, credibility regression methods (dot lines) perform better than the LC (solid lines) and CBD (dashed lines) models. An alternative way to see how close the credibility forecasts are to the the actual mortality trend, Figure 5 illustrates the intercept and the slope of the actual rates and the forecasted ones for some ages, under the best performing methods (based on AFE_x) with credibility (FC-MEM for males and RC-MEM for females) and without credibility (LC, CBD).

The trend lines for the RC-MEM and FC-MEM forecasts can be easily extracted using the ordinary least squares method. Recall that, the intercept and the slope for the LC and CBD models is given by Equations (2) and (4), respectively (Remark 1), while for the credibility method RC by (21) and for FC by (28). The illustrated results in Figure 5 indicate that intercepts and slopes of the FC-MEM (for males) and RC-MEM (for females) lines are closer to the actual ones, which set the best starting point for the forecasts.

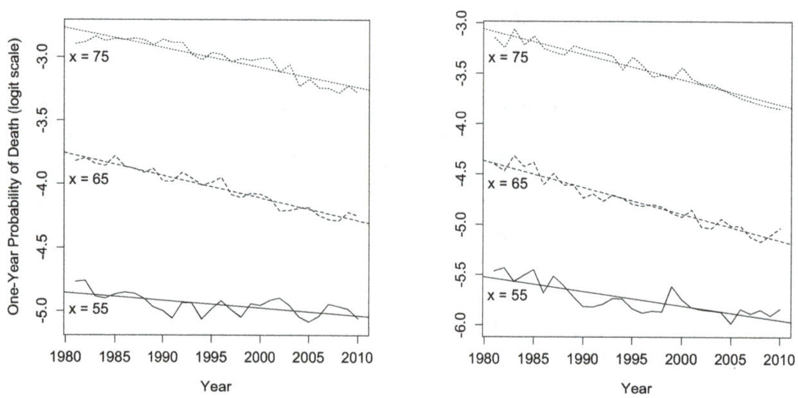

Figure 3. Linear trend of the observed logit $q(t,x)$ of the period 1981–2010 in Greece, for males (**left**) and females (**right**) at the age of 55, 65 and 75.

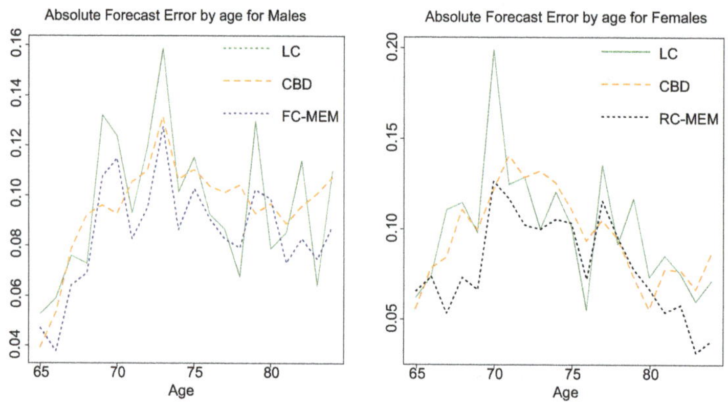

Figure 4. AFE values against age of logit $q(2000+h,x)$, $h=1,\ldots,10$ between the actual rates and the rates produced from the best performing models with and without credibility for males (**left**) and females (**right**) over [2001, 2010], fitted to pension ages [65, 84] for years [1981, 2000].

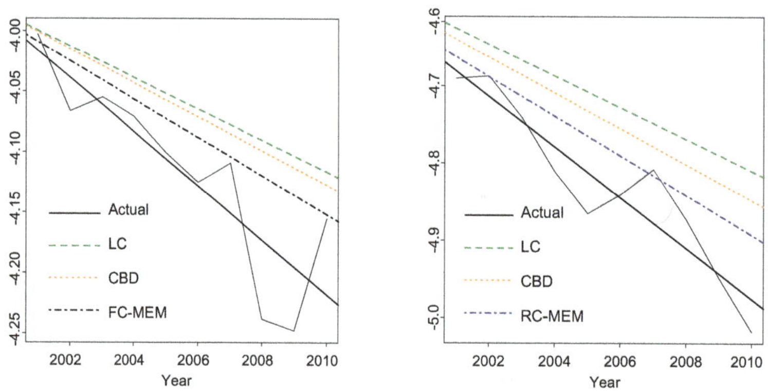

Model \ Trend	Intercept	Slope
Actual	−4.0028	−0.0225
LC	−3.9957	−0.0130
CBD	−3.9959	−0.0141
FC-MEM	−4.0023	−0.0159

Model \ Trend	Intercept	Slope
Actual	−4.6515	−0.0328
LC	−4.6084	−0.0205
CBD	−4.6198	−0.0232
RC-MEM	−4.6403	−0.0256

Figure 5. Intercept and slope estimates of logit $q(2000+h,x)$ for $h=1,\ldots,10$ and ages $x=66$ for males and $x=67$ for females, with credibility (dot-dashed lines for FC-MEM and RC-MEM) and without credibility (dashed lines for LC and dot lines for CBD). Solid lines show the actual mortality and its trend.

5.2. Applying the Bühlmann Credibility Approach

Tsai and Lin (2017a) proposed a Bühlmann credibility approach to forecast mortality rates for both genders in Japan, the United Kingdom and the United States. This model can be directly obtained from the more general regression model, presented in Section 3.3, if we set $\mathbf{Z}_x = \begin{pmatrix} 1 & 1 & \dots & 1 \end{pmatrix}'$ and $\mathbf{W}_x = \mathbf{I}$ for $x = x_0, \dots, x_{k-1}$. Then, from (27), $\boldsymbol{\beta}_x$ is equal to $\overline{\mathbf{Y}}_x$ and the model parameters, which are scalars now, can be estimated by

$$\widehat{s}^2 = \frac{1}{(x_{k-1} - x_0 + 1)(t_{n-1} - t_0)} \sum_{x=x_0}^{x_{k-1}} \sum_{t=t_0}^{t_{n-1}} \left(Y_{t,x} - \overline{Y}_x \right) , \tag{36}$$

$$\widehat{b} = \frac{1}{x_{k-1} - x_0 + 1} \sum_{x=x_0}^{x_{k-1}} \overline{\mathbf{Y}}_x = \frac{1}{(x_{k-1} - x_0 + 1)(t_{n-1} - t_0 + 1)} \sum_{x=x_0}^{x_{k-1}} \sum_{t=t_0}^{t_{n-1}} Y_{t,x} = \overline{Y} , \tag{37}$$

$$\widehat{u} = \frac{1}{x_{k-1} - x_0} \sum_{x=x_0}^{x_{k-1}} \left(\overline{\mathbf{Y}}_x - \overline{Y} \right) - \frac{\widehat{s}^2}{t_{n-1} - t_0 + 1} , \tag{38}$$

$$\widehat{K} = \left[(t_{n-1} - t_0 + 1) \, \widehat{u} \right] \left[\widehat{s}^2 + (t_{n-1} - t_0 + 1) \, \widehat{u} \right]^{-1} . \tag{39}$$

The Bühlmann credibility estimates for one year ahead can be obtained by

$$\widehat{Y}_{t_{n-1}+1,x} = \widehat{K} \, \overline{\mathbf{Y}}_x + (1 - \widehat{K}) \, \overline{Y}, \ \text{ for } x = x_0, \dots, x_{k-1} . \tag{40}$$

In contrast to the credibility regression approaches, which aim to capture the downward trend of $m(t,x)$s over t, for the Bühlmann credibility approach to be applied, this downward trend must be eliminated. For this reason, Tsai and Lin (2017a) applied the Bühlmann credibility model on the time series of mortality rate changes rather than the mortality rate levels, i.e., $Y_{t,x} = \log m(t,x) - \log m(t-1,x)$, for $t_1, \dots, t_{n-1}$. Then, they proposed two strategies for estimating $Y_{t+h,x}$, $h = 2, \dots, H$. The first strategy expands fitting window (EW) by one year, similarly with the EEM regression method, described in Section 4 and the second one moves fitting window (MW) by one year, similarly with the MEM regression method. In what follows, we compare the forecasting performance between the Bühlmann and the credibility regression methods on Greek data. To be consistent with the Bühlmann modelling framework of Tsai and Lin (2017a), age fitting spans [21, 85] and [56, 85] were selected and forecast errors were also evaluated under the averaged *MAPFE* values, which is defined by$MAPFE_{avg} = \frac{1}{H \times (x_{k-1} - x_0 + 1)} \sum_{h=1}^{H} \sum_{x=x_0}^{x_{k-1}} \frac{|\widehat{m}(t_{n-1}+h,x) - m(t_{n-1}+h,x)|}{|m(t_{n-1}+h,x)|} \times 100$.

Error values for each gender were evaluated by fitting $Y_{t,x}$s on [1982, 2000], [1986, 2000], and [1990, 2000] period spans. Comparison of averaged *MAFE*, *RMSFE* and *MAPFE*[4] results between Bühlmann and credibility regression methods is given for both genders in Table 4 (a)–(c) for ages [21, 85] and Table 5 (a)–(c) for ages [56, 85].

The results indicate that credibility regression methods produce the smallest *MAFE*, *RMSFE* and *MAPFE* values for the majority of the selected fitting periods for both age spans. More precisely, the FC-MEM method has the best average performance according to *MAFE* and *MAPFE* values for ages [21, 85], while the RC-MEM method seems to be more appropriate to capture future mortality trends for older ages [56, 85]. We note that the smallest values in average are produced by different regression methods, depending on which measure is used. Such inconsistencies are expected due to the nature of *MAFE*, *RMSFE* and *MAPFE* formulas. That was also pointed out by (Tsai and Yang 2015, p. 9).

[4] To distinguish one from the other, MAFE and *RMSFE* averaged error values are rounded to four decimal points, while, for *MAPFE* values, two decimal points are enough.

Table 4. *MAFE, RMSFE* and *MAPFE* values of forecast errors over the period [2001, 2010] for ages [21, 85].

(a) *MAFE* Values

$MAFE_{[21,85]}$		Bühlmann Methods		Regression Methods – RC			Regression Methods – FC		
Fitting Period	Gender	EW	MW	*SEM*	*MEM*	*EEM*	*SEM*	*MEM*	*EEM*
[1982, 2000]	Male	0.2348	0.2334	0.1404	0.1287	0.1379	0.1444	0.1361	0.1460
	Female	0.0930	0.0931	0.0816	0.0882	0.0843	0.0791	0.0780	0.0790
[1986, 2000]	Male	0.2170	0.2294	0.1329	0.1321	0.1306	0.1364	0.1358	0.1373
	Female	0.0918	0.0919	0.0782	0.0852	0.0909	0.0741	0.0805	0.0747
[1990, 2000]	Male	0.2355	0.2258	0.1399	0.1392	0.1369	0.1434	0.1422	0.1423
	Female	0.0954	0.0933	0.0836	0.0839	0.0879	0.0798	0.0818	0.0802
Average		0.1613(8)	0.1612(7)	0.1094(2)	0.1096(4)	0.1114(6)	0.1095(3)	0.1091(1)	0.1099(5)

(b) *RMSFE* Values

$RMSFE_{[21,85]}$		Bühlmann Methods		Regression Methods – RC			Regression Methods – FC		
Fitting Period	Gender	EW	MW	*SEM*	*MEM*	*EEM*	*SEM*	*MEM*	*EEM*
[1982, 2000]	Male	0.4980	0.4948	0.2633	0.2342	0.2566	0.2756	0.2564	0.2799
	Female	0.1795	0.1795	0.1613	0.1884	0.1730	0.1540	0.1581	0.1541
[1986, 2000]	Male	0.4584	0.4861	0.2447	0.2387	0.2386	0.2564	0.2532	0.2591
	Female	0.1767	0.1772	0.1633	0.1781	0.1999	0.1484	0.1643	0.1502
[1990, 2000]	Male	0.4997	0.4765	0.2578	0.2574	0.2472	0.2704	0.2666	0.2668
	Female	0.1849	0.1802	0.1640	0.1761	0.1767	0.1567	0.1674	0.1570
Average		0.3329(8)	0.3324(7)	0.2091(1)	0.2122(5)	0.2153(6)	0.2103(2)	0.2110(3)	0.2112(4)

(c) *MAPFE* Values

$MAPFE_{[21,85]}$		Bühlmann Methods		Regression Methods – RC			Regression Methods – FC		
Fitting Period	Gender	EW	MW	*SEM*	*MEM*	*EEM*	*SEM*	*MEM*	*EEM*
[1982, 2000]	Male	11.90	11.86	11.97	11.24	11.80	11.95	11.43	12.00
	Female	13.75	13.76	11.66	11.83	11.69	11.66	11.54	11.66
[1986, 2000]	Male	11.30	11.71	12.05	10.76	11.73	11.86	10.72	11.90
	Female	13.71	13.72	11.52	11.82	11.89	11.56	11.73	11.55
[1990, 2000]	Male	11.93	11.60	10.81	9.81	10.60	10.57	9.71	10.52
	Female	13.83	13.77	11.84	11.79	12.08	12.05	11.83	11.99
Average		12.73(7)	12.74(8)	11.64(6)	11.21(2)	11.63(5)	11.61(4)	11.16(1)	11.60(3)

Table 5. *MAFE, RMSFE* and *MAPFE* values of forecast errors over the period [2001, 2010] for ages [56, 85].

(a) *MAFE* Values

$MAFE_{[56,85]}$		Bühlmann Methods		Regression Methods – RC			Regression Methods – FC		
Fitting Period	Gender	EW	MW	*SEM*	*MEM*	*EEM*	*SEM*	*MEM*	*EEM*
[1982, 2000]	Male	0.3599	0.3503	0.3272	0.3012	0.3210	0.3262	0.3036	0.3255
	Female	0.1686	0.1623	0.1717	0.1633	0.1735	0.1711	0.1595	0.1709
[1986, 2000]	Male	0.3233	0.3430	0.2893	0.2958	0.2886	0.2946	0.2991	0.2937
	Female	0.1481	0.1539	0.1534	0.1601	0.1617	0.1495	0.1573	0.1511
[1990, 2000]	Male	0.3745	0.3641	0.2958	0.2934	0.2937	0.2999	0.2954	0.2973
	Female	0.1670	0.1646	0.1617	0.1616	0.1613	0.1601	0.1625	0.1615
Average		0.2569(8)	0.2564(7)	0.2332(3)	0.2293(1)	0.2333(4)	0.2336(6)	0.2296(2)	0.2334(5)

Table 5. *Cont.*

(b) *RMSFE* Values

$RMSFE_{[56,85]}$		Bühlmann Methods		Regression Methods – RC			Regression Methods – FC		
Fitting Period	Gender	EW	MW	*SEM*	*MEM*	*EEM*	*SEM*	*MEM*	*EEM*
[1982, 2000]	Male	0.5411	0.5261	0.4670	0.4213	0.4524	0.4700	0.4305	0.4679
	Female	0.2358	0.2282	0.2368	0.2242	0.2366	0.2389	0.2202	0.2381
[1986, 2000]	Male	0.4852	0.5159	0.4065	0.4138	0.3987	0.4221	0.4224	0.4185
	Female	0.2120	0.2178	0.2151	0.2235	0.2271	0.2089	0.2192	0.2107
[1990, 2000]	Male	0.5636	0.5472	0.4139	0.4130	0.4072	0.4291	0.4184	0.4195
	Female	0.2338	0.2307	0.2243	0.2246	0.2236	0.2217	0.2257	0.2232
Average		0.3786(8)	0.3777(7)	0.3273(4)	0.3201(1)	0.3243(3)	0.3318(6)	0.3227(2)	0.3297(5)

(c) *MAPFE* Values

$MAPFE_{[56,85]}$		Bühlmann Methods		Regression Methods – RC			Regression Methods – FC		
Fitting Period	Gender	EW	MW	*SEM*	*MEM*	*EEM*	*SEM*	*MEM*	*EEM*
[1982, 2000]	Male	9.53	9.34	9.48	9.17	9.54	9.29	8.97	9.31
	Female	9.93	9.72	9.98	9.81	10.36	9.65	9.43	9.69
[1986, 2000]	Male	8.82	9.20	8.78	8.97	8.99	8.61	8.85	8.66
	Female	9.23	9.45	9.14	9.42	9.62	8.84	9.26	8.98
[1990, 2000]	Male	9.82	9.61	8.85	8.74	9.00	8.62	8.74	8.78
	Female	9.88	9.81	9.49	9.33	9.46	9.32	9.37	9.48
Average		9.54(8)	9.52(7)	9.29(5)	9.24(4)	9.50(6)	9.06(1)	9.10(2)	9.15(3)

5.3. Application in Insurance-Related Products

In this section, we apply the mortality forecasts obtained from the Lee–Carter, the Cairns–Blake–Dowd and the credibility regression models to calculate life premiums, reflecting the appropriateness of each model in pricing applications. Denote $A^{1}_{t_{n-1}+1,x:\overline{K}|}$ as the fully discrete life insurance premium, payable at the end of the year of death, if it occurs within a term of K years and $A_{t_{n-1}+1,x:\overset{1}{\overline{K}|}}$ as the pure endowment, payable at the end of K years in case of being alive. Both products are issued to an insured aged x in year $t_{n-1}+1$. Net premiums (NP) are obtained (see Bozikas and Pitselis 2018) by

$$A^{1}_{t_{n-1}+1,x:\overline{K}|} = \sum_{k=0}^{K-1} {}_kp_{t_{n-1}+1,x} \cdot q(t_{n-1}+1+k, x+k) \,.\, (1+i)^{-(k+1)} \,, \tag{41}$$

$$A_{t_{n-1}+1,x:\overset{1}{\overline{K}|}} = {}_Kp_{t_{n-1}+1,x} \cdot (1+i)^{-K} \,, \tag{42}$$

where ${}_kp_{t_{n-1}+1,x}$ denotes the k-year survival probability for age x in year $t_{n-1}+1$, while its estimate is given by ${}_k\widehat{p}_{t_{n-1}+1,x} = \widehat{p}_{t_{n-1}+1,x} \cdot \ldots \cdot \widehat{p}_{t_{n-1}+1+k-1,x+k-1}$, $k = 1, \ldots, K-1$ and similarly for ${}_K\widehat{p}_{t_{n-1}+1,x}$, where i is the interest rate and ${}_0\widehat{p}_{t_{n-1}+1,x} = 1$. In addition, to see the performance on a life annuity product, typically used for pension applications, denote $\ddot{a}_{t_{n-1}+1,x:\overline{K}|}$ as the discrete life annuity-due at age x in year $t_{n-1}+1$, payable annually for up to K years. Its actuarial present value (APV) can be obtained by

$$\ddot{a}_{t_{n-1}+1,x:\overline{K}|} = \sum_{k=0}^{K-1} {}_kp_{t_{n-1}+1,x} \cdot (1+i)^{-k} \,. \tag{43}$$

Then, we apply the estimated mortality rates obtained from the LC, CBD and credibility methods, fitted to 1981–2000 rates, to calculate the NPs and APVs for ages 55–74 with $K = 10$, assuming $i = 4\%$.

The errors between forecasted values and those produced from the observed mortality rates for the years 2001–2010 are evaluated using *MAFE* and *RMSFE*, which are defined by

$$MAFE_{avg} = \frac{1}{20}\sum_{x=55}^{74}\left|\widehat{A}_{\substack{1\\2001,x:\overline{10}|}} - A_{\substack{1\\2001,x:\overline{10}|}}\right| \times 100\,, \tag{44}$$

$$RMSFE_{avg} = \sqrt{\frac{1}{20}\sum_{x=55}^{74}(\widehat{A}_{\substack{1\\2001,x:\overline{10}|}} - A_{\substack{1\\2001,x:\overline{10}|}})^2 \times 100}\,. \tag{45}$$

Similarly, *MAFE* and *RMSFE* formulas are adjusted for pure endowment or annuity products by replacing $A_{\substack{1\\t_{n-1}+1,x:\overline{K}|}}$ with $A_{\substack{\quad 1\\t_{n-1}+1,x:\overline{K}|}}$ or $\ddot{a}_{t_{n-1}+1,x:\overline{K}|}$ in Equations (44) and (45). Table 6 presents the averaged error values in ranking order for a 10 year forecasted life insurance, pure endowment and life annuity for both genders, aged 55–74 in 2001–2010. In addition, Figure 6 illustrates the absolute forecast error values against each corresponding age (AFE$_x$) for the top LC, CBD, RC and FC credibility regression methods for males and females, according to Table 6 values. For each model, AFE$_x$ is obtained from $AFE_x = \left|\widehat{A}_{\substack{1\\x,2001:\overline{10}|}} - A_{\substack{1\\x,2001:\overline{10}|}}\right| \times 100.$

Table 6. *MAFE* and *RMSFE* values (ranking order in brackets) for a 10-year forecasted life insurance, a pure endowment and a life annuity for males and females of ages 55–74 during 2001–2010.

(a) Life Insurance

$MAFE_{avg}$	Mortality Models				Random Coefficients (RC)			Fixed Coefficients (FC)		
Gender	LC	LC-Poisson	CBD	CBD-Poisson	*SEM*	*MEM*	*EEM*	*SEM*	*MEM*	*EEM*
Male	1.6019(8)	1.5640(7)	1.7151(10)	1.6794(9)	1.5000(6)	1.4169(2)	1.4924(5)	1.4735(3)	1.3932(1)	1.4741(4)
Female	1.0264(6)	1.0269(7)	1.2141(10)	1.1079(9)	1.0262(5)	0.9317(2)	1.0346(8)	0.9898(3)	0.8840(1)	0.9910(4)
$RMSFE_{avg}$	Mortality Models				Random Coefficients (RC)			Fixed Coefficients (FC)		
Gender	LC	LC-Poisson	CBD	CBD-Poisson	*SEM*	*MEM*	*EEM*	*SEM*	*MEM*	*EEM*
Male	1.8423(8)	1.8043(7)	1.9401(10)	1.9089(9)	1.7125(6)	1.6143(2)	1.7043(5)	1.6871(3)	1.5989(1)	1.6875(4)
Female	1.2320(8)	1.2294(7)	1.4023(10)	1.2918(9)	1.2133(5)	1.0965(2)	1.2215(6)	1.1744(3)	1.0494(1)	1.1756(4)

(b) Pure Endowment

$MAFE_{avg}$	Mortality Models				Random Coefficients (RC)			Fixed Coefficients (FC)		
Gender	LC	LC-Poisson	CBD	CBD-Poisson	*SEM*	*MEM*	*EEM*	*SEM*	*MEM*	*EEM*
Male	1.1439(8)	1.1139(7)	1.2417(10)	1.2044(9)	1.0722(6)	1.0153(2)	1.0681(5)	1.0512(3)	0.9942(1)	1.0518(4)
Female	0.7181(7)	0.7192(8)	0.8894(10)	0.7923(9)	0.7340(5)	0.6717(2)	0.7463(6)	0.7026(3)	0.6297(1)	0.7038(4)
$RMSFE_{avg}$	Mortality Models				Random Coefficients (RC)			Fixed Coefficients (FC)		
Gender	LC	LC-Poisson	CBD	CBD-Poisson	*SEM*	*MEM*	*EEM*	*SEM*	*MEM*	*EEM*
Male	1.3274(8)	1.2975(7)	1.4104(10)	1.3786(9)	1.2347(6)	1.1659(2)	1.2303(5)	1.2150(3)	1.1535(1)	1.2154(4)
Female	0.8745(8)	0.8717(7)	1.0310(10)	0.9319(9)	0.8774(5)	0.7968(2)	0.8889(6)	0.8440(3)	0.7552(1)	0.8451(4)

(c) Life Annuity

$MAFE_{avg}$	Mortality Models				Random Coefficients (RC)			Fixed Coefficients (FC)		
Gender	LC	LC-Poisson	CBD	CBD-Poisson	*SEM*	*MEM*	*EEM*	*SEM*	*MEM*	*EEM*
Male	5.4466(8)	5.2602(7)	6.3032(10)	5.7857(9)	5.1642(6)	4.9260(2)	5.1561(5)	5.0331(3)	4.7893(1)	5.0369(4)
Female	2.9140(7)	2.9361(8)	4.4471(10)	3.5932(9)	3.1527(5)	2.9479(2)	3.2151(6)	2.9656(3)	2.7024(1)	2.9721(4)
$RMSFE_{avg}$	Mortality Models				Random Coefficients (RC)			Fixed Coefficients (FC)		
Gender	LC	LC-Poisson	CBD	CBD-Poisson	*SEM*	*MEM*	*EEM*	*SEM*	*MEM*	*EEM*
Male	6.6138(7)	6.4342(8)	7.2583(10)	6.8729(9)	6.1786(6)	5.8730(2)	6.1608(5)	6.0681(3)	5.7919(1)	6.0704(4)
Female	3.7013(7)	3.7218(8)	5.1510(10)	4.3300(9)	3.9187(5)	3.6344(2)	3.9846(6)	3.7084(3)	3.3878(1)	3.7155(4)

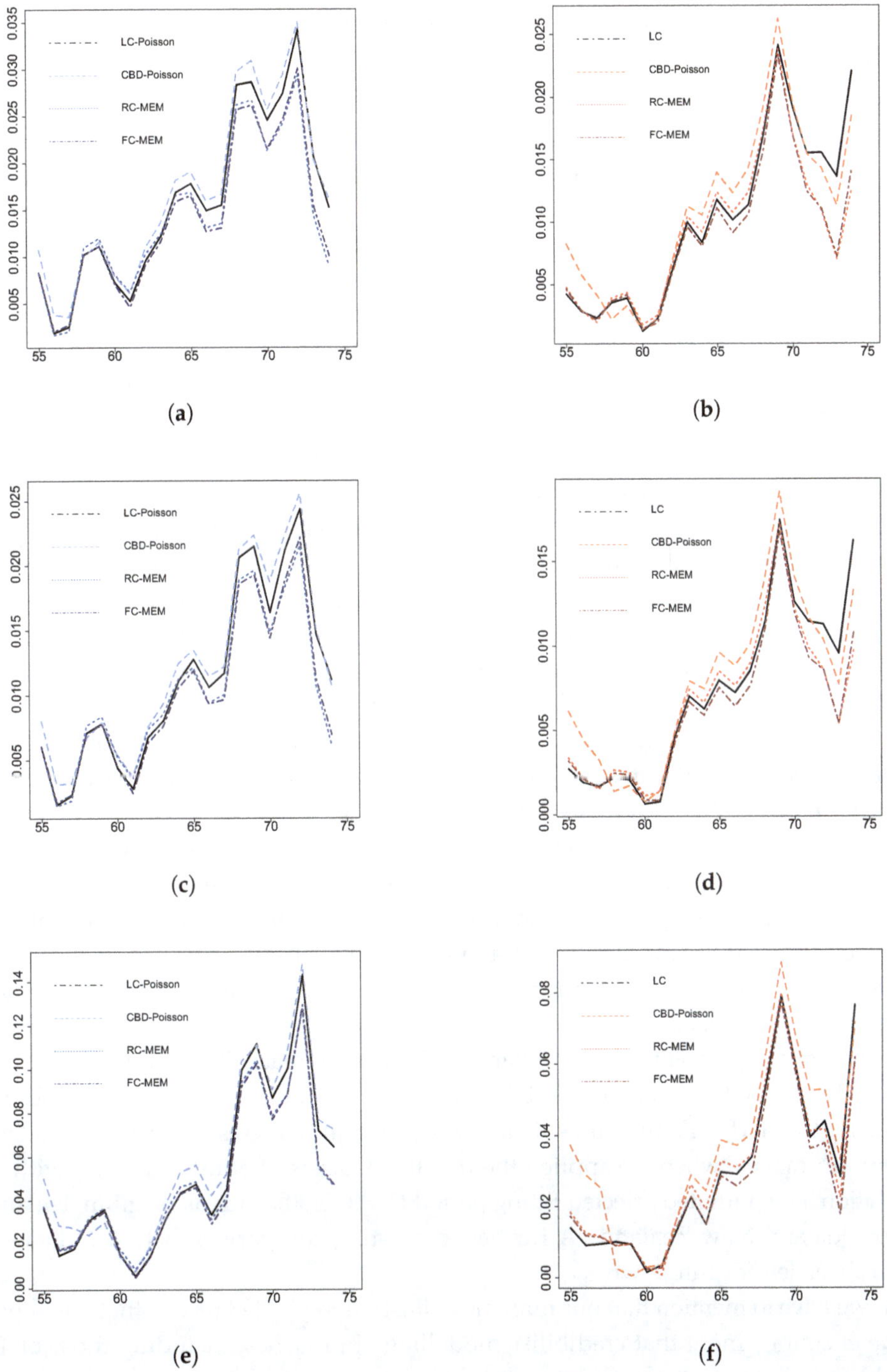

Figure 6. AFE values against age of life insurance and annuity products for the top LC, CBD and credibility regression models for males (left panels) and females (right panels): (**a**) life insurance AFEs for males; (**b**) life insurance AFEs for females; (**c**) pure endowment AFEs for males; (**d**) pure endowment AFEs for females; (**e**) life annuity AFEs for males; and (**f**) life annuity AFEs for females.

According to *MAFE* and *RMSFE* values for both genders and insurance products in Table 6, credibility regression models produce better insurance-related forecasts in comparison with the LC and CBD modelling methods. We can easily observe that for each gender, error measures coincide in the same ranking order for all insurance products. In particular, measures show that credibility regression methods under a moving fitting span outperform LC and CBD methods in aggregate, with FC-MEM being dominant and RC-MEM following. This fact is also evident in Figure 6, where absolute error values against age for the MEM regression models lie on the lower levels for all the insurance products. Nevertheless, the FC-SEM should also be a good modelling choice for pricing insurance-related products.

6. Concluding Remarks

Credibility regression techniques seem to be of special interest and particularly useful for mortality datasets of a relatively short historical period of observations (limited data), as they can efficiently capture the underlying mortality trend for a given age, using all the information gained from populations of other ages. This paper proposes mortality modelling approaches embedded, for the first time, in a credibility regression framework. In our illustration on Greek data, credibility regression approaches resulted in better forecasts for both genders (in terms of *MAFE* and *RMSFE* measures), compared to the Lee–Carter and Cairns–Blake–Dowd models, as well as the Bühlmann credibility approach (Tsai and Lin 2017a). Finally, their performance was also evaluated on insurance-related applications.

Specifically, in Section 3, we proposed a credibility regression mortality framework with randomly varying coefficients and a special case with fixed coefficients. To estimate future mortality rates, we presented extrapolation methods for each credibility approach in Section 4. The applicability of our modelling approaches was comparatively illustrated on Greek male and female data in Section 5, accompanied with an explanation of the credibility effects in mortality modelling and a pricing application on insurance-related products. From our analysis, we concluded that, in aggregate, credibility modelling methods performed better than the LC and CBD methods. Forecasting accuracy results indicate that, for the whole age fitting span, fixed coefficients credibility methods performed better on average, while, for higher ages, the RC-MEM should also be a good choice. In addition, the FC-MEM performed a bit better in aggregate on pricing insurance-related products.

Furthermore, we noted that FC-SEM credibility forecasts were closer to observed rates for the same periods, when we used population exposure to risk as weights, i.e., $W_x = \text{diag}\left[E(t_0, x), \ldots, E(t_{n-1}, x)\right]$, for $x = x_0, \ldots, x_{k-1}$, but weighted regression is restricted for use only under the SEM, as $E(t, x)$s are practically unknown for the upcoming years. Additionally, during the estimation procedure for the random regression models, we observed that, if we use the MINQUE estimator (Remark 2) instead of (20), error values for all the credibility modelling methods become even smaller for both genders.

For the sake of comparability, the Bühlmann credibility approach (Tsai and Lin 2017a) was applied on our dataset in Section 5, where the credibility regression methods resulted to better forecasts based on *MAFE*, *RMSFE* and *MAPFE* measures. In addition, credibility regression methods had a very good forecasting performance, when we applied them to the datasets of other countries (with a relatively small population[5]) for a limited selected fitting period (1980–2000), such as Belgium, Finland, Norway, Ireland, Slovakia and New Zealand. A further forecasting comparison between datasets of other countries has been left for future work.

Finally, we have to mention that our numerical illustration yielded results that are fully applicable and provide encouragement that credibility modelling approaches, including those of Tsai (2017a, 2017b), could contribute to future mortality projection studies.

Author Contributions: The authors contributed equally to this work.

Funding: This research received no external funding.

Acknowledgments: Part of this work was presented at the 10th Conference in Actuarial Science & Finance on Samos. The first author acknowledges the financial support from the Hellenic Foundation for Research and Innovation (HFRI) and the General Secretariat for Research and Technology (GSRT), under the HFRI PhD Fellowship grant (GA. no. 1286). The second author acknowledges the partial support from the University of Piraeus Research Center.

---

[5] According to the World Bank database (https://data.worldbank.org/indicator/SP.POP.TOTL), total population counts for 2016 were 11.35 million for Belgium, 5.50 for Finland, 5.23 for Norway, 4.77 for Ireland, 5.43 for Slovakia and 4.69 for New Zealand.

Conflicts of Interest: The authors declare no conflict of interest.

References

Bozikas, Apostolos, and Georgios Pitselis. 2018. An Empirical Study on Stochastic Mortality Modelling under the Age-Period-Cohort Framework: The Case of Greece with Applications to Insurance Pricing. *Risks* 6: 44. [CrossRef]

Brouhns, Natacha, Michel Denuit, and Jeroen K. Vermunt. 2002. A Poisson log-bilinear regression approach to the construction of projected lifetables. *Insurance: Mathematics and Economics* 31: 373–93. [CrossRef]

Bühlmann, Hans. 1967. Experience Rating and Credibility. *ASTIN Bulletin* 4: 199–207. [CrossRef]

Bühlmann, Hans, and Alois Gisler. 2005. *A Course in Credibility Theory and Its Applications.* Berlin and Heidelberg: Springer.

Cairns, Andrew J. G., David Blake, and Kevin Dowd. 2006. A two-factor model for stochastic mortality with parameter uncertainty: Theory and calibration. *Journal of Risk and Insurance* 73: 687–718. [CrossRef]

Cairns, Andrew J. G., David Blake, Kevin Dowd, Guy D. Coughlan, David Epstein, Alen Ong, and Igor Balevich. 2009. A quantitative comparison of stochastic mortality models using data from England and Wales and the United States. *North American Actuarial Journal* 13: 1–35. [CrossRef]

De Vylder, F. Etienne. 1978. Parameter estimation in credibility theory. *ASTIN Bulletin* 10: 99–112. [CrossRef]

Gong, Maxwell, Zhuangdi Li, Maria Milazzo, Kristen Moore, and Matthew Provencher. 2018. Credibility Methods for Individual Life Insurance. *Risks* 6: 144. [CrossRef]

Goovaerts, Marc. J., Rob Kaas, A. E. Van Heerwaarden, and T. Bauwelinckx. 1990. *Effective Actuarial Methods.* Amsterdam: North-Holland.

Greene, William H. 2012. *Econometric Analysis,* International ed. London: Pearson Education Limited.

Hachemeister, Charles. 1975. Credibility for Regression Models with Application to Trend (Reprint). In *Credibility: Theory and Applications.* Edited by P. Kahn. New York: Academic Press, Inc., pp. 307–48.

Hansen, Hendrik. 2013. The forecasting performance of mortality models. *AStA Advances in Statistical Analysis* 97: 11–31. [CrossRef]

Hardy, M. R., and H. H. Panjer. 1998. A credibility approach to mortality risk. *Astin Bulletin* 28: 269–83. [CrossRef]

Hildreth, Clifford, and James P. Houck. 1968. Some Estimators for a Linear Model with Random Coefficients. *Journal of the American Statistical Association* 63: 584–95.

Hsiao, Cheng. 1986. Analysis of Panel Data. In *Econometric Society Monographs.* New York: Cambridge University Press.

Huang, Fei, and Bridget Browne. 2017. Mortality forecasting using a modified Continuous Mortality Investigation Mortality Projections Model for China I: Methodology and country-level results. *Annals of Actuarial Science* 11: 20–45. [CrossRef]

Human Mortality Database. 2017. University of California, Berkeley (USA) and Max Planck Institute for Demographic Research (Germany). Available online: www.mortality.org (accessed on 20 April 2018).

Klugman, Stuart A., Harry H. Panjer, and Gordon E. Willmot. 2012. *Loss Models: From Data to Decisions*, 4th ed. New York: John Wiley & Sons.

Lee, Ronald D., and Lawrence R. Carter. 1992. Modeling and Forecasting U.S. Mortality. *Journal of the American Statistical Association* 87: 659–71. [CrossRef]

Ledolter, Johannes, Stuart Klugman, and Chang-Soo Lee. 1991. Credibility models with time-varying trend components. *Astin Bulletin* 21: 73–91. [CrossRef]

Li, Hong, and Yang Lu. 2018. A Bayesian non-parametric model for small population mortality. *Scandinavian Actuarial Journal* 2018: 605–28. [CrossRef]

Li, Nan, Ronald Lee, and Shripad Tuljapurkar. 2004. Using the Lee–Carter Method to Forecast Mortality for Populations with Limited Data. *International Statistical Review* 72: 19–36. [CrossRef]

Luan, Xiang. 2015. *A Pseudo Non-Parametric Buhlmann Credibility Approach to Modeling Mortality Rates.* Master's thesis, Department of Statistics and Actuarial Science, Simon Fraser University, Burnaby, BC, Canada.

Norberg, Ragnar. 1980. Empirical bayes credibility. *Scandinavian Actuarial Journal* 1980: 177–94. [CrossRef]

Pitselis, Georgios. 2004. Credibility models with cross-section effect and with both cross-section and time effects. *Blätter der DGVFM* 26: 643–63. [CrossRef]

Plat, Richard. 2009. On stochastic mortality modeling. *Insurance: Mathematics and Economics* 45: 393–404.

R Core Team. 2017. *A Language and Environment for Statistical Computing*. Vienna: R Foundation for Statistical Computing. Available online: https://www.r-project.org/ (accessed on 10 February 2018).

Rao, C. Radhakrishna. 1973. *Linear Statistical Inference and Its Applications*, 2nd ed. New York: Wiley.

Renshaw, Arthur E., and Steven Haberman. 2006. A cohort-based extension to the Lee-Carter model for mortality reduction factors. *Insurance: Mathematics and Economics* 38: 556–70. [CrossRef]

Salhi, Yahia, Pierre-E. Thérond, and Julien Tomas. 2016. A credibility approach of the Makeham mortality law. *European Actuarial Journal* 6: 61–96. [CrossRef]

Salhi, Yahia, and Pierre-E. Thérond. 2018. Age-Specific Adjustment of Graduated Mortality. *ASTIN Bulletin* 48: 543–69. [CrossRef]

Schinzinger, Edo, Michel M. Denuit, and Marcus C. Christiansen. 2016. A multivariate evolutionary credibility model for mortality improvement rates. *Insurance: Mathematics and Economics* 69: 70–81. [CrossRef]

Shang, Han Lin, Heather Booth, and Rob J. Hyndman. 2011. Point and interval forecasts of mortality rates and life expectancy: A comparison of ten principal component methods. *Demographic Research* 25: 173–214. [CrossRef]

Tsai, Cary Chi-Liang, and Tzuling Lin. 2017a. A Bühlmann credibility approach to modeling mortality rates. *North American Actuarial Journal* 21: 204–27. [CrossRef]

Tsai, Cary Chi-Liang, and Tzuling Lin. 2017b. Incorporating the Bühlmann credibility into mortality models to improve forecasting performances. *Scandinavian Actuarial Journal* 2017: 419–40. [CrossRef]

Tsai, Cary Chi-Liang, and Shuai Yang. 2015. A Linear Regression Approach to Modeling Mortality Rates of Different Forms. *North American Actuarial Journal* 19: 1–23. [CrossRef]

Van Berkum, Frank, Katrien Antonio, and Michel Vellekoop. 2016. The impact of multiple structural changes on mortality predictions. *Scandinavian Actuarial Journal* 2016: 581–603. [CrossRef]

Zhao, Bojuan Barbara. 2012. A modified Lee-Carter model for analysing short-base-period data. *Population Studies* 66: 39–52. [CrossRef] [PubMed]

8

The $W, Z/\nu, \delta$ Paradigm for the First Passage of Strong Markov Processes without Positive Jumps

Florin Avram [1,*], **Danijel Grahovac** [2] **and Ceren Vardar-Acar** [3]

1 Laboratoire de Mathématiques Appliquées, Université de Pau, 64012 Pau, France
2 Department of Mathematics, University of Osijek, 31000 Osijek, Croatia; dgrahova@mathos.hr
3 Department of Statistics, Middle East Technical University, Ankara 06800, Turkey; cvardar@metu.edu.tr
* Correspondence: florin.avram@univ-Pau.fr

Abstract: As is well-known, the benefit of restricting Lévy processes without positive jumps is the "W, Z scale functions paradigm", by which the knowledge of the scale functions W, Z extends immediately to other risk control problems. The same is true largely for strong Markov processes X_t, with the notable distinctions that (a) it is more convenient to use as "basis" differential exit functions ν, δ, and that (b) it is not yet known how to compute ν, δ or W, Z beyond the Lévy, diffusion, and a few other cases. The unifying framework outlined in this paper suggests, however, via an example that the spectrally negative Markov and Lévy cases are very similar (except for the level of work involved in computing the basic functions ν, δ). We illustrate the potential of the unified framework by introducing a new objective (33) for the optimization of dividends, inspired by the de Finetti problem of maximizing expected discounted cumulative dividends until ruin, where we replace ruin with an optimally chosen Azema-Yor/generalized draw-down/regret/trailing stopping time. This is defined as a hitting time of the "draw-down" process $Y_t = \sup_{0 \le s \le t} X_s - X_t$ obtained by reflecting X_t at its maximum. This new variational problem has been solved in a parallel paper.

Keywords: first passage; drawdown process; spectrally negative process; scale functions; dividends; de Finetti valuation objective; variational problem

---

1. A Brief Review of First Passage Theory for Strong Markov Processes without Positive Jumps and Their Draw-Downs

Motivation. First passage times intervene in the control of reserves/risk processes. The rough idea is that when below low levels a, the reserves should be replenished at some cost, and when above high levels b, the reserves should be invested to yield dividends—see for example Albrecher and Asmussen (2010). There is a wide variety of first passage control problems (involving absorption, reflection and other boundary mechanisms), and it has been known for a long while that these problems are simpler in the "completely asymmetric" case when all jumps go in the same direction. In recent years it has become clearer that most first passage problems can be reduced to the two basic problems of going up before down, or vice versa, and that their answers may usually be ergonomically expressed in terms of two basic "scale functions" W, Z (Albrecher et al. (2016); Avram et al. (2004, 2007, 2015, 2017a, 2017b, 2018a, 2018b); Avram and Zhou (2017); Bertoin (1997); Ivanovs and Palmowski (2012); Kyprianou (2014); Landriault et al. (2017b); Li et al. (2017); Li and Zhou (2018); Suprun (1976)). The proofs require typically not much more than the strong Markov property; it is natural, therefore, to develop extensions to strong Markov processes. This has been achieved already in particular spectrally negative cases such as random walks Avram and Vidmar (2017), Markov additive processes Ivanovs and Palmowski (2012), Lévy processes with Ω state-dependent killing Ivanovs and Palmowski (2012), certain Lévy processes with state-dependent drift Czarna et al. (2017), and is in fact possible in general.

However, characterizing the functions W, Z is still an open problem, even for simple classic processes such as the Ornstein-Uhlenbeck and the Feller branching diffusion with jumps.

Let X_t denote a one-dimensional strong Markov process without positive jumps, defined on a filtered probability space $(\Omega, \{\mathcal{F}_t\}_{t\geq 0}, \mathbb{P})$. Denote its first passage times above and below by

$$T_{b,+} = T_{b,+}(X) = \inf\{t \geq 0 : X_t > b\}, \quad T_{a,-} = T_{a,-}(X) = \inf\{t \geq 0 : X_t < a\},$$

with $\inf \emptyset = +\infty$.

Recall that first passage theory for diffusions and spectrally negative or spectrally positive Lévy processes is considerably simpler than that for processes which may jump both ways. For these two families, a large variety of first passage problems may be reduced to the computation of two monotone "scale functions" W, Z (by simple arguments such as the strong Markov property). See Albrecher et al. (2016); Avram et al. (2004, 2007, 2015, 2017a, 2018a); Avram and Zhou (2017); Bertoin (1997); Ivanovs and Palmowski (2012); Li and Zhou (2018); Suprun (1976) for the introduction and applications of W, Z in the Lévy case. For diffusions, the most convenient basic functions are the monotone solutions φ_+, φ_- of the Sturm-Liouville equation—see Borovkov (2012). Finally, for spectrally negative or spectrally positive Lévy processes and diffusions, off-shelf computer programs could easily produce the answer to a large variety of problems, once approximations for the basic functions associated with the process have been produced. This continues to be true in principle for non-homogeneous Markov processes with one-sided jumps (by a simple application of the strong Markov property at the smooth crossing exit from an interval). However, there are very few papers proposing methods to compute W, Z for non-Lévy processes (see though Czarna et al. (2017), and Jacobsen and Jensen (2007), where the case of Ornstein-Uhlenbeck processes with phase-type jumps is studied).

The two sided exit functions. The most important first passage functions are the solutions of the two-sided upward and downward exit problems from a bounded interval $[a, b]$:

$$\begin{cases} \overline{\Psi}^b_{q,\theta}(x,a) := \mathbb{E}_x \left[e^{-qT_{b,+} - \theta(X_{T_{b,+}} - b)} 1_{\{T_{b,+} < T_{a,-}\}} \right] \\ \Psi^b_{q,\theta}(x,a) := \mathbb{E}_x \left[e^{-qT_{a,-} + \theta(X_{T_{a,-}} - a)} 1_{\{T_{a,-} < T_{b,+}\}} \right] \end{cases} \quad q,\ \theta \geq 0,\ a \leq x \leq b. \tag{1}$$

We will also call them killed survival and ruin first passage probabilities, respectively. Note that these are functions of five variables, very hard to compute in general. For processes with one-sided jumps, one of the exits must be smooth (without overshoot); in this case, the parameter θ is unnecessary and will be omitted. Also, when $a = 0$, it will be omitted, to simplify the notation.

For diffusions and Lévy processes with one-sided jumps, the two sided exit functions have well-known explicit formulas.

For spectrally negative Lévy processes, the simplest is the smooth survival probability, whose factors are:

$$\overline{\Psi}^b_q(x,a) = \frac{W_q(x-a)}{W_q(b-a)} = e^{-\int_x^b \nu_q(s-a)ds}. \tag{2}$$

$W_q(x)$ is called the scale function Bertoin (1998); Suprun (1976)[1]. We will assume throughout that W_q is differentiable (see Chan et al. (2011) for information on the smoothness of scale functions). Then, $\nu_q(s) = \frac{W_q'(s)}{W_q(s)}$ is the logarithmic derivative of W_q, and may be interpreted as the "survival function of excursions lengths" Bertoin (1998). The non-smooth ruin probability has a more complicated explicit formula involving a second scale function Z_q Avram et al. (2004)—see Remark 1 below.

[1] The fact that the survival probability has the multiplicative structure (2) is equivalent to the absence of positive jumps, by the strong Markov property.

The draw-down/regret/loss/process. Motivated by applications in statistics, mathematical finance and risk theory, there has been increased interest recently in the study of the running maximum and of the draw-down/regret/loss/process reflected at the maximum, defined by

$$Y_t = \overline{X}_t - X_t, \quad \overline{X}_t := \sup_{0 \le t' \le t} X_s.$$

Of equal interest is the infimum, and the draw-up/gain/process reflected at the infimum, defined by

$$\underline{Y}_t = X_t - \underline{X}_t, \quad \underline{X}_t = \inf_{0 \le t' \le t} X_s.$$

See Landriault et al. (2015, 2017a); Mijatovic and Pistorius (2012) for references to the numerous applications of draw-downs and draw-ups.

Draw-down and draw-up times are first passage times for the reflected processes:

$$\begin{aligned} \tau_d &:= \inf\{t \ge 0 : \overline{X}_t - X_t > d\}, \\ \underline{\tau}_d &:= \inf\{t \ge 0 : X_t - \underline{X}_t > d\},\ d > 0. \end{aligned} \tag{3}$$

Such times turn out to be optimal in several stopping problems, in statistics Page (1954) in mathematical finance/risk theory—see for example Avram et al. (2004); Carr (2014); Lehoczky (1977); Shepp and Shiryaev (1993); Taylor (1975)—and in queueing. More specifically, they figure in risk theory problems involving capital injections or dividends at a fixed boundary, and idle times until a buffer reaches capacity in queueing theory.

Remark 1. *The second scale function Z Avram et al. (2004); Ivanovs and Palmowski (2012); Pistorius (2004) useful for solving the spectrally negative non-smooth ruin probability (and many other problems) is best defined via the solution of the non-smooth total discounted "regulation" problem.*

Let $X_t^{[0} = X_t + L_t$ denote the process X_t modified by Skorohod reflection at 0, with regulator $L_t = -\underline{X}_t$, let $E_x^{[0}$ denote expectation for this process and let

$$T_b^{[0} = T_{b,+} \mathbb{1}_{\{T_{b,+} < T_{0,-}\}} + \underline{\tau}_b \mathbb{1}_{\{T_{0,-} < T_{b,+}\}} \tag{4}$$

denote the first passage to b of $X_t^{[0}$.

(a) The Laplace transform of the total regulation ("capital injections/bailouts") into the process reflected non-smoothly at 0, until the first smooth up-crossing of a level b, may be factored as (Ivanovs and Palmowski 2012, Thm. 2):

$$\mathbb{E}_x^{[0}\left[e^{-qT_b^{[0}-\theta L_{T_b^{[0}}}\right] = \begin{cases} \dfrac{Z_{q,\theta}(x)}{Z_{q,\theta}(b)}, & \theta < \infty \\ \mathbb{E}_x\left[e^{-qT_b^{[0}}; T_{b,+} < T_{0,-}\right] = \dfrac{W_q(x)}{W_q(b)}, & \theta = \infty \end{cases}, \tag{5}$$

with $Z_{q,\theta}(x)$ determined up to a multiplying constant.

(b) Decomposing (5) *at $\min(T_b^+, T_{0,-})$ yields a formula* (1) *for the ruin probability Ivanovs and Palmowski (2012). Indeed:*

$$\mathbb{E}_x^{[0}\left[e^{-qT_b^{[0}-\theta L_{T_b^{[0}}}\right] = \frac{Z_{q,\theta}(x)}{Z_{q,\theta}(b)} = \frac{W_q(x)}{W_q(b)} + \mathbb{E}_x\left[e^{-qT_{0,-}+\theta X_{T_{0,-}}}; T_{0,-} < T_{b,+}\right] \frac{Z_{q,\theta}(0)}{Z_{q,\theta}(b)} \Longrightarrow \tag{6}$$

$$\Psi_{q,\theta}^b(x) Z_{q,\theta}(0) = \mathbb{E}_x\left[e^{-qT_{0,-}+\theta X_{T_{0,-}}}; T_{0,-} < T_{b,+}\right] Z_{q,\theta}(0) = Z_{q,\theta}(x) - W_q(x) W_q(b)^{-1} Z_{q,\theta}(b). \tag{7}$$

To simplify this formula, it is customary to choose $Z_{q,\theta}(0) = 1$.

For non-homogeneous spectrally negative Markov processes, it is possible Avram et al. (2017a) to extend the equalities (2), (7) to analogue expressions involving scale functions of two variables

$$\overline{\Psi}_q^b(x,a) = \frac{W_q(x,a)}{W_q(b,a)}, \qquad \Psi_{q,\theta}^b(x,a) = Z_{q,\theta}(x,a) - W_q(x,a)W_q(b,a)^{-1}Z_{q,\theta}(b,a). \tag{8}$$

However, it is simpler to start, following Landriault et al. (2017b), with differential versions, whose existence will be assumed throughout this paper.

Assumption 1. *For all $q,\theta \geq 0$ and $y \leq x$ fixed, assume that $\overline{\Psi}_q^b(x,y)$ and $\Psi_{q,\theta}^b(x,y)$ are differentiable in b at $b = x$, and in particular that the following limits exist:*

$$\nu_q(x,y) := \lim_{\varepsilon \downarrow 0} \frac{1 - \overline{\Psi}_q^{x+\varepsilon}(x,y)}{\varepsilon} \tag{9}$$

and

$$\delta_{q,\theta}(x,y) := \lim_{\varepsilon \downarrow 0} \frac{\Psi_{q,\theta}^{x+\varepsilon}(x,y)}{\varepsilon} \tag{10}$$

Remark 2. *A necessary condition for Assumption 1 to hold is that X is upward regular and creeping upward at every x in the state space—see (Landriault et al. 2017b, Rem. 3.1). Within this class, it seems difficult to provide examples where Assumption 1 is not satisfied.*

It turns out that the differentiability of the two-sided ruin and survival probabilities as functions of the upper limit provides a method for computing other first passage quantities; for example, (12) and (23) below may be computed by solving the first order ODE's in Theorem 2. Informally, we may say that the pillar of first passage theory for spectrally negative Markov processes is proving the existence of ν, δ.

In the Lévy case note that by (2) $\nu_q(x,y) = \frac{W_q'(x-y)}{W_q(x-y)} = \nu_q(x-y)$, and $\delta_{q,\theta}(x,y) = \delta_{q,\theta}(x-y)$ where Avram et al. (2017a)

$$\delta_{q,\theta}(x) := Z_{q,\theta}(x) - W_q(x)\frac{Z_{q,\theta}'(x)}{W_q'(x)}. \tag{11}$$

Remark 3. *For diffusions, $W_q(x,a)$ is a certain Wronskian–see for example Borovkov (2012). Also, for Langevin type processes with decreasing state-dependent drifts, $W_q(x,a)$ solves a certain renewal equation Czarna et al. (2017). The case of Ornstein-Uhlenbeck/Segerdahl-Tichy processes with exponential jumps is currently under study in Avram and Garmendia (2019). Some information about the generalization to Ornstein-Uhlenbeck processes with phase-type jumps can be found in Jacobsen and Jensen (2007). Beyond that, computing $W_q(x,a)$ or $\nu_q(x,a)$ is an open problem. This is an important problem, and we conjecture that the method of Jacobsen and Jensen (2007) may be extended, at least to affine diffusions with phase-type jumps, and possibly to all diffusions with phase-type jumps.*

The drawdown exit functions. Recently, control results with drawdown times τ_d replacing classic first passage times started being investigated—see for example Landriault et al. (2017a); Mijatovic and Pistorius (2012). Two natural objects of interest for studying τ_d are the two sided exit times

$$T_{b+,d} = \min(\tau_d, T_{b,+}), \qquad T_{a-,d} = \min(\tau_d, T_{a,-}).$$

In terms of the two-dimensional process $t \mapsto (X_t, Y_t)$, these are the first exit times from the regions $(-\infty, b] \times [0,d]$ and $[a,\infty) \times [0,d]$.

Fundamental in the study of say $T_{b+,d}$ are the following two Laplace transforms UbD/DbU (up-crossing before draw-down/draw-down before up-crossing), which are analogues of the killed survival and ruin probabilities :

$$\begin{aligned} UbD^b_{q,\theta,d}(x) &= \mathbb{E}_x\left[e^{-qT_{b,+}-\theta(X_{T_{b,+}}-b)};T_{b,+}<\tau_d\right] = \mathbb{E}_x\left[e^{-qT_{b,+}-\theta(X_{T_{b,+}}-b)};\overline{X}_{\tau_d}>b\right] \\ DbU^b_{q,\theta,d}(x) &= \mathbb{E}_x\left[e^{-q\tau_d-\theta(Y_{\tau_d}-d)};\tau_d<T_{b,+}\right] = \mathbb{E}_x\left[e^{-q\tau_d-\theta(Y_{\tau_d}-d)};\overline{X}_{\tau_d}<b\right]. \end{aligned} \tag{12}$$

For spectrally negative Lévy processes, these have again simple formulas:

1.
$$UbD^b_{q,d}(x) := \mathbb{E}_x\left[e^{-qT_{b,+}};T_{b,+}\le\tau_d\right] = e^{-(b-x)\frac{W_q'(d)}{W_q(d)}}, \tag{13}$$

2. The function DbU may be obtained by integrating the fundamental law (Mijatovic and Pistorius 2012, Thm 1), (Landriault et al. 2017a, Thm 3.1)[2]

$$\begin{aligned} \delta_{q,\theta}(d,x,s) &:= \mathbb{E}_x\left[e^{-q\tau_d-\theta(Y_{\tau_d}-d)};\overline{X}_{\tau_d}\in ds\right] = \left(\nu_q(d)\,e^{-\nu_q(d)(s-x)_+}\,ds\right)\delta_{q,\theta}(d) \\ \Leftrightarrow \mathbb{E}_x\left[e^{-q\tau_d-\theta(Y_{\tau_d}-d)-\vartheta(\overline{X}_{\tau_d}-x)}\right] &= \frac{\nu_q(d)}{\vartheta+\nu_q(d)}\delta_{q,\theta}(d) \end{aligned} \tag{14}$$

where $\delta_{q,\theta}(d)$ is given by (11). Integrating yields

$$DbU^b_{q,\theta,d}(x) = \left(1-e^{-(b-x)\frac{W_q'(d)}{W_q(d)}}\right)\delta_{q,\theta}(d). \tag{15}$$

Remark 4. *The probabilistic interpretation of ν_q, the logarithmic derivative of W_q. Taking $a=0$ for simplicity, the last formula in (2) has the interesting interpretation as the probability that no arrival has occurred between times x and b, for a non-homogeneous Poisson process of rate $\nu_q(s), s\in[x,b]$. Alternatively, differentiating (2) yields*

$$\frac{d}{ds}\overline{\Psi}^b_q(s)-\nu_q(s)\overline{\Psi}^b_q(s)=0, \qquad \overline{\Psi}^b_q(b)=1. \tag{16}$$

This equation coincides the Kolmogorov equation for the probability that a deterministic process $\widetilde{Y}_s=s$, killed at rate $\nu_q(s)$, reaches b before killing, when starting at s. It turns out, by excursion theory, that such a process $\widetilde{Y}_s$ may be constructed by excising the negative excursions from X_t, and by taking the running maximum s as time parameter.

The logarithmic derivative $\nu_q(s)$ will be needed below in the de Finetti problem (17), where we will use the fact that the expected dividends $v_q(b)$ paid at a fixed barrier b, starting from b, equal the expected discounted time until killing, which is exponential with parameter $\nu_q(b)$, being therefore simply the reciprocal of the killing parameter $\nu_q(b)$:

$$v_q(b) := \mathbb{E}_b\left[\int_0^{T^{b]}_{0,-}} e^{-qt}d(\overline{X}_t-b)\right] = \nu_q(b)^{-1}. \tag{17}$$

---

2 Please note that (Mijatovic and Pistorius 2012, Thm. 1) give a more complicated "sextuple law" with two cases, and that (Landriault et al. 2017a, Thm 3.1) use an alternative to the function $Z_q(x,\theta)$, so that some computing is required to get (11) and (14).

We see in the equation above and others that ν_q may serve as a convenient alternative characteristic of a spectrally negative Markov process, replacing W_q. Just as W_q, it may be extended to the case of generalized drawdown killing introduced in Avram et al. (2017b); Li et al. (2017).

Contents. We start in Section 2 by presenting a pedagogic first passage example illustrating the W, Z paradigm: the first time

$$T_R = T_{a,b,d} = T_{a,-} \wedge T_{b,+} \wedge \tau_d. \tag{18}$$

when (X, Y) with X Lévy leaves a rectangular region $R = [a, b] \times [0, d]$.

Remark 5. *Please note that letting $a \to -\infty, b \to \infty$ reduces $T_{a,b,d}$ to τ_d, and letting $d \to \infty, b \to \infty$ reduces $T_{a,b,d}$ to $T_{a,-}$. Hence both classic first passage and drawdown times appear as special cases of $T_{a,b,d}$. For finite a, b, d, our region has two classic and one drawdown exit boundary.*[3]

In Section 3 we provide geometric considerations which reduce computations of the Laplace transforms of the "three-sided" exit times of (X, Y) to that of Laplace transforms of two-sided exit problems involving $T_{a,-}$, $T_{b,+}$ and τ_d (like (1) and (12))—see Figure 1.

Only the strong Markov property is used; however, for the sake of simple notations we restricted the exposition to the family of Lévy processes (which have also the convenient feature that the scale functions W, Z may be computed by inverting Laplace transforms Avram et al. (2004, 2015); Bertoin (1998); Ivanovs and Palmowski (2012); Kyprianou (2014)).

In Section 4 we enlarge the framework to that of generalized drawdown times Avram et al. (2017b); Li et al. (2017). This immediately entails that ν, δ become functions of two variables defined in (9) and (10), and the extension to the spectrally negative Markov case becomes natural. We turn therefore to exits from certain trapezoidal-type regions in Section 5, under the spectrally negative Markov model.

In Section 6 we consider processes reflected at an upper barrier and formulate a Finetti's optimal dividends type objective with combined ruin and generalized drawdown stopping; this involves adding one reflecting vertex to our trapezoidal region. Included here is a new variational problem for de Finetti's dividends with generalized drawdown stopping (33); since the solution is not immediate even in the Lévy case, this has been provided in the parallel paper Avram and Goreac (2018).

2. Geometric Considerations Concerning the Joint Evolution of a Lévy Process and Its Draw-Down in a Rectangle

To study the process (X_t, Y_t), it is useful to start with its evolution in a rectangular region $R := [a, b] \times [0, d] \subset \mathbb{R} \times \mathbb{R}_+$, where $a < b$ and $d > 0$. Define

$$T_R = T_{a,b,d} := \inf\{t : (X_t, Y_t) \notin R\} = \tau_d \wedge T_{a,-} \wedge T_{b,+}.$$

A sample path of (X, Y), where X is chosen to be a spectrally negative Lévy process, and the region R is depicted in Figure 1.

---

[3] Choosing a, b, d optimally in various control problems involving optimal dividends and capital injections should be of interest, and will be pursued in further work.

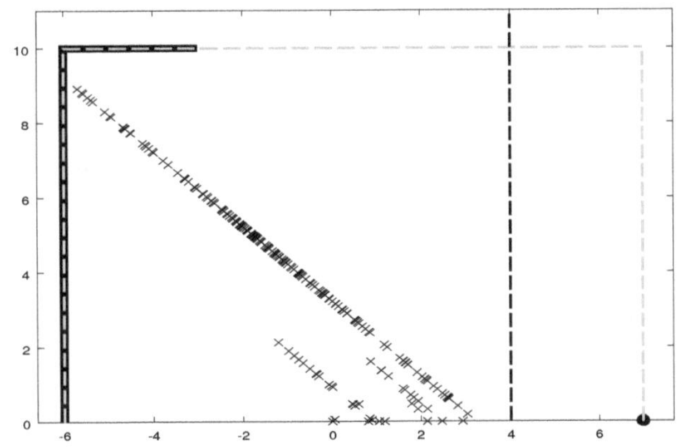

Figure 1. A sample path of (X,Y) with X a spectrally negative Lévy process. The region R has $d=10$, $a=-6$ and $b=7$; the dark boundary shows the possible exit points of (X,Y) from R. The base of the red line separates R in two parts with different behavior.

As is clear from the figure and from its definition, the process (X,Y) has very particular dynamics on R: away from the boundary $\partial_1 := \{(x_1,x_2) \in \mathbb{R}\times\mathbb{R}_+ : x_2 = 0\}$ it oscillates during negative excursions from the maximum on line segments $l_{\overline{X}_t}$ where, for $c\in\mathbb{R}$, $l_c := \{(x_1,x_2)\in\mathbb{R}\times\mathbb{R}_+ : x_1+x_2 = c\}$.

As $\overline{X}_t$ increases, the line segment $l_{\overline{X}_t}$ on which (X,Y) oscillates advances to the right—continuously, in the spectrally negative case, and in general possibly with jumps.

On ∂_1, we observe the Markovian upward ladder process, i.e., the maximum $\overline{X}$ with downward excursions excised, with extra spatial killing upon exiting R. If only time killing was present, with $d=\infty$, this would be a killed drift subordinator, with Laplace exponent $\kappa(s) = s+\Phi_q$ (as a consequence of the Wiener-Hopf decomposition Kyprianou (2014)). In the rectangle, in the spectrally negative case, the ladder process becomes a killed drift with generator $\mathcal{G}\varphi(s) := \varphi'(s) - \nu_q(d)\varphi(s)$ Albrecher et al. (2014); Avram et al. (2017b). Finally, with generalized drawdown (when the upper boundary is replaced by one determined by certain parametrizations $(\widehat{d}(s), d(s))$—see below), the generator will have state-dependent killing:

$$\mathcal{G}\varphi(s) := \varphi'(s) - \nu_q(d(s))\varphi(s). \tag{19}$$

Several functionals (ruin, dividends, tax, etc.) of the original process may be expressed as functionals of the killed ladder process. This explains the prevalence of first order ODE's—see (25) for one example—when working with spectrally negative processes. Several implications for T_R are immediately clear from these dynamics: for example, the process (X,Y) can leave R only through $\partial R \cap \{(x_1,x_2)\in\mathbb{R}\times\mathbb{R}_+ : x_1 \le b-d\}$ or through the point $(b,0)$ (see the shaded region in Figure 1). Also,

1. If $b \le a+d$, it is impossible for the process to leave R through the upper boundary of ∂R and for these parameter values T_R reduces to $T_{a,-}\wedge T_{b,+}$. Here it suffices to know the functions (1) to obtain the Laplace transform of T_R.
2. If $a+d\le x$, it is impossible for the process to leave R through the left boundary of ∂R, and T_R reduces to $T_{b,+}\wedge\tau_d$. Here it suffices to apply the spectrally negative drawdown formulas provided in Landriault et al. (2017a); Mijatovic and Pistorius (2012).
3. In the remaining case $x\le a+d\le b$, both drawdown and classic exits are possible. For the latter case, see Figure 1. The key observation here is that drawdown [classic] exits occur iff X_t does [does not] cross the line $x_1 = d+a$. The final answers will combine these two cases.

3. The Three Laplace Transforms of the Exit Time out of a Rectangle for Lévy Processes without Positive Jumps

In this section we provide Laplace transforms of T_R and of the eventual overshoot at T_R. One can break down the analysis of T_R to nine cases, depending on which of the three exit boundaries $T_{a,-}$, $T_{b,+}$ or τ_d occurred, and on the three relations between x, a, b and d described above.

The following results are immediate applications of the strong Markov property and of known first passage and draw-down results.

Theorem 1. *Consider a spectrally negative Lévy process X with differentiable scale function W_q. Then, for fixed $d \geq 0$ and $a \leq x \leq b$, letting UbD, DbU denote the functions defined in* (13), (15), *we have:*

	$a+d \leq x \leq b$	$x \leq a+d \leq b$	$b \leq a+d$
$\mathbb{E}_x\left[e^{-qT_{b,+}}; T_{b,+} \leq \min(\tau_d, T_{a,-})\right] =$	$UbD^b_{q,d}(x)$	$\overline{\Psi}_q^{(a+d)}(x,a)UbD^b_{q,d}(a+d)$	$\overline{\Psi}_q^b(x,a)$
$\mathbb{E}_x\left[e^{-qT_{a,-}+\theta(X_{T_{a,-}}-a)}; T_{a,-} \leq \min(\tau_d, T_{b,+})\right] =$	0	$\Psi_{q,\theta}^{(a+d)}(x,a)$	$\Psi^b_{q,\theta}(x,a)$
$\mathbb{E}_x\left[e^{-q\tau_d-\theta(Y_{\tau_d}-d)}; \tau_d \leq \min(T_{b,+}, T_{a,-})\right] =$	$DbU^b_{q,\theta,d}(x)$	$\overline{\Psi}_q^{(a+d)}(x,a)DbU^b_{q,\theta,d}(a+d)$	0

(20)

Proof. Please note that in the third column the d boundary is invisible and does not appear in the results, and in the first column the a boundary is invisible and does not appear in the results. These two cases follow therefore by applying already known results.

The middle column holds by breaking the path at the first crossing of $a+d$. The main points here are that

1. the middle case may happen only if X_t visits a before $a+d$;
2. the first case (exit through b) and the third case (drawdown exit) may happen only if X_t visits first $a+d$, with the drawdown barrier being invisible, and that subsequently the lower first passage barrier a becomes invisible.

The results follow then due to the smooth crossing upward and the strong Markov property. □

Proof. Let us check the first and third row of the second column. Applying the strong Markov property at $T_{a+d,+}$ yields

$$\begin{aligned}\mathbb{E}_x\left[e^{-qT_{b,+}}; T_{b,+} \leq \min(\tau_d, T_{a,-})\right] &= \mathbb{E}_x\left[e^{-qT_{b,+}}; T_{a+d,+} \leq T_{a,-}\right]\mathbb{E}_{a+d}\left[e^{-qT_{b,+}}; T_{b,+} \leq \tau_d\right] \\ &= \frac{W_q(x-a)}{W_q(d)} e^{-(b-a-d)\frac{W_q'(d)}{W_q(d)}}\end{aligned}$$

and

$$\begin{aligned}\mathbb{E}_x\left[e^{-q\tau_d-\theta(Y_{\tau_d}-d)}; \tau_d \leq \min(T_{b,+}, T_{a,-})\right] &= \mathbb{E}_x\left[e^{-q\tau_d-\theta(Y_{\tau_d}-d)}; T_{a+d,+} \leq T_{a,-}\right]\mathbb{E}_{a+d}\left[e^{-q\tau_d-\theta(Y_{\tau_d}-d)}; \tau_d \leq T_{b,+}\right] \\ &= \frac{W_q(x-a)}{W_q(d)}\delta_{q,\theta}(d)\left(1-e^{-(b-a-d))\frac{W_q'(d)}{W_q(d)}}\right).\end{aligned}$$

□

4. Generalized Draw-Down Stopping for Processes without Positive Jumps

Generalized drawdown times appear naturally in the Azema Yor solution of the Skorokhod embedding problem Azéma and Yor (1979), and in the Dubbins-Shepp-Shiryaev, and

Peskir-Hobson-Egami optimal stopping problems Dubins et al. (1994); Egami and Oryu (2015); Hobson (2007); Peskir (1998). Importantly, they allow a unified treatment of classic first passage and drawdown times (see also Avram et al. (2018b) for a further generalization to taxed processes)—see Avram et al. (2017b); Li et al. (2017). The idea is to replace the upper side of the rectangle R by a parametrized curve

$$(x_1, x_2) = (\widehat{d}(s), d(s)), \quad \widehat{d}(s) = s - d(s),$$

where $s = x_1 + x_2$ represents the value of $\overline{X}_t$ during the excursion which intersects the upper boundary at (x_1, x_2) (see Figure 2). Alternatively, parametrizing by x yields

$$y = h(x), \quad h(x) = \widehat{d}^{-1}(x) - x.$$

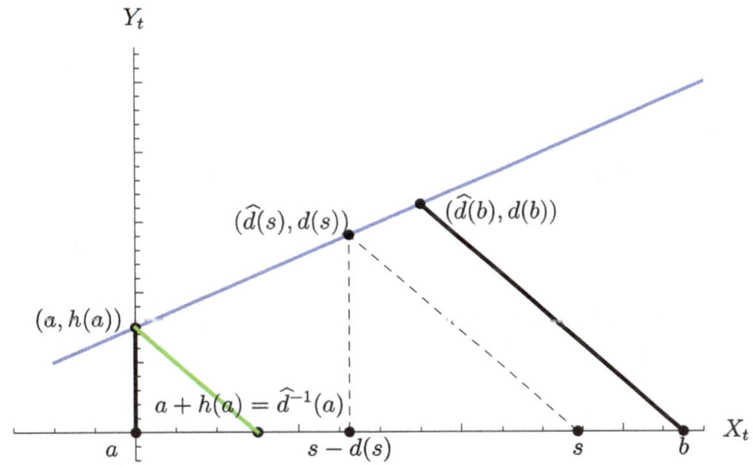

Figure 2. Affine drawdown exit of (X, Y) $d(s) = \frac{1}{3}s + 1$.

Definition 1. *Li et al. (2017) For any function $d(s) > 0$ such that $\widehat{d}(s) = s - d(s)$ is nondecreasing, a generalized drawdown time is defined by*

$$\tau_{\widehat{d}(\cdot)} := \inf\{t \geq 0 : Y_t > d(\overline{X}_t)\} = \inf\left\{t \geq 0 : X_t < \widehat{d}(\overline{X}_t)\right\}. \tag{21}$$

Such times provide a natural unification of classic and drawdown times.

Introduce

$$\widetilde{Y}_t := Y_t - d(\overline{X}_t), \; t \geq 0$$

to be called draw-down type process. Please note that we have $\widetilde{Y}_0 = -\widehat{d}(X_0) < 0$, and that the process $\widetilde{Y}_t$ is in general non-Markovian. However, it is Markovian during each negative excursion of X_t, along one of the oblique lines in the geometric decomposition sketched in Figure 1.

Example 1. *With affine functions*

$$d(s) = (1 - \xi)s + d \Leftrightarrow \widehat{d}(s) = \xi s - d, \quad \xi \in [0, 1], d > 0, \tag{22}$$

we obtain the affine draw-down/regret times studied in Avram et al. (2017b).

Affine drawdown times reduce to a classic drawdown time (3) *when $\xi = 1$, $d(s) = d$, and to a ruin time when $\xi = 0$, $\widehat{d}(s) = -d$, $d(s) = s + d$. When ξ varies, we are dealing with the pencil of lines passing through $(x_1, x_2) = (-d, d)$. In particular, for $\xi = 1$ we obtain the rectangle case from section 3, and for $\xi = 0$ we have an infinite strip with a vertical boundary at $x_1 = -d$.*

One of the merits of affine drawdown times is that they allow unifying the classic first passage theory with the drawdown theory Avram et al. (2017b); in particular, the generalized drawdown functions (23) *below unify the classic and drawdown survival and ruin probabilities (and have relatively simple formulas as well—see Avram et al. (2017a)).*

Introduce now generalized drawdown analogues of the drawdown survival and ruin probabilities (12) for which we will use the same notation:

$$UbD^b_{q,\widehat{d}(\cdot)}(x) = \mathbb{E}_x\left[e^{-qT_{b,+}}; T_{b,+} \le \tau_{\widehat{d}(\cdot)}\right]$$
$$DbU^b_{q,\theta,\widehat{d}(\cdot)}(x)) = \mathbb{E}_x\left[e^{-q\tau_{\widehat{d}(\cdot)}-\theta \widetilde{Y}_{\tau_{\widehat{d}(\cdot)}}}; \tau_{\widehat{d}(\cdot)} < T^+_b\right]. \tag{23}$$

Remark 6. *In the spectrally negative case, these functions may be represented as integrals:*

$$UbD^b_{q,\widehat{d}(\cdot)}(x) = e^{-\int_x^b \nu_q(s,\widehat{d}(s))ds},$$
$$DbU^b_{q,\theta,\widehat{d}(\cdot)}(x) = \int_x^b e^{-\int_x^y \nu_q(s,\widehat{d}(s))ds}\nu_q(y,\widehat{d}(y))\delta_{q,\theta}(y,\widehat{d}(y))dy, \tag{24}$$

where $\nu_q(y,\widehat{d}(y))$, $\delta_{q,\theta}(y,\widehat{d}(y))$ are defined in (9), (10).

This is already apparent in (Landriault et al. 2017b, Cor 3.1), and may be easily understood probabilistically from Figure 2: the first equation is the probability of no occurrence in a non-homogeneous Poisson process, and the second decomposes the transform of the deficit, by conditioning on the point $y \in [x,b]$ where the maximum occurred.

We provide now a heuristic proof valid for the Lévy case when $\nu_q(y,\widehat{d}(y)) = \nu_q(y-\widehat{d}(y)) = \nu_q(d(y))$ and $\delta_{q,\theta}(y,\widehat{d}(y)) = \delta_{q,\theta}(y-\widehat{d}(y)) = \delta_{q,\theta}(d(y))$.

1. *Due to creeping, UbD is a product of infinitesimal events*

$$\overline{\Psi}^{y+\epsilon}_q(y, y-d(y)) = \frac{W_q(d(y))}{W_q(d(y)+\epsilon)} \sim 1-\epsilon\nu_q(d(y)) \sim e^{-\epsilon\nu_q(d(y))}.$$

   Taking product, with $\epsilon = \mathrm{d}y$, yields (24).

2. *Informally, we condition on the density $\overline{X}_t \in \mathrm{d}y$. The integrand of DbU is obtained multiplying survival infinitesimal events up to level y by an infinitesimal termination event in $[y, y+\mathrm{d}y]$. The probability of this event, conditioned on survival up to y, is given by the deficit formula*

$$\Psi^{y+\epsilon}_{q,\theta}(y, y-d(y)) = Z_{q,\theta}(d(y)) - W_q(d(y))\frac{Z_{q,\theta}(d(y)+\epsilon)}{W_q(d(y)+\epsilon)}$$
$$\sim \epsilon(-Z'_{q,\theta}(d(y)) + \nu_q(d(y))Z_{q,\theta}(d(y)) = \epsilon\nu_q(d(y))\delta_{q,\theta}(d(y))$$

   For a rigorous (rather intricate) proof, see Avram et al. (2018b).

The end result for generalized drawdown times is (Avram et al. 2018b, Thm1):

Theorem 2. *Consider a process X for which the functions $\Psi, \overline{\Psi}$ are differentiable in the upper variable b. Assume $d(x) > 0$ and $\widehat{d}(x) = x - d(x)$ nondecreasing. Then, $\forall q,\theta \ge 0, b \in \mathbb{R}$, the functions $UbD(x) = UbD^b_q(x,\widehat{d}(\cdot))$, $DbU(x) = DbU^b_{q,\theta}(x,\widehat{d}(\cdot))$ satisfy (24). Alternatively, they satisfy the ODE's*

$$UbD'(y) - \nu_q(y,\widehat{d}(y))UbD(y) = 0, \quad UbD(b) = 1, \tag{25}$$

$$DbU'(y) - \nu_q(y,\widehat{d}(y))DbU(y) + \delta_{q,\theta}(y,\widehat{d}(y)) = 0, \quad DbU(b) = 0. \tag{26}$$

Remark 7. *The operator involved in the ODE's above is the generator of the upward ladder process, under time and spatial killing, and with the downward excursions excised. Once this known, variations involving different boundary conditions are easily obtained as well.*

5. The Three Laplace Transforms of the Exit Time out of a Curved Trapezoid, for Processes without Positive Jumps

We will replace now the classic drawdown time in Section 3 by a generalized one. Similar geometric considerations, with $d(\cdot), a+h(a)$ replacing $d, a+d$ in Theorem 1, yield:

Theorem 3. *Consider a spectrally negative Lévy process X with differentiable scale function W_q. Then, for $a \le x \le b$ and $d(\cdot)$ satisfying the conditions of Definition 1, we have:*

	$a+h(a) \le x$	$x \le a+h(a) \le b$	$b \le a+h(a)$
$\mathbb{E}_x\left[e^{-qT_{b,+}}; T_{b,+} \le \min(\tau_{\widehat{d}(\cdot)}, T_{a,-})\right] =$	$UbD^b_{q,\widehat{d}(\cdot)}(x)$	$\overline{\Psi}_q^{a+h(a)}(x,a)UbD^b_{q,\widehat{d}(\cdot)}(a+h(a))$	$\overline{\Psi}_q^b(x,a)$
$\mathbb{E}_x\left[e^{-qT_{a,-}+\theta(X_{T_{a,-}}-a)}; T_{a,-} \le \min(\tau_{\widehat{d}(\cdot)}, T_{b,+})\right] =$	0	$\Psi_{q,\theta}^{a+h(a)}(x,a)$	$\Psi_{q,\theta}^b(x,a)$
$\mathbb{E}_x\left[e^{-q\tau_{\widehat{d}(\cdot)}-\theta(Y_{\tau_{\widehat{d}(\cdot)}}-d)}; \tau_{\widehat{d}(\cdot)} \le \min(T_{b,+}, T_{a,-})\right] =$	$DbU^b_{q,\theta,\widehat{d}(\cdot)}(x)$	$\overline{\Psi}_q^{a+h(a)}(x,a)DbU^b_{q,\theta,\widehat{d}(\cdot)}(a+h(a))$	0

Proof. Note that if $b \le a+h(a)$ (narrow band), it is again impossible for the process to leave R through the upper boundary of ∂R, and T_R reduces to $T_{a,-} \wedge T_{b,+}$, and nothing changes. Similarly, if $a+h(a) \le x$ (flat band), it is impossible for the process to leave R through the left boundary of ∂R, and T_R reduces to $T_{b,+} \wedge \tau_d$. Finally, the two zones in the intermediate case are separated by $a+h(a)$ (instead of $a+d$). □

6. de Finetti's Optimal Dividends for Spectrally Negative Markov Processes with Generalized Draw-Down Stopping

In this section, we revisit the de Finetti's optimal dividend problem for spectrally negative Markov processes with the point b becoming a reflecting boundary, instead of absorbing, as it was in Section 3.

Define the Skorokhod reflected/constrained process at first passage times below or above by:

$$X_t^{[a} = X_t + L_t, \quad X_t^{b]} = X_t - U_t. \tag{27}$$

Here

$$L_t = L_t^{[a} = -(\underline{X}_t - a)_-, \quad U_t = U_t^{b]} = (\overline{X}_t - b)_+ \tag{28}$$

are the minimal "Skorohod regulators" constraining X_t to be bigger than a, and smaller than b, respectively.

Let now

$$V^{b]}(x) = V^{b]}_{q,\widehat{d}(\cdot)}(x) := \mathbb{E}_x\left[\int_0^{\tau_{\widehat{d}(\cdot)} \wedge T_{a,-}} e^{-qt} dU_t^{b]}\right] \tag{29}$$

denote the present value of all dividend payments at b, until the first passage time either below a, or below the drawdown boundary for the process $X_t^{b]}$ reflected at b, starting from $x \le b$ (a generalization of the famous de Finetti objective). By the strong Markov property, it holds that

$$V^{b]}(x) = \mathbb{E}_x\left[e^{-qT_{b,+}}; T_{b,+} \le \min(\tau_{\widehat{d}(\cdot)}, T_{a,-})\right] v(b), \quad v(b) = v_q(b, \widehat{d}(b)) := \mathbb{E}_b\left[\int_0^{\tau_{\widehat{d}(\cdot)}} e^{-qt} dU_t^{b]}\right]. \tag{30}$$

Remark 8. *The function $v(b)$, the expected discounted time until killing for the reflected process, when starting from b, equals the time the process reflected at b spends at point $(b,0)$ in Figure 2, before a downward excursion beyond $\widehat{d}(b)$ kills the process. In the Lévy case, it is well-known Kyprianou (2014) that this time is exponential with parameter $\nu_q(b,\widehat{d}(b))$, and thus its expectation is the reciprocal of the killing parameter $\nu_q(b,\widehat{d}(b))$, i.e.,*

$$v(b) = \nu_q(b,\widehat{d}(b))^{-1} \tag{31}$$

Excursion theoretic arguments show that (31) continues to hold in the spectrally negative Markov case (for a proof under a similar setup, see (Czarna et al. 2018, sct. 4)).

Furthermore, by (Avram et al. 2018b, Thm. 1) included above as (24), it holds that

$$\mathbb{E}_x\left[e^{-qT_{b,+}}1_{\{T_{b,+}<\tau_{d(\cdot)}\}}\right] = e^{-\int_x^b \nu_q(z,\widehat{d}(z))\mathrm{d}z}. \tag{32}$$

When $a=-\infty$, we arrive finally to an explicit formula

$$V^{b]}(x) = \frac{e^{-\int_x^b \nu_q(y,\widehat{d}(y))\mathrm{d}s}}{\nu_q(b,\widehat{d}(b))} \tag{33}$$

expressing the expected dividends in terms of $\nu_q(y,\widehat{d}(y))$. Please note that in the Lévy case Equation (33) simplifies to:

$$V^{b]}(x) = \frac{W_q(d(x))}{W_q(d(b))}\nu_q(d(b))^{-1}$$

(using $x - l(x) = d(x)$), which checks with (Wang and Zhou 2018, Lem. 3.1–3.2).

The problem of choosing a drawdown boundary to optimize dividends in (33) is solved in Avram and Goreac (2018) via Pontryagin's maximum principle.

7. Example: Affine Draw-Down Stopping for Brownian Motion

Consider optimizing expected dividends $V^{b]}(x)$ given in Equation (29) with respect to the optimal dividend barrier b for Brownian motion with drift $X(t) = \sigma B_t + \mu t$ and with affine drawdown stopping $d(x) = (1-\xi)x + d$, where $\xi \in [0,1]$, $d \geq 0$, $a \leq x \leq b$.

Please note that if $a + h(a) > b$, where $h(x) = d(x)/\xi$, then the drawdown constraint is invisible, and the problem reduces to the classical de Finetti objective. Hence, we consider $a + h(a) \leq b$.

The scale function of Brownian motion is

$$W_q(x) = \frac{2e^{-\mu x/\sigma^2}}{\Delta}\sinh(x\Delta/\sigma^2) = \frac{1}{\Delta}[e^{(-\mu+\Delta)x/\sigma^2} - e^{-(\mu+\Delta)x/\sigma^2}],$$

where $\Delta = \sqrt{\mu^2 + 2q\sigma^2}$. Assume that $x \geq a + h(a) = a + \frac{d(a)}{\xi} = \frac{a+d}{\xi}$, then as a special case of spectrally negative Levy process, the expected dividends for Brownian motion equals

$$V^{b]}(x) = \mathbb{E}_x\left[e^{-qT_{b,+}}; T_{b,+} \leq \min(\tau_{\widehat{d}(\cdot)}, T_{a,-})\right]v(b) = \left(\frac{W_q(d(x))}{W_q(d(b))}\right)^{\frac{1}{1-\xi}}\frac{W_q(d(b))}{W_q'(d(b))}, \tag{34}$$

see (Avram et al. 2017b, Thm. 1.1), with tax parameter $\gamma = 0$, and (Avram et al. 2017b, Rem. 7), with tax parameter $\gamma = 1$. The barrier influence function which must be optimized in b becomes

$$BI(b,d,\xi) = \frac{W_q((1-\xi)x+d)^{1-\frac{1}{1-\xi}}}{W_q'((1-\xi)x+d)} = \frac{\sigma^2}{2}\frac{e^{x\mu/\sigma^2}\operatorname{csch}\left(x\sqrt{\mu^2+2q\sigma^2}/\sigma^2\right)}{\coth\left((d+x-x\xi)\sqrt{\mu^2+2q\sigma^2}/\sigma^2\right) - \mu/\sqrt{\mu^2+2q\sigma^2}}. \tag{35}$$

The critical point b^* satisfies

$$\frac{W_q''W_q}{(W_q')^2}((1-\xi)b^*+d) = -\frac{\xi}{1-\xi}, \tag{36}$$

that is b^* satisfies

$$-\frac{q\sigma^2+\mu^2+\mu\sqrt{2q\sigma^2+\mu^2}\sinh\left(\frac{2b^*\sqrt{2q\sigma^2+\mu^2}}{\sigma^2}\right)-(q\sigma^2+\mu^2)\cosh\left(\frac{2b^*\sqrt{2q\sigma^2+\mu^2}}{\sigma^2}\right)}{\left(\sqrt{2q\sigma^2+\mu^2}\cosh\left(\frac{b^*\sqrt{2q\sigma^2+\mu^2}}{\sigma^2}\right)-\mu\sinh\left(\frac{b^*\sqrt{2q\sigma^2+\mu^2}}{\sigma^2}\right)\right)^2} = -\frac{\xi}{1-\xi}.$$

In Figure 3 given below, we have an illustration of plot of barrier influence function and its derivative for Brownian motion with drift $\mu = 1/2$ and $\sigma = 1$.

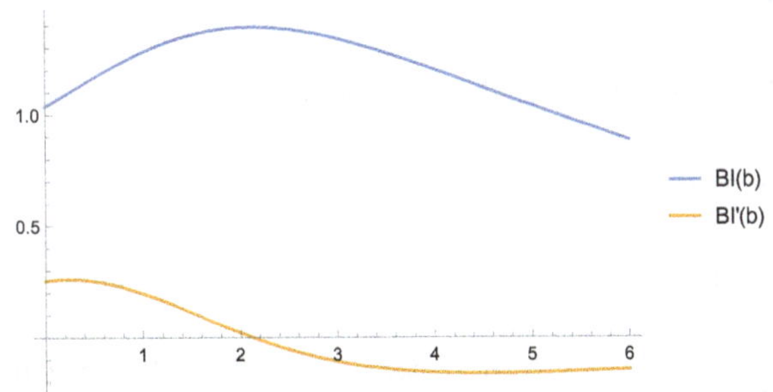

Figure 3. Optimizing dividends with affine drawdown stopping where $\mu = 1/2$, $q = 1/10$, $\sigma = 1$, $\xi = 1/3$, $b = 20$, $d = 1$. The critical point $b^* = 2.12445$.

Remark 9. *Please note that once ξ is fixed, we get nontrivial results for the optimal barrier. However, if we maximize over ξ as well, the optimum is achieved by the classical de Finetti solution $\xi = 0 \Longrightarrow W_q''(b^*+d) = 0$, corresponding to forced stopping below $-d$ (d is just a shift of the origin, with respect to the classical solution $W_q''(b^*) = 0$) Avram and Goreac (2018). In the diffusion case, it is not yet known whether examples in which the generalized de Finetti problem improves on the classic de Finetti solution are possible.*

Remark 10. *Let us note now that Equation (36) holds in fact for any spectrally negative Lévy process. Similar computations may be therefore performed for any spectrally negative Levy process, by plugging exact or approximate formulas for the scale function into the function*

$$\frac{W_q''W_q}{(W_q')^2} \tag{37}$$

which is required to solve (36).

The easiest case is the Cramér-Lundberg process with phase-type claims, since in this case the scale function is a sum of exponentials. For example, for a Cramér-Lundberg process with premium rate $c > 0$, Poisson arrivals of intensity λ and exponential claims with mean $1/\mu$, the scale function is $W_q(x) = c^{-1}(\frac{\mu+\Delta_+}{\Delta_+-\Delta_-}e^{\Delta_+ x} - \frac{\mu+\Delta_-}{\Delta_+-\Delta_-}e^{\Delta_- x})$, $x \geq 0$, where $\Delta_\pm = \frac{q+\lambda-\mu c \pm \sqrt{(q+\lambda-\mu c)^2+4cq\mu}}{2c}$, and similar computations may be performed (see also (Wang and Zhou 2018, Example 5.2)).

Author Contributions: Conceptualization, F.A.; Formal analysis, F.A. and C.V.-A.; Project administration, F.A.; Supervision, F.A.; Validation, D.G., C.V.-A.; Writing—original draft, F.A. and C.V.-A.; Writing—review, editing, D.G., C.V.-A.

Funding: This work is supported by the Scientific and Technological Research Council of Turkey, TUBITAK Project No. 117F273.

Acknowledgments: We thank Ali Devin Sezer for useful discussions.

Conflicts of Interest: The authors declare no conflict of interest.

References

Albrecher, Hansjörg, and Sören Asmussen. 2010. *Ruin Probabilities*. Singapore: World Scientific, vol. 14.

Albrecher, Hansjörg, Florin Avram, Corina Constantinescu, and Jevgenijs Ivanovs. 2014. The tax identity for Markov additive risk processes. *Methodology and Computing in Applied Probability* 16: 245–58. [CrossRef]

Albrecher, Hansjörg, Jevgenijs Ivanovs, and Xiaowen Zhou. 2016. Exit identities for Lévy processes observed at Poisson arrival times. *Bernoulli* 22: 1364–82. [CrossRef]

Avram, Florin, and J. P. Garmendia. 2019. Some first passage theory for the Segerdahl-Tichy risk process, and open problems. Forthcoming.

Avram, Florin, and Dan Goreac. 2018. A pontryaghin maximum principle approach for the optimization of dividends/consumption of spectrally negative Markov processes, until a generalized draw-down time. *arXiv* arXiv:1812.08438.

Avram, Florin, Andreas E. Kyprianou, and Martijn R. Pistorius. 2004. Exit problems for spectrally negative Lévy processes and applications to (Canadized) Russian options. *The Annals of Applied Probability* 14: 215–38.

Avram, Florin, Zbigniew Palmowski, and Martijn R. Pistorius. 2007. On the optimal dividend problem for a spectrally negative Lévy process. *The Annals of Applied Probability* 17: 156–80. [CrossRef]

Avram, Florin, Zbigniew Palmowski, and Martijn R. Pistorius. 2015. On Gerber–Shiu functions and optimal dividend distribution for a Lévy risk process in the presence of a penalty function. *The Annals of Applied Probability* 25: 1868–935. [CrossRef]

Avram, Florin, Danijel Grahovac, and Ceren Vardar-Acar. 2017a. The W, Z scale functions kit for first passage problems of spectrally negative Lévy processes, and applications to the optimization of dividends. *arXiv* arXiv:1706.06841.

Avram, Florin, Nhat Linh Vu, and Xiaowen Zhou. 2017b. On taxed spectrally negative Lévy processes with draw-down stopping. *Insurance: Mathematics and Economics* 76: 69–74. [CrossRef]

Avram, Florin, José-Luis Pérez, and Kazutoshi Yamazaki. 2018a. Spectrally negative Lévy processes with Parisian reflection below and classical reflection above. *Stochastic Processes and Their Applications* 128: 255–90. [CrossRef]

Avram, Florin, Bin Li, and Shu Li. 2018b. A unified analysis of taxed draw-down spectrally negative Markov processes. Forthcoming.

Avram, Florin, and Matija Vidmar. 2017. First passage problems for upwards skip-free random walks via the Φ, W, Z paradigm. *arXiv* arXiv:1708.06080.

Avram, Florin, and Xiaowen Zhou. 2017. On fluctuation theory for spectrally negative Lévy processes with parisian reflection below, and applications. *Theory of Probability and Mathematical Statistics* 95: 17–40. [CrossRef]

Azéma, Jacques, and Marc Yor. 1979. Une solution simple au probleme de Skorokhod. In *Séminaire de Probabilités XIII*. Berlin: Springer, pp. 90–115.

Bertoin, Jean. 1997. Exponential decay and ergodicity of completely asymmetric Lévy processes in a finite interval. *The Annals of Applied Probability* 7: 156–69. [CrossRef]

Bertoin, Jean. 1998. *Lévy Processes*. Cambridge: Cambridge University Press, vol. 121.

Borovkov, Alexandr. 2012. *Stochastic Processes in Queueing Theory*. Berlin: Springer Science & Business Media, vol. 4.

Carr, Peter. 2014. First-order calculus and option pricing. *Journal of Financial Engineering* 1: 1450009. [CrossRef]

Chan, Terence, Andreas E. Kyprianou, and Mladen Savov. 2011. Smoothness of scale functions for spectrally negative Lévy processes. *Probability Theory and Related Fields* 150: 691–708. [CrossRef]

Czarna, Irmina, José-Luis Pérez, Tomasz Rolski, and Kazutoshi Yamazaki. 2017. Fluctuation theory for level-dependent Lévy risk processes. *arXiv* arXiv:1712.00050.

Czarna, Irmina, Adam Kaszubowski, Shu Li, and Zbigniew Palmowski. 2018. Fluctuation identities for omega-killed Markov additive processes and dividend problem. *arXiv* arXiv:1806.08102.

Dubins, Lester E., Larry A. Shepp, and Albert Nikolaevich Shiryaev. 1994. Optimal stopping rules and maximal inequalities for Bessel processes. *Theory of Probability & Its Applications* 38: 226–61.

Egami, Masahiko, and Tadao Oryu. 2015. An excursion-theoretic approach to regulator's bank reorganization problem. *Operations Research* 63: 527–39. [CrossRef]

Hobson, David. 2007. Optimal stopping of the maximum process: A converse to the results of Peskir. *Stochastics An International Journal of Probability and Stochastic Processes* 79: 85–102. [CrossRef]

Ivanovs, Jevgenijs, and Zbigniew Palmowski. 2012. Occupation densities in solving exit problems for Markov additive processes and their reflections. *Stochastic Processes and Their Applications* 122: 3342–60. [CrossRef]

Jacobsen, Martin, and Anders Tolver Jensen. 2007. Exit times for a class of piecewise exponential Markov processes with two-sided jumps. *Stochastic Processes and Their Applications* 117: 1330–56. [CrossRef]

Kyprianou, Andreas. 2014. *Fluctuations of Lévy Processes with Applications: Introductory Lectures*. Berlin: Springer Science & Business Media.

Landriault, David, Bin Li, and Shu Li. 2015. Analysis of a drawdown-based regime-switching Lévy insurance model. *Insurance: Mathematics and Economics* 60: 98–107. [CrossRef]

Landriault, David, Bin Li, and Hongzhong Zhang. 2017a. On magnitude, asymptotics and duration of drawdowns for Lévy models. *Bernoulli* 23: 432–58. [CrossRef]

Landriault, David, Bin Li, and Hongzhong Zhang. 2017b. A unified approach for drawdown (drawup) of time-homogeneous Markov processes. *Journal of Applied Probability* 54: 603–26. [CrossRef]

Lehoczky, John P. 1977. Formulas for stopped diffusion processes with stopping times based on the maximum. *The Annals of Probability* 5: 601–7. [CrossRef]

Li, Bo, Linh Vu, and Xiaowen Zhou. 2017. Exit problems for general draw-down times of spectrally negative Lévy processes. *arXiv* arXiv:1702.07259.

Li, Bo, and Xiaowen Zhou. 2018. On weighted occupation times for refracted spectrally negative Lévy processes. *Journal of Mathematical Analysis and Applications* 466: 215–37. [CrossRef]

Mijatovic, Aleksandar, and Martijn R Pistorius. 2012. On the drawdown of completely asymmetric Lévy processes. *Stochastic Processes and Their Applications* 122: 3812–36. [CrossRef]

Page, Ewan S. 1954. Continuous inspection schemes. *Biometrika* 41: 100–15. [CrossRef]

Peskir, Goran. 1998. Optimal stopping of the maximum process: The maximality principle. *Annals of Probability* 26: 1614–40. [CrossRef]

Pistorius, Martijn R. 2004. On exit and ergodicity of the spectrally one-sided Lévy process reflected at its infimum. *Journal of Theoretical Probability* 17: 183–220. [CrossRef]

Shepp, Larry, and Albert N. Shiryaev. 1993. The Russian option: Reduced regret. *The Annals of Applied Probability* 3: 631–40. [CrossRef]

Suprun, V. N. 1976. Problem of destruction and resolvent of a terminating process with independent increments. *Ukrainian Mathematical Journal* 28: 39–51. [CrossRef]

Taylor, Howard M. 1975. A stopped Brownian motion formula. *The Annals of Probability* 3: 234–46. [CrossRef]

Wang, Wenyuan, and Xiaowen Zhou. 2018. General drawdown-based de Finetti optimization for spectrally negative Lévy risk processes. *Journal of Applied Probability* 55: 513–42. [CrossRef]

9

Machine Learning in Banking Risk Management

Martin Leo *, Suneel Sharma and K. Maddulety

SP Jain School of Global Management, Sydney 2127, Australia; sunil2500@gmail.com (S.S.); k.maddulety@spjain.org (K.M.)
* Correspondence: amaleo@yahoo.com

Abstract: There is an increasing influence of machine learning in business applications, with many solutions already implemented and many more being explored. Since the global financial crisis, risk management in banks has gained more prominence, and there has been a constant focus around how risks are being detected, measured, reported and managed. Considerable research in academia and industry has focused on the developments in banking and risk management and the current and emerging challenges. This paper, through a review of the available literature seeks to analyse and evaluate machine-learning techniques that have been researched in the context of banking risk management, and to identify areas or problems in risk management that have been inadequately explored and are potential areas for further research. The review has shown that the application of machine learning in the management of banking risks such as credit risk, market risk, operational risk and liquidity risk has been explored; however, it doesn't appear commensurate with the current industry level of focus on both risk management and machine learning. A large number of areas remain in bank risk management that could significantly benefit from the study of how machine learning can be applied to address specific problems.

Keywords: risk management; bank; machine learning; credit scoring; fraud

---

1. Introduction

Since the global financial crisis, risk management in banks has gained more prominence, and there has been a constant focus on how risks are being detected, measured, reported and managed. Considerable research (Van Liebergen 2017; Deloitte University Press 2017; Helbekkmo et al. 2013; MetricStream 2018; Oliver Wyman 2017), both in academia and industry, has focused on the developments in banking and risk management and the current and emerging challenges. In tandem, there has been a growing influence of machine learning in business applications, with many solutions already implemented and many more being explored.

McKinsey & Co highlighted that risk functions in banks, by 2025, would need to be fundamentally different from what they are today. The broadening and deepening of regulations, evolving customer expectations and the evolution of risk types are expected to drive the change within risk management. New products, services and risk management techniques are being enabled through the application of evolving technologies and advanced analytics. Machine learning, identified as one of the technologies with important implications for risk management, can enable the building of more accurate risk models by identifying complex, nonlinear patterns within large datasets. The predictive power of these models can grow with every bit of information added, thus enhancing predictive power over time. It is expected that machine learning will be applied across multiple areas within a bank's risk organisation. Machine learning has also been recommended as an initiative that could help in the transformation of the risk management function at banks.

The paper seeks to study the extent to which machine learning, which has been highlighted as an emergent business enabler, has been researched in the context of risk management within the banking industry and, subsequently, to identify potential areas for further research. The aim of this review paper is to assess, analyse and evaluate machine-learning techniques that have been applied to banking risk management, and to identify areas or problems in risk management that have been inadequately explored and make suggestions for further research.

To determine the risks specific to banks, as an alternate to leveraging on existing literature, this paper provides a taxonomy of risks that is developed based on a review of bank annual reports. An analysis of the available literature was carried out to evaluate the areas of banking risk management where machine-learning techniques have been researched. The research evaluated the risk areas where machine learning has been implemented in the risk types and the specific risk methodology they addressed. The analysis also identified the machine learning algorithms being used, both for specific areas and in general.

Section 2.1 provides an overview of risk management at banks, the key risk types and risk management tools and methodologies. Section 2.2 gives a quick introduction to machine learning and its use. Section 3 begins by providing an overview of the research methodology. The section further examines the existing research around the application of machine learning in the management of risk at banks. It provides an analysis of the areas where the application of machine learning has been studied, highlighting areas where there is little to no academic study. Section 4 discusses the key observations from the review, stressing the potential challenges and topics that could be addressed in the future. Section 5 summarises the general findings from the study. The paper concludes by listing additional areas or problems in banking risk management where the application of machine learning can be further researched.

2. Theoretical Background

2.1. *Risk Management at Banks*

The bank's management's pursuit to increase returns for its owners comes at the cost of increased risk. Banks are faced with various risks—interest rate risk, market risk, credit risk, off-balance-sheet risk, technology and operational risk, foreign exchange risk, country or sovereign risk, liquidity risk, liquidity risk and insolvency risk. Effective management of these risks is key to a bank's performance. Also, given these risks and the role that banks play in financial systems, they are subject to regulatory attention (Saunders et al. 2006). The regulators require banks to hold capital for the many risks that arise and are carried due to a bank's varied operations. The Basel standards for the determination of capital requirements were developed in 1998, and since then, have developed and evolved. Capital is required for each of the main risk types. Credit risk has traditionally been the greatest risk facing banks, and usually the one requiring the most capital. Market risk arises primarily from the trading operations of a bank, while operational risk is the risk of losses from internal system failures or external events. In addition to calculating regulatory capital, most large banks also calculate economic capital, which is based on a bank's models rather than on prescriptions from regulators (Hull 2012). The main risks that banks face are credit, market, and operational risks, with other types of risk including liquidity, business, and reputational risk. Banks are actively engaged in risk management to monitor, manage and measure these risks (Apostolik et al. 2009).

Market risk can be defined as the risk of losses "owing to movements in the level or volatility of market prices" (Jorion 2007). Market risk includes interest rate risk, equity risk, foreign exchange risk and commodity risk. Interest risk can be defined as the potential loss due to movements in interest rates. Equity risk can be defined as the potential loss consequent to an adverse change in the price of a stock. Foreign exchange risk can be defined as the risk that the value of the assets or liabilities of a bank changes due to fluctuations in the currency exchange rate. Commodity risk can be defined as the potential loss due to an adverse change in the price of commodities held. The market risk framework of the Basel accord consists of an internal models approach and a standardised approach. To capture tail risk better, the revised framework also saw a shift in the measure of risk under stress from the Value-at-Risk (VaR) to Expected Shortfall (ES) (Basel Committee on Banking Supervision 2006).

Credit can be defined as the risk of potential loss to the bank if a borrower fails to meet its obligations (interest, principal amounts). Credit risk is the single largest risk banks face (Apostolik et al. 2009). The Basel Accord allows banks to take the internal ratings-based approach for credit risk. Banks can internally develop their own credit risk models for calculating expected loss. The key risk parameters to be estimated are probability of default (PD), loss given default (LGD) and exposure at default (EAD). Expected Loss = $PD \times LGD \times EAD$ (Basel Committee on Banking Supervision 2005a, 2005b).

Liquidity risk, treated separately from the other risks, takes two forms—asset liquidity risk and funding liquidity risk. A bank is exposed to asset-liquidity risk when a transaction cannot be executed at the prevailing market prices, which could be a consequence of the size of the position relative to the normal trading lot size. Funding liquidity risk refers to the inability to meet cash flow obligations, and is also known as cash flow risk (Jorion 2007). Banks are required to establish a robust liquidity risk management framework that would ensure sufficient liquidity is maintained, including the ability to withstand a range of stress events. A sound process for the identification, measurement, monitoring and control of liquidity risk should be implemented (Basel Committee on Banking Supervision 2008).

Operational risk is defined by BCBS as the risk of loss resulting from "inadequate or failed internal processes, people and systems or from external events" and is a "fundamental element of risk management" at banks. This definition includes legal risk, but excludes strategic and reputational risk. It is considered inherent in all banking products, activities, processes and systems (Basel Committee on Banking Supervision 2011). In the annual reports, operational risk was varyingly presented and included a number of sub risks, and could be referred to more as non-financial risk. It included, among many others, fraud risk, cyber security, clients products and business practices, information and resiliency risk, money laundering and financial crime risks, vendor and outsourcing risks, technology risk, business disruption risks. In some instances, banks have reported compliance and legal risk also under operational risk.

To determine the risks specific to banks, as an alternate to leveraging the existing literature, a review was done of bank annual reports. Based on the review, a taxonomy was charted of the various risk types that banks typically seek to manage as part of their business and the methodologies and tools in use. The annual reports of 10 leading banks were reviewed to determine which risk areas were specifically being reported on by these banks. The review also included identifying the specific tools, methodologies or risk management framework components that were in use. To get wider coverage, the list of banks included a representative from each region—US, predominantly globally operating banks, European banks, and also an Asian bank. Also, these banks operated a wide ranging of banking business lines—investment banking, securities trading, consumer or retail banking and corporate banking. While there were differences in the way the risks were discussed and presented, including sub risks, the top risks were largely the same and included credit risk management, market risk management, liquidity risk, operational risk.

A chart (Figure 1) depicting the taxonomy of the various risk types discussed in bank annual reports and also the various methodologies or tools (Figure 2) implemented to manage these risks is included below.

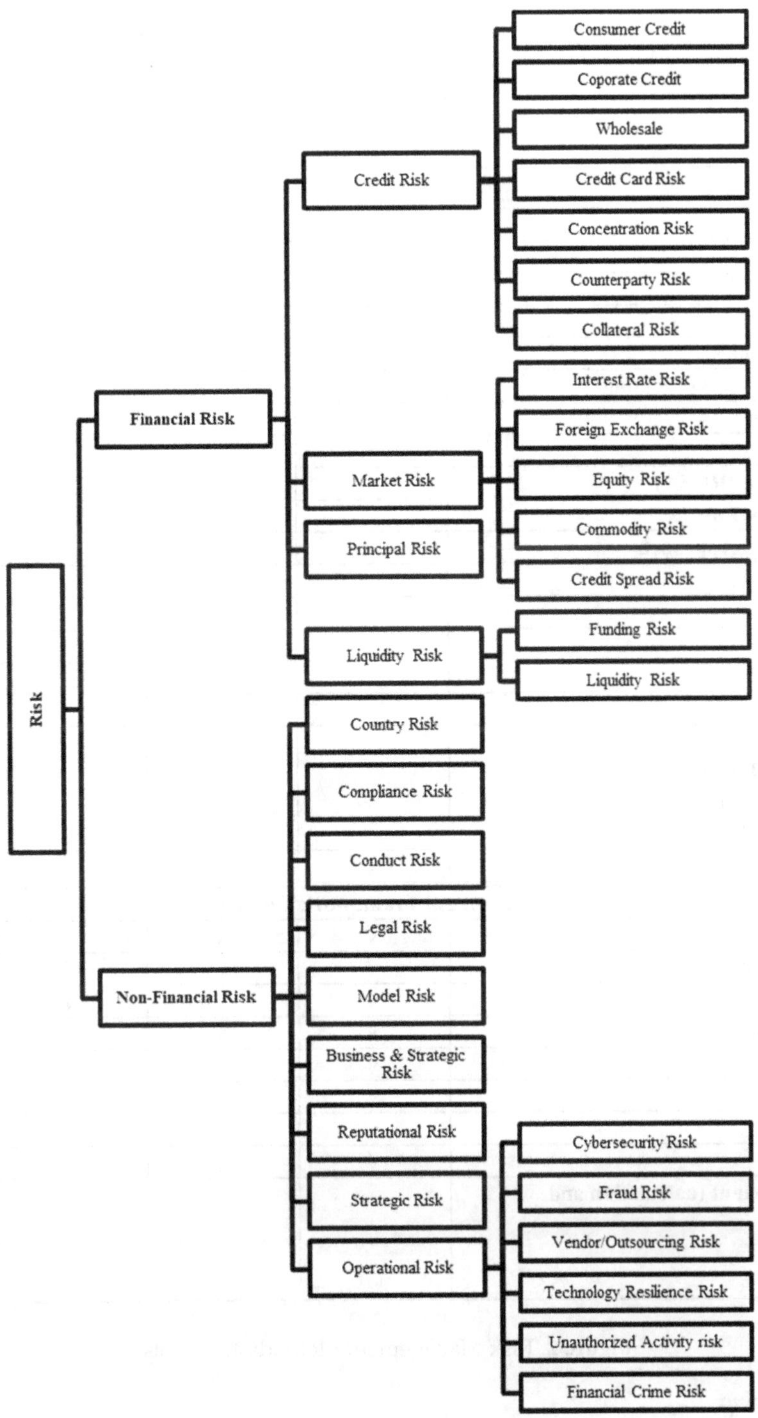

Figure 1. Taxonomy of risks.

The chief risk officer has access to risk insight and intelligence that was more retrospective in nature, such as incident analyses focusing on understanding what happened and why. Now, increasingly, they are gearing up with tools that allow for a look ahead that facilitates the predicting of potential risk incidents. Data mining, scenario modelling and forecasting are built-in features of most risk management solutions. Cognitive (pattern recognition by visualising and identifying apparent and later trends in historical data) and algorithmic (establishing causal relationships between diverse events and data sets) intelligence is making way for augmented (natural language processing and machine learning) and assistive (contextual virtual intelligent assistance) intelligence that augments and accelerates decision making (MetricStream 2018).

	Market Risk	Credit Risk	Liquidity Risk	Non-Financial Risk (Operational Risk)
Risk Management Tools				
Risk Limits	√	√	√	
Credit Risk limits		√		
Value at Risk	√			
Earnings at Risk	√			
Expected Shortfall	√			
Economic Value Stress Testing	√			
Economic Capital	√	√	√	√
Risk Sensitivities	√			
Risk Assessment (RCSA)				√
Operational Risk Losses				√
Loss Distribution Approach				√
Scenario Analysis	√	√	√	√
Tail Risk Capture	√	√	√	√
Stress Testing	√	√	√	√
Scoring Models		√		
Rating Models		√		
Exposure - Probability of Default - Loss Given Default - Exposure at Default		√		
Back Testing	√	√	√	
Risk Management Framework Components				
Risk Appetite	√	√	√	√
Risk Identification	√	√	√	√
Risk Assessment	√	√	√	√
Risk Measurement	√	√	√	√
Risk Testing	√	√	√	√
Risk Monitoring	√	√	√	√
Risk reporting	√	√	√	√
Risk Oversight	√	√	√	√
Capital Management (calculation and allocation) - CCAR - ICAAP	√	√	√	√

Figure 2. Risk Management Methods and Tools.

2.2. *Machine Learning*

Machine learning has been explained as lying at the intersection of computer science, engineering and statistics. It has been highlighted as a tool that can be applied to various problems, especially in fields that require data to be interpreted and acted upon (Awad and Khanna 2015). Machine learning delivers the capability to detect meaningful patterns in data, and has become a common tool for almost any task faced with the requirement of extracting meaningful information from data sets. When faced with the requirement of extracting meaningful information from data, and the consequent complexity of patterns to be studied, a programmer may not be able to provide explicit and detailed specification on the execution process. Machine learning addresses this challenge by "endowing programs" with the ability to "learn and adapt". The machine learning programs learn and improve, and can be applied when the problem that has to be dealt has the dual challenge of complexity and the need for adaptability (Shalev-Shwartz and Ben-David 2014).

Machine learning tools that are driving the advances in search engines and self-driving cars can be adopted and applied to the financial sector. A variety of technological developments have contributed to the financial sector being able to explore and mine a voluminous data infrastructure that includes diverse sets of unstructured forms of financial data about markets and consumers. Economists are increasingly adopting machine learning, in conjunction with other tools and expertise to evaluate complex relationships, despite machine learning's limitations in being able to determine causality. The adoption of machine learning has been motivated by the potential opportunities for cost reduction, improved productivity and improved risk management. New regulations have also pushed the banks to automate with the need to have efficient regulatory compliance (Financial Stability Board 2017).

Data driven and computational-based, machine learning algorithms rely less on assumptions about the data, including about the distribution. While they are considered more robust and better at addressing complex non-linear relationships, they also are seen as being difficult to interpret (Galindo and Tamayo 2000).

Recent years have seen a surge in the amount of data gathered within financial institutions (FI). A big push towards the digitalisation of services and increased regulatory reporting requirements has resulted in a large amount of unstructured data being created and/or collected at a high frequency. This data comes from various sources, including consumer apps, client interactions, metadata and other external data sources. The desire to enhance their analytical capabilities and automate across business lines, including risk management, by managing and mining these increased volumes and a variety of data has led financial institutions to explore powerful and analytical solutions, a consequence of which is the rise in interest and the popularity of machine learning and artificial intelligence within the FI community (Van Liebergen 2017). Machine learning is widely seen in the financial services sector as having the potential to deliver the analytical capability that FIs desire. Machine learning is capable of impacting every aspect of the FI's business model—improving insight into client preferences, risk management, fraud detection, conduct monitoring, client support automation and even automated identity verification when coupled with biometrics.

Van Liebergen (2017) introduces the field, and through discussions with the Institute of International Finance and technology ventures, explains use cases within financial institutions. He discusses applications in the area of credit risk modelling, detection of credit card fraud and money laundering and surveillance of conduct breaches at FIs. He also highlights that Machine learning seeks to predict "out-of-sample" while learning "found in-sample" (past) correlations, while falling short of providing an explanation for the analysed relationship. This could create complexities around model development and evaluation.

Machine learning also plays a role at the Securities and Exchange Commission (SEC) in the risk assessment process in identifying misconduct. While this is applicable from a supervisory perspective and for the oversight of systemic risks, it can also serve as a guide for a bank on how similar machine learning techniques can be applied in risk assessments for the detection of misconduct (internal or external) including risk assessments on corporate issuers or counterparties (Bauguess 2015). In computational finance, machine learning has great potential and could be variedly used, ranging from the comprehensive exploratory data analysis to the presentation/visualisation of modelling results (Kanevski and Timonin 2010).

Some of the cons of machine learning, as argued, are that they are more "black box" in nature, with results at times being difficult to interpret. It is argued that they are also sensitive to outliers, resulting in the overfitting of the data and counterintuitive predictions. They are also argued to have the pros of being able to be a better fit for non-linear relationships between the explanatory variables and explained variables, and also that the ability for them to apply a broader set of variables tends to improve accuracy (Bacham and Zhao 2017).

3. Materials and Methods

To carry out the review of literature that researches the application of machine learning in bank risk management, two sets of key words were used in the search for related papers. The search for papers was done using the scholar.google.com, SSRN and ProQuest databases. The search was largely focused on papers after 2007 to capture developments since the global financial crisis; however papers prior to that period were also included if they were referenced in other recent papers.

The first group of words was 'machine learning', in line with the topic. The second group comprised terms that were identified from the review of the bank annual reports. This includes risk types, as listed in the risk taxonomy and risk management tools or methods that were identified from the bank annual reports. Taxonomy is as shown in Figure 1, and methods as in Figure 2.

The search and review was limited to conference papers, journal articles and selected theses (post graduate or doctoral). The review has not considered articles, white papers, vendor papers or web articles that have just made reference to machine learning without providing details on how, or that made references to the application of any specific algorithm, though many such articles did come up in the search. In particular, there are a large number of articles, web and magazines, and publications that include machine learning as a solution or as a generic and general recommendation without providing further details on how a given specific problem can be addressed.

The review has looked at only papers that have analysed the topic with a level of depth, namely, by making references to specific algorithms or providing a design or model for how ML can be implemented. Articles or papers or conference proceedings that have made only a cursory or a general reference to the application of ML in the risk management space have not been considered for this research. It is noted that there are many references available where the authors or speakers have proposed that ML or AI can be applied in the management of risk; however, many of them stop short of providing clarity on *which* algorithms, or fail to provide examples of how ML/AI has been applied in a test or industry setup.

The methodological framework for this research was determined by analysing the various problem areas related to machine learning and risk management in banks. The articles were classified to understand: (i) the risk area they focused on; (ii) the risk management tool or risk management framework component they targeted; or (iii) the algorithms that were applied/studied/proposed. The survey was also seeking to review papers that focused more on risk assessment and measurement.

Risk areas such as cybersecurity and fraud risk have been dealt with widely; however, the focus in this review has been only on cases where they specifically relate to banking risk management use cases. Papers that focus the research on operational matters, such as credit risk management solutions that address the operational process of credit review and approval, or tools that are focused on supporting traders and trading risk managers in the order and trade management process, have not been considered. Additionally, operational risk management solutions that fit within the operational process to mitigate operational events/incidents (e.g., robotics process automation, STP, anomaly detection) have not been researched.

An overview of the papers that were reviewed is included in Appendix A.

3.1. Credit Risk

The assessment of credit risk remains an important and challenging research topic in the field of finance, with initial efforts dating back to the last century. On the back of the global financial crisis events and the consequent increased regulatory focus, the credit risk assessment process has seen an increased interest within the academic and business community. The general approach to credit risk assessment has been to apply a classification technique on past customer data, including on delinquent customers, to analyse and evaluate the relation between the characteristics of a customer and their potential failure. This could be used to determine classifiers that can be applied in the categorisation of new applicants or existing customers as good or bad (Wang et al. 2005).

Credit risk evaluation occupies an important place within risk management. Techniques such as Logistic regression and discriminant analysis are traditionally used in credit scoring to determine likelihood of default. Support Vector machines are successful in classifying credit card customers who default. They were also found to be competitive in discovering features that are most significant in determining risk of default when tested and compared against the traditional techniques (Bellotti and Crook 2009). Credit risk modelling for the calculation of credit loss exposure involves the estimation of the Probability of Default (PD), the Exposure at Default (EAD) and the Loss Given Default (LGD). This is emphasised by the Basel II accord. Predominant methods to develop models for PD are classification and survival analysis, with the latter involving the estimation of whether the customer would default and when the default could occur. Classifier algorithms were found to perform significantly more accurately than standard logistic regression in credit scoring. Also, advanced methods were found to perform extremely well on credit scoring data sets such as artificial neural networks, performing better than extreme learning machine (Lessmann et al. 2015).

Through the Basel accord requirements, the need to allocate capital in an efficient and profitable manner has lead FIs to build credit scoring models to assess the default risk of their customers. Again, SVM has been shown to yield significantly better results in credit scoring (Van Gestel et al. 2003). An accurate prediction of estimated probability of default delivers more value to risk management in comparison to a binary classification of clients as either credible or not-credible. A number of techniques are used in credit scoring, such as discriminant analysis, logistic regression, Bayes classifier, nearest neighbour, artificial neural networks and classification trees. Artificial neural networks have been shown to perform classifications more accurately than the other five methods (Yeh and Lien 2009)

Methods and models are being constantly developed to address a significant issue at banks, namely, the correct classification of customers and the estimation of credit risk. The various approaches applied in these methods seek to increase the accuracy of creditworthiness predictions that could lead to a bigger and profitable loan portfolio. Neural networks have proven to be of significant value in the credit risk decision process, and their application in company distress predictions was reported to be beneficial in credit risk evaluation (Wójcicka 2017).

While credit risk is the most researched and evaluated risk area for the application of machine learning, this is not a new phenomenon. Dating as far back as 1994, Altman and colleagues conducted an analysis comparing traditional statistical methods of distress and bankruptcy prediction with alternative neural network algorithm, and concluded that a combined approach of the two improved accuracy significantly (Aziz and Dowling 2018).

Hand and Henley (1997) argued that "credit scoring is the term used to describe formal statistical methods which are used for classifying applicants for credit into "good" and "bad" risk classes". Credit scoring models are multivariate statistical models applied to economic and financial indicators to predict the default risk of individuals or companies. These indicators are assigned a weight relative of importance in predictions, and are fed as input to arrive at an index of creditworthiness. This numerical score serves as a measure of the borrower's probability of default. The support vector machine technique was concluded as being the most widely applied in credit risk evaluations. Hybrid SVM models have been proposed to improve the performance by adding methods for the reduction in the feature subset. These, however, only classify, and don't provide an estimation of the probability of default (Keramati and Yousefi 2011).

The dramatic growth in consumer credit has increased the importance of credit scoring models. The bulk of the research appears to be focussed on credit scoring techniques, as seen in the number of papers focussing on this area (Ala'raj and Abbod 2016a; Ala'Raj and Abbod 2016b; Bellotti and Crook 2009; Cao et al. 2013; Van Gestel et al. 2003; Guegan et al. 2018; Huang et al. 2007; Keramati and Yousefi 2011; Lai et al. 2006; Lessmann et al. 2015; Van-Sang and Nguyen 2016; Malhotra and Malhotra 2003; Wang et al. 2015; Wójcicka 2017). Predominantly, the focus is on classification and the application of algorithms that enable this. A number of papers evaluate the various algorithms in an attempt to identify the most efficient and accurate prediction algorithm. The papers make a case that machine learning delivers comparable accuracy and is better equipped to capture non-linear relationships common to credit risk (Bacham and Zhao 2017; Hamori et al. 2018; Zhang 2017).

Zhou and Wang (2012) propose allocating weights to decision trees for better prediction. They put forward an improved random forest algorithm for predictions. The algorithm, during aggregation, allocates weights which are calculated based on out-of-bag errors in training to the decision trees in the forest. They attempt to address the binary classification problem, and their experiment shows that the proposed algorithm beats the original random forest and other popular classification algorithms (SVM, KMM, C4.5) in terms of balanced and overall accuracy metrics.

Some papers focus on a comparison against traditional statistical methods to highlight the efficiency in applying machine learning algorithms. Galindo and Tamayo (2000) research, through a comparative analysis of statistical and machine learning classification techniques, the credit portfolios of institutions to find accurate predictions of individual risk. They built more than 9000 models as part of the study and ranked the performance of the various algorithms. They show that the CART decision tree models provided the best estimates for default, with neural networks coming second. Hamori et al. (2018) studied and compared the prediction accuracy and classification ability of bagging, random forest, boosting with neural network methods in analysing default payment data. They found boosting to be superior among the studied machine learning methods.

A number of researchers have also evaluated the application of hybrid techniques and ensemble methods to study credit scoring (Bastos 2014; Hamori et al. 2018; Raei et al. 2016). In a hybrid system, one technique is employed for the final prediction after the use of several heterogeneous techniques in the analysis (Chen et al. 2016). In dealing with credit scoring problems, ensemble learning, using regularised logistic regression, can be applied. A method of applying clustering and bagging algorithms to balance and diversify the data, followed by lasso-logistic regression ensemble to evaluate credit risks, was found to outperform many popular credit-scoring models (Wang et al. 2015).

Khandani et al. (2010), to improve classification rates of credit card holder delinquencies and defaults, constructed a nonlinear, non-parametric forecast model. The consumer credit risk model was able to identify subtle non-linear relationships in massive datasets. These relationships were typically reportedly difficult to detect when using standard consumer credit-default models such as logit, discriminant analysis or credit scores. This allows for credit line risk management, the forecasting of aggregate consumer credit delinquencies and the forecasting of consumer credit cycle.

Yu et al. (2016) propose a novel multistage deep belief network based extreme machine learning as promising tool for credit risk assessment. The framework of multistage ensemble learning paradigms, working at three stages, is shown to outperform typical single classification techniques and similar multistage ensemble learning paradigms with high prediction accuracy.

"Support Vector Machine" (SVM) is a supervised machine-learning algorithm, and while it is widely used in classification problems, it is relatively new to credit scoring. In this algorithm, each data item is plot as a point in n-dimensional space, the value of each feature is the value of a particular coordinate (n—is number of features). Classification is performed by finding the hyper-plane that is the frontier that segregates two classes (Ray 2015). The SVM has been applied as is or in some varied form to design a credit risk evaluation and credit scoring models (Bellotti and Crook 2009; Cao et al. 2013; Van Gestel et al. 2003; Huang et al. 2007; Lai et al. 2006). Harris (2013) compares SVM-based credit scoring models using broad (<90 days past due) and narrow (>90 days past due), the latter being the more traditional approach. It was found that models built using a broader definition were more accurate, allowing for improvements in prediction accuracy.

Wang et al. (2005) propose a new "fuzzy support vector machine". The algorithm seeks to discriminate good creditors from bad ones through more generalisation while preserving the ability of the fuzzy SVM to be insensitive to outliers. They present a bilateral weighted fuzzy SVM with results that show promising application in credit analysis. Huang et al. (2007) constructed a credit scoring model to evaluate an applicant's credit score from input features based on a hybrid SVM constructed using three strategies.

Yeh and Lien (2009), in their paper, have acknowledged that forecasting the probability of default (PD) is a challenge facing practitioners and researchers, and it needs more study. A few papers have the objective of going beyond just classification, so as to predict the probability of default (PD) or recovery rates (RR) (Bastos 2014; Raei et al. 2016). TheILeast squares vector machine technique, when incorporated into a two-state model, followed by a regression step, for predicting recovery rates, was also reported to show improvement compared to traditional statistical regression models (Yao et al. 2017). Support Vector regression techniques could also be applied to increase the predictive ability of loss given default for corporate bonds outperforming statistical models (Yao et al. 2015). These papers stop short of being able to provide a quantitative value, as they seem to approach more from a classification perspective.

Raei et al. (2016) research a new hybrid model for estimating the probability of default of corporate customers in a commercial bank. They present the hybrid mode as one that can address the 'black box'—model obtained not understandable in terms of parameters—criticism of neural networks. The research combines a two-stage approach, i.e., combining comprehensibility of logit models with the predictive power of non-linear techniques like neural networks. The overall accuracy of this hybrid model was shown outperform both the base models. Low default portfolios (LDP) are those that are considered as very low risk. LDPs have a class imbalance problem as, in a class of defaulters, they are contained in smaller numbers than in a class of good payers. Gradient boosting and random forest classifiers were found to perform well in dealing with samples that exhibited a class imbalance problem (Brown and Mues 2012).

Banks seek to develop efficient models that can assess the likelihood of counterparty defaults. Barboza et al. (2017) test machine learning models to predict bankruptcy one year prior to the event comparing the performance with results from traditional methods. They report significant predictive accuracy being achieved, and also suggest that ML techniques can easily be applied for substantial classification accuracy in comparison to traditional mechanisms. Despite the concerns around the explanatory ability of the model, given the complexity of bankruptcy models, machine learning could prove to be an important aid. Yang et al. (2011) also explore a novel method to predict bankruptcy, proposing a combined method of partial least squares (PLS) -based feature selection with SVM for information fusion. A bank could benefit from the model's ability to select the financial indicators which are most relevant in the prediction process, and also from its high level of prediction accuracy.

There are also a few papers that research the area of stress testing in credit risk management (Islam et al. 2013). Stress testing requires the modelling of the link between macro-economic developments and banking variables to determine the impact of extreme scenarios on a bank. More frequently, bottom-up approaches are used where predictions about future profits/losses are made on mostly disaggregated portfolio levels, making it data intensive and difficult to identify the exact drives of loses. Predictions on an aggregated portfolio using a top down method can complement this process. A supervised learning algorithm that does not need a pre-specified model is the Least Absolute Shrinkage and Selection Operator (Lasso) method. A more involved version of the Lasso is Adaptive Lasso, which possesses attractive convergence properties. Adaptive Lasso can be used in the absence of theoretical models, as in the case of top-down stress testing, to discover a parsimonious top-down model from a set of thousand possible specifications. It was shown to give sparse, approximately unbiased solutions, by searching for variables that describe the behaviour of credit loss rates best resulting in a parsimonious description of the relation between macro-economy and credit loss rates. A key issue is the need for substantial amounts of data to train a model (Blom 2015).

Model selection and forecasting have become a challenge as stress scenarios become more comprehensive, encompassing an increasing number of primary variables. Machine learning techniques for identifying patters and relationships between data can facilitate model selection and forecasting. These techniques don't seem to be widely applied in stress testing. When there are a large number of potential covariates and the number of observations is small, lasso regressions are found to be suited to building forecasting models. They are likely to outperform traditional statistical models in forecasting the performance indicators required in applied stress testing. An advantage of the Lasso-type estimators is that they can handle complications arising from the high dimensional nature of stress tests (Chan-Lau 2017). The Multivariate Adaptive Regression Splines (MARS), a machine learning technique, can be viewed as a generalisation of stepwise linear regression of the classification and regression tree (CART) method. Stress testing statistical regression models such as Vector Autoregression (VAR) is a common modelling approach which is known to be unable to explain the phenomenon of fat-tailed distributions. An empirical test of these models found that the MARS model exhibited greater accuracy in model testing and superior out-of-sample performance, with MARS producing more reasonable forecasts (Jacobs 2018). Probabilistic graphs may be used for modelling and assessments of credit concentration risk with a tree-augmented Bayesian network providing a better understanding of the risk. This was also found to be suitable for stress testing analyses, with the ability to provide estimates of risk of losses consequent to changes in a borrowers financial condition (Pavlenko and Chernyak 2009). EMA workbench is a software toolbox, developed by a team at Technische Universiteit Delft, TBM Faculty (Policy Analysis Section). Particular machine learning algorithms and advanced visualisation tools are used to perform multiple experiments and analyse the results, providing the ability to explore possible uncertainties and identify causes based on the inputs.

Neural networks, Support Vector Models and Random Forest appear to be the most researched algorithms in the credit risk management area.

3.2. Market Risk

Risk can be measured by the standard deviation of unexpected outcomes, also called volatility. Value at Risk (VAR) calculates the worst loss over a target horizon that will not be exceeded with a given level of confidence and captures the combined effect of underlying volatility and exposure to financial risks (Jorion 2007). Volatility forecasting in the financial markets is important in the areas of risk management and asset pricing, among others. By using NN models, the performance of the volatility estimation method can be improved (Monfared and Enke 2014).

Zhang et al. (2017) propose a model that is based on the Generalized Autoregressive Conditional Heteroskedastic (GARCH) model and Extreme Machine Learning (ELM) algorithm to estimate volatility. The model predicts the volatility of target time series using GELM-RBF and extrapolating the predicted volatilities allows for the calculation of VaR with improved performance in terms of accuracy and efficiency. The model utilises a stochastic mapping method that doesn't require the Gaussian likelihood for estimation and is a not linear data driver model.

Market risk also includes interest rate and equity risk. Interest rate curves, which is the relation between the interest rate and the time to maturity of the debt for a given borrower in a given currency, is widely used in financial engineering and market risk management. A clustering method called the "Gaussian Mixture Model" can be used to develop nonlinear models of the evolution of the parameters and then to forecast interest rate curves. This can allow for better visualisation of interest rates (Kanevski and Timonin 2010). Machine learning clustering methods designed to address Stochastic Differential Equation (SDE) can be applied to develop anticipatable VAR models that aim at being a leading risk measure of market regime change. This can partially address some of the complexity introduced by the challenging regulatory environment, such as scenario coherence (Mahdavi-Damghani and Roberts 2017).

3.3. Liquidity Risk

A number of liquidity risk problems can be solved through the use of machine learning. Measurement of liquidity risk, the analysis of key factors including the study of the interconnections between the factors can be achieved through the use of machine learning. For the purposes of estimating a risk measure Artificial Neural Networks (ANN), a genetic algorithm can be applied. ANN can be used in the approximation of the general risk trend and determination of the most influential factors. The probability that a liquidity risk event will occur can be estimated by the application of Bayesian Networks. The ANN and the BN implementations were capable of distinguishing the most critical liquidity risk factors measuring the risk by a functional approximation and a distributional estimation, respectively (Tavana et al. 2018).

3.4. Operational Risk

Machine learning is also applied in operational areas that enable the mitigation of risk, i.e., detection and/or prevention of risks. In the area of operational risk, aside from cyber security cases, machine learning is predominantly focused on problems related to fraud detection and suspicious transactions detection.

Khrestina et al. (2017), in their paper, propose a prototype for the generation of a report that allows for the detection of suspicious transactions. The prototype uses a logistical regression algorithm. It is noteworthy that they have also included a survey of six software solutions that are currently implemented at various banks for the automation of suspicious transaction detection and monitoring processes. While the authors make a reference to algorithms, it is unclear whether these products apply machine learning techniques, and if so, with which algorithms. No further research was done on these products as this was not in the scope of the paper.

One such area where an intelligent system based on machine learning is known to add value is in the defence against spammers where the attackers' techniques evolve. Losses from spam potentially include lost productivity, disrupted communications, malware attacks and theft of data, including financial loss. Proofpoint's MLX technology uses advanced machine learning techniques to provide comprehensive spam detection that guards against the threat of spam. Millions of messages can be analysed by the technology, which also automatically refines the detection algorithm to identify and detect newer threats (Proofpoint 2010). While it was not in scope for this research, being more of an operational control to manage risk, it has been highlighted as a case of how machine learning is used in managing cybersecurity risks.

In money laundering, criminals route money through various transactions, layering them with legitimate transactions to conceal the true source of the funds. The funds typically originate from criminal or illegal activities, and can be further used in other illegal activities including the financing of terrorist activities. There has been extensive research on detecting financial crimes using traditional statistical methods, and more recently, using machine-learning techniques. Clustering algorithms identify customers with similar behavioural patterns and can help to find groups of people working together to commit money laundering (Sudjianto et al. 2010). A major challenge for banks, given the large volume of transactions per day and the non-uniform nature of many, is to be able to sort through all the transactions and identify those that are of suspicious nature. Financial institutions utilise anti-money laundering systems to filter and classify transactions based on degrees of suspiciousness. Structured processes and intelligent systems are required to enable the detection of these money laundering transactions (Kannan and Somasundaram 2017).

Money laundering is another area that poses a significant challenge to financial institutions, given the high volumes and complexity of transactions coupled with the dynamic and fast evolving nature of financial crimes, and the need to do so on real-time data sets. In the area of financial crime detection, there has been a significant amount of research in the application of statistical learning and data mining for developing classification models to flag suspicious transactions. A C5.0 algorithm was applied to predict risk levels based on the different customer potential risk factors to create the set of rules for cluster allocation. The key factors were used to characterise transaction profiles. The model reportedly provided a 99.6% correct classification rate on the test data. The number of alerted cases was reported to have reduced from the close to 30% of transactions to less than 1% (Villalobos and Silva 2017).

Credit card fraud is significantly increasing annually, costing consumers and the industry billions of dollars. Fraudsters are constantly finding newer techniques to perpetrate the crime. In order to manage the increasing fraud risk and minimise losses, banks have fraud detection systems in place.

The systems are oriented towards increasing the detection rate while minimising the false positive rate. Models are estimated based on samples of fraudulent and legitimate transactions in supervised detection methods while in unsupervised detection methods outliers or unusual transactions are identified as potential cases of fraud. Both seek to predict the probability of fraud in a given transaction. Some reported challenges in credit card fraud detection are the non-availability of real data sets, unbalanced data sets, size of the data sets and the dynamic behaviour of fraudster. Bayesian algorithms, K-Nearest neighbor, Support Vector machines (SVM) and bagging ensemble classifier based on decision tree have been varyingly used in fraud detection systems. A comparative evaluation showed that the bagging ensemble classifier based on decision tree algorithms works well, as it is independent of attribute values, and is also able to handle class imbalance (Zareapoor and Shamsolmoali 2015). False alarms, namely transactions labelled as fraudulent that are in fact legitimate, are significant, causing concerns for customers and delaying the detection of actual fraud transactions. Large Canadian banks rely heavily on NN scores, ranging from 1 to 999, with 1 being the lowest chance of a fraudulent transaction, determined by neural network algorithms. Reportedly, 20% of transactions with a NN score greater than or equal to 990 are fraudulent, causing fraud analysts to inefficiently spend time investigating legitimate transactions. A meta-classifier (a multiple algorithm learning technique) applied to a post-neural network was shown to provide quantifiable savings improvements with a larger percentage of fraudulent transactions being caught (Pun and Lawryshyn 2012).

Also, in the areas of operational risk, there are a few papers on fraud risk detection in credit cards and online banking. They concern credit card fraud detection in domains not specifically related to bank risk management or the banking industry. One would note that the algorithms they refer to were SVM, KNN, Naïve Bayes Classifier, Bagging ensemble classifier based on decision tree (Dal Pozzolo 2015; Pun and Lawryshyn 2012; Vaidya and Mohod 2014).

4. Discussion

Credit scoring involves the assignment of a numerical value to the firm (or client) indicating whether the firm (or client) is likely to default or not. Most of the research has been focused on addressing this area by handling it as a classification problem, predicting a prospective customer as "good" or "bad" so as to facilitate the credit decision and management of credit risk. There is therefore a dominance of classification related algorithms. Many papers have gone beyond only providing a classification of creditors, and have addressed how to predict of the probability of default or recovery rate i.e., estimating the probability of default (PD), loss given default (LGD), exposure at default (EAD). It would be of significant value to banks and their risk management functions to have research and models for predicting or estimating the PD, LGD, EAD, and therefore, estimating the credit loss exposure.

Machine learning techniques have been proven to perform better than traditional statistical techniques, both in classification and also predictive accuracy. The support vector machine is seen to be a widely tested and proven machine learning approach. Much empirical work is based on observational data. Selection mechanisms could result in non-random samples, either due to sample design or the behaviour of the sampled units. In the former, data are usually missing, and in the latter, there is a self-selection of the sample units. This leads to sample selection bias (Arezzo and Guagnano 2018). When the sample data being studied has a proportional representation of certain dependent variable outcomes (e.g., default, fraudulent transaction) different from their proportional representation in the population they are drawn from, it is said to be 'choice based'. This 'choice based' sampling induces a bias in the estimation (Greene 1992). As machine learning bases much of the modelling upon learning from available data, it could be prone to the same problems and biases that affect traditional statistical methods. As machine-learning methods are compared to traditional statistical techniques, it would be beneficial to evaluate and understand how problems inherent to traditional statistical research methods fare when treated by machine learning techniques.

The application of machine learning for market risk management also doesn't appear to have been adequately studied. Many papers have researched market volatility or market risk from a portfolio or investment risk management perspective. However, from a bank risk management perspective, the papers appear limited. Further research on this, especially from the point of view of stress testing or tail end risk capture, is merited. Liquidity risk that has, since the financial crisis, attracted a lot of attention from regulators, has a few use cases researched.

In the operational risk area, studies have been predominantly focused on fraud and suspicious transaction detection—problems that are typically addressed by classification algorithms. Clustering analysis, Bayesian networks, decision, classification trees, SVM are commonly noted in the application of machine learning algorithms. Neural networks have also been referred to as a very prevalent and prominent technique in credit card fraud detection.

Much of the other areas of non-financial risk management, country risk management, compliance risk management—aside from money laundering related uses—cases haven't been explored adequately. Conduct risk, which has become a key risk and assumed a high priority for regulators and banks driven by the spate of conduct issues in Europe, US and Asia Pacific also seems to be lacking in research papers, though machine learning is offered as a solution to manage conduct risk (Oliver Wyman 2017). Furthermore, many of the standard risk management tools such as risk assessments, risk monitoring and risk reporting appear as areas that could significantly benefit from further research.

Dataset sources used by researchers for their studies are varied, with some receiving data from commercial banks or from databases provided by financial services providers (e.g., Moody's), and with some researchers conducting their studies using publicly-available data. Problems highlighted are that the data can be highly skewed (e.g., low default rates), data incompleteness and data integrity (e.g., may not be labelled correctly or as expected (Khandani et al. 2010). A wider availability of real world data sets would definitely encourage more research in evaluating the many problems faced by risk management functions.

5. Conclusions

The future of machine learning in the banking and financial industry is well recognised, and it is expected that the field of risk management will also seek to apply machine learning techniques to enhance their capabilities. Despite being critiqued for operating like a black box, the ability of machine learning techniques to analyse volumes of data without being constrained by assumptions of distribution and deliver much value in exploratory analysis, classification and predictive analytics, is significant. This offers the potential to transform the area of risk management. Machine learning, identified as one of the technologies with important implications for risk management, can enable the building of more accurate risk models by identifying complex, nonlinear patterns within large datasets. This paper has presented an assessment, analysis and evaluation of the research around the application of machine learning in risk management within the banking industry. Most of the research appears to be focused around credit risk management. One could attribute this to the fact that credit risks is considered the most significant risk to a banking organisation. More specifically from a methodology perspective, credit risk management problems researched have been around credit scoring; it would go a long way to research how machine learning can be applied to quantitative areas for better computations of credit risk exposure by predicting probabilities of default, loss given default given the many complexities and the varied factors that are involved. Market risk has seen some research with machine learning being used to forecast volatility, interest rate curves, and market regime change. Liquidity risk, despite the increased attention in the industry post the concern from Regulators, has seen limited research. Given the implications to a bank's profitability and solvency as a consequence of a liquidity risk event materialising, liquidity risk would be a very good candidate to be research extensively, more notably, research around predicting liquidity risk events in isolation or as a network of factors or events. Operational risk has also seen very limited research. Research has focused on application of machine learning to prevent or detect operational risk events; however, there is very limited application to operational risk management practices especially in the areas of risk identification, assessments, monitoring, reporting. Given the vast amounts of operational data available (internal to a bank) machine learning could be applied in effectively developing operational risk management capabilities, which has predominantly relied on qualitative factors to measure, report and manage risk. The review has shown that areas of stress testing, tail risk capture, scenario analysis—areas that rely on predictive analysis of large volumes of data —have also seen only limited research. The advantages and disadvantages of the different machine learning techniques in solving specific risk management problems can also be further evaluated and studied to maximise the value.

The review has showed that the application of machine learning in the management of banking risks such as credit risk, market risk, operational risk and liquidity risk has been explored; however, it doesn't appear commensurate with the current industry level of focus on both risk management and machine learning. In areas of market risk, operational risk, and liquidity risk research appear lacking, and there is significant potential for further study. The application of machine learning could be further researched for some areas where analysis or modelling on volumes of data with complex and non-linear computations is required. As one of a group of topics that requires a lot of analysis of different data types to predict potential events or estimate losses, these include tail risk analysis and stress testing. Measuring and reporting technology risk is still a new area and could be further researched, especially as this risk is rising up the charts and senior managers and risk managers in bank are starting to seek more insight into what the technology risk is. As banks look to mature their enterprise risk management capabilities, it would be beneficial to study how machine learning can be applied in the aggregation of risks, and enhancing risk reporting capabilities. While areas such as conduct risk could also be researched, it is noted that these areas would benefit more from application in the operational area such, as behaviour monitoring and activity monitoring. While these go towards managing risk (risk mitigation, risk detection) at the bank, they are not the risk management systems (risk measurement, risk assessment) that are the focus of this research.

In conclusion, while there has been research on the application of machine learning in risk management over the years, it still falls short and is not on par across the various areas of risk management or risk methodologies. There still remain a large number of areas as highlighted above in bank risk management that could significantly benefit from study on how machine learning can be applied to address specific problems.

Author Contributions: Conceptualization, M.L.; Formal analysis, M.L.; Investigation, M.L.; Methodology, M.L.; Supervision, S.S and K.M.; Writing—original draft, M.L.; Writing—review & editing, S.S, K.M. and M.L.

Funding: This research received no external funding.

Conflicts of Interest: The authors declare no conflict of interest.

Appendix A

The table provides a list of the papers that have been reviewed classifying then by the risk type, including the risk management method/tool addressed and the algorithms referred to in the application.

Risk Type	Risk Management Method/Tool	Reference	Algorithm
Compliance Risk Management	Risk Monitoring	Mainelli and Yeandle 2006	SVM
Credit Risk Management—Concentration Risk	Stress Testing	Pavlenko and Chernyak 2009	Bayesian Networks
Credit Risk Management—Consumer Credit	Exposure (PD, LGD, EAD)	Yeh and Lien 2009	Bayesclassifier, Nearest neighbor, ANN, Classification trees
Credit Risk Management—Consumer Credit	Scoring Models	Bellotti and Crook 2009	SVM
Credit Risk Management—Consumer Credit	Scoring Models	Galindo and Tamayo 2000	CART, NN, KNN
Credit Risk Management—Consumer Credit	Scoring Models	Wang et al. 2015	Lasso logistic regression
Credit Risk Management—Consumer Credit	Scoring Models	Hamori et al. 2018	Bagging, Random Forest, Boosting
Credit Risk Management—Consumer Credit	Scoring Models	Harris 2013	SVM
Credit Risk Management—Consumer Credit	Scoring Models	Huang et al. 2007	SVM
Credit Risk Management—Consumer Credit	Scoring Models	Keramati and Yousefi 2011	NN, Bayesian Classifier, DA, Logistic Regression, KNN, Decision tree, Survival Analysis, Fuzzy Rule based system, SVM, Hybrid mode
Credit Risk Management—Consumer Credit	Scoring Models	Khandani et al. 2010	CART
Credit Risk Management—Consumer Credit	Scoring Models	Lai et al. 2006	SVM
Credit Risk Management—Consumer Credit	Scoring Models	Lessmann et al. 2015	Multiple algos assessed
Credit Risk Management—Consumer Credit	Scoring Models	Van-Sang and Nguyen 2016	Deep Learning
Credit Risk Management—Consumer Credit	Scoring Models	Yu et al. 2016	Deep belief network, Extreme Machine Learning
Credit Risk Management—Consumer Credit	Scoring Models	Wang et al. 2005	SVM, Fuzzy SVM
Credit Risk Management—Consumer Credit	Scoring Models	Zhou and Wang 2012	Random Forest
Credit Risk Management—Coporate Credit	Exposure (PD, LGD, EAD)	Bastos 2014	Bagging
Credit Risk Management—Coporate Credit	Exposure (PD, LGD, EAD)	Barboza et al. 2017	Neural Network, SVM, Boosting, Bagging, Random Forest

Risk Type	Risk Management Method/Tool	Reference	Algorithm
Credit Risk Management—Coporate Credit	Exposure (PD, LGD, EAD)	Raei et al. 2016	Neural Networks
Credit Risk Management—Coporate Credit	Exposure (PD, LGD, EAD)	Yang et al. 2011	SVM
Credit Risk Management—Coporate Credit	Exposure (PD, LGD, EAD)	Yao et al. 2017	SVR
Credit Risk Management—Coporate Credit	Scoring Models	Ala'Raj and Abbod 2016b	Multiclassifer system (MCS)—Ensemble—neural networks (NN), support vector machines (SVM), random forests (RF), decision trees (DT) and naïve Bayes (NB).
Credit Risk Management—Coporate Credit	Scoring Models	Ala'raj and Abbod 2016a	GNG, MARS
Credit Risk Management—Coporate Credit	Scoring Models	Bacham and Zhao 2017	ANN, Random Forest
Credit Risk Management—Coporate Credit	Scoring Models	Cao et al. 2013	SVM
Credit Risk Management—Coporate Credit	Scoring Models	Van Gestel et al. 2003	SVM
Credit Risk Management—Coporate Credit	Scoring Models	Guegan et al. 2018	Elastic Net, random forest, Boosting, NN
Credit Risk Management—Coporate Credit	Scoring Models	Malhotra and Malhotra 2003	NN
Credit Risk Management—Coporate Credit	Scoring Models	Wójcicka 2017	Neural networks
Credit Risk Management—Coporate Credit	Scoring Models	Zhang 2017	KNN, Random Forest
Credit Risk Management—Corporate Credit	Stress Testing	Blom 2015	Lasso regression
Credit Risk Management—Corporate Credit	Stress Testing	Chan-Lau 2017	Lasso regression
Credit Risk Management—Credit Card Risk	Exposure (PD, LGD, EAD)	Yao et al. 2017	SVM
Credit Risk Management—Cross-risk	Stress Testing	Jacobs 2018	MARS
Credit Risk Management—Wholesale	Stress Testing	Islam et al. 2013	Cluster analysis
Liquidity Risk Management—Liquidity Risk	Risk Limits	Gotoh et al. 2014	vSVM
Liquidity Risk Management—Liquidity Risk	Risk Monitoring	Sala 2011	ANN

Risk Type	Risk Management Method/Tool	Reference	Algorithm
Liquidity Risk Management—Liquidity Risk	Scoring Models	Tavana et al. 2018	ANN, Bayesian Networks
Management—Consumer Credit	Scoring Models	Brown and Mues 2012	Gradient, Boosting, Random Forest, Least Squares—SVM
Market Risk Management—Equity Risk	Value at Risk	Zhang et al. 2017	GELM
Market Risk Management—Equity Risk	Value at Risk	Mahdavi-Damghani and Roberts 2017	Cluster analysis
Market Risk Management—Equity Risk	Value at Risk	Monfared and Enke 2014	NN
Market Risk Management—Interest Rate Risk	Value at Risk	Kanevski and Timonin 2010	SOM, Gaussian Mixtures, Cluster Analysis
Operational Risk Management—Cybersecurity	Risk Assessment (RCSA)	Peters et al. 2017	Non-linear clustering method
Operational Risk Management—Fraud Risk	Operational Risk Losses	Pun and Lawryshyn 2012	Neural Networks, k-Nearest Neighbor, Naïve Bayesian, Decision Tree
Operational Risk Management—Fraud Risk	Operational Risk Losses	Sharma and Choudhury 2016	SOM
Operational Risk Management—Fraud Risk	Risk Monitoring	Ngai et al. 2011	neural networks, Bayesian belief network, decision trees
Operational Risk Management—Fraud Risk	Risk Monitoring	Sudjianto et al. 2010	SVM, Classification Trees, Ensemble Learning, CART, C4.5, Bayesian belief networks, HMM
Operational Risk Management—Money Laundering/Financial Crime	Risk Monitoring	Khrestina et al. 2017	logistic regression

References

Ala'raj, Maher, and Maysam F. Abbod. 2016a. A New Hybrid Ensemble Credit Scoring Model Based on Classifiers Consensus System Approach. *Expert Systems with Applications* 64: 36–55. [CrossRef]

Ala'Raj, Maher, and Maysam F. Abbod. 2016b. Classifiers Consensus System Approach for Credit Scoring. *Knowledge-Based Systems* 104: 89–105. [CrossRef]

Apostolik, Richard, Christopher Donohue, Peter Went, and Global Association of Risk Professionals. 2009. *Foundations of Banking Risk: An Overview of Banking, Banking Risks, and Risk-Based Banking Regulation.* New York: John Wiley.

Arezzo, Maria, and Giuseppina Guagnano. 2018. Response-Based Sampling for Binary Choice Models with Sample Selection. *Econometrics* 6: 12. [CrossRef]

Awad, Mariette, and Rahul Khanna. 2015. Machine Learning in Action: Examples. *Efficient Learning Machines.* [CrossRef]

Aziz, Saqib, and Michael M. Dowling. 2018. AI and Machine Learning for Risk Management. *SSRN Electronic Journal.* [CrossRef]

Bacham, Dinesh, and Janet Zhao. 2017. Machine Learning: Challenges and Opportunities in Credit Risk Modeling. Available online: https://www.moodysanalytics.com/risk-perspectives-magazine/managing-disruption/spotlight/machine-learning-challenges-lessons-and-opportunities-in-credit-risk-modeling (accessed on 2 April 2018).

Barboza, Flavio, Herbert Kimura, and Edward Altman. 2017. Machine learning models and bankruptcy prediction. *Expert Systems with Applications* 83: 405–17. [CrossRef]

Basel Committee on Banking Supervision. 2005a. *Guidance on Paragraph 468 of the Framework Document*. Basel: Bank for International Settlements.

Basel Committee on Banking Supervision. 2005b. *An Explanatory Note on the Basel II IRB Risk Weight Functions*. Basel: Bank for International Settlements.

Basel Committee on Banking Supervision. 2006. *Minimum Capital Requirements for Market Risk*. Basel: Bank for International Settlements.

Basel Committee on Banking Supervision. 2008. *Principles for Sound Liquidity Risk Management and Supervision*. Basel: Bank for International Settlements.

Basel Committee on Banking Supervision. 2011. *Principles for the Sound Management of Operational Risk*. Basel: Bank for International Settlements, pp. 1–27.

Bastos, João A. 2014. Ensemble Predictions of Recovery Rates. *Journal of Financial Services Research* 46: 177–93. [CrossRef]

Bauguess, Scott W. 2015. *The Hope and Limitations of Machine Learning in Market Risk Assessment*. Washington, DC: U.S. Securities and Exchange Commission.

Bellotti, Tony, and Jonathan Crook. 2009. Support Vector Machines for Credit Scoring and Discovery of Significant Features. *Expert Systems with Applications*. [CrossRef]

Blom, Tineke. 2015. Top down Stress Testing: An Application of Adaptive Lasso to Forecasting Credit Loss Rates. Master's Thesis, Faculty of Science, Hongkong, China.

Brown, Iain, and Christophe Mues. 2012. An experimental comparison of classification algorithms for imbalanced credit scoring data sets. *Expert Systems with Applications* 39: 3446–53. [CrossRef]

Cao, Jie, Hongke Lu, Weiwei Wang, and Jian Wang. 2013. A Loan Default Discrimination Model Using Cost-Sensitive Support Vector Machine Improved by PSO. *Information Technology and Management* 14: 193–204. [CrossRef]

Chan-Lau, Jorge. 2017. Lasso Regressions and Forecasting Models in Applied Stress Testing. *IMF Working Papers* 17: 1. [CrossRef]

Chen, Ning, Bernardete Ribeiro, and An Chen. 2016. Financial Credit Risk Assessment: A Recent Review. *Artificial Intelligence Review* 45: 1–23. [CrossRef]

Dal Pozzolo, Andrea. 2015. Adaptive Machine Learning for Credit Card Fraud Detection. Unpublished doctoral dissertation, Université libre de Bruxelles, Faculté des Sciences—Informatique, Bruxelles.

Deloitte University Press. 2017. *Global Risk Management Survey*, 10th ed. Deloitte University Press: Available online: https://www2.deloitte.com/tr/en/pages/risk/articles/global-risk-management-survey-10th-ed.html (accessed on 4 October 2018).

Financial Stability Board. 2017. Artificial Intelligence and Machine Learning in Financial Services. Market Developments and Financial Stability Implications. *Financial Stability Board*. November 1. Available online: http://www.fsb.org/2017/11/artificial-intelligence-and-machine-learning-in-financial-service/ (accessed on 2 July 2018).

Galindo, Jorge, and Pablo Tamayo. 2000. Credit Risk Assessment Using Statistical and Machine Learning: Basic Methodology and Risk Modeling Applications. *Computational Economics* 15: 107–43. [CrossRef]

Gotoh, Jun-ya, Akiko Takeda, and Rei Yamamoto. 2014. Interaction between financial risk measures and machine learning methods. *Computational Management Science* 11: 365–402. [CrossRef]

Greene, William H. 1992. A Statistical Model for Credit Scoring. NYU Working Paper No. EC-92-29. Available online: https://ssrn.com/abstract=1867088 (accessed on 8 April 1992).

Guegan, Dominique, Peter Addo, and Bertrand Hassani. 2018. Credit risk analysis using machine and deep learning models. *Risks* 6: 38.

Hamori, Shigeyuki, Minami Kawai, Takahiro Kume, Yuji Murakami, and Chikara Watanabe. 2018. Ensemble Learning or Deep Learning? Application to Default Risk Analysis. *Journal of Risk and Financial Management* 11: 12. [CrossRef]

Hand, David J., and William E. Henley. 1997. Statistical Classification Methods in Consumer Credit Scoring: A Review. *Journal of the Royal Statistical Society Series A: Statistics in Society*. [CrossRef]

Harris, Terry. 2013. Quantitative credit risk assessment using support vector machines: Broad versus Narrow default definitions. *Expert Systems with Applications* 40: 4404–13. [CrossRef]

Helbekkmo, Hans, Alok Kshirsagar, Andreas Schlosser, Francesco Selandari, Uwe Stegemann, and Joyce Vorholt. 2013. *Enterprise Risk Management—Shaping the Risk Revolution*. New York: McKinsey & Co., Available online: www.rmahq.org (accessed on 18 June 2018).

Huang, Cheng Lung, Mu Chen Chen, and Chieh Jen Wang. 2007. Credit Scoring with a Data Mining Approach Based on Support Vector Machines. *Expert Systems with Applications* 33: 847–56. [CrossRef]

Hull, John. 2012. *Risk Management and Financial Institutions*. New York: John Wiley and Sons, vol. 733.

Islam, Tushith, Christos Vasilopoulos, and Erik Pruyt. 2013. Stress—Testing Banks under Deep Uncertainty. Paper presented at the 31st International Conference of the System Dynamics Society, Cambridge, MA, USA, July 21–25; Available online: http://repository.tudelft.nl/islandora/object/uuid:c162de43-4235-4d29-8eed-3246df87e119?collection=education (accessed on 17 July 2018).

Jacobs, Michael, Jr. 2018. The validation of machine-learning models for the stress testing of credit risk. *Journal of Risk Management in Financial Institutions* 11: 218–43.

Jorion, Philippe. 2007. *Value at Risk: The New Benchmark for Managing Financial Risk*. New York: McGraw-Hill.

Kanevski, Mikhail F., and Vadim Timonin. 2010. Machine learning analysis and modeling of interest rate curves. Paper presented at the 18th European Symposium on Artificial Neural Networks ESANN, Bruges, Belgium, April 28–30; Available online: https://www.elen.ucl.ac.be/Proceedings/esann/esannpdf/es2010-17.pdf (accessed on 18 June 2018).

Kannan, Somasundaram, and K. Somasundaram. 2017. Autoregressive-Based Outlier Algorithm to Detect Money Laundering Activities. *Journal of Money Laundering Control* 20: 190–202. [CrossRef]

Keramati, Abbas, and Niloofar Yousefi. 2011. A proposed classification of data mining techniques in credit scoring. Paper presented at the 2011 International Conference of Industrial Engineering and Operations Management, Kuala Lumpur, Malaysia, January 22–24.

Khandani, Amir E., Adlar J. Kim, and Andrew W. Lo. 2010. Consumer credit-risk models via machine-learning algorithms. *Journal of Banking & Finance* 34: 2767–87.

Khrestina, Marina Pavlovna, Dmitry Ivanovich Dorofeev, Polina Andreevna Kachurina, Timur Rinatovich Usubaliev, and Aleksey Sergeevich Dobrotvorskiy. 2017. Development of Algorithms for Searching, Analyzing and Detecting Fraudulent Activities in the Financial Sphere. *European Research Studies Journal* 20: 484–98.

Lai, Kin Keung, Lean Yu, Ligang Zhou, and Shouyang Wang. 2006. Credit risk evaluation with least square support vector machine. In *International Conference on Rough Sets and Knowledge Technology*. Berlin/Heidelberg: Springer, pp. 490–95.

Lessmann, Stefan, Bart Baesens, Hsin Vonn Seow, and Lyn C. Thomas. 2015. Benchmarking State-of-the-Art Classification Algorithms for Credit Scoring: An Update of Research. *European Journal of Operational Research* 247: 124–36. [CrossRef]

Mahdavi-Damghani, Babak, and Stephen Roberts. 2017. A Proposed Risk Modeling Shift from the Approach of Stochastic Differential Equation towards Machine Learning Clustering: Illustration with the Concepts of Anticipative and Responsible VaR. *SSRN Electronic Journal*. [CrossRef]

Mainelli, Michael, and Mark Yeandle. 2006. Best execution compliance: New techniques for managing compliance risk. *The Journal of Risk Finance* 7: 301–12. [CrossRef]

Malhotra, Rashmi, and D. K. Malhotra. 2003. Evaluating Consumer Loans Using Neural Networks. *Omega* 31: 83–96. [CrossRef]

MetricStream. 2018. The Chief Risk Officer's Role in 2018 and Beyond Managing the Challenges and Opportunities of a Digital Era New Roles of the CRO. Available online: https://www.metricstream.com/insights/chief-risk-officer-role-2018.htm (accessed on 23 June 2018).

Monfared, Soheil Almasi, and David Enke. 2014. Volatility Forecasting Using a Hybrid GJR-GARCH Neural Network Model. *Procedia Computer Science* 36: 246–53. [CrossRef]

Ngai, Eric W. T., Yong Hu, Yiu Hing Wong, Yijun Chen, and Xin Sun. 2011. The Application of Data Mining Techniques in Financial Fraud Detection: A Classification Framework and an Academic Review of Literature. *Decision Support Systems* 50: 569. [CrossRef]

Oliver Wyman. 2017. Next Generation Risk Management. Available online: https://www.oliverwyman.com/content/dam/oliver-wyman/v2/publications/2017/aug/Next_Generation_Risk_Management_Targeting_A-Technology_Dividend.pdf (accessed on 1 May 2018).

Pavlenko, Tatjana, and Oleksandr Chernyak. 2009. Bayesian Networks for Modeling and Assessment of Credit Concentration Risks. *International Statistical Conference Prague*. Available online: http://www.czso.cz/conference2009/proceedings/data/methods/pavlenko_paper.pdf (accessed on 21 July 2018).

Peters, Gareth, Pavel V. Shevchenko, Ruben Cohen, and Diane Maurice. 2017. Statistical Machine Learning Analysis of Cyber Risk Data: Event Case Studies. Available online: https://ssrn.com/abstract=3073704 (accessed on 18 June 2018).

Proofpoint. 2010. MLX Whitepaper "Machine Learning to Beat Spam Today and Tomorrow". Available online: https://www.excelmicro.com/datasheets/Proofpoint-White-Paper-MLX-Technology.pdf (accessed on 2 May 2018).

Pun, Joseph, and Yuri Lawryshyn. 2012. Improving credit card fraud detection using a meta-classification strategy. *International Journal of Computer Applications* 56: 41–46. [CrossRef]

Raei, Reza, Mahdi Saeidi Kousha, Saeid Fallahpour, and Mohammad Fadaeinejad. 2016. A Hybrid Model for Estimating the Probability of Default of Corporate Customers. *Iranian Journal of Management Studies* 9: 651–73.

Ray, Sunil. 2015. Understanding Support Vector Machine Algorithm from Examples (along with Code). Available online: https://www.analyticsvidhya.com/blog/2017/09/understaing-support-vector-machine-example-code/ (accessed on 16 August 2018).

Sala, Jordi Petchamé. 2011. Liquidity Risk Modeling Using Artificial Neural Network. Master's thesis, Universitat Politècnica de Catalunya, Barcelona, Spain.

Saunders, Anthony, Marcia Millon Cornett, and Patricia Anne McGraw. 2006. *Financial Institutions Management: A Risk Management Approach*. New York: McGraw-Hill.

Shalev-Shwartz, Shai, and Shai Ben-David. 2014. *Understanding Machine Learning: From Theory to Algorithms*. Cambridge: Cambridge University Press. [CrossRef]

Sharma, Shashank, and Arjun Roy Choudhury. 2016. Fraud Analytics: A Survey on Bank Fraud Prediction Using Unsupervised Learning Based Approach. *International Journal of Innovation in Engineering Research and Technology* 3: 1–9.

Sudjianto, Agus, Sheela Nair, Ming Yuan, Aijun Zhang, Daniel Kern, and Fernando Cela-Díaz. 2010. Statistical Methods for Fighting Financial Crimes. *Technometrics* 52: 5–19. [CrossRef]

Tavana, Madjid, Amir Reza Abtahi, Debora Di Caprio, and Maryam Poortarigh. 2018. An Artificial Neural Network and Bayesian Network Model for Liquidity Risk Assessment in Banking. *Neurocomputing* 275: 2525–54. [CrossRef]

Vaidya, Avanti H., and Sudhir W. Mohod. 2014. Internet Banking Fraud Detection using HMM and BLAST-SSAHA Hybridization. *International Journal of Science and Research (IJSR)* 3: 574–9.

Van Gestel, Ir Tony, Bart Baesens, Ir Joao Garcia, and Peter Van Dijcke. 2003. A support vector machine approach to credit scoring. In *Forum Financier—Revue Bancaire Et Financiaire Bank En Financiewezen*. Bruxelles: Larcier, pp. 73–82. Available online: http://citeseerx.ist.psu.edu/viewdoc/download?doi=10.1.1.93.6492&rep=rep1&type=pdf (accessed on 7 July 2018).

Van Liebergen, Bart. 2017. Machine Learning: A Revolution in Risk Management and Compliance? *Journal of Financial Transformation* 45: 60–67.

Van-Sang, Ha, and Ha-Nam Nguyen. 2016. Credit Scoring with a Feature Selection Approach Based Deep Learning. In *MATEC Web of Conferences*. Les Ulis: EDP Sciences, volume 54, p. 05004. Available online: https://www.matec-conferences.org/articles/matecconf/abs/2016/17/matecconf_mimt2016_05004/matecconf_mimt2016_05004.html (accessed on 19 July 2018).

Villalobos, Miguel Agustín, and Eliud Silva. 2017. A Statistical and Machine Learning Model to Detect Money Laundering: An Application. Available online: http://hddavii.eventos.cimat.mx/sites/hddavii/files/Miguel_Villalobos.pdf (accessed on 21 June 2018).

Wang, Yongqiao, Shouyang Wang, and Kin Keung Lai. 2005. A New Fuzzy Support Vector Machine to Evaluate Credit Risk. *IEEE Transactions on Fuzzy Systems* 13: 820–31. [CrossRef]

Wang, Hong, Qingsong Xu, and Lifeng Zhou. 2015. Large Unbalanced Credit Scoring Using Lasso-Logistic Regression Ensemble. *PLoS ONE* 10: e0117844. [CrossRef] [PubMed]

Wójcicka, Aleksandra. 2017. Neural Networks vs. Discriminant Analysis in the Assessment of Default. *Electronic Economy*, 339–49. [CrossRef]

Yang, Zijiang, Wenjie You, and Guoli Ji. 2011. Using partial least squares and support vector machines for bankruptcy prediction. *Expert Systems with Applications* 38: 8336–42. [CrossRef]

Yao, Xiao, Jonathan Crook, and Galina Andreeva. 2015. Support vector regression for loss given default modelling. *European Journal of Operational Research* 240: 528–38. [CrossRef]

Yao, Xiao, Jonathan Crook, and Galina Andreeva. 2017. Enhancing two-stage modelling methodology for loss given default with support vector machines. *European Journal of Operational Research* 263: 679–89. [CrossRef]

Yeh, I. Cheng, and Chehui Lien. 2009. The Comparisons of Data Mining Techniques for the Predictive Accuracy of Probability of Default of Credit Card Clients. *Expert Systems with Applications*. [CrossRef]

Yu, Lean, Zebin Yang, and Ling Tang. 2016. A Novel Multistage Deep Belief Network Based Extreme Learning Machine Ensemble Learning Paradigm for Credit Risk Assessment. *Flexible Services and Manufacturing Journal* 28: 576–92. [CrossRef]

Zareapoor, Masoumeh, and Pourya Shamsolmoali. 2015. Application of Credit Card Fraud Detection: Based on Bagging Ensemble Classifier. *Procedia Computer Science* 48: 679–86. [CrossRef]

Zhang, Wenhao. 2017. Machine Learning Approaches to Predicting Company Bankruptcy. *Journal of Financial Risk Management* 6: 364–74. [CrossRef]

Zhang, Heng Guo, Chi Wei Su, Yan Song, Shuqi Qiu, Ran Xiao, and Fei Su. 2017. Calculating Value-at-Risk for High-Dimensional Time Series Using a Nonlinear Random Mapping Model. *Economic Modelling* 67: 355–67. [CrossRef]

Zhou, Lifeng, and Hong Wang. 2012. Loan Default Prediction on Large Imbalanced Data Using Random Forests. *TELKOMNIKA Indonesian Journal of Electrical Engineering*. [CrossRef]

10

Can Sustainable Investment Yield Better Financial Returns: A Comparative Study of ESG Indices and MSCI Indices

Mansi Jain, Gagan Deep Sharma * and Mrinalini Srivastava

School of Management Studies, Guru Gobind Singh Indraprastha University, Sector 16C, Dwarka, New Delhi 110078, India; guptamansi007@gmail.com (M.J.); mrinalinisrivastava26@gmail.com (M.S.)
* Correspondence: angrishgagan@gmail.com

Abstract: 'Sustainable investment'—includes a variety of asset classes selected while caring for the causes of environmental, social, and governance (ESG). It is an investment strategy that seeks to combine social and/ or environmental benefits with financial returns, thus linking investor's social, ethical, ecological and economic concerns Under certain conditions, these indices also help to attract foreign capital, seeking international participation in the local capital markets. The purpose of this paper is to study whether the sustainable investment alternatives offer better financial returns than the conventional indices from both developed and emerging markets. With an intent to maintain consistency, this paper comparatively analyzes the financial returns of the Thomson Reuters/S-Network global indices, namely the developed markets (excluding US) ESG index—TRESGDX, emerging markets ESG index—TRESGEX, US large-cap ESG index—TRESGUS, Europe ESG index—TRESGEU, and those of the usual markets, namely MSCI world index (MSCI W), MSCI All Country World Equity index (MSCI ACWI), MSCI USA index (MSCI USA), and MSCI Europe Australasia Far East index (MSCI EAFE), MSCI Emerging Markets index (MSCI EM) and MSCI Europe index (MSCI EU). The study also focusses on the inter-linkages between these indices. Daily closing prices of all the benchmark indices are taken for the five-year period of January 2013–December 2017. Line charts and unit-root tests are applied to check the stationary nature of the series; Granger's causality model, auto-regressive conditional heteroskedasticity (ARCH)-GARCH type modelling is performed to find out the linkages between the markets under study followed by the Johansen's cointegration test and the Vector Error Correction Model to test the volatility spillover between the sustainable indices and the conventional indices. The study finds that the sustainable indices and the conventional indices are integrated and there is a flow of information between the two investment avenues. The results indicate that there is no significant difference in the performance between sustainable indices and the traditional conventional indices, being a good substitute to the latter. Hence, the financial/investment managers can obtain more insights regarding investment decisions, and the study further suggests that their portfolios should consider both the indices with the perspective of diversifying the risk and hedging, and reap benefits of the same. Additionally, corporate executives shall use it to benchmark their own performance against peers and track news as well.

Keywords: sustainability indices; socially responsible investment; index returns; financial markets; ARCH; Johansen's cointegration; VECM

JEL Classification: G11; G15; G19; Q56; M14

1. Introduction

'Sustainable investment' includes a variety of asset classes selected while caring for the causes of environmental, social, and governance (ESG). It is an investment strategy that seeks to combine social and/or environmental benefits with financial returns, thus linking investor's social, ethical, ecological, and economic concerns (Brzeszczynski and McIntosh 2014). Nowadays, corporate sustainability has become a crucial aspect of a company's business strategy. Companies have begun to realize business benefits from the responsible practices, and even investors focus more on 'value' having realized that a company's sustainability strategy may result in better risk-adjusted returns (Vives and Wadhwa 2012).

Sustainability indices differ from the conventional market indices and also assist analysts and investors in monitoring the firm's sustainability performance, as only those companies that out-perform their peers in an in-depth analysis of economic, environmental, and social criteria are included in sustainability index categorizing as the industry sustainability leaders (del Mar Miralles-Quiros et al. 2017). Extant literature has studied the return and volatility linkages and comparisons among the general market indices and sustainability indices. For example, Charlo et al. (2015); Lopez et al. (2007); Santis et al. (2016); de Souza Cunha and Samanez (2013) and Tularam et al. (2010) study the sustainable indices in terms of their risks and returns, and their impact on the market as a whole. The sustainable and the conventional indices are also compared by evaluating the performance of the companies included in each of these indices based on their respective financial ratio analysis and overall business performance (Martinez-Ferrero and Frias-Aceituno 2015; Pilar Marti et al. 2015; Ransariya and Bhayani 2015; Skare and Golja 2012).

The history of sustainable indices is considerably short, since Domini 400 social index launched in May 1990 by Kinder, Lydenberg, Domini, and Co., becoming the world's first sustainability index. (Guerard 1997a, 1997b). The growing acceptance of sustainable indices, also known as socially responsible investments (SRIs), has led to the establishment of a number of other sustainable indices, which now includes offerings from the Dow Jones, E. Capital, Ethibel, FTSE4Good, Humanix, Jantzi, KLD Analytics, and Vigeo (Fowler and Hope 2007).

Most of the studies on socially responsible investments concentrate on the performance of sustainable or socially responsible mutual funds. The socially responsible mutual funds have been the focus of many researchers, while the sustainable indices have not received the same level of attention in academic research (Fowler and Hope 2007). The results of the academic research on the performance of socially responsible mutual funds are varied. A number of studies report minimal difference in risk-adjusted returns between ethical and conventional funds (Fowler and Hope 2007; Guerard 1997a). Sustainable investments can indeed provide diversification gains for conventional stock portfolios globally (Balcilar et al. 2017; Brzeszczynski and McIntosh 2014).

The present paper aims to study whether the returns from the sustainable indices are co-integrated with the returns from the conventional indices. This paper also studies the volatility and the volatility spillover between the two set of indices. Finally, it attempts to suggest if the investors and portfolio managers can reap the benefits by diversifying their investments among the conventional and sustainable indices. This paper is organized as follows—the present study, the second section reviews the literature, the third section elaborates the research methodology, the fifth section presents the empirical analysis, and the sixth section concludes.

2. Literature Review

The development of sustainable indices presages well for the growing interest in sustainable and societal issues. A good amount of research has studied the return and volatility linkages and comparisons among the general market indices and sustainability indices. For example, Charlo et al. (2015, 2017); Fowler and Hope (2007); Lopez et al. (2007); Mensi et al. (2017); Santis et al. (2016); Schmid et al. (2017); de Souza Cunha and Samanez (2013); la Torre et al. (2016), and Tularam et al. (2010) study the sustainable indices in terms of their risks and returns, and their impact on the market as a whole. Sustainable investment is a potential solution to social and ecological issues that transforms the financial markets to have more accountability of their impacts and hence, more research in this field is required to develop it as an applied field of investment (Talan and Sharma 2019).

On the methodological front, researchers employ simple methods like calculating correlations, exponential smoothening to more complex methods, such as different forms of auto-regressive conditional heteroskedasticity (ARCH), and various other econometric models (such as VaR). Some of their interesting applications are evident in the studies by Balcilar et al. (2017); Bianconi et al. (2013); Mensi et al. (2017); Ortas et al. (2014); Park and Jei (2010); Sadorsky (2014); Seo et al. (2009), and Tse (1999). Sadorsky (2014) employs multi-variate GARCH models to study the volatilities and conditional correlation between a stock price index comprising of socially responsible companies, oil prices, and gold prices and concludes that social and responsible investment exhibits similar results received on investing in the S&P 500. On the other hand, Tse (1999) examines the price discovery process and the volatility spillover between the Dow Jones Industrial Average (DJIA) index and the index futures, based on a bivariate EGARCH model, indicating a significant bi-directional flow of information between the two indices.

Some existing literature comparatively analyses the relationship of corporate social responsibility and financial performance of companies listed on sustainable indices and those listed on general indices. A recent study by Alshehhi et al. (2018) use content analysis to examine the literature concerning the impact of corporate sustainability on corporate financial performance and find that 78% of the publications opine a positive relationship between corporate social responsibility and financial performance. Lopez et al. (2007) study the difference in the performance indicators between European firms that have adopted corporate social responsibilities (CSR) and others that have not, selecting the firms listed on the Dow Jones Sustainability Index and others on the Dow Jones Global Index. On similar lines, Gallego-Alvarez et al. (2014); Patari et al. (2012); Pilar Marti et al. (2015); Rajnoha et al. (2016, 2017) and Skare and Golja (2012) analyze the financial performance of companies with respect to their adoption of social responsibilities. Santis et al. (2016) evaluate the performance of companies listed in the corporate sustainability index in comparison with the performance of companies listed in the Sao Paulo Stock Exchange Index. Similarly, Pilar Marti et al. (2015) analyze the firms listed on the Stoxx Europe 600 Index and the Stoxx Europe Sustainability Index. Considering the growth in the amount of funds invested in the Socially Responsible Investments globally to around US$6.5 trillion, while around US$55 billion is placed in the Australian market, Tularam et al. (2010) examine the relationship of the Australian SRI market with fourteen other markets, namely—Canada, Denmark, France, Germany, Hong Kong, Ireland, Japan, Netherlands, Norway, South Africa, Sweden, Switzerland, United Kingdom, and the United States during the period 1994–2009, using the DCC-GARCH model.

The relationship between social, environmental and financial performance in companies has been a subject of debate but the results obtained so far are not conclusive (Lassala et al. 2017). Stock exchanges have created indices for more sustainable business, with a growing number of companies joining them—the return generated by firms in this profile remains controversial. Santis et al. (2016) compare the companies listed in the corporate sustainability index with companies listed in the Sao Paulo Stock Exchange Index and conclude that characteristics such as the sectoral classification have more influence on firms' financial performance than their investments in sustainable initiatives. Lo and Sheu (2007) and Skare and Golja (2012) examine the impact of the CSR practices on the financial performance of the firm and conclude that CSR firms, on average, perform better financially than the non-CSR firms, and by adopting sustainable practices, they are in a better position to be rewarded by the investors with a higher valuation. Charlo et al. (2015) study the Spanish sustainability index, the FTSE4Good IBEX (the sustainable market index created by partnership between Financial Times Stock Exchange (FTSE) Group and Bolsas y Mercados Espanoles, Spanish stock exchange market) and opine that socially responsible corporations obtain higher profits, for the same level of systematic risk and show greater sensitivity to market information. Likewise, Liket and Maas (2016), utilize the data from 2006–2009, for a sample of Dow Jones Sustainability Index and conclude that corporate social performance has little impact on the company's financial performance, company size, and profitability. Additionally, Fowler and Hope (2007) highlight that the entry of the Dow Jones and FTSE (the FTSE4Good sustainable market indices launched by Financial Times Stock Exchange Group) in the market of sustainable responsible indices and the increase in index licensees, indicate the growing interest of companies and the fund managers using the money under management in the sustainable indices.

Considering the pre-crisis period from 2003–2007 that marked the increase in Socially Responsible Investment worldwide, Ortas and Moneva (2011) examined the market reaction to the company's inclusion in, and exclusion from, the Dow Jones Sustainability Stoxx Index, and opine that investors value the non-excluded companies more in achieving a good level of corporate social performance and corporate financial performance. Consistently, Lopez et al. (2007) study the pre-crisis period from 1999–2004 and conclude that corporate social responsibility practices have a negative impact on the company's financial performance over the short term, which eventually decreases over the longer time frame. With a post-crisis period from 2012–2016, Alexandre and Francisco (2018) examine the sustainable practices of the firms listed on the Corporate Sustainability Index, with respect to the Brazilian stock market and find that environmental, human resource, and organizational management as the baseline for the implementation of the sustainable practices.

On the other hand, relating to the 2008–2013 time frame, involving the global financial crisis of 2008, Ortas et al. (2014) find that social and responsible investment strategies as less risky in comparison to the conventional investment avenues, specifically during the periods of maximum market instability. Studying the same crisis of 2008, del Mar Miralles-Quiros et al. (2017) find that investors value companies with sustainability leadership, which is proxied by its inclusion in the Dow Jones Sustainability Index Europe. Other studies considering the period of market crisis, include Antonakakis et al. (2016); Brzeszczynski and McIntosh 2014; Mensi et al. (2017); Ransariya and Bhayani (2015); Schmid et al. (2017); de Souza Cunha and Samanez (2013), and la Torre et al. (2016).

There is immense research on the U.S.' Sustainability Indices (Antonakakis et al. 2016; Mensi et al. 2017; Giannarakis et al. 2011; Lopez et al. 2007; Mensi et al. 2017; la Torre et al. 2016), Europe's Sustainability Index (Charlo et al. 2015, 2017; Lopez et al. 2007; del Mar Miralles-Quiros et al. 2017; Ortas et al. 2014; Pilar Marti et al. 2015; Stolowy and Paugam 2018), and Australian markets (Lokuwaduge and Heenetigala 2017; Tularam et al. 2010). However, not much of the literature is available on the economies of developing countries (Talan and Sharma 2019). Alshehhi et al. (2018) comment on the literature trends relating to the relationship between corporate sustainability and corporate financial performance, and opine that the number of similar publications from the developing countries lags behind those of the developed countries, indicating the need for more research in the economies of the developing economies. This paper incorporates this field of study.

An extensive survey of the literature reveals that, although there are papers that evaluate sustainable indices, namely the Dow Jones Sustainability Index (Antonakakis et al. 2016; Giannarakis et al. 2011; Hsu et al. 2008; Lopez et al. 2007; del Mar Miralles-Quiros et al. 2017; Skare and Golja 2012), FTSE4Good-IBEX (Charlo et al. 2015, 2017; Lassala et al. 2017; Ortas et al. 2014), and the IPC sustainability (IPCS) index (la Torre et al. 2016), corporate environmental sustainability reporting (CESR) index (Ortas et al. 2015); no studies have evaluated the relationship between the Thomson Reuters Sustainable Indices and their conventional alternatives namely the MSCI stock market indices worldwide.

Most of the published research has focused on the returns of the sustainable indices compared with the traditional market indices (Fowler and Hope 2007; Mensi et al. 2017; de Souza Cunha and Samanez 2013; la Torre et al. 2016; Vives and Wadhwa 2012), or the financial performance of the companies listed on the sustainability index relative to the companies listed on the conventional market indices. (Alexandre and Francisco 2018; Alshehhi et al. 2018; Lassala et al. 2017; Santis et al. 2016). However, the extant literature does not include the understating of the volatility spillovers and the inter-dependency between the sustainable indices and the conventional market indices (Sadorsky 2014). Modelling and forecasting volatility is an essential component of the modern day financial market because precise estimates of volatility, and the information on the interdependency of the two set of indices, shall assist in derivative pricing, portfolio optimization, risk management, and hedging. (Balcilar et al. 2017; Mensi et al. 2017). Balcilar et al. (2017) opines that in comparison to the conventional stocks, sustainable investment options improve the risk/return profile of the portfolios. This raises the need for an understanding about the volatility dynamics and the inter-relatedness between the sustainable and the conventional indices. Hence, the novelty of this paper lies in the fact that it examines the financial returns and the volatility spillover between these afore-mentioned sustainable indices and the conventional market indices, thereby addressing an important gap in the literature.

3. Methodology

This article comparatively analyzes the financial returns of the S-Network global indices, namely the developed markets (excluding the US) ESG index (TRESGDX), emerging markets ESG index (TRESGEX), US large-cap ESG index (TRESGUS), and Europe ESG index (TRESGEU), and their reciprocating alternatives from both the developed and the emerging markets, namely MSCI World index (MSCI W), MSCI All Country World Equity index (MSCI ACWI), MSCI USA index (MSCI USA), MSCI Europe Australasia Far East index (MSCI EAFE), MSCI Emerging Markets index (MSCI EM), and MSCI Europe index (MSCI EU). The study also focusses on the volatility and volatility spillover between these indices. Daily closing prices of all the benchmark indices are taken for the five-year period from the 1 January 2013 to 31 December 2017, on the lines of the period selection in extant literature, which uses five year data (Alexandre and Francisco 2018; Tse 1999; Ortas and Moneva 2011; Ortas et al. 2014; de Souza Cunha and Samanez 2013; la Torre et al. 2016).

The paper takes the log of the ten series and arrives at their respective daily returns. These return series are evaluated for their stationarity, and all further analysis are performed on their daily return values i.e., the log of the ten series. These variables are named as r_m_w, r m_acwi, r_m_usa, r_m_eafe, r_m_em, r_m_eu, r_ tdx, r_tex, r_tus, and r_teu. Data analysis starts with the computation of the descriptive statistics, which includes the presentation of mean, median, standard deviation, skewness, kurtosis, Jarque-Bera statistic, and coefficient of variation. The paper then proceeds with the econometric analysis, along with the respective line graphs of the series. Augmented Dickey-Fuller (ADF) unit root test is applied to examine whether or not the series are stationary. The following equation explains the basic concept of the unit root testing:

$$y_t = py_{t-1} + x_t' + \varepsilon_t, \tag{1}$$

where x_t' are optional exogenous repressors, which consist of a constant, r and d are the parameters to be estimated, and ε_t is assumed to be white noise. If $|p| \geq 1$, then y is a non-stationary series. If $|p| \leq 1$, then y is a stationary series. Hence, we evaluate the hypothesis of stationary by testing whether the absolute value of $|p|$ is less than one.

The standard Dicky-Fuller test is carried out by estimating Equation (2) after subtracting y_{t-1} from both sides of the equation,

$$\Delta y_t = \alpha y_{t-1} + x_t' + \varepsilon_t. \tag{2}$$

This is followed with the Granger causality check to assess the volatility of the series. The paper applies the auto-regressive conditional heteroscedasticity (ARCH) family model. The relevant ARCH family model is chosen, using Akaike Information Criterion (AIC) and Schwarz Information Criterion SIC as benchmarks, where the model with lowest AIC and SIC values is chosen to be applied in individual series, which is also evident in the studies by Bildirici and Ersin (2009); Su (2010); Dimitriou et al. (2013); Kalu (2015); Kenourgios and Dimitriou (2015); Tse (1999) and Wang and Moore (2008). To study the return linkages between both the set of indices, the Johansen's cointegration test is applied. Finally, the vector error correction model (VECM) is applied to test the volatility spillover between the sustainable indices and their conventional alternatives, on the lines of extant literature which employs

VECM model to test volatility spillover (Abdullah et al. 2016; Bellalah et al. 2016; Huo and Ahm 2018; Sehgal et al. 2015; Humpe and Macmillan 2007).

The series are further tested for ARCH effect that is the serial correlation of the heteroscedasticity. The ARCH effect measures the risk of an asset while this while this helps detect the time-varying phenomenon in the conditional volatility, thereby suggesting different types of models (ARCH/GARCH) to capture these dynamics (Figure 1).

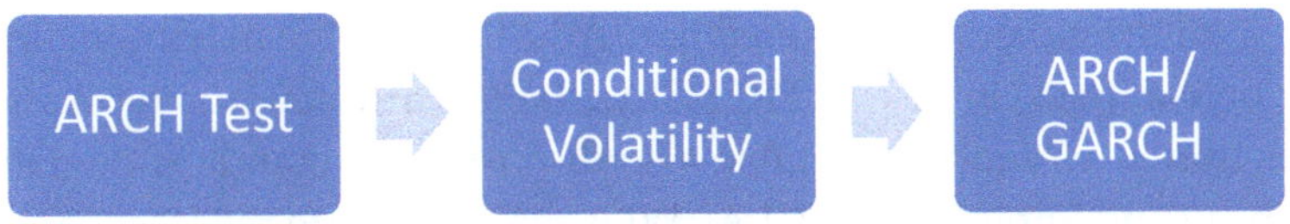

Figure 1. Methodology to test the ARCH effect.

As detailed further in Section 4 of this paper, the p-value of the chi-square leads to the rejection of the null hypothesis—'there is no ARCH effect' indicates the presence of ACRH effect in all the series. Therefore, we proceed to apply the ARCH/GARCH modelling. The most appropriate ARCH family model is chosen on the basis of the AIC and SIC values. As per the AIC and SIC value criterion, the lower the values of AIC and SIC, the better the model. Out of the ARCH (5,0), GARCH (1,1), TARCH and EGARCH models, EGARCH reported the lowest AIC and SIC values for all the ten series. The EGARCH model, also known as the exponential GARCH model was proposed by Nelson (1991). The EGARCH model can be explained by the following equation (Su and Fleisher 1998; Brooks 2008; Su 2010):

$$\ln\left(\sigma_t^2\right) = \omega + \beta \ln\left(\sigma_{t-1}^2\right) + \gamma \frac{u_{t-1}}{\sqrt{\sigma_{t-1}^2}} + \alpha \left[\frac{|u_{t-1}|}{\sqrt{\sigma_{t-1}^2}} - \sqrt{\frac{2}{\pi}} \right]. \quad (3)$$

EGARCH model is advocated for various reasons; first, since $\log\left(\sigma_t^2\right)$ is modelled, even if the parameters are negative, $\left(\sigma_t^2\right)$ will be positive. Hence, there is no need to impose non-negativity constraints on the model parameters. Second, asymmetries are allowed. If the relationship between volatility and returns is negative, γ will be negative. The α parameter represents a magnitude effect of the model, the "GARCH" effect. β measures the conditional volatility. When β is relatively large, then volatility takes a long time to die out. EGARCH model also exhibits the leverage effect, which is a negative correlation between the past return and future volatility of return.

The article further applies Johansen's cointegration analysis on the series under reference to check for the cointegration among them. This test also enables the examination of the volatility spillover between the sustainability indices and the conventional indices in the market. The co-integration test is applied on the absolute series (which is of a non-stationarity nature), rather than the return series.

The co-integration test is followed up by the VECM. A VECM model is restricted VAR designed for use with non-stationary series that are cointegrated. The VECM has cointegration relations, so that the long run behavior of the extraneous variables can be eliminated from converging to their cointegrating relations while adjusting the short-run dynamics. VECM can be stated as:

$$\Delta x_t = x_{t-1} + \sum_{i=1}^{p-1} \phi * \Delta x_{t-i} + \varepsilon_t. \quad (4)$$

If $\Pi = 0$, then there is no cointegration.

4. Results

In order to get comparative insights into the risks and returns from the sustainability indices and the conventional indices under reference, this paper computes descriptive statistics i.e., the mean, median, minimum, maximum, standard deviation, skewness, and kurtosis for understanding the behavior of the series, along with the p-value of Jarque-Bera statistic to check for the normality of the series.

Table 1 shows that the average daily returns of MSCI ACWI, MSCI EAFE, MSCI EM, MSCI EU, MSCI USA, MSCI W, TRESGDX, TRESGEU, TRESGEX, TRESGUS are 0.0317 per cent, 0.0185 per cent, 0.0068 per cent, 0.0163 per cent, 0.0480 per cent, 0.0347 per cent, 0.0186 per cent, 0.0197 per cent, 0.0051 per cent, and 0.0524 per cent respectively, concluding that MSCI USA gives the highest average return on a daily basis. Average annual returns for the ten indices are found to be 8.26 per cent, 4.84 per cent, 1.77 per cent, 4.24 per cent, 12.5 per cent, 9.04 per cent, 4.52 per cent, 5.15 per cent, 1.35 per cent, and 13.64 per cent, respectively. This depicts that on average, TRESGUS provides the highest return out of all the indices under reference. Additionally, the maximum and minimum value is the highest and lowest (both) in case of TRESGEU. Table 1 also reports the skewness and kurtosis values of the series under reference. The table also discusses the standard deviation of the various indices under the study and imply that MSCI ACWI is the series with the least variations, followed by MSCI World and MSCI USA, while on the other hand, TRESGEU exhibits the highest variation in its values. The Jarque-Bera probability value is 0.00000 for all ten indices, which indicates that the null hypothesis of normality can be rejected for all ten indices, concluding that the series under reference are non-normal. The application of the augmented-Dicky Fuller (ADF) unit root test on all the ten series reveal the rejection of the null hypothesis i.e., series have a unit root, concluding that the series under reference are stationary. As suggested by existing literature (see for example, Kuwornu and Owusu-Nantwi 2011; S Sharma and Mishra 2015; Sharma and Gupta 2015), we proceed by applying the econometric analysis on the reference series.

The following are line graphs of the various indices, representing the stationarity of the series under study.

Figure 2 presents the combined graph of returns of all ten market indices during the study period from 2013–2017. It is evident that the indices are quite volatile and highly inter-dependent throughout the concerned time period.

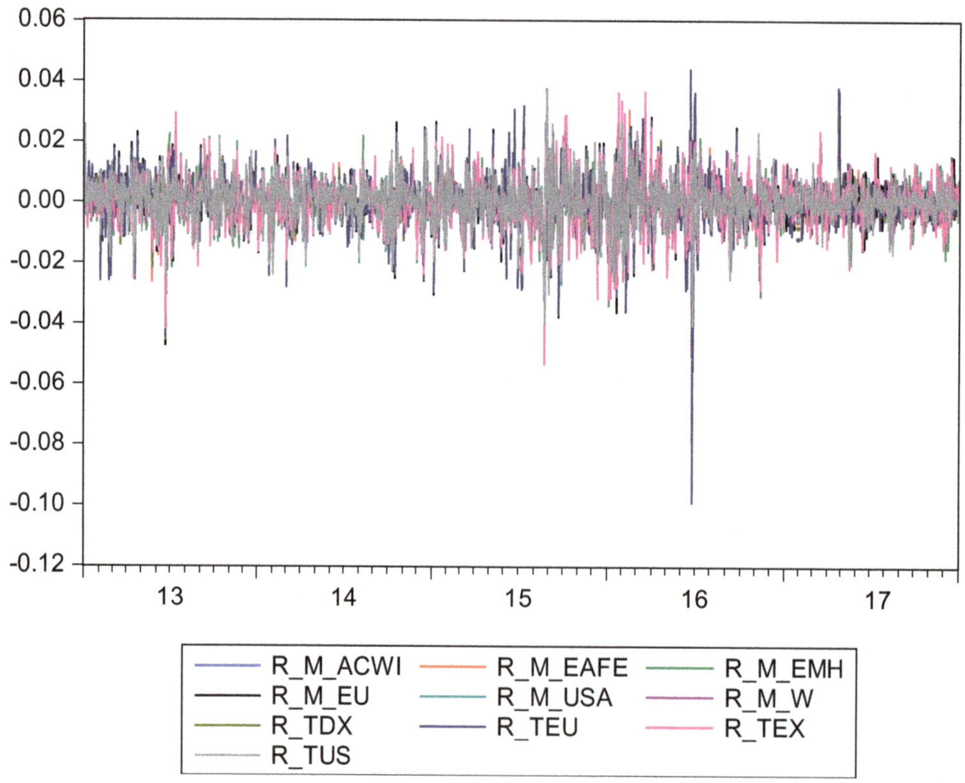

Figure 2. Consolidated graph of the ten indices.

Table 1. Descriptive statistics of the sustainable and conventional indices.

Statistics	R_M_ACWI	R_M_EAFE	R_M_EM	R_M_EU	R_M_USA	R_M_W	R_TDX	R_TEU	R_TEX	R_TUS
Mean	0.000317	0.000186	0.000068	0.000163	0.000480	0.000347	0.000187	0.000198	0.000052	0.000524
Median	0.000497	0.000356	0.000441	0.000123	0.000277	0.000563	0.000371	0.000400	0.000138	0.000374
Maximum	0.026212	0.035626	0.032220	0.043212	0.037691	0.025652	0.037064	0.044109	0.036928	0.036073
Minimum	−0.048806	−0.073647	−0.051282	−0.091786	−0.040445	−0.050287	−0.082237	−0.098918	−0.053383	−0.040615
Std. Dev.	0.006469	0.007862	0.008586	0.009607	0.007391	0.006553	0.008137	0.009646	0.009068	0.007507
Skewness	−0.817664	−0.907482	−0.328174	−0.880051	−0.431247	−0.815105	−1.039662	−1.035854	−0.242739	−0.442586
Kurtosis	8.530125	11.194234	5.339575	11.568677	6.084535	8.421365	13.325701	13.711232	5.402859	5.946921
Jarque-Bera	1804.169366	3821.346034	320.313797	4151.220495	556.510322	1738.646813	6018.695544	6456.968810	326.011146	513.631891
Probability	0.000000	0.000000	0.000000	0.000000	0.000000	0.000000	0.000000	0.000000	0.000000	0.000000

Further, Granger's causality test is applied to check the causality between the reference series. In case of MSCI ACWI and MSCI EAFE, the results exhibited the rejection of the null hypothesis i.e., MSCI EAFE does not Granger cause MSCI ACWI and vice-versa, hence Granger causality runs both ways between MSCI EAFE and MSCI ACWI. This index exhibits the same behavior with certain other indices, namely MSCI USA and TRESGUS. MSCI World is seen to witness Granger causality running both ways, with the maximum indices under study namely with MSCI EU, MSCI USA, TRESGUS and TRESGEU. The same is the case for MSCI EM with MSCI EAFE, MSCI USA, and TRESGUS. The same phenomena are also evident between MSCI EAFE and MSCI USA. On the other hand, we accept the null hypothesis that MSCI EM does not Granger cause MSCI ACWI, but the other way around, results reveal rejection of the same hypothesis. The same phenomena are present where Granger causality runs one way from MSCI ACWI to MSCI EU, TRESGDX, TRESGEU, and TRESGEX. There is one way causality that runs from MSCI USA to MSCI EU, TRESGDX, TRESGEU, and TRESGEX. MSCI World Granger cause TRESGDX, TRESGEX, MSCI ACWI, MSCI EAFE, and MSCI EM, thereby resulting in one way causality. TRESGDX value reveals one way Granger causality with TRESGEU, MSCI EAFE, MSCI EM, and MSCI EU, while TRESGEU value causes one way Granger causality with MSCI EU, MSCI EAFE, and MSCI EM. The MSCI EU Index statistic reveals one way Granger causality with MSCI EAFE and MSCI EM. In case of the sustainable indices, TRESGEX statistic reveals one-way causality to MSCI EAFE, MSCI EM, MSCI EU, TRESGDX and TRESGEU, while TRESGUS value exhibits one way Granger causality to MSCI EU, MSCI EAFE, TRESGDX, TRESGEX, and TRESGEU. Clearly, MSCI World, MSCI ACWI, TRESGEX, and TRESGUS statistics reveal one way Granger causality on the maximum number of indices under reference.

To check for the volatility behavior of the index series, the ARCH family models are applied on the data series, the stationarity of which is already proven through the ADF unit root test.

In line with the discussion presented under Section 3 of this paper, we proceed with the EGARCH analysis.

Table 2 indicates that all the values of β are statistically significant (at 95% level of confidence). The values of β for all the series are more than 0.9 implying that volatility is quite high and takes a longer time to die out, with the β value being relatively low for both the US indices i.e., MSCI USA and TRESGUS.

All the values of α in Table 2 are statistically significant (at 95% level of confidence) and relatively larger than 0.1 throughout the markets, except for the emerging market indices, namely MSCI EM and TRESGEX, and MSCI ACWI, which means that the volatility is sensitive to market events for these indices.

Additionally, the values of leverage effect as measured by γ are negative and statistically significant at 95% level of confidence throughout the markets, which indicates that good news generates less volatility in the market than the bad news.

The overall analysis of Table 2 indicates that both the sustainable indices and the conventional indices are volatile throughout the period under study, with the US indices being relatively less volatile, and hence taking time to die down. For majority of indices, the values report sensitivity to the market events, except in the case of both the emerging market indices and the MSCI ACWI. Also, the leverage effect is observed to be negative and is statistically significant for all the indices.

This paper further applies Johansen's co-integration analysis on the series under reference to check for the co-integration among them. Table 3 tests the null hypothesis that no co-integrating equation exists between the series under reference. The trace statistic value of 3866.44 is observed to be greater than the corresponding critical value i.e., 239.23. Therefore, the H_0 of no co-integrating equation is rejected, while results reveal the acceptance of H_0 of 'at most 10' cointegrating equation at 0.05 level.

Table 2. Auto-regressive conditional heteroskedasticity (ARCH) and GARCH Coefficients for the sustainable and conventional market indices.

Coefficients	MSCI ACWI	MSCI EAFE	MSCI EM	MSCI EU	MSCI USA	MSCI W	TRESGDX	TRESGEU	TRESGEX	TRESGUS
Ω	−0.321344 *	−0.304368 *	−0.251332 *	−0.401082 *	−0.725725 *	−0.369354 *	−0.313757 *	−0.447815 *	−0.199743 *	−0.699055 *
A	0.091134 *	0.129268 *	0.084865 *	0.151492 *	0.101944 *	0.101830 *	0.130717 *	0.161361 *	0.080939 *	0.104174 *
γ	−0.145660 *	−0.091401 *	−0.081596 *	−0.122241 *	−0.255610 *	−0.157770 *	−0.105855 *	−0.116434 *	−0.078737 *	−0.214269 *
B	0.975582 *	0.979192 *	0.9809162 *	0.969728 *	0.935471 *	0.971559 *	0.978237 *	0.965585 *	0.985769 *	0.938017 *

(* indicates statistically significant values at 95% level of confidence)

Table 3. Results from Johansen's cointegration analysis: Trace statistics.

Trace Statistic Test Analysis			
Hypothesized No. of CE(s)	**Trace Statistic**	**Critical Value**	**Probability**
None *	3866.443	239.2354149	1.0000
At most 1 *	3172.861	197.3708726	1.0000
At most 2 *	2571.371	159.5296978	1.0000
At most 3 *	2067.848	125.6154331	1.0000
At most 4 *	1681.732	95.75366142	1.0000
At most 5 *	1321.34	69.81888745	1.0000
At most 6 *	964.1827	47.85612716	0.0001
At most 7 *	679.2532	29.79707334	0.0001
At most 8 *	423.0889	15.49471288	0.0001
At most 9 *	206.8152	3.841465501	0.0000
Trace test indicates 10 cointegrating eqn(s) at the 0.05 level			

* denotes rejection of the hypothesis at the 0.05 level.

Similarly, the results of the maximum eigenvalue statistic (Table 4) exhibit that at no cointegrating equation, maximum eigen statistic is 693.58 which is greater than the corresponding critical value 64.50. Therefore, the H_0 of no co-integrating equation is rejected which means that there is at least one co-integrating equation. Clearly, the results indicate, at most, 10 co-integrating equation at the 0.05 level of significance. Hence, in both the tests, there is at most 10 co-integrating equations.

Table 4. Results from Johansen's co-integration analysis: Max Eigen value.

Max-Eigen Statistic Test Analysis			
Hypothesized No. of CE(s)	**Max-Eigen Statistic**	**Critical Value**	**Probability**
None *	693.5813	64.50471706	0.0001
At most 1 *	601.4906	58.43353809	0.0001
At most 2 *	503.5226	52.36260958	0.0001
At most 3 *	386.1161	46.23141975	0.0001
At most 4 *	360.3923	40.07757358	0.0001
At most 5 *	357.1572	33.87686662	0.0001
At most 6 *	284.9295	27.58433779	0.0001
At most 7 *	256.1643	21.1316163	0.0001
At most 8 *	216.2737	14.26460015	0.0001
At most 9 *	206.8152	3.841465501	0.0000
Max-eigenvalue test indicates 10 cointegrating eqn(s) at the 0.05 level			

* denotes rejection of the hypothesis at the 0.05 level.

To further explain the co-integrating equations, the application of VECM model is adopted. The results of the VECM are summarized below in Tables 5 and 6.

From the application of VECM, it is observed that the integration of the series with the other is established at 0.95 per cent confidence level, if the value in the table is more than 1.96. Table 6 exhibits that the returns at R_M_ACWI, at the lag of 1 highly influences the returns from all the four sustainable indices, as well as the R_M_USA, R_M_EAFE and R_M_EU. Additionally, it continues to impact the returns of the same indices at the lag of 2, but with a lower value. RM_EAFE affects all the indices, barring R_M_ACWI and R_M_EMH at the lag of 1, but the impact reduces to few indices at the second lag. R_M_EMH strongly controls the returns from R_M_EMH series, however at the second lag, the impact becomes disbursed to other indices. Similar to R_M_EAFE, the R_M_EU and R_M_USA series influence the returns of all the indices, barring returns from the R_M_W series at the lag of 1, and continues the impact with the same consistency at the second lag as well. The R_M_W series is observed to impact the returns from all the other indices at the lag of 1, barring only R_M_ACWI, R_M_EAFE and R_M_EMH in the second lag. R_TDX influences the returns from all the indices, except for R_M_EMH and R_M_W at lag 1, while its impacts become completed eroded from the sustainable indices in the second lag. The other sustainable indices, namely R_TEX, R_TEU, and R_TUS, continue to impact the returns from the sustainable indices at the second lag. Overall, it is observed that the returns from the sustainable indices are more influenced by the index series in comparison to the conventional indices. The degree of impact on the returns of the sustainable indices is also evident to be higher relative to the regular stock market indices.

Table 5. Results from vector error correction model applied for conventional and sustainable analysis.

Cointegrating Equation:	CointEq1
R_M_ACWI(-1)	1
R_M_EAFE(-1)	−0.74763
	0.10105
	[−7.39859]
R_M_EMH(-1)	0.007435
	0.045223
	[0.16441]
R_M_EU(-1)	−0.28586
	0.091493
	[−3.12436]
R_M_USA(-1)	−1.67062
	0.123721
	[−13.5031]
R_M_W(-1)	1.685899
	0.055261
	[30.5078]
R_TDX(-1)	−0.26932
	0.126472
	[−2.12950]
R_TEU(-1)	0.287319
	0.111044
	[2.58743]
R_TEX(-1)	−0.12065
	0.043545
	[−2.77063]
R_TUS(-1)	0.121102
	0.115707
	[1.04663]
C	0.0000

Table 6. Results from vector error correction model applied for conventional and sustainable analysis (cont.).

Error Correction:	R_M_ACWI	R_M_EAFE	R_M_EMH	R_M_EU	R_M_USA	R_M_W	R_TDX	R_TEU	R_TEX	R_TUS
CointEq1	0.736677	0.946760	0.618470	1.340643	0.959434	−0.212965	1.120551	1.409968	0.922008	1.00906
	[13.2352]	[14.2665]	[7.97963]	[15.8324]	[13.5111]	[−3.14913]	[15.6791]	[16.0778]	[10.9755]	[14.0928]
R_M_ACWI(-1)	−1.374503	−0.589217	−0.087382	−1.093818	−1.130714	0.118807	−1.304169	−1.524877	−1.409849	−1.1659
	[−12.1086]	**[−4.35358]**	[−0.55281]	**[−6.33392]**	**[−7.80768]**	[0.86142]	**[−8.94783]**	**[−8.52601]**	**[−8.22917]**	**[−7.98423]**
R_M_ACWI(-2)	−0.628400	−0.390677	−0.026475	−0.715141	−0.646387	−0.199913	−0.845569	−1.062302	−0.725599	−0.70484
	[−5.58006]	**[−2.90969]**	[−0.16883]	**[−4.17423]**	**[−4.49903]**	[−1.46108]	**[−5.84776]**	**[−5.98709]**	**[−4.26911]**	**[−4.86545]**
R_M_EAFE(-1)	0.087640	−0.688309	−0.105306	0.379313	0.435293	−0.350167	0.473366	0.675112	0.286409	0.483455
	[1.07760]	**[−7.09849]**	[−0.92987]	**[3.06574]**	**[4.19528]**	**[−3.54373]**	**[4.53306]**	**[5.26863]**	**[2.33335]**	**[4.62104]**
R_M_EAFE(-2)	−0.098151	−0.367400	−0.180250	0.150803	0.166000	−0.185008	0.304902	0.463962	0.048373	0.213946
	[−1.28784]	**[−4.04325]**	[−1.69845]	[1.30064]	[1.70725]	**[−1.99795]**	**[3.11576]**	**[3.86379]**	[0.42054]	**[2.18221]**
R_M_EMH(-1)	−0.004320	−0.029468	−0.763402	−0.038819	0.085490	0.046642	0.021354	0.015046	0.024437	0.081653
	[−0.10926]	[−0.62509]	**[−13.8653]**	[−0.64534]	[1.69474]	[0.97089]	[0.42061]	[0.24152]	[0.40950]	[1.60533]
R_M_EMH(-2)	−0.076091	−0.086778	−0.374056	−0.136414	−0.037985	−0.040145	−0.087042	−0.124474	−0.065490	−0.03646
	[−2.00729]	[−1.92006]	**[−7.08641]**	**[−2.36548]**	[−0.78543]	[−0.87163]	[−1.78832]	**[−2.08411]**	[−1.14470]	[−0.74763]
R_M_EU(-1)	0.294354	0.327710	0.301212	−0.457878	0.285485	0.058422	0.327254	0.330196	0.486127	0.276698
	[4.65233]	**[4.34426]**	**[3.41888]**	**[−4.75698]**	**[3.53677]**	[0.75999]	**[4.02831]**	**[3.31235]**	**[5.09082]**	**[3.39964]**
R_M_EU(-2)	0.230447	0.258244	0.228179	−0.131006	0.169973	0.149546	0.193588	0.183684	0.322795	0.159692
	[3.69891]	**[3.47663]**	**[2.63020]**	[−1.38222]	**[2.13847]**	**[1.97563]**	**[2.42002]**	[1.87127]	**[3.43294]**	[1.99256]
R_M_USA(-1)	0.941462	0.981942	0.595525	1.531117	0.960135	0.152218	1.487172	1.889525	1.488173	1.540357
	[6.06351]	**[5.30436]**	**[2.75443]**	**[6.48203]**	**[4.84704]**	[0.80689]	**[7.45968]**	**[7.72394]**	**[6.35056]**	**[7.71205]**
R_M_USA(-2)	0.384111	0.498706	−0.000059	0.972258	0.478913	0.227933	0.793742	1.161054	0.475613	0.840649
	[2.68021]	**[2.91865]**	[−0.00030]	**[4.45938]**	**[2.61934]**	[1.30902]	**[4.31349]**	**[5.14196]**	**[2.19889]**	**[4.55988]**
R_M_W(-1)	−0.348390	−0.585089	−0.267813	−0.943563	−0.758486	−0.275057	−0.821950	−1.124089	−0.631536	−0.81406
	[−4.76246]	**[−6.70831]**	**[−2.62911]**	**[−8.47847]**	**[−8.12711]**	**[−3.09469]**	**[−8.75082]**	**[−9.75283]**	**[−5.72006]**	**[−8.65063]**

Table 6. *Cont.*

Error Correction:	R_M_ACWI	R_M_EAFE	R_M_EMH	R_M_EU	R_M_USA	R_M_W	R_TDX	R_TEU	R_TEX	R_TUS
R_M_W(-2)	−0.057066	−0.092593	0.058356	−0.225887	−0.345998	−0.197078	−0.221487	−0.332262	−0.128850	−0.36697
	[−1.31976]	[−1.79606]	[0.96920]	**[−3.43391]**	**[−6.27211]**	**[−3.75131]**	**[−3.98935]**	**[−4.87710]**	**[−1.97441]**	**[−6.59748]**
R_TDX(-1)	0.322296	0.457619	0.117940	0.621904	0.299253	0.161904	−0.347859	0.526113	0.353620	0.256833
	[3.36120]	**[4.00285]**	[0.88330]	**[4.26328]**	**[2.44625]**	[1.38971]	**[−2.82541]**	**[3.48243]**	**[2.44350]**	**[2.08218]**
R_TDX(-2)	0.300381	0.450584	0.343373	0.532713	0.028027	0.170556	−0.088961	0.291506	0.259776	−0.00272
	[3.17838]	**[3.99884]**	**[2.60921]**	**[3.70516]**	[0.23245]	[1.48535]	[−0.73311]	[1.95770]	[1.82125]	[−0.02236]
R_TEU(-1)	−0.301910	−0.352806	−0.189503	−0.457573	−0.323894	−0.086087	−0.357368	−1.227176	−0.442376	−0.29391
	[−3.69700]	**[−3.62355]**	[−1.66648]	**[−3.68310]**	**[−3.10884]**	[−0.86763]	**[−3.40821]**	**[−9.53771]**	**[−3.58923]**	**[−2.79779]**
R_TEU(-2)	−0.251712	−0.383223	−0.301987	−0.423034	−0.076115	−0.099668	−0.260673	−0.671500	−0.316513	−0.05605
	[−3.13122]	**[−3.99842]**	**[−2.69780]**	**[−3.45913]**	[−0.74217]	[−1.02045]	**[−2.52549]**	**[−5.30177]**	**[−2.60879]**	[−0.54207]
R_TEX(-1)	0.138911	0.117200	0.241235	0.146299	0.097100	−0.028691	0.116771	0.121810	−0.413448	0.105173
	[3.67918]	**[2.60357]**	**[4.58844]**	**[2.54704]**	**[2.01583]**	[−0.62544]	**[2.40872]**	**[2.04767]**	**[−7.25557]**	**[2.16544]**
R_TEX(-2)	0.117043	0.101496	0.082126	0.158859	0.144143	0.039767	0.135784	0.177266	−0.131234	0.151615
	[3.17040]	**[2.30592]**	[1.59758]	**[2.82855]**	**[3.06044]**	[0.88659]	**[2.86454]**	**[3.04760]**	**[−2.35534]**	**[3.19256]**
R_TUS(-1)	−0.194259	0.030356	−0.097868	−0.094454	−0.571217	−0.324109	−0.003114	−0.128533	−0.155513	−1.1008
	[−1.56243]	[0.20478]	[−0.56529]	[−0.49937]	**[−3.60116]**	**[−2.14555]**	[−0.01951]	[−0.65614]	[−0.82875]	**[−6.88263]**
R_TUS(-2)	−0.134289	−0.063854	0.137801	−0.359083	−0.307028	−0.193912	−0.091307	−0.307831	0.086649	−0.62727
	[−1.07768]	[−0.42980]	[0.79417]	[−1.89419]	[−1.93130]	[−1.28080]	[−0.57068]	[−1.56793]	[0.46073]	**[−3.91317]**
C	−0.000001	0.000003	0.000009	0.000005	−0.000008	−0.000009	0.000003	0.000003	0.000003	0.0000
	[−0.00485]	[0.01668]	[0.04092]	[0.02131]	[−0.03972]	[−0.04296]	[0.01182]	[0.01204]	[0.01388]	[−0.04383]

Note: The values in bold are statistically significant at 5% confidence level.

5. Conclusions and Implications

Analysts and investors usually employ sustainability indices as an integrated measure of a firm's sustainability performance, considering that only those companies that outperform their peers in an in-depth analysis of economic, environmental, and social criteria, are included in sustainability index. This thereby categorizes them as industry sustainability leaders (del Mar Miralles-Quiros et al. 2017).

This study concludes that over the period of five years, TRESGUS provides the highest return out of all the indices under reference on an average. On the other hand, MSCI ACWI is the least risky series, followed by MSCI World and MSCI USA, while TRESGEU exhibits the highest variation in its values. The study finds TRESGUS as a favourable investment option, offering the highest return with a convenient level of risk.

Additionally, the paper finds evidence of bi-directional volatility spillover between the sustainable indices and the conventional indices. The results from the sustainable indices impact their alternatives and vice-versa. In general, it is evident that there is a flow of information between the two sets of indices and hence, these markets are integrated with each other. The information from one index can be used to predict the behaviour of the other index. Accordingly, financial managers and professionals can obtain more insights regarding investment decisions, and the study further suggests that their portfolios should consider both the indices, with the perspective of diversifying the risk and hedging, and reap benefits of the same (Balcilar et al. 2017; Sadorsky 2014). Additionally, the government may use such information, while drafting public policies, and civil societies may employ them in monitoring and controlling the social and environmental responsibility of firms. Similar results are evident in the study by Charlo et al. (2017), where the findings exhibit no significant difference between the two groups of companies listed in the sustainability index and the traditional market index, and responsible companies provide similar returns to those of the conventional companies.

Theses finding contradict the popular belief (Hong and Kacperczyk 2009; Lee et al. 2010; Lopez et al. 2007; de Souza Cunha and Samanez 2013) that the sustainable investment options yield lower financial returns as against traditional investment options.

The results indicate that there is no significant difference in the performance between sustainable indices and the traditional conventional indices, being a good substitute to the latter, and this is partially similar to the findings of other studies for instance, Charlo et al. (2017); Santis et al. (2016) and la Torre et al. (2016).

Author Contributions: Conceptualization, G.D.S and M.J.; Methodology, M.J. and G.D.S.; Validation, G.D.S. and M.S.; Formal Analysis, G.D.S. and M.J.; Data Curation, M.J. and G.D.S.; Writing–Original Draft Preparation, M.J.; Writing – Review and Editing, M.J., M.S. and G.D.S.; and Supervision, G.D.S.

Funding: This research received no external funding.

Conflicts of Interest: The authors declare no conflict of interest.

References

Abdullah, Ahmad Monir, Buerhan Saiti, and Mansur Masih. 2016. The impact of crude oil price on Islamic stock indices of South East Asian countries: Evidence from MGARCH-DCC and wavelet approaches. *Borsa Istanbul Review* 16: 219–32. [CrossRef]

Alexandre, Alamo, and Antonio Carlos De Francisco. 2018. Organizational Sustainability Practices: A Study of the Firms Listed by the Corporate Sustainability Index. *Sustainability* 10: 226. [CrossRef]

Alshehhi, Ali, Haitham Nobanee, and Nilesh Khare. 2018. The Impact of Sustainability Practices on Corporate Financial Performance: Literature Trends and Future Research Potential. *Sustainability* 10: 494. [CrossRef]

Antonakakis, Nikolaos, Vassilios Babalos, and Clement Kyei. 2016. Predictability of sustainable investments and the role of uncertainty: Evidence from a non-parametric causality-in-quantiles test. *Applied Economics* 48: 4655–65. [CrossRef]

Balcilar, Mehmet, Riza Demirer, and Rangan Gupta. 2017. Do Sustainable Stocks Offer Diversification Benefits for Conventional Portfolios? An Empirical Analysis of Risk Spillovers and Dynamic Correlations. *Sustainability* 9: 1799. [CrossRef]

Bellalah, Makram, Mondher Bellalah, and Haifa Boussada. 2016. Modeling Transmissions of Volatility Shocks: Application to CDS Spreads during the Euro Area Sovereign Crisis. *International Journal of Business* 21: 1–25.

Bianconi, Marcelo, Joe A Yoshino, and Mariana O Machado de Sousa. 2013. BRIC and the US financial crisis: An empirical investigation of stock and bond markets. *Emerging Markets Review* 14: 76–109. [CrossRef]

Bildirici, Melike, and Özgür Ömer Ersin. 2009. Improving forecasts of GARCH family models with the artificial neural networks: An application to the daily returns in Istanbul Stock Exchange. *Expert Systems with Applications* 36: 7355–62. [CrossRef]

Brooks, Chris. 2008. *Introductory Econometrics for Finance*. Finance. Cambridge: Cambridge University Press. [CrossRef]

Brzeszczynski, Janusz, and Graham McIntosh. 2014. Performance of Portfolios Composed of British SRI Stocks. *Journal of Business Ethics* 120: 335–62. [CrossRef]

Charlo, Maria J., Ismael Moya, and Ana M Munoz. 2015. Sustainable Development and Corporate Financial Performance: A Study Based on the FTSE4Good IBEX Index. *Business Strategy and the Environment* 24: 277–88. [CrossRef]

Charlo, Maria J., Ismael Moya, and Ana M Munoz. 2017. Sustainable Development in Spanish Listed Companies: A Strategic Approach. *Corporate Social Responsibility and Environmental Management* 24: 222–34. [CrossRef]

de Souza Cunha, F. A., and C. P. Samanez. 2013. Performance Analysis of Sustainable Investments in the Brazilian Stock Market: A Study About the Corporate Sustainability Index (ISE). *Journal of Business Ethics* 117: 19–36. [CrossRef]

del Mar Miralles-Quiros, Maria, Jose Luis Miralles-Quiros, and Irene Guia Arraiano. 2017. Sustainable Development, Sustainability Leadership and Firm Valuation: Differences across Europe. *Business Strategy and the Environment* 26: 1014–28. [CrossRef]

Dimitriou, Dimitrios, Dimitris Kenourgios, and Theodore Simos. 2013. Global Financial Crisis and Emerging Stock Market Contagion: A Multivariate FIAPARCH-DCC Approach. *International Review of Financial Analysis* 30: 46–56. [CrossRef]

Fowler, Stephen J., and Chris Hope. 2007. A Critical Review of Sustainable Business Indices and their Impact. *Journal of Business Ethics* 76: 243–52. [CrossRef]

Gallego-Alvarez, Isabel, Isabel M Garcia-Sanchez, and Cleber da Silva Vieira. 2014. Climate Change and Financial Performance in Times of Crisis. *Business Strategy and the Environment* 23: 361–74. [CrossRef]

Giannarakis, Grigoris, Nikolaos Litinas, and Nikolaos Sariannidis. 2011. Evaluation of corporate social responsibility performance standards. *African Journal of Business Management* 5: 7367–74. [CrossRef]

Guerard, John B, Jr. 1997a. Additional Evidence on the Cost of Being Socially Responsible in Investing. *The Journal of Investing* 6: 31–36. [CrossRef]

Guerard, John B, Jr. 1997b. Is there a cost to being socially responsible in investing. *The Journal of Investing* 6: 11–18. [CrossRef]

Hong, Harrison, and Marcin Kacperczyk. 2009. The price of sin: The effects of social norms on markets. *Journal of Financial Economics* 93: 15–36. [CrossRef]

Hsu, Chih-Chiang, Chih-Ping Tseng, and Yaw-Huei Wang. 2008. Dynamic hedging with futures: A copula-based GARCH model. *Journal of Futures Markets* 28: 1095–116. [CrossRef]

Humpe, Andreas, and Peter Macmillan. 2007. *Can Macroeconomic Variables Explain Long Term Stock Market Movements? A Comparison of the US and Japan*. Rochester: SSRN, vol. 44. Available online: https://www.st-andrews.ac.uk/~{}wwwecon/CDMA/papers/wp0720.pdf (accessed on 28 December 2018).

Huo, Rui, and Abdullahi Dahir Ahm. 2018. Relationships between Chinese stock market and its index futures market: Evaluating the impact of QFII scheme. *Research in International Business and Finance* 44: 135–52. [CrossRef]

Kalu, Emenike O. 2015. Dynamic Correlation between Stock Market Returns and Crude Oil Prices: Evidence from a Developing Economy. *Indonesian Capital Market Review* 7: 102–12. [CrossRef]

Kenourgios, Dimitris, and Dimitrios Dimitriou. 2015. Contagion of the Global Financial Crisis and the real economy: A regional analysis. *Economic Modelling* 44: 283–93. [CrossRef]

Kuwornu, John K. M., and Victor Owusu-Nantwi. 2011. Macroeconomic Variables and Stock Market Returns: Full Information Maximum Likelihood Estimation. *Research Journal of Finance and Accounting* 2: 49–64.

la Torre, Oscar, Evaristo Galeana, and Dora Aguilasocho. 2016. The use of the sustainable investment against the broad market one. A first test in the Mexican stock market. *European Research on Management and Business Economics* 22: 117–23. [CrossRef]

Lassala, Carlos, Andreea Apetrei, and Juan Sapena. 2017. Sustainability matter and financial performance of companies. *Sustainability* 9: 1498. [CrossRef]

Lee, Darren D., Jacquelyn Humphrey, Karen L. Benson, and Jason Ahn. 2010. Socially Responsible Investment Fund Performance: The Impact of Screening Intensity. *Accounting and Finance* 50: 351–70. [CrossRef]

Liket, Kellie, and Karen Maas. 2016. Strategic Philanthropy: Corporate Measurement of Philanthropic Impacts as a Requirement for a "Happy Marriage" of Business and Society. *Business and Society* 55: 889–921. [CrossRef]

Lo, Shih-Fang, and Her-Jiun Sheu. 2007. Is corporate sustainability a value-increasing strategy for business? *Corporate Governance-An International Review* 15: 345–58. [CrossRef]

Lokuwaduge, Chitra Sriyani De Silva, and Kumudini Heenetigala. 2017. Integrating Environmental, Social and Governance (ESG) Disclosure for a Sustainable Development: An Australian Study. *Business Strategy and the Environment* 26: 438–50. [CrossRef]

Lopez, M Victoria, Arminda Garcia, and Lazaro Rodriguez. 2007. Sustainable development and corporate performance: A study based on the Dow Jones Sustainability Index. *Journal of Business Ethics* 75: 285–300. [CrossRef]

Martinez-Ferrero, Jennifer, and Jose Valeriano Frias-Aceituno. 2015. Relationship Between Sustainable Development and Financial Performance: International Empirical Research. *Business Strategy and the Environment* 24: 20–39. [CrossRef]

Mensi, Walid, Shawkat Hammoudeh, Idries Mohammad Wanas Al-Jarrah, Ahmet Sensoy, and Sang Hoon Kang. 2017. Dynamic risk spillovers between gold, oil prices and conventional, sustainability and Islamic equity aggregates and sectors with portfolio implications. *Energy Economics* 67: 454–75. [CrossRef]

Nelson, Daniel B. 1991. Conditional heteroskedasticity in asset returns: A new approach. *Econometrica* 59: 347–70. [CrossRef]

Ortas, Eduardo, and Jose M Moneva. 2011. Sustainability stock exchange indexes and investor expectations: Multivariate evidence from DJSI-Stoxx. *Journal of Finance and Accounting* 40: 395–416. [CrossRef]

Ortas, Eduardo, Jose M Moneva, Roger Burritt, and Joanne Tingey-Holyoak. 2014. Does Sustainability Investment Provide Adaptive Resilience to Ethical Investors? Evidence from Spain. *Journal of Business Ethics* 124: 297–309. [CrossRef]

Ortas, Eduardo, Isabel Gallego-Alvarez, and Igor Alvarez Etxeberria. 2015. Financial Factors Influencing the Quality of Corporate Social Responsibility and Environmental Management Disclosure: A Quantile Regression Approach. *Corporate Social Responsibility and Environmental Management* 22: 362–80. [CrossRef]

Park, Sung Yong, and Sang Young Jei. 2010. Estimation and Hedging Effectiveness of Time-Varying Hedge Ration: Flexible Bivariate GARCH Approaches. *Journal of Futures Markets* 30: 71–99. [CrossRef]

Patari, Satu, Ari Jantunen, Kalevi Kylaheiko, and Jaana Sandstrom. 2012. Does Sustainable Development Foster Value Creation? Empirical Evidence from the Global Energy Industry. *Corporate Social Responsibility and Environmental Management* 19: 317–26. [CrossRef]

Pilar Marti, Carmen, Maria Rosa Rovira-Val, and Lisa Geneva Johanna Drescher. 2015. Are Firms that Contribute to Sustainable Development Better Financially? *Corporate Social Responsibility and Environmental Management* 22: 305–19. [CrossRef]

Rajnoha, Rastislav, Petra Lesnikova, and Antonin Koraus. 2016. From Financial Measures To Startegic Performance Measurement System And Corporate Sustainability: Emperical Evidence From Slovakia. *Economics and Sociology* 9: 134–52. [CrossRef] [PubMed]

Rajnoha, Rastislav, Petra Lesnikova, and Vladimir Krajcik. 2017. Influence of Business Performance Measuremnet Systems and Corporate Sustainability Concept To Overall Business Performance: "Save The Planet And Keep Your Performance". *E and M Ekonomie A Management* 20: 111–28. [CrossRef]

Ransariya, Shailesh N., and Sanjay J. Bhayani. 2015. Relationship between Corporate Social Responsibility and Financial Performance of RIL. *Pacific Business Review International* 7: 66–75.

Sadorsky, Perry. 2014. Modeling volatility and conditional correlations between socially responsible investments, gold and oil. *Economic Modelling* 38: 609–18. [CrossRef]

Santis, Paula, Andrei Albuquerque, and Fabiane Lizarelli. 2016. Do sustainable companies have a better financial performance? A study on Brazilian public companies. *Journal of Cleaner Production* 133: 735–45. [CrossRef]

Schmid, Jochen, Marieta Olaru, and Ana-Maria Verjel. 2017. The effect of sustainable investments on the economic objectives of the company in relation to the total quality management. *Amfiteatru Economic* 19: 939–50.

Sehgal, Sanjay, Wasim Ahmad, and Florent Deisting. 2015. An investigation of price discovery and volatility spillovers in India's foreign exchange market. *Journal of Economic Studies* 42: 261–84. [CrossRef]

Seo, Joo Hwan, Sung Yong Park, and Larry Yu. 2009. The analysis of the relationships of Korean outbound tourism demand: Jeju Island and three international destinations. *Tourism Management* 30: 530–43. [CrossRef]

Sharma, Gagan Deep, and Mansi Gupta. 2015. Does the pre-open auction market improve efficiency of price discovery in stock markets? Evidence from India. *Indian Journal of Finance* 9. [CrossRef]

S Sharma, Gagan Deep, and Namish Mishra. 2015. Return Linkages and Volatility Spillover Effect Between Stock Markets and Currency Markets. *Review of Market Integration* 7: 175–97. [CrossRef]

Skare, Marinko, and Tea Golja. 2012. Corporate Social Responsibility and Corporate Financial Performance—Is There A Link? *Ekonomska Istrazivanja-Economic Research* 25: 215–42. [CrossRef]

Stolowy, Herve, and Luc Paugam. 2018. The expansion of non-financial reporting: An exploratory study. *Accounting and Business Research* 48: 525–48. [CrossRef]

Su, Chang. 2010. *Application of EGARCH Model to Estimate Financial Volatility of Daily Returns: The Empirical Case of China*. Gothenburg: University of Gothenburg.

Su, Dongwei, and Belton M. Fleisher. 1998. Risk, Return and Regulation in Chinese Stock Markets. *Journal of Economics and Business* 50: 239–56. [CrossRef]

Talan, Gaurav, and Gagan Sharma. 2019. Doing Well by Doing Good: A Systematic Review and Research Agenda for Sustainable Investment. *Sustainability* 11: 353. [CrossRef]

Tse, Yiuman. 1999. Price Discovery and Volatility Spillovers in the DJIA Index and Futures Markets. *J. Futures Mark.* 19: 911–30. [CrossRef]

Tularam, Gurudeo Anand, Eduardo Roca, and Victor S H Wong. 2010. Investigation of Socially Responsible Investment Markets (SRI) Using Dynamic Conditional Correlation (DCC) Method: Implications for Diversification. *Journal of Mathematics and Statistics* 6: 385–94. [CrossRef]

Vives, Antonio, and Baljit Wadhwa. 2012. Sustainability indices in emerging markets: Impact on responsible practices and financial market development. *Journal of Sustainable Finance and Investment* 2: 318–37. [CrossRef]

Wang, Ping, and Tomoe Moore. 2008. Stock market integration for the transition economies: Time-varying conditional correlation approach. *The Manchester School* 76: 116–33. [CrossRef]

11

Efficient Retirement Portfolios: Using Life Insurance to Meet Income and Bequest Goals in Retirement

Fangyuan Dong [1], Nick Halen [2], Kristen Moore [3,*] and Qinglai Zeng [4]

1 Paid Growth Analyst, Airbnb, Inc., 888 Brennan St., San Francisco, CA 94103, USA; keiradong1020@gmail.com
2 Strategy, Research and Analytics, New York Life, 51 Madison Avenue, New York, NY 10010, USA; Nick_Halen@newyorklife.com
3 Department of Mathematics, University of Michigan, 2074 East Hall, 530 Church Street, Ann Arbor, MI 48109-1043, USA
4 People Advisory Services, Ernst & Young LLP, 155 North Wacker Drive, Chicago, IL 60606, USA; qinglai318@gmail.com
* Correspondence: ksmoore@umich.edu

Abstract: Life Insurance Retirement Plans (LIRPs) offer tax-deferred cash value accumulation, tax-free withdrawals (if properly structured), and a tax-free death benefit to beneficiaries. Thus, LIRPs share many of the tax advantages of other retirement savings vehicles but with less restrictive limitations on income and contributions. Opinions are mixed about the effectiveness of LIRPs; some financial advisers recommend them enthusiastically, while others are more skeptical. In this paper, we examine the potential of LIRPs to meet both income and bequest needs in retirement. We contrast retirement portfolios that include a LIRP with those that include only investment products with no life insurance. We consider different issue ages, face amounts, and withdrawal patterns. We simulate market scenarios and we demonstrate that portfolios that include LIRPs yield higher legacy potential and smaller income risk than those that exclude it. Thus, we conclude that the inclusion of a LIRP can improve financial outcomes in retirement.

Keywords: life insurance retirement plan; simulation; efficient frontier

1. Introduction

Retirees face significant financial risk and competing financial objectives. Pfau (2014) summarizes them as lifestyle, longevity, legacy, and liquidity. In retirement, individuals need steady income to fund their day-to-day expenses (lifestyle), they face the risk of outliving their retirement savings (longevity), they may wish to leave a bequest to heirs (legacy), and they must have reserves for healthcare costs or other unforeseen expenses (liquidity). They must construct and manage their portfolios to address both their need for secure lifetime income and wealth accumulation.

In the United States, employer-sponsored retirement plans fall broadly into two categories: Defined Benefit (DB) and Defined Contribution (DC). For both types of plans, employers and employees make contributions to fund future benefits. In a DB plan, the employee's retirement benefit is calculated on the basis of factors such as age, length of service, final average salary, etc. The retirement benefits may be paid as a life annuity; thus, they offer retirees the prospect of a secure lifetime income. The employer manages the investment fund and assumes all investment and longevity risks. In a DC plan, the participants choose among a set of investment options according to their time horizon and risk tolerance. They contribute to their retirement account and, upon retirement, they must manage their nest egg to fund their retirement. Because of the upside potential of equities markets, DC plans offer the potential for significant wealth accumulation. However, the plan participant bears all of the investment and longevity risk and thus might have insufficient income in retirement or might outlive their savings.

The shift from DB retirement plans, under which retirees can receive guaranteed income for life, toward DC plans is well documented (EBRI 2016). A prudent investor should add longevity-protected vehicles such as life annuities and life insurance to manage longevity risk and to protect against downside market risk.

There is considerable literature on using life annuities to manage income risk (see Chen and Milevsky (2003), Milevsky et al. (2006), and the references contained therein). In a different vein, Bayraktar et al. (2014, 2015) and Bayraktar and Young (2016) used stochastic optimal control to determine strategies to maximize the probability of reaching a bequest goal.

Pfau (2014) considered combinations of investment portfolios, annuities, and life insurance and examined their performance relative to income and legacy wealth. The annuity, along with withdrawals from the investment fund, provided income, and the life insurance provided bequest.

In this paper, we examine the potential of life insurance to meet both income and bequest needs in retirement. In particular, we examine the effectiveness of Life Insurance Retirement Plans (LIRPs) in a retirement portfolio.

LIRPs and Other Retirement Savings Vehicles

In the United States, there are several different mechanisms through which investors can save for retirement while enjoying certain tax advantages. In this section, we will briefly discuss some of these vehicles, including 401(k) and related plans, Individual Retirement Accounts (IRAs), and Roth IRAs, and we will contrast them with LIRPs.

A 401(k) plan is a tax-qualified, employer-sponsored DC plan as defined in subsection 401(k) of the United States Internal Revenue Code. Employees contribute a portion of their paycheck to their 401(k) plan. Often, employers provide a proportional match of the employee's contribution. Often, employees can choose how to invest their retirement funds from among a menu of investment options offered by the employer. The contributions and investment earnings are tax-deferred; investors do not incur income tax liability until they begin withdrawing funds in retirement, presumably when they are in a lower tax bracket. Nonprofit and governmental employers may offer 403(b) and 457(b) plans, respectively, which share many of the features of 401(k) plans.

An IRA is a self-directed, not an employer-sponsored, retirement savings plan. Contributions to an IRA are tax-deductible, and the investment earnings are tax-deferred. As with a 401(k) plan, individuals only pay taxes when they withdraw the funds at retirement. A Roth IRA is also a self-directed retirement savings plan. Unlike traditional IRAs, contributions are taxable as income; however, the investment earnings and withdrawals are tax-free—not tax-deferred—subject to certain conditions.

The 401(k) plans, IRAs, and Roth IRAs are subject to various income and contribution limits and early withdrawal penalties. A concise overview of traditional and Roth IRAs is given in Spors (2018). We refer the reader to McGill et al. (2010) and Allen et al. (2014) for more detailed information.

Under a LIRP, investors contribute premiums to fund a cash value life insurance policy. Generally speaking, the strategy is to overfund the policy, that is, to pay a large amount of premium for a low face-amount policy. Careful planning is important. If the policy is too overfunded, it will be classified as a Modified Endowment Contract, or MEC, instead of as life insurance for the purposes of taxation. Policyholders can meet their income needs via withdrawals and policy loans. Contributions are not tax-deductible; however, the cash value accumulation is tax-deferred, and withdrawals are tax-free. Moreover, beneficiaries receive a tax-free death benefit upon the death of the policyholder. Thus, a properly structured LIRP (one that is not classified as a MEC) offers tax-deferred cash value accumulation, tax-free withdrawals, and a tax-free death benefit to beneficiaries. In other words, LIRPs share many of the tax advantages of a Roth IRA. More significantly, the limits on income, contributions, and withdrawals are considerably less restrictive than for Roth IRAs (again, subject to MEC limits).

Opinions are mixed about the effectiveness of LIRPs. Ikokwu (2013) enthusiastically recommends LIRPs, describing them as a "turbo charged Roth IRA without the limitations." McKnight (2012) points out that if a LIRP is properly structured, the cost can be lower than the annual expenses in a typical 401(k). Moreover, LIRPs can insulate investors from rising tax rates, and some insurance companies allow policyholders to access death benefit proceeds to pay for long-term care. Bloink and Byrnes (2011) are more skeptical. They point out that if investors are not savvy, the policy could become classified as a MEC, which would eliminate the tax advantages on policy loans. Moreover, if the policy lapses with outstanding loans, the amount of the loan is taxable. In addition, they point to surrender fees, the cost of insurance, and other charges. They conclude LIRPs offer the greatest benefit and fewer drawbacks for high-net-worth investors who have already maximized other tax-advantaged retirement savings plans.

In this paper, we contrast retirement portfolios that include a LIRP with those that include only investment products with no life insurance. In other words, we contrast strategies that include, say, a mutual fund only with those that include both a mutual fund and a LIRP. We consider different issue ages, face amounts, and withdrawal patterns. We simulate market scenarios and, using the Efficient Income Frontier (EIF) of Milevsky (2008) and Pfau (2013), we demonstrate that portfolios that include LIRPs yield higher legacy potential and smaller income risk than those that exclude it. Thus, we conclude that the inclusion of a LIRP can improve financial outcomes in retirement.

2. Methodology and Assumptions

2.1. Overview

Let (x) represent an individual aged x and let $T(x)$ be the future lifetime random variable for (x).

We assume that (x) is endowed with initial wealth E_x. We set E_{35} = 50K, E_{45} = 200K, and E_{55} = 500K, and we assume further that (x) can invest E_x in a mutual fund and purchase life insurance.

We define the following:

- FA = face amount of the life insurance;
- n = number of premium payments;
- E_x = endowment of wealth of (x) at time 0;
- FB = mutual fund balance at age 65;
- α = percentage of accumulated mutual fund balance (FB) to withdraw at age 65. Beyond age 65, the mutual fund withdrawals are increased for inflation;
- m = number of annual withdrawals from the life insurance product.

We fix all of the values except FB a priori and we also fix values for the pre- and postretirement tax rate and the loan interest rate.

We define the premium burden to be the present value of future life insurance premiums divided by E_x.

We perform our calculations using two disjoint models: Our Excel-based market model for the market and mutual fund calculations, and New York Life's (NYL's) illustration system for the insurance calculations.

We compute premiums and dividends using the illustration system, with dividends being added to the policy's cash value. Moreover, we use the illustration system to compute the amount of each annual withdrawal from the life insurance product.

We fix an allocation strategy for the mutual fund and we simulate 250 market outcome scenarios. Please see Section 2.5 for more information about the asset allocation strategies.

In the decumulation phase, we assume that the retiree will follow a systematic withdrawal plan; in other words, they desire an annual income that is a fixed percentage α of their mutual fund balance FB at age 65, increased for inflation thereafter. If they are also using a LIRP, we assume that for the first

m years of retirement, they take withdrawals (or loans) from the life insurance product. Thus, they can decrease the amount that they withdraw from the mutual fund, thereby preserving the fund value.

We examine whether the retiree has adequate income and bequest using the metrics described in Section 2.2 below and we compare the performance of the resulting portfolios.

2.2. *Mortality Assumption and Measures of Portfolio Performance*

We measure the performance of the portfolio using two metrics: Income risk and legacy potential. Income risk measures how often, in 250 scenarios, income sources (both the mutual fund and the income provided by the life insurance product) were depleted before the 75th percentile of $T(x)$. Legacy potential is the sum of the mutual fund value plus the death benefit at the 50th percentile of $T(x)$. Mortality is based on the Society of Actuaries Annuity 2012 Basic Mortality Table with Improvement Scale G2. Thus, for example, according to our mortality table, the 50th percentile of $T(35)$ is 45 and the 75th percentile is 51. For (35), income risk masures how often, in 250 trials, income is depleted before age 86, while legacy potential measures the mutual fund value plus death benefit at age 80.

In the retirement period, retirees are exposed not only to investment risk but also to longevity risk, withdrawal rate risk, inflation risk, and sequence of returns risk. The income risk metric incorporates all of these.

We can visualize portfolio performance by plotting legacy potential versus income risk and then identifying "efficient" portfolios, i.e., portfolios that maximize legacy potential while minimizing income risk. In Section 3, we see that the inclusion of a life insurance product in a retirement portfolio can improve financial outcomes and we identify which face amounts, withdrawal patterns, issue ages, and asset allocation strategies are most efficient.

We describe the life insurance product that we modeled and elaborate on our assumptions below.

2.3. *The Insurance Product—Limited Pay Whole Life (LPWL)*

In our modeling, we construct the LIRP with NYL's Custom Whole Life (CWL) product. CWL is a participating (dividend-paying), cash value, limited payment whole life (LPWL) policy. Policyholders can customize the duration of their premium payments. Subject to the limitations of an MEC, the accumulation of the cash value is tax-deferred, the death benefit is tax-free, and policyholders can use partial surrenders and policy loans to supplement their income.

2.4. *Issue Ages (X)*

We consider policies issued at ages 35, 45, and 55 and assume that retirement occurs at age 65.

2.5. *The Portfolio*

We consider a portfolio that consists of a mutual fund and possibly a life insurance product for the LIRP. The life insurance product is described in Section 2.3.

For the mutual fund, we examine four different allocations between stocks and bonds.

- Moderate strategy: 30% stocks, 70% bonds
- Balanced strategy: 50% stocks, 50% bonds
- Growth strategy: 70% stocks, 30% bonds
- Aggressive strategy: 90% stocks, 10% bonds

We did initial testing to determine the optimal preretirement asset allocations. We describe the asset allocations that we used in our simulations in Table 1 below.

Then, we varied the postretirement asset allocation and examined the portfolio performance with and without the LIRP.

Table 1. Preretirement asset allocation.

Age	Preretirement Asset Allocation
35	Aggressive
45	Age 45–55: Aggressive; Age 55–65: Moderate
55	Balanced

2.6. Simulation of Market Outcomes

We assume that the stock and bond returns are correlated, lognormally distributed random variables. We use the @Risk software package to implement Monte Carlo simulation. We simulate 250 market return scenarios, each of which had a 60-year time frame. Our assumptions are summarized in Table 2 below.

Table 2. Market parameters.

	Stock	Bond
Mean Return	7%	3%
Standard Deviation	15%	5.5%
Correlation		20%

2.7. Number of Premium Payments (N)

For policies issued at ages 35 and 45, we assume a 20-year premium payment period. For 55 year olds, we assume a 10-year premium payment period. We compute the premium on the basis of the face amount and the number of years of level premium payments using the illustration software.

2.8. Face Amounts (FA)

For each issue age, we consider six different face amounts. For the 35-year-old case, we look into a range of face amounts from $50,000 to $100,000. For the 45-year-old case, the range of face amount is from $100,000 to $200,000. For the 55-year-old case, the range of face amount is $100,000 to $400,000. We assume lower face amounts for younger individuals because they were endowed with lower initial wealth E_x.

2.9. Number of Withdrawals (M)

As a supplement to mutual funds, the life insurance product allows policyholders to take out a certain amount of money as an income source for their retirement living expenses. We examine withdrawal periods ranging from 10 to 25 years. The money withdrawn will subsequently decrease the accumulated cash value as well as the death benefit. We use the illustration software to compute the withdrawal amount, cash value, loan interest, and death benefit.

3. Results

In this section, we present our numerical results. We first present a case study for illustration, and then, more generally, we contrast numerous portfolios that include a LIRP with those that exclude it. Moreover, we contrast the results for different face amounts, withdrawal patterns, and issue ages. Specifically, we plot legacy potential versus income risk and identify an Efficient Income Frontier (EIF), which consists of portfolios that best maximize legacy potential while minimizing income risk.

3.1. Case Study

Consider a single male aged 55 who has initial wealth of $500,000 to invest in mutual funds. He considers using a LIRP to optimize his retirement portfolio. Upon retirement at age 65, he makes withdrawals according to a systematic withdrawal plan with the initial withdrawal amount equal to 3.5% of the initial mutual fund balance, increased for inflation thereafter.

As we described in Section 2.5, prior to retirement, he invests according to the balanced allocation strategy. In Tables 3 and 4, we show selected values of the income risk and legacy potential, respectively, that result if the investor chooses the face amount and number of withdrawals shown in the header row and column. We assume the balanced asset allocation after retirement as well.

For example, if the investor buys life insurance with 100K face amount and withdraws 10 years of income during retirement, the income risk is 20%, and the legacy potential is $530,067.

Now, we contrast the results for the growth and aggressive asset allocation strategies. In Figure 1, we show the allocation of E_x among stocks (blue), bonds (red), and life insurance premiums (green). For example, for the growth strategy, the premium burden, or present value of future life insurance premiums, is 41% of the initial endowment E_x. The remaining 59% is allocated 70/30 to stocks and bonds.

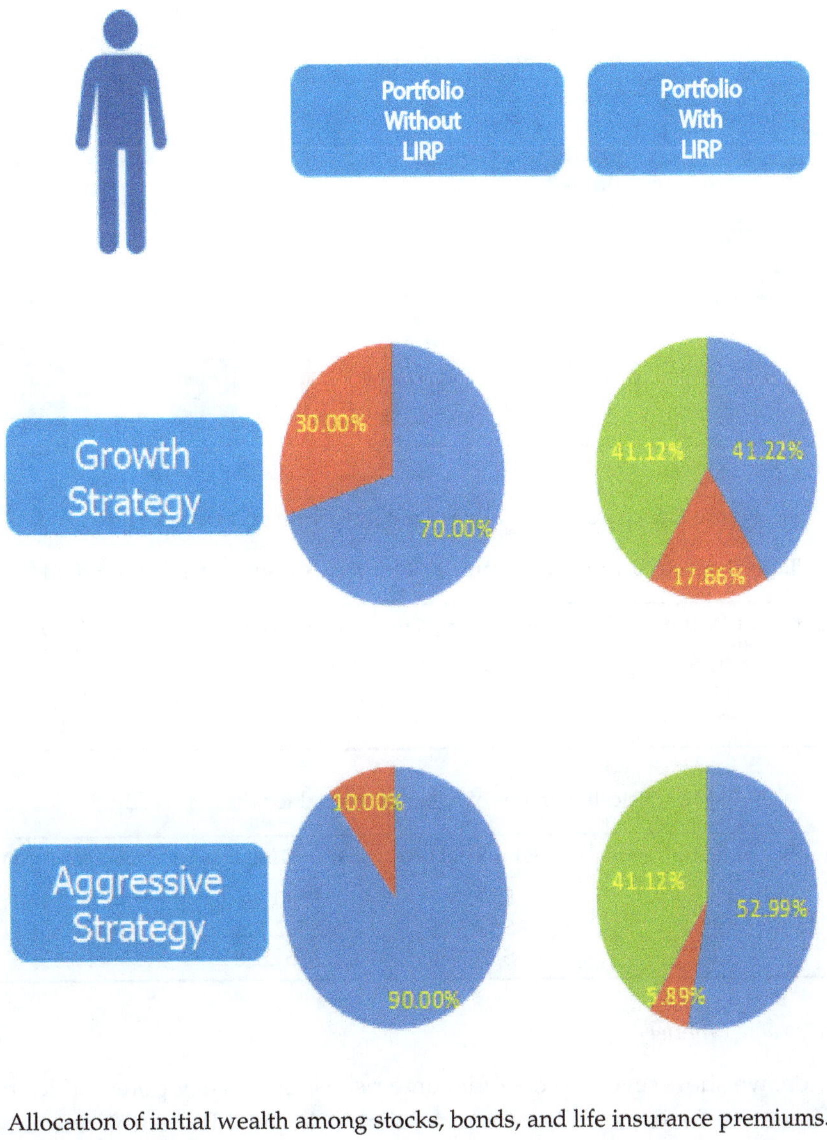

Figure 1. Allocation of initial wealth among stocks, bonds, and life insurance premiums. LIRP: Life Insurance Retirement Plans.

In Figure 2 we show the values of income risk and legacy potential with and without a LIRP for fixed values of the face amount and number of withdrawals. We see that under both asset allocation strategies, despite the initial outlay of premiums, the inclusion of the LIRP decreases the income risk and increases the legacy potential. The aggressive strategy produces higher legacy potential but also increases income risk compared to the growth strategy.

Figure 2. Income risk and legacy potential with and without LIRP.

Table 3. Selected values of income risk for the case study. *FA*: face amount

Number of Withdrawals	*FA* = $100,000	*FA* = $160,000	*FA* = $220,000
10	20%	20%	20%
11	19%	19%	20%
12	19%	19%	19%

Table 4. Selected values of legacy potential for the case study.

Number of Withdrawals	*FA* = $100,000	*FA* = $160,000	*FA* = $220,000
10	$530,067	$560,036	$592,848
11	$531,625	$562,516	$594,654
12	$532,988	$564,898	$596,886

3.2. The Efficient Income Frontier

In this section, we show several plots of income risk versus legacy potential for portfolios that consist only of a mutual fund, as well as for those that include a LIRP and a mutual fund. As the graphs show, the portfolios that include the LIRP often dominate those that exclude it.

In Figure 3, the issue age is fixed at 55. We first remark that because we wish to maximize legacy potential and minimize income risk, the optimal, or most efficient, portfolios are those in the "northwest" section of the graph. For portfolios that include only a mutual fund, there are only four portfolios corresponding to the four postretirement asset allocation strategies: Moderate, balanced, growth, and aggressive. We connect these four portfolios with the orange curve. We color-code other portfolios according to the postretirement investment strategy: For example, the purple dots represent portfolios which include a LIRP and in which the mutual fund is a growth fund. Each purple dot represents a different face amount or withdrawal strategy. The black curve is the EIF; in other words, it connects some of the most efficient portfolios.

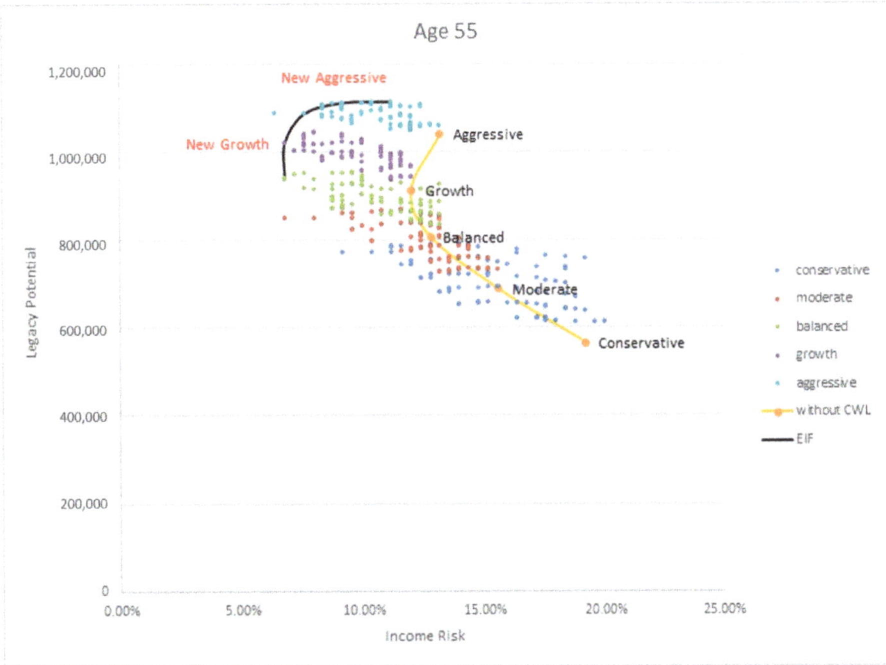

Figure 3. Income risk versus legacy potential for all portfolios and Efficient Income Frontier (EIF).

In Figure 4, again, we consider a 55 year old. We color-code the dots on the graph according to the face amount of the life insurance. For example, all of the red dots correspond to portfolios with a $400K life insurance policy but with one of the 16 different income withdrawal patterns and one of the four different postretirement asset allocation strategies within the mutual fund. We see that the highest face amounts occupy the northwest corner of graph; thus, we conclude that higher face amounts produce more efficient portfolios than lower face amounts.

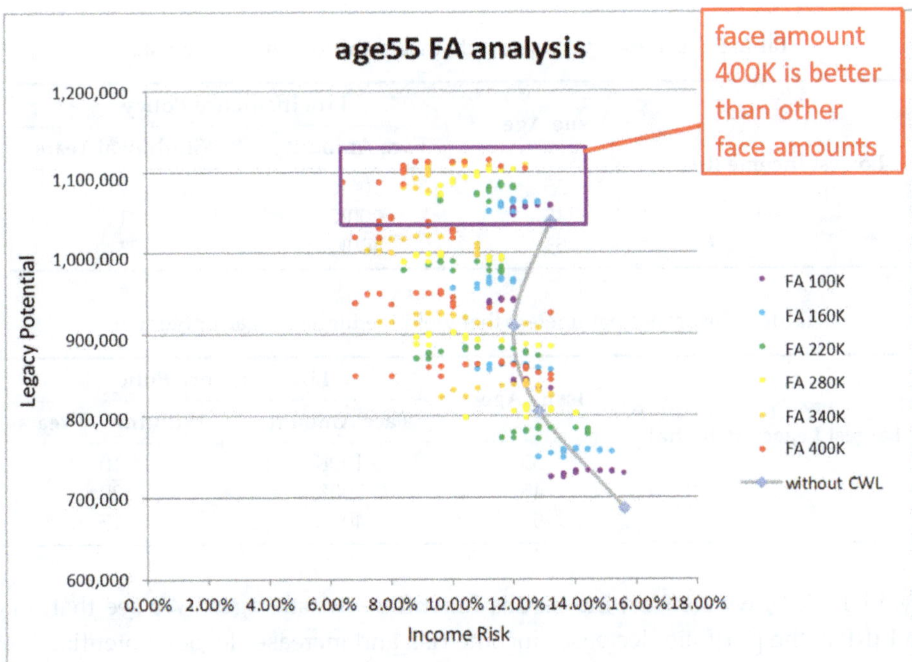

Figure 4. Analysis of face amounts.

In Figure 5, the issue age is again fixed at 55. This time, we color-code the portfolios according to the number of withdrawals from the life insurance product. Thus, the red dots correspond to portfolios with 22–25 annual withdrawals from the life insurance but with different face amounts for the life insurance and asset allocations within the mutual fund. We see that for a fixed value of the legacy potential, the longest withdrawal patterns (red dots) produce the lowest income risk.

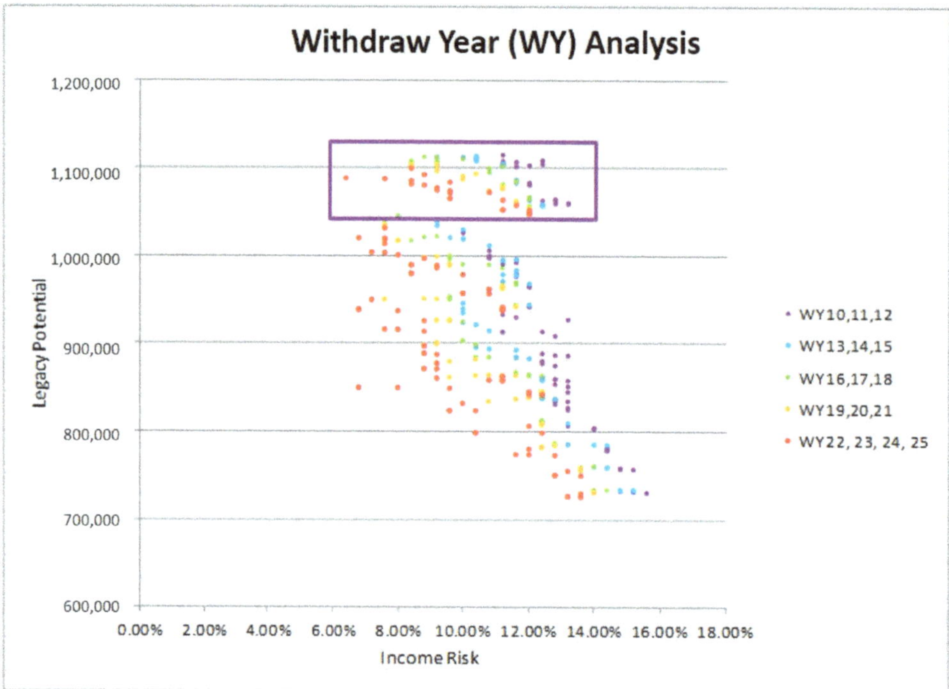

Figure 5. Analysis of withdrawal years.

In Table 5, we summarize the combinations of face amount and withdrawal patterns that minimize income risk for issue ages 35, 45, and 55. In Table 6, we summarize the combinations of face amount and withdrawal pattern that maximize legacy potential for these issue ages.

Table 5. Insurance parameters that yield the lowest income risk.

Lowest Income Risk	Issue Age	Life Insurance Policy	
		Face Amount	Withdrawal Years
	35	100K	12
	45	200K	21
	55	400K	23

Table 6. Insurance parameters that yield the highest legacy potential.

Largest Legacy Potential	Issue Age	Life Insurance Policy	
		Face Amount	Withdrawal Years
	35	100K	10
	45	200K	22
	55	400K	17

Finally, in Table 7, we contrast the results for different issue ages. We see that, in each case, including a LIRP in the portfolio decreases income risk and increases legacy potential. We note that, in our tests, the effect is more pronounced at ages 45 and 55 than at 35.

Table 7. Issue age comparison.

Issue Age	Initial Asset	Face Amount	Premium Burden	Lowest Income Risk		Largest Legacy Potential	
				Without LIRP	With LIRP	Without LIRP	With LIRP
35	50K	100K	67.63%	14.4%	13%	1,144,719	1,208,479
45	200K	200K	44.30%	11.6%	4.8%	1,291,259	1,515,885
55	500K	400K	41.21%	12%	6.8%	1,039,859	1,114,554

4. Conclusions and Directions for Future Work

In this paper, we considered different asset allocation strategies, face amounts, and withdrawal strategies and examined the income risk and legacy potential of the various portfolios under simulated pre- and postretirement market outcomes. We demonstrated that portfolios that include a LIRP in addition to mutual funds often outperform portfolios without a LIRP.

There are several avenues for further investigation. First, our metrics of portfolio performance, income risk, and legacy potential, are based on percentiles of the future lifetime random variable $T(x)$. It would be worthwhile to compare the results if we simulated outcomes from $T(x)$ as well as market outcomes. This would allow us to compute the probability of depleting the income source prior to death (or probability of lifetime ruin) and the probability of reaching a bequest goal. These more sophisticated metrics are used in Chen and Milevsky (2003), Milevsky et al. (2006), Young (2004), Bayraktar et al. (2014, 2015), and Bayraktar and Young (2016).

Moreover, beyond the simulation approach that we used here, it would be interesting to investigate this problem via stochastic optimal control. For example, one might try to determine the premium strategy to optimize a value function based on the probability of ruin and the probability of meeting a bequest goal.

We chose to use the LPWL product for our modeling to balance sophistication (dividends, cash value, flexible duration of premium payments) with model tractability. More sophisticated products such as Universal Life (UL), Indexed Universal Life (IUL), and Variable Universal Life (VUL) are more commonly used as investment vehicles than general account whole life products. In future modeling, we would like to examine how portfolios that include, for example, a VUL-based LIRP perform compared to those that exclude a LIRP. We expect that a VUL-based LIRP will improve portfolio performance beyond our results here.

Author Contributions: Conceptualization, N.H.; methodology, F.D., N.H. and Q.Z.; validation, N.H.; formal analysis, F.D., N.H., and Q.Z.; investigation, F.D., N.H., K.M., and Q.Z.; writing—original draft preparation, F.D., K.M., and Q.Z.; writing—review and editing, K.M.; supervision, N.H.; funding acquisition, K.M.

Funding: This research was funded by a Center of Actuarial Excellence Grant from the Society of Actuaries.

Acknowledgments: This project is part of the Industry Partnership Program (IPP) at the University of Michigan, under which students work with both academic and practicing actuaries on problems that are directly relevant to the industry. The authors gratefully acknowledge the support of the Society of Actuaries under the Center of Actuarial Excellence Grant as well as New York Life (NYL) for their participation in the IPP.

Conflicts of Interest: The authors declare no conflict of interest.

References

Allen, Everett, Jr., Joseph Melone, Jerry Rosenbloom, and Dennis Mahoney. 2014. *Retirement Plans: 401 (k) s, IRAs and Other Deferred Compensation Approaches*, 11th ed. New York: McGraw-Hill Education, ISBN 978-0-07-337743-8.

Bayraktar, Erhan, and Virginia R. Young. 2016. Optimally investing to reach a bequest goal. *Insurance: Mathematics and Economics* 70: 1–10. [CrossRef]

Bayraktar, Erhan, S. David Promislow, and Virginia R. Young. 2014. Purchasing Life Insurance to Reach a Bequest Goal. *Insurance: Mathematics and Economics* 58: 204–16.

Bayraktar, Erhan, S. David Promislow, and Virginia R. Young. 2015. Purchasing Term Life Insurance to Reach a Bequest Goal: Time-Dependent Case. *North American Actuarial Journal* 19: 224–36. [CrossRef]

Bloink, Robert, and William H. Byrnes. 2011. Life Insurance Retirement Plans: Alternative or Rip-off? Available online: http://www.thinkadvisor.com/2011/11/25/life-insurance-retirement-plans-alternative-or-rip?&slreturn=1479162075 (accessed on 20 December 2018).

Chen, Peng, and Moshe A. Milevsky. 2003. Merging Asset Allocation and Longevity Insurance: An Optimal Perspective on Payout Annuities. *Journal of Financial Planning* 16: 52–62.

EBRI. 2016. FAQs about Benefits—Retirement Issues. Available online: https://www.ebri.org/publications/benfaq/index.cfm?fa=retfaq14 (accessed on 30 June 2016).

Ikokwu, Ike. 2013. What's a LIRP and Why You Should Own One. *Huffington Post*. June 15. Available online: http://www.huffingtonpost.com/ike-ikokwu/whats-a-lirp-and-why-you-_b_3084702.html. (accessed on 20 December 2018).

McGill, Dan M., Kyle N. Brown, John J. Haley, Sylvester J. Schieber, and Mark J. Warshawsky. 2010. *Fundamentals of Private Pensions*, 9th ed. Oxford and New York: Oxford University Press.

McKnight, David C. 2012. What Is a LIRP? Available online: https://www.thinkadvisor.com/2012/05/11/whats-a-l-i-r-p-2/ (accessed on 20 December 2018).

Milevsky, Moshe A. 2008. Are You a Stock or a Bond? Create Your Own Pension Plan for a Secure Financial Future. Upper Saddle River: FT Press.

Milevsky, Moshe A., Kristen S. Moore, and Virginia R. Young. 2006. Asset Allocation and Annuity-Purchase Strategies to Minimize the Probability of Financial Ruin. *Mathematical Finance* 16: 647–71. [CrossRef]

Pfau, Wade. 2013. A Broader Framework for Determining an Efficient Frontier for Retirement Income. *Journal of Financial Planning* 26: 44–51.

Pfau, Wade. 2014. Optimizing Retirement Income by Combining Actuarial Science and Investments. One America White Paper. Available online: https://www.owrsfirm.com/wp-content/uploads/OA_WP_Opt-Ret_Inc_05-15_web.pdf (accessed on 20 December 2018).

Spors, Kelly. 2018. Traditional IRA vs. Roth IRA. Available online: https://www.rothira.com/traditional-ira-vs-roth-ira. (accessed on 20 December 2018).

Young, Virginia R. 2004. Optimal Investment Strategy to Minimize the Probability of Lifetime Ruin. *North American Actuarial Journal* 8: 105–26. [CrossRef]

12

Model-Free Stochastic Collocation for an Arbitrage-Free Implied Volatility

Fabien Le Floc'h [1,*] **and Cornelis W. Oosterlee** [1,2]

1 Delft Institute of Applied Mathematics, TU Delft, 2628 XE Delft, The Netherlands
2 CWI-Centrum Wiskunde & Informatica, 1098 XE Amsterdam, The Netherlands; C.W.Oosterlee@cwi.nl
* Correspondence: F.L.Y.LeFloch@tudelft.nl

Abstract: This paper explores the stochastic collocation technique, applied on a monotonic spline, as an arbitrage-free and model-free interpolation of implied volatilities. We explore various spline formulations, including B-spline representations. We explain how to calibrate the different representations against market option prices, detail how to smooth out the market quotes, and choose a proper initial guess. The technique is then applied to concrete market options and the stability of the different approaches is analyzed. Finally, we consider a challenging example where convex spline interpolations lead to oscillations in the implied volatility and compare the spline collocation results with those obtained through arbitrage-free interpolation technique of Andreasen and Huge.

Keywords: stochastic collocation; implied volatility; quantitative finance; arbitrage-free; risk neutral density; B-spline

1. Introduction

Financial markets provide option prices for a discrete set of strike prices and maturity dates. In order to price over-the-counter vanilla options with different strikes, or to hedge complex derivatives with vanilla options, it is useful to have a continuous arbitrage-free representation of the option prices, or equivalently of their implied volatilities. For example, the variance swap replication of Carr and Madan consists in integrating a specific function over a continuum of vanilla put and call option prices (Carr and Madan 2001; Carr and Lee 2009). More generally, Breeden and Litzenberger (1978) have shown that any path-independent claim can be valued by integrating over the probability density implied by market option prices. An arbitrage-free representation is also particularly important for the Dupire local volatility model (Dupire 1994), where arbitrage will translate to a negative local variance. In this paper, we describe a new technique to interpolate the market option prices in an arbitrage-free manner.

A rudimentary, but popular, representation is to interpolate market implied volatilities with a cubic spline across option strikes. Unfortunately, this may not be arbitrage-free as it does not preserve the convexity of option prices in general. A typical convex interpolation of the call option prices by quadratic splines or rational splines is also not satisfactory in general since it may generate unrealistic oscillations in the corresponding implied volatilities, as evidenced in (Jäckel 2014). Kahalé (2004) designs an arbitrage-free interpolation of the call prices, which however requires convex input quotes, employs two embedded non-linear minimizations, and it is not proven that the algorithm for the interpolation function of class C^2 converges. In reality, it is often not desirable to strictly interpolate option prices as those fluctuate within a bid-ask spread. Interpolation will lead to a noisy estimate of the probability density (which corresponds to the second derivative of the undiscounted call option price).

More recently, Andreasen and Huge (2011) have proposed to calibrate the discrete piecewise constant local volatility corresponding to a single-step finite difference discretization of the forward

Dupire equation. In their representation of the local volatility, the authors use as many constants as the number of market option strikes for an optimal fit. It is thus sometimes considered to be "non-parametric". Their technique works well but often yields a noisy probability density estimate, as the prices are typically over-fitted. Furthermore the output of their technique is a discrete set of option prices, which, while relatively dense, must still be interpolated carefully to obtain the price of options whose strike falls in between nodes.

This paper considers another approach, based on the stochastic collocation technique of Grzelak and Oosterlee (2017). Instead of collocating on a polynomial as in Le Floc'h and Oosterlee (2019), we explore various ways to use a monotonic spline, including B-spline parametrizations. This allows for a richer representation, with as many parameters as there are market option strikes. A direct consequence is the ability to capture more complex implied probability distributions, such as multi-modal distributions. We pay attention to avoid over-fitting by adding some appropriate regularization. This is reminiscent of the penalized B-spline technique for volatility modelling of Corlay (2016), where a B-spline parameterization of the Radon–Nikodym derivative of the underlying's risk-neutral probability density with respect to a roughly calibrated base model is used. Concretely, Corlay's method translates to an explicit probability density representation where the probability density is a spline multiplied by a base probability density function, such as the lognormal or normal probability density function. Corlay's technique however limits the implied volatility shapes allowed, and often requires the use of a more elaborate base probability density function, such as the one stemming from the SVI[1] parameterization of Gatheral (2004), to properly fit the market in practice. We will see that the stochastic collocation on a spline is more flexible and can fit the market very well when collocating to a simple Gaussian variable.

The outline of the paper is as follows. Section 2 presents how to apply the stochastic collocation on a monotonic cubic spline, while still preserving the first moment exactly. The collocation on an exponential spline is explored in Section 3, which results in analytical formulas not only for the price of vanilla options but also for the price of variance swaps. Section 4 considers B-spline representations which take into account the monotonicity and the martingale constraints explicitly. Section 5 details the calibration towards market option prices of each kind of representation. Section 6 explains how to filter the market quotes so that the spline collocation technique can be applied directly. The filtering may be used independently of the B-spline collocation. Finally, Section 7 explores the stability of the calibration on concrete market data, for the different parametrizations considered. We compare the quality of fit and the implied probability density with the Andreasen–Huge technique, regularized. In Section 8, we look at a challenging example of Jäckel (2014), where interpolation splines applied to call prices lead to oscillations in the interpolation.

2. Spline Collocation

Collocation methods are commonly used to solve ordinary or partial differential equations (LeVeque 2007). The underlying principle is to solve the equations in a specific finite dimensional space of solutions, such as polynomials up to a certain degree. In contrast, the stochastic collocation method (Mathelin and Hussaini 2003) consists in mapping a physical random variable Y to a point X in an artificial stochastic space. Collocation points x_i are used to approximate the function mapping X to Y, $F_X^{-1} \circ F_Y$, typically by a polynomial, where F_X, F_Y are respectively the cumulative distribution functions (CDF) of X and Y. Thus, only a small number of inversions of Y (and evaluations of F_Y) are used. This allows the problem to be solved in the "cheaper" artificial space.

---

1 SVI stands for Stochastic Volatility Inspired. The SVI model consists in five parameters which define the scaled sum of a linear function with a multiquadric function.

In the context of option price interpolation, the stochastic collocation allows us to interpolate the market CDF in a better set of coordinates. In particular, we follow Grzelak and Oosterlee (2017) and use a Gaussian distribution for X.

In (Grzelak and Oosterlee 2017), the stochastic collocation is applied to the survival distribution function G_Y, where $G_Y(y) = 1 - F_Y(y)$ with F_Y being the cumulative density function of the asset price process. When the survival density function is known for a range of strikes, their method can be summarized by the following steps:

1. Given a set of collocation strikes y_i, $i = 0, \ldots, N$, compute the survival density p_i at those points: $p_i = G_Y(y_i)$.
2. Project on the Gaussian distribution by transforming the p_i using the inverse cumulative normal distribution Φ^{-1} resulting in $x_i = \Phi^{-1}(1 - p_i)$.
3. Interpolate (x_i, y_i) with a monotonic and derivable function g on $\mathbb{R}$. Grzelak and Oosterlee (2017) use a Lagrange polynomial for g but the technique can be applied to any derivable and monotonic function. Further on, we will consider a monotonic spline.
4. Price by integrating the density with the integration variable $x = \Phi^{-1}(1 - G_Y(y))$, using the approximation g to map the coordinates x to the strikes y.

In order to illustrate the mapping involved in the stochastic collocation technique, we consider four options with strikes $y_0 = 40$, $y_1 = 70$, $y_2 = 120$, $y_3 = 215$ and maturity time $T = 2$ in the Black–Scholes model with constant volatility $\sigma = 20\%$ and forward price to maturity $F = 100$. Figure 1a details the mapping from the four market strikes y_i to the cumulative probability density p_i (step 1) and Figure 1b shows the mapping from the coordinate x_i to y_i (step 2). The initial goal of step 3 is to find a smooth function that approximates the theoretical mapping in the coordinates from x to y well. The mapping function only needs to be monotonic, and to conserve the first moment, in order for the collocation method to be arbitrage-free. The figures show the mapping with the Black–Scholes model, which constitutes the reference, and with the B-spline collocation presented in this paper, based on the four options. The cumulative density for the B-spline collocation is obtained after computing the optimal collocation B-spline in the x, y coordinates, based on the four points $(x_i, y_i)_{i=0,\ldots,3}$.

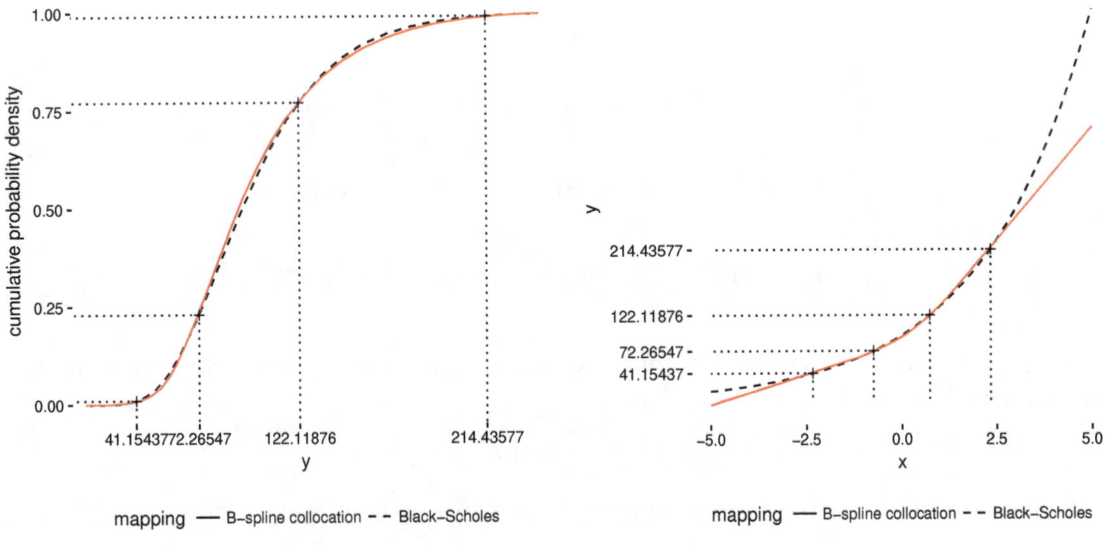

(**a**) Cumulative probability density from strike prices y_i

(**b**) x_i from y_i

Figure 1. Mapping in the stochastic collocation technique for the Black–Scholes model with volatility $\sigma = 20\%$.

In reality, we are really interested in minimizing the error in terms of option prices (or equivalently implied volatilities). The discrete set of reference option prices either come directly from the financial markets, or from a prior model. This is where step 4 also becomes critical.

Let us now detail step 4. The undiscounted price of an option with strike price K is obtained by integrating over the probability density Breeden and Litzenberger (1978):

$$C(K) = \int_0^{+\infty} \max(y - K, 0) f(y) dy,$$

where f is the probability density implied by the options prices. We then perform the change of variable $x = \Phi^{-1}(1 - G_Y(y))$ to obtain

$$C(K) = \int_{\Phi^{-1}(0)}^{\Phi^{-1}(1)} \max\left(G_Y^{-1}(1 - \Phi(x)) - K, 0\right) \phi(x) dx.$$

As $g(x) \approx G_Y^{-1}(1 - \Phi(x))$, we have

$$\begin{aligned} C(K) &\approx \int_{-\infty}^{\infty} \max(g(x) - K, 0) \phi(x) dx \\ &= \int_{x_K}^{\infty} (g(x) - K) \phi(x) dx, \end{aligned} \tag{1}$$

where $\phi(x)$ is the Gaussian density function and

$$x_K = g^{-1}(K). \tag{2}$$

The change of variables is valid when the survival density is continuous and its derivative is integrable. In particular, it is not necessary for the derivative to be continuous.

When g is a piecewise cubic polynomial defined on the knots $(x_i, y_i)_{i=0,\dots,N}$, the call option price can be obtained analytically. Let $g(x) = g_i(x) = a_i + b_i(x - x_i) + c_i(x - x_i)^2 + d_i(x - x_i)^3$ for $x \in [x_i, x_{i+1}]$, and k the index such that $y_k \leq K < y_{k+1}$, assuming that $0 \leq i < N$ exists, Equation (1) becomes

$$\begin{aligned} C(K) &= I(\tilde{x}_{-1}, x_0) + I(\tilde{x}_N, \infty) - K\Phi(-\tilde{x}_k) \\ &+ \sum_{i=k}^{N-1} \left[a_i - (b_i + d_i(\tilde{x}_i^2 + 3))x_i + c_i(x_i^2 + 1)\right] (\Phi(-\tilde{x}_i) - \Phi(-\tilde{x}_{i+1})) \\ &+ \sum_{i=k}^{N-1} \left[b_i + c_i(\tilde{x}_i - 2x_i) + d_i(3x_i^2 - 3\tilde{x}_i x_i + \tilde{x}_i^2 + 2)\right] \phi(\tilde{x}_i) \\ &- \sum_{i=k}^{N-1} \left[b_i + c_i(\tilde{x}_{i+1} - 2x_i) + d_i(3x_i^2 - 3x_i\tilde{x}_{i+1} + \tilde{x}_{i+1}^2 + 2)\right] \phi(\tilde{x}_{i+1}), \end{aligned} \tag{3}$$

with $\tilde{x}_k = g^{-1}(K)$, $\tilde{x}_{-1} = x_0$ and $\tilde{x}_i = x_i$ for $i > k$. The integral I corresponding to the left and right extrapolations is defined by

$$I(a, b) = \int_a^b g(x)\phi(x) dx.$$

In the case of a linear extrapolation with slope s and starting at the point (x, y), we have

$$I_L(a, b) = (y - sx)(\Phi(b) - \Phi(a)) - s(\phi(b) - \phi(a)).$$

with the abuse of notation $\Phi(\infty) = 1, \Phi(-\infty) = 0$ and $\phi(\infty) = \phi(-\infty) = 0$. We use $s = s_L$, and $x = x_0, y = y_0$ for the left wing extrapolation, and $s = s_R$, and $x = x_N, y = y_N$ for the right wing extrapolatioin.

When $K < y_0$ and in the case of a linear extrapolation, Equation (3) is still valid, but with $\tilde{x}_{-1} = \frac{K-y_0}{s_L} + x_0$. When $K > y_N$, $C_K = I_R(\tilde{x}_N, \infty)$ with $\tilde{x}_N = \frac{K-y_N}{s_R} + x_N$.

The cut-off point $\tilde{x}_k = g_k^{-1}(K)$ can be found analytically through Cardano's formula (Nonweiler 1968).

The first moment is given by

$$\begin{aligned} M_1(g) = &I(-\infty, x_0) + I(x_N, \infty) \\ &+ \sum_{i=0}^{N-1} \left[a_i - (b_i + d_i(x_i^2+3))x_i + c_i(x_i^2+1)\right] (\Phi(x_{i+1}) - \Phi(x_i)) \\ &+ \sum_{i=0}^{N-1} \left[b_i - c_i x_i + d_i(x_i^2+2)\right] \phi(x_i) \\ &- \sum_{i=0}^{N-1} \left[b_i + c_i(x_{i+1} - 2x_i) + d_i(3x_i^2 - 3x_i x_{i+1} + x_{i+1}^2 + 2)\right] \phi(x_{i+1}) . \end{aligned} \quad (4)$$

In practice, the preservation of the martingale property (and the put-call parity relation) imposes $M_1 = F$ where F is the market forward price to maturity T.

The put option price is calculated through the put-call parity relation, namely

$$C(K) - P(K) = F - K, \quad (5)$$

where $P(K)$ is the undiscounted price today of a put option of maturity T, and F is the forward price to maturity.

When put option prices are very small, and assuming that the first moment equals exactly the forward price, it is preferable to use a more direct approach. Equation (5) does not allow to compute prices below machine epsilon. Using the same change of variables as for the call option (Equation (1)), we have for a put option with strike K:

$$\begin{aligned} P(K) &= \int_0^{+\infty} \max(K - y, 0) f(y) dy \\ &= \int_{-\infty}^{x_K} (g(x) - K)\phi(x) dx . \end{aligned}$$

This leads to

$$\begin{aligned} P(K) = &K\Phi(\tilde{x}_k) - I(-\infty, \tilde{x}_{-1}) - I(\tilde{x}_N, x_N) \\ &+ \sum_{i=0}^{k-1} \left[a_i - (b_i + d_i(x_i^2+3))x_i + c_i(x_i^2+1)\right] (\Phi(\tilde{x}_{i+1}) - \Phi(\tilde{x}_i)) \\ &+ \sum_{i=0}^{k-1} \left[b_i + c_i(\tilde{x}_i - 2x_i) + d_i(3x_i^2 - 3x_i\tilde{x}_i + \tilde{x}_i^2 + 2)\right] \phi(\tilde{x}_i) \\ &- \sum_{i=0}^{k-1} \left[b_i + c_i(\tilde{x}_{i+1} - 2x_i) + d_i(3x_i^2 - 3x_i\tilde{x}_{i+1} + \tilde{x}_{i+1}^2 + 2)\right] \phi(\tilde{x}_{i+1}) , \end{aligned} \quad (6)$$

with $\tilde{x}_k = g^{-1}(K)$, $\tilde{x}_{-1} = x_0$ and $\tilde{x}_i = x_i$ for $0 \le i < k$.

3. Exponential Spline Collocation

3.1. Vanilla Options

Instead of interpolating on the strikes (the points $(x_i, y_i)_{i=0,...,N}$), we will interpolate the log strikes (the points $(x_i, \ln y_i)_{i=0,...,N}$) with a piecewise polynomial. This presupposes that the strikes are strictly positive and that the probability of the asset being negative equals zero. The undiscounted call price of an option with strike K is then

$$C(K) = \int_{-\infty}^{\infty} \max(e^{g(x)} - K, 0)\phi(x)dx\,, \quad (7)$$

where g is a monotonic piecewise polynomial function interpolating $(x_i, \ln y_i)_{i=0,\dots,N}$. We cannot obtain a closed-form formula for a general g function, if we assume that g is a quadratic spline. Let $(\bar{x}_j)_{j=0,\dots,M}$ be the spline knots, and $g(x) = a_j + b_j(x - \bar{x}_j) + c_j(x - \bar{x}_j)^2$ on $[\bar{x}_j, \bar{x}_{j+1}]$, with k the index such that $\bar{y}_k \leq K < \bar{y}_{k+1}$, we have then

$$\begin{aligned} C(K) &= I(\tilde{x}_{-1}, \tilde{x}_0) + I(\tilde{x}_M, \infty) + K\Phi(-\tilde{x}_k) \\ &+ \sum_{j=k}^{M-1} e^{a_j - b_j\bar{x}_j + c_j\bar{x}_j^2 + \frac{1}{2}m_j^2} \frac{\Phi\left(\tilde{x}_{j+1}\sqrt{1-2c_j} - m_j\right) - \Phi\left(\tilde{x}_j\sqrt{1-2c_j} - m_j\right)}{\sqrt{1-2c_j}}, \end{aligned}$$

with $m_j = \frac{b_j - 2c_j\bar{x}_j}{\sqrt{1-2c_j}}$ and defining $\tilde{x}_k = g^{-1}(\ln K)$, $\tilde{x}_i = \bar{x}_i$ for $i > k$. When $1 - 2c_j < 0$, we can use the imaginary error function erfi as we have for $a, b \in \mathbb{R}$,

$$-i\frac{\Phi(ib\sqrt{2c_j - 1}) - \Phi(ia\sqrt{2c_j - 1})}{\sqrt{2c_j - 1}} = \frac{\operatorname{erfi}\left(b\sqrt{\frac{2c_j-1}{2}}\right) - \operatorname{erfi}\left(a\sqrt{\frac{2c_j-1}{2}}\right)}{2\sqrt{2c_j - 1}}.$$

For a linear extrapolation with slope s and passing by the point (x, y), corresponding to $g(u) = s(u - x) + y$, we find

$$\begin{aligned} I(a,b) &= \int_a^b e^{s(u-x)+y}\phi(u)du \\ &= e^{y - sx + \frac{1}{2}s^2}\left(\Phi(b - s) - \Phi(a - s)\right), \end{aligned} \quad (8)$$

with some abuse of notation $\Phi(-\infty) = 0$, $\Phi(\infty) = 1$. The left wing extrapolation corresponds to $x = \bar{x}_0$ and $y = \bar{y}_0$, with $s = s_L$ a free parameter and the right wing extrapolation corresponds to $x = \bar{x}_M, y = \bar{y}_M$ with $s = s_R$. In order to keep the continuity of the derivative at the boundaries, we choose $s_R = g'(x_N)$ and $s_L = g'(x_0)$.

The first moment is given by

$$\begin{aligned} M_1 &= \int_{-\infty}^{\infty} e^{g(x)}\phi(x)dx \\ &= I(-\infty, \bar{x}_0) + I(\bar{x}_M, \infty) \\ &+ \sum_{j=0}^{M-1} e^{a_j - b_j\bar{x}_j + c_j\bar{x}_j^2 + \frac{1}{2}m_j^2} \frac{\Phi\left(\bar{x}_{j+1}\sqrt{1-2c_j} - m_j\right) - \Phi\left(\bar{x}_j\sqrt{1-2c_j} - m_j\right)}{\sqrt{1-2c_j}} \\ &= I(-\infty, \bar{x}_0) + I(\bar{x}_M, \infty) \\ &+ \sum_{j=0}^{M-1} e^{a_j + \frac{b_j^2 - 2b_j\bar{x}_j + 2c_j\bar{x}_j^2}{2(1-2c_j)}} \frac{\Phi\left(\bar{x}_{j+1}\sqrt{1-2c_j} - m_j\right) - \Phi\left(\bar{x}_j\sqrt{1-2c_j} - m_j\right)}{\sqrt{1-2c_j}}. \end{aligned} \quad (9)$$

3.2. Variance Swap

Variance swaps contracts allow a buyer to receive the future realized variance of the price changes until a specific maturity date against a fixed strike price, paid at maturity. Conventionally, these price changes are daily log returns of a specific stock, equity index, or exchange rate based upon the most commonly used closing price (or exchange rate reset price). Variance swaps became particularly popular after Demeterfi et al. showed that a single contract could be statically replicated by a portfolio of vanilla options (Demeterfi et al. 1999). In the absence of jumps[2] and assuming the observations to be continuous, the problem of pricing a variance swap can be reduced to the pricing of a log-contract. The price V of a variance swap, by continuous replication, has a particularly simple closed-form expression with the exponential spline parametrization. For a newly issued variance swap with zero strike, and a transition probability density f from $t = 0$ to $t = T$, following Carr and Lee (2009), we have

$$V(0,T) = -\frac{2}{T}\int_0^{\infty} \ln\left[\frac{y}{F(0,T)}\right] f(y)dy \qquad (10)$$
$$= -\frac{2}{T}\int_{-\infty}^{\infty} (g(x) - \ln F(0,T))\, \phi(x)dx\,.$$

In Equation (10), $\tilde{g} = g - F(0,T)$ is a piecewise quadratic spline. The value of the integral corresponds to the first moment of the collocation variable with the spline $\tilde{g}$, which is given explicitly by Equation (4). The standard replication formula from Carr and Madan (2001) implies to choose an integration cut-off and to use of a numerical quadrature, typically an adaptive Gauss–Lobatto quadrature. This is not necessary with the exponential spline collocation approach. The price of the variance swap can be adjusted by changing the slope of the linear extrapolation. This allows for a fast joint calibration of the collocating B-spline to market option prices and variance swaps. The market variance swap prices give some additional information on the tail of the distribution, not covered by vanilla options.

4. B-Spline Collocation

We recall that the goal of the stochastic collocation is to find a smooth monotonic function to represent the function g mapping the abscissas $(x_i)_{i=0,\dots,N}$ to the ordinates (the strikes) $(y_i)_{i=0,\dots,N}$ (see Figure 1b), by minimizing the error in option prices in a least-squares sense. From the previous sections, we now know how to price vanilla options by collocating on a spline, which passes through the specific points $(x_i, y_i)_{i=0,\dots N}$. We can then choose to optimize either the abscissas or the ordinates of those points in order to minimize the least squares error in option prices, on the condition that we use a monotonicity preserving spline and make sure to conserve the first moment in the optimization.

Instead of using an exact interpolation function on a set of points, and optimizing this interpolation through the choice of points, we can rely on a B-spline representation and optimize directly the B-spline coefficients. The method will work both on the direct strikes, or on the log strikes. We consider a quadratic B-spline representation, that is, B-splines of order $k = 3$. The B-spline representation of g on $N + 1 + k$ knots reads (De Boor 1978)

$$g(x) = \sum_{i=0}^{N} \alpha_i B_{i,3}(x)\,. \qquad (11)$$

We choose the nearly optimal knots $t_{i+3} = \frac{x_{i+1}+x_{i+2}}{2}$ for $i = 0, \dots, N-3$ according to (De Boor 1978, p. 193) with the boundary knots $t_0 = t_1 = t_2 = x_0$ and $t_{N+1} = t_{N+2} = t_{N+3} = x_N$. This choice of knots ensures that g is C^1 on $[x_0, x_N]$.

Because the derivative of the equivalent piecewise polynomial representation is linear between two distinct knots, g will be monotonically increasing on an interval $[t_{i-1}, t_i]$ if and only if the derivative at the endpoints is positive. Thus, g will be monotonically increasing on the interval $[x_0, x_N]$ if and only if $\alpha_i - \alpha_{i-1} > 0$ for $i = 1, \dots, N$ in Equation (11).

---

2 Although such a hypothesis may seem very strong, most practitioners value the variance swaps by replication.

It is then particularly simple to impose the monotonicity constraints when we optimize the coefficients α_i during the calibration to market quotes. Furthermore, a least-squares fit of g directly to some input $(x_i, y_i)_{i=0,...,N}$ reduces to a simple quadratic programming problem:

$$\tilde{\alpha} = \arg\min_{\alpha \in \mathbb{R}^{N+1}} \frac{1}{2}\alpha^T Q \alpha + q^T \alpha \tag{12}$$

subject to $\alpha_i - \alpha_{i-1} > 0$ for $i = 1, ..., N$, with $Q = P^T P$, $q = -P^T y$ and P the matrix defined by $P_{i,j} = B_{i,3}(y_j)$. In particular, P is a banded matrix (De Boor 1978).

The quadratic programming problem is fast to solve using a standard optimization library such as CVXOPT (Andersen et al. 2013), OSQP (Stellato et al. 2017), or quadprog (Turlach and Weingessel 2007), when compared to the total time taken to calibrate the spline. This will allow starting the optimization from a reasonable initial guess.

In order to price an option or to evaluate the first moment, we simply transform the B-spline representation to a piecewise quadratic polynomial (De Boor 1978, p. 117–19) and rely on Sections 2 and 3 in this paper, for respectively a direct B-spline collocation, and an exponential B-spline collocation.

In the case of the direct B-spline collocation, the first moment is a linear combination of the B-spline coefficients. Indeed, the first moment is a linear combination of the piecewise polynomial coefficients in Equation (4) and the piecewise polynomial coefficients themselves are a linear combination of the B-spline coefficients:

$$a_j = \frac{t_{j+2} - t_{j+1}}{t_{j+3} - t_{j+1}} \left(\alpha_{j+1} - \alpha_j\right) + \alpha_j \,, \tag{13}$$

$$b_j = 2\frac{\alpha_{j+1} - \alpha_j}{t_{j+3} - t_{j+1}} \,, \tag{14}$$

$$c_j = \frac{1}{t_{j+3} - t_{j+2}} \left(\frac{\alpha_{j+2} - \alpha_{j+1}}{t_{j+4} - t_{j+2}} + \frac{\alpha_j - \alpha_{j+1}}{t_{j+3} - t_{j+1}} \right) . \tag{15}$$

We can thus add the martingale constraint directly to the quadratic programming problem as an additional equality constraint.

5. Calibration of the Spline Collocation to Market Quotes

We wish to minimize the weighted ℓ_2 error norm between the volatilities implied from the prices obtained by spline collocation and the market implied volatilities. For this, we can optimize the location of either the spline knots abscissas x_i or the spline knots ordinates y_i, or in the case of the B-spline representation, the coefficients α_i.

5.1. Coordinate Transformation

In order to preserve the order of the knots, we rely on the following mapping:

$$\begin{cases} z_i = x_i - x_{i-1} \,, \text{ for } i > 0 \,, \\ z_0 = x_0 \,, \end{cases}$$

and enforce $z_i \geq 0$ as box constraints in the least-squares minimization. Box constraints can be added in a relatively straightforward manner to any Levenberg-Marquardt algorithm, such as the one of Klare and Miller (2013), through the projection technique described in (Kanzow et al. 2004).

We use the same mapping if the ordinates or the B-spline coefficients are optimized, using y_i, respectively α_i, instead of x_i in the above equations.

5.2. Moment Conservation

We also wish to preserve the first moment exactly in order for the spline representation to be fully arbitrage-free. Let $M_1(g)$ be the first moment computed by Equation (4) and F be the market forward price to the option maturity time T. In order to make M_1 match F, we shift the coefficient a_i of each piecewise polynomial $(g_i)_{i=0,\dots,N-1}$ and use

$$\hat{a}_i = a_i + F - M_1\,, \text{ for } 0 \leq i \leq N\,. \tag{16}$$

For the exponential spline representation on $M+1$ unique knots, the adjustment is almost the same, but based on the log values we use

$$\hat{a}_i = a_i + \ln F - \ln M_1\,, \text{ for } 0 \leq i \leq M\,. \tag{17}$$

The new spline $\hat{g}$ with updated coefficients $\hat{a}_i$ will satisfy exactly $M_1 = F$.

With this adjustment, there is a fundamental difference between the optimization of the abscissas x_i and the ordinates y_i: when the abscissas are optimized, the adjustment will also implicitly adjust the y_i as we have $y_i = \hat{a}_i$. Furthermore, when optimizing the ordinates y_i or the B-spline coefficients α_i, the first coordinate y_0 (respectively α_0) can be directly deduced from the martingale adjustment. Indeed, the adjustment only impacts the value of z_0 and has no effect on $z_i = u^{-1}(y_i - y_{i-1})$ for $i > 0$. This allows to reduce the number of dimensions of the optimization problem by one.

5.3. Choice of Coordinates

In our experiments, the optimization of the abscissas $(x_i)_{i=0,\dots,N}$ appeared to be the least stable. In particular, the outcome was highly dependent on the initial guess. Only with a proper regularization and a good smooth initial guess (for example, the constant Bachelier guess) was the outcome satisfactory.

In comparison, the optimization of the ordinates $(y_i)_{i=0,\dots,N}$ was found to be more stable, and the optimization of the B-spline coefficients was the most stable of all choices. One reason for this stability, is the initial guess for the B-spline coefficients respects the martingale constraint. Another is that the B-spline formulation is simply more stable than the piecewise-polynomial version (De Boor 1978). Values from the B-spline representation are obtained from a linear combination of the coefficients, while values obtained from the monotonic cubic spline representation are neither a linear combination of the abscissas nor of the ordinates, because of the monotonicity constraint.

The flexibility of choosing a different variety of monotonic splines such as the cubic spline of Hyman (1983) or Huynh (1993) when optimizing the knots abscissas or ordinates does not translate to a better fit of the reference option prices. In some specific cases, such as the one we explore in Section 8, the optimization the abscissas led to a better fit, but this consists in fitting towards the prices of a pre-existing model at hypothetical strikes, and not directly towards the market prices.

From now on, for clarity, we will thus focus only on the B-spline or exponential B-spline collocations where the B-spline coefficients are optimized.

5.4. Regularization

We will see through real examples that it can be useful to add regularization to the minimization as well, in order to avoid an implied probability density with many spikes. An interesting candidate for the regularization is to minimize the strain energy of the beam that is forced to pass through the given data points (Glass 1966):

$$E = \sum_{i=0}^{m} \mu_i^2 \left(\sigma(\xi, K_i) - \sigma_i\right)^2 + \lambda^2 \sum_{i=0}^{m-1} \frac{\mu_i^2 g''(x_i)^2}{[1 + g'(x_i)^2]^{\frac{5}{2}}}(x_{i+1} - x_i)\,, \tag{18}$$

where $\sigma(\xi, K)$ is the implied volatility corresponding to the option prices obtained with the spline collocation and σ_i is the market implied volatility at strike K_i. For the maturity T considered, $m+1$ is the number of market strikes. We allow the number of strikes to be greater than or equal to the number of spline interpolation nodes $N+1$. The parameter ξ represents a specific spline configuration on $N+1$ nodes. For a B-spline, we have $\xi = (\alpha_j)_{j=0,\dots,N}$, where $(\alpha_j)_{j=0,\dots,N}$ are the coefficients of the B-spline representation.

The first term of the objective E corresponds to the square of the root mean square error (RMSE), while the second term is the regularization. The regularization parameter λ controls the smoothness of the spline interpolation.

In the case of the B-spline representation, Eilers and Marx (1996) propose a simpler regularization. Their penalized spline (P-spline) minimizes the total variation of the second derivative. This regularization, expressed in terms of the B-spline coefficients, reads

$$E = \sum_{i=0}^{m} \mu_i^2 \left(\sigma(\xi, K_i) - \sigma_i\right)^2 + \lambda^2 \sum_{j=1}^{N-1} \frac{4\mu_i^2}{(t_{j+2} - t_{j+1})^2} \left(\frac{\alpha_{j+1} - \alpha_j}{t_{j+3} - t_{j+1}} + \frac{\alpha_{j-1} - \alpha_j}{t_{j+2} - t_j} \right)^2, \tag{19}$$

where $(t_j)_{j=0,\dots,N+3}$ are the spline knots. In particular, the latter regularization is linear in the coefficients $(\alpha_j)_{j=0,\dots,N}$ and can thus be directly included in the quadratic programming problem described in Section 4.

6. Making Market Call Prices Arbitrage-Free

For each strike and maturity, at a given time, the market quotes two prices for an option contract: the bid price and the ask price. In order to calibrate directly the collocation spline to the market quotes, we need a single estimate of the implied cumulative probability density. It is common practice to use the average of the bid and ask prices, the mid price for this purpose. Alternatively, we could also build two distinct representations: one for the bid prices and one or the ask prices.

When considered separately, the bid, ask, or mid prices are not guaranteed to be arbitrage-free in theory: there can be theoretical arbitrages within the bid-ask spread that cannot be taken advantage of in practice. Like most financial models, the collocation method is really only well defined in the absence of arbitrage: the implied cumulative probability density needs to be monotonic. We will explore in this section different ways to smooth the quotes and make them arbitrage-free. The goal is to obtain a good initial guess of the implied cumulative probability density in order to calibrate the spline nodes to the market prices afterwards.

6.1. No-Arbitrage Properties

Let $(y_i)_{i=0,\dots,m}$ be the market strikes and $(c_i)_{i=0,\dots,m}$ the undiscounted market call option prices corresponding to each strike, with $y_0 < y_1 < \dots < y_n$. Lemma 1 of Kahalé (2004) states that there is no arbitrage in those prices if and only if

$$-1 < \frac{c_i - c_{i-1}}{y_i - y_{i-1}} < \frac{c_{i+1} - c_i}{y_{i+1} - y_i} < 0\,, \text{ for } i = 1, \dots, m-1\,. \tag{20}$$

To be more precise, we should also have $\max(F - y_i, 0) < c_i < F$, where F is the underlying forward price to the option maturity.

6.2. A Quadratic Programming Problem

When the undiscounted call option prices c_i contain some arbitrage, we need to solve the following quadratic programming problem:

$$\tilde{c} = \underset{z \in \mathbb{R}^{n+1}}{\arg\min} \, \|W \cdot (z - c)\|_2^2 \tag{21}$$

subject to

$$-1 < \frac{z_i - z_{i-1}}{y_i - y_{i-1}} < \frac{z_{i+1} - z_i}{y_{i+1} - y_i} < 0\,, \text{ for } i = 1, ..., m-1\,, \tag{22}$$

where W is a diagonal matrix of weights. For equal weights W is the identity matrix I_{n+1}. We can include information on the bid-ask spread, for example by taking w_i to be the inverse of the bid-ask spread at strike y_i.

We have

$$\|W \cdot (z - c)\|_2^2 = z^T W^T W z - 2(W^T W c)^T z + (Wc)^T Wc\,.$$

The minimization problem can thus be formulated as a quadratic programming problem:

$$\tilde{c} = \underset{z \in \mathbb{R}^{n+1}, Gz \leq h}{\arg\min} \; \frac{1}{2} z^T Q z + q^T z \tag{23}$$

with

$$Q = W^T W\,,$$
$$q = -W^T W c\,,$$

and the elements $G_{i,j}$ of the matrix G, that specifies the linear constraints in (23), are

$$G_{i,i-1} = -\frac{1}{y_i - y_{i-1}}\,, \quad G_{i,i} = \frac{1}{y_i - y_{i-1}} + \frac{1}{y_{i+1} - y_i}\,, \quad G_{i,i+1} = -\frac{1}{y_{i+1} - y_i}\,,$$

for $i = 1, ..., n-1$, and

$$G_{0,0} = \frac{1}{y_1 - y_0}\,, \quad G_{0,1} = -\frac{1}{y_1 - y_0}\,,$$
$$G_{n,n} = \frac{1}{y_n - y_{n-1}}\,, \quad G_{n,n-1} = -\frac{1}{y_n - y_{n-1}}\,.$$

and the vector h by $h_0 = 1.0 - \epsilon$, $h_i = -\epsilon$ for $i > 0$. The constant ϵ defines a maximum acceptable slope and ensures that the call prices are strictly convex.

In order to tune the smoothing of option prices, we could add a Tikhonov regularization, using the matrix of second order differences as Tikhonov matrix. This is, however, not necessary for the B-spline collocation, as we already add a regularization when computing the B-spline representation based on the initial guess.

Once the quadratic programming problem has been solved[3], we can estimate the call price slope c'_i at each strike y_i using the parabola that passes through the three points c_{i-1}, c_i, c_{i+1} (see Le Floc'h and Oosterlee (2019)):

$$c'_i \approx \frac{l_i(y_{i+1} - y_i) + l_{i+1}(y_i - y_{i-1})}{y_{i+1} - y_{i-1}} \text{ where } l_i = \frac{c_i - c_{i-1}}{y_i - y_{i-1}} \tag{24}$$

for $i = 1, ..., m-1$, and with $c'_0 = l_1$, $c'_m = l_m$. It will lead to $-1 < c'_i < 0$ and increasing c'_i assuming that the call prices c_i obeys the conditions of lemma 1 of Kahalé (2004). This gives a direct estimate of the survival density $p_i = -c'_i$ and thus of the abscissa x_i.

Another approach to find an initial guess is to rely on a very rough estimate, which may be a good starting point for the optimization. A straightforward initial guess for the implied cumulative

3 We used quadprog (Turlach and Weingessel 2007) in our numerical examples.

probability density is to consider the density implied by a flat Bachelier volatility. The at-the-money market implied volatility is a natural choice. For a given option price, the Bachelier implied volatility σ_N can be found in closed form using the rational expansions of Le Floc'h (2016). The collocation points can then be obtained directly:

$$x_i = -\frac{F - y_i}{\sigma\sqrt{T}} . \quad (25)$$

With a constant Bachelier volatility, x is an affine function of y and vice-versa.

7. Example of Calibration on TSLA Options

We consider options on the stock with ticker TSLA expiring on 17 January 2020 as of 15 June 2018. We first imply the forward price from the put-call parity relation at-the-money and then imply the Black–Scholes volatility from the mid price for each option strike (Table A1). In this example, the options mid prices are not arbitrage free.

We will measure the RMSE between the volatilities implied by the calibrated stochastic collocation and the market implied volatilities, with and without regularization. We use equal weights in this example. Although it is not particularly realistic, it has the advantage of making the plots of the implied volatility more explicit.

The calibration consists firstly in computing an arbitrage-free (convex) set of call option prices from the market mid quotes according to Section 6.2, secondly in computing the B-spline initial guess following Section 4, and thirdly in minimizing the error measure represented by Equation (18) with a Levenberg–Marquardt minimizer.

7.1. B-Spline

With a small (or zero) regularization parameter λ, the resulting implied probability density possesses many spurious spikes (Figure 2a). The use of a larger regularization parameter λ, during the non-linear minimization of the objective E described in Equation (18), helps smoothing the spikes, but it increases the RMSE slightly (see Table 1).

Table 1. Root mean square error (RMSE) of the collocation method implied volatilities against the market implied volatilities of the TSLA 1 m options as of 18 June 2018.

Method	Regularization	RMSE	Time (ms)
Exponential B-spline collocation	$\lambda = 1 \times 10^{-3}$	0.00437	43
B-spline collocation	$\lambda = 6 \times 10^{-6}$	0.00397	71
Andreasen–Huge	none	0.00356	890
Exponential B-spline collocation	$\lambda = 1 \times 10^{-7}$	0.00345	150
B-spline collocation	$\lambda = 1 \times 10^{-10}$	0.00326	37
Schumarker quadratic spline	none	0.00313	0.5

In Table 1, we also compute the RMSE with a simple convexity preserving quadratic spline (Schumaker 1983) on the filtered market option prices (Equation (23)). This interpolation leads to a positive and piecewise-constant probability density. On convex prices, the interpolation is exact. The RMSE is thus purely due to the filtering of the market quotes by quadratic programming.

Andreasen and Huge (2011) propose a different non-parametric arbitrage-free volatility interpolation, where a discrete local volatility is calibrated to market option prices in a one-step finite-difference discretization of the forward Dupire partial differential equation. The number of free parameters corresponds effectively to the number of quotes, as in the spline collocation, and their technique will also tend to overfit. It is known to lead to a nearly exact interpolation on arbitrage-free option prices. It does however not lead to a more accurate representation of the market implied volatilities than the B-spline collocation with a small regularization constant. The corresponding implied probability density also possesses spikes.

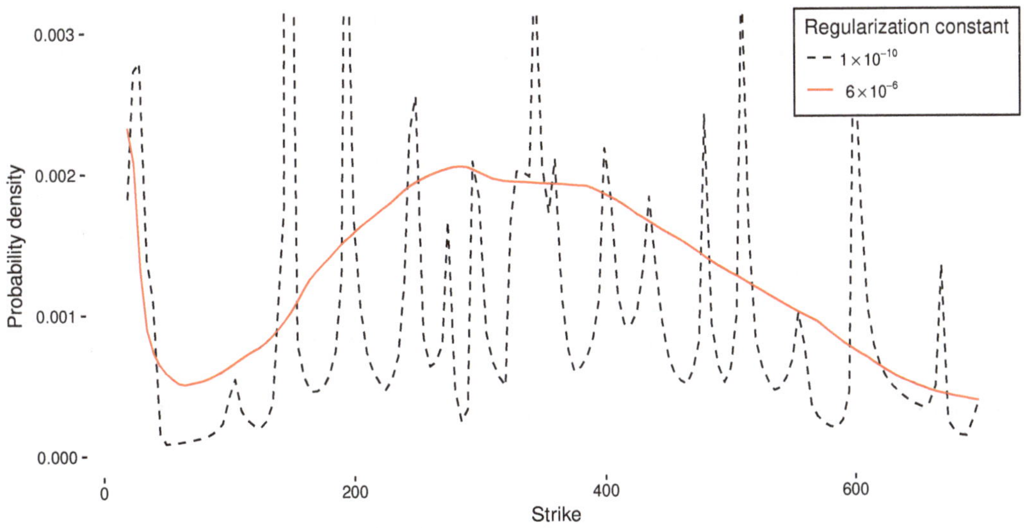

(**a**) Probability density implied by the prices obtained with a calibrated B-spline collocation

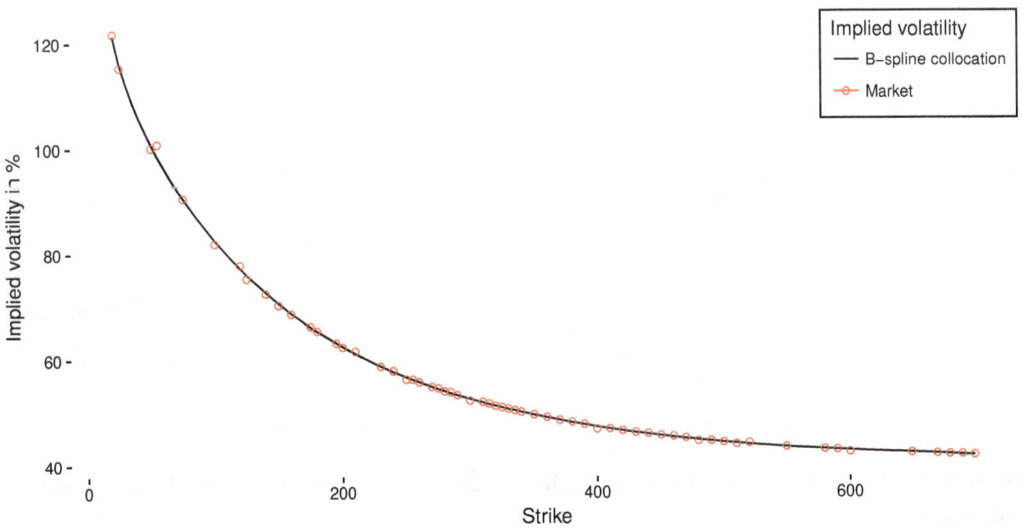

(**b**) Volatility smile implied by the prices obtained with B-spline collocation with regularization $\lambda = 6 \times 10^{-6}$

Figure 2. Implied probability density and implied volatility for the B-spline collocation, calibrated to 1 m TSLA options.

The B-spline collocation is not only at least as accurate as the technique of Andreasen and Huge (2011) on this example, it is also significantly faster. In the latter, the involved finite difference grid must be relatively large (we used 800 points) and the corresponding tridiagonal system must be solved for each set of piecewise constant volatilities considered by the minimizer. Furthermore, the B-spline collocation offers a continuous interpolation of the option prices. In the technique of Andreasen and Huge (2011), options prices are given only at the finite difference grid points. Another careful[4] arbitrage-free interpolation must be used to compute the price in between grid points. Finally, the B-spline collocation offers the ability to tune the probability density smoothness against the RMSE.

The optimal regularization parameter can be found using the L-curve method (Hansen 1992). On Figure 3b we plot the L-curve for the calibrated B-spline collocation, that is the regularization

4 In practice, we solve the Fokker-Planck forward PDE instead of the Dupire forward PDE, and then integrate the option payoff on the known probability density as in Hagan et al. (2014); Le Floc'h and Kennedy (2017) in order to obtain arbitrage-free prices everywhere.

norm against residual norm, in logarithmic scale, or equivalently, the second sum against the first sum of Equation (19), varying the regularization parameter λ. For most regularization techniques, such a curve is L-shaped, because, on linear problems, the regularization norm is a strictly decreasing function of the regularization parameter λ, and the residual norm is a strictly increasing function of λ. A good regularization parameter will achieve a good compromise between the two errors, and will correspond to a regularized solution near the "corner" of the L-curve. On non-linear least-squares problems in general, the regularization and residual norms will not be strictly monotonic, they will however be nearly monotonic and the L-curve method may still be applied (Aster et al. 2018, p. 241).

Our choice $\lambda = 6 \times 10^{-6}$ is the point located in the corner of the L-curve (see Figure 3b). Performing multiple calibrations to find the optimal regularization parameter, following one of the algorithms of Hansen and O'Leary (1993), may be time-consuming. An alternative is to apply the L-curve method to the B-spline initial guess based on the convex option prices[5] (Figure 3a).

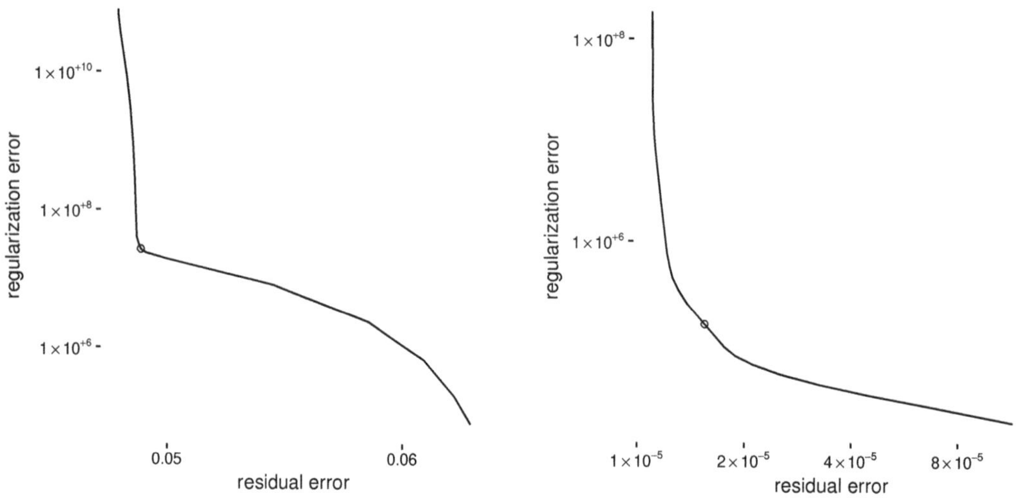

(**a**) Initial guess on convex prices (**b**) Calibrated collocation

Figure 3. L-curves of the B-spline corresponding to the initial guess, and the calibration result on TSLA options.

7.2. Exponential B-Spline

The exponential B-spline initial guess does not preserve the first moment. As a consequence, its calibration tends to be less stable than the calibration of the regular B-spline. The choice of initial guess plays then an important role, and the inclusion of the regularization in the calculation of the exponential B-spline initial guess is particularly important. The RMSE in the implied volatilities is comparable to the one obtained by the Andreasen and Huge technique, and is larger than the RMSE of the regular B-spline collocation (Table 1). In spite of the larger error, the implied probability density is not as smooth as the one implied from the regular B-spline collocation (Figure 4). A smoother initial guess, such as the constant Bachelier volatility, is then preferable.

5 We use inverse Vega weights to fit the B-spline guess to the option prices.

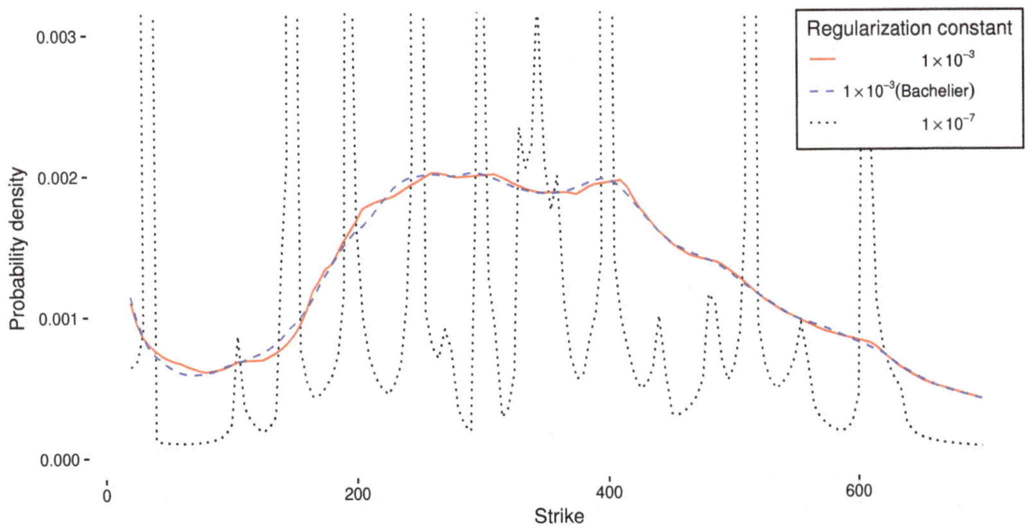

Figure 4. Implied probability density for the exponential B-spline collocation, calibrated to 1 m TSLA options, with different regularization constants.

7.3. Starting from Arbitrage-Free Prices

It is also interesting to take the filtered convex option prices (from Equation (23)) as a basis to compare the different techniques. We expect the RMSE to be lower, eventually zero, if the interpolation is exact at the market strikes. For example, the convexity-preserving Schumaker quadratic spline results in an RMSE of exactly zero (but the associated implied probability density is a staircase). The B-spline collocation results in an RMSE of around 0.0005 without regularization constant. This is lower than the RMSE produced by the Andreasen–Huge technique. In theory, their technique should be able to attain a lower RMSE, but the number of strikes, and thus the number of constants to optimize is relatively large on our problem and this creates difficulties for the numerical optimization. The collocation on an exponential B-spline leads to an RMSE similar to the one obtained with the Andreasen–Huge technique (Table 2). Of course, with a small regularization constant, the corresponding probability density possesses many spikes and is not very practical.

Table 2. Root mean square error (RMSE) of the collocation method implied volatilities against the implied volatilities of the TSLA 1 m options as of 18 June 2018, based on convexity adjusted prices.

Method	Regularization	RMSE	Time (ms)
Exponential B-spline collocation	$\lambda = 10^{-3}$	0.00287	35
B-spline collocation	$\lambda = 6 \times 10^{-6}$	0.00239	39
Exponential B-spline collocation	$\lambda = 10^{-7}$	0.00118	160
Andreasen–Huge	none	0.00112	890
B-spline collocation	$\lambda = 10^{-10}$	0.00042	78
Schumaker quadratic spline	none	0	0.02

On other market data, for example, options on NFLX from July 2018, the same conclusions can be drawn.

8. A More Extreme Example—Wiggles in the Implied Volatility

Jäckel (2014) shows that undesired oscillations can appear in the graph of the implied volatility against the option strikes when the option prices are interpolated by a monotonic and convex spline. Table A2 in Appendix A presents a concrete example[6]. Here, the option quotes are not direct market quotes, but the solution of a sparse finite difference discretization of a local stochastic volatility model: the market never quotes so far out-of-the-money option prices. His data has a few interesting properties:

- some of the option prices are extremely small: the interpolation must be very accurate numerically.
- the option prices are free of arbitrage. In theory, an arbitrage-free interpolation can be exact.
- a cubic spline interpolation on the volatilities or the variances, often used by practitioners, is not arbitrage-free.
- a convexity preserving C^1-quadratic, or C^2-rational spline results in strong oscillations in the implied volatility.

The interpolation proposed in (Jäckel 2014) possesses unnatural spikes at the points of clamping, in particular, the implied density is not continuous.

For this example, the B-spline collocation leads to a relatively large RMSE when compared to Andreasen–Huge method. As a consequence, we can see an oscillation of small amplitude in the corresponding implied volatility for large strikes (Figure 5b). This is very mild compared to the spline interpolations presented in (Jäckel 2014). The higher error is mostly located in the left wing. The exponential B-spline collocation results in a much lower RMSE, albeit still larger than the Andreasen and Huge technique (Table 3). The volatility implied by the exponential B-spline collocation does not oscillate.

The optimal implied probability density is relatively smooth, but possesses a few visible modes (Figure 5a). This makes the monotonic polynomial collocation of Le Floc'h and Oosterlee (2019) ineffective, even when using a high degree polynomial. Polynomials of degree seven and higher lead to a RMSE larger than one vol point.

Table 3. Root mean square error (RMSE) of the collocation method implied volatilities against the implied volatilities of Table A2 in Appendix A.

Method	Regularization	RMSE	Time (ms)
Septic polynomial	none	1×10^{-2}	230
B-spline	$\lambda = 10^{-12}$	2×10^{-4}	10
Exponential B-spline	$\lambda = 10^{-7}$	6×10^{-5}	10
Andreasen–Huge (800 nodes)	none	1×10^{-6}	25
Andreasen–Huge (3200 nodes)	none	9×10^{-8}	67
Schumaker convex spline	none	0	0.02

It is possible to obtain a better fit with the B-spline collocation with a better choice of knots, for example, if we compute the knots implied by the calibrated B-spline collocation, and calibrate one more time. In Table 4, we denote this technique as "Best". It improves significantly the accuracy on the example of Peter Jäckel, but not on the filtered and non filtered TSLA market option quotes, where the different choices for the initial knots lead to a very similar RMSE.

On Peter Jäckel's example, the optimal implied probability density is relatively smooth everywhere, and especially for strike moneyness larger than one. Figure 6 shows however that the probability density implied by technique of Andreasen and Huge (2011) exhibits a staircase shape when zoomed-in. This is due to the interpolation in between the finite difference grid nodes. In contrast, the probability density implied by the (exponential) B-spline collocation stays very smooth, and is continuous by construction.

---

[6] We are grateful to Peter Jäckel for kindly providing this data.

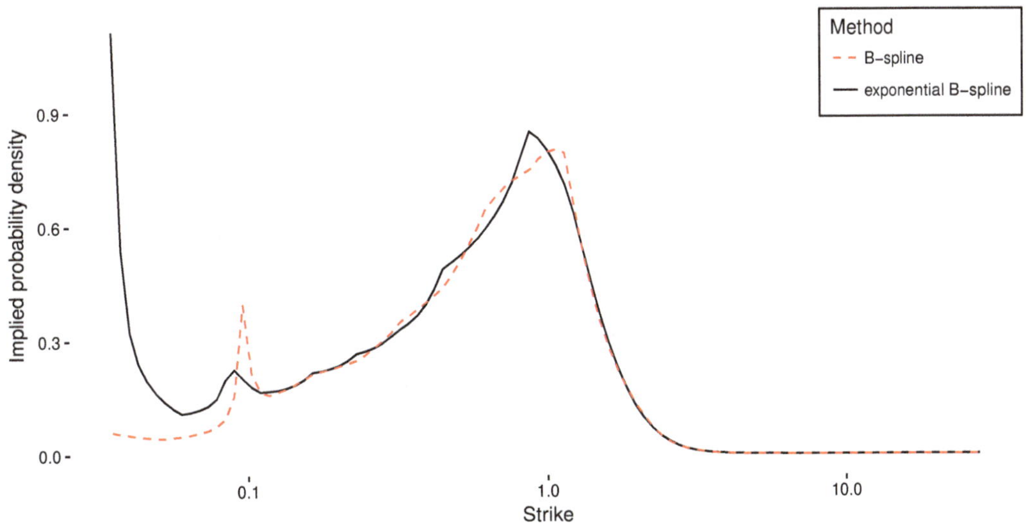

(**a**)Probability density

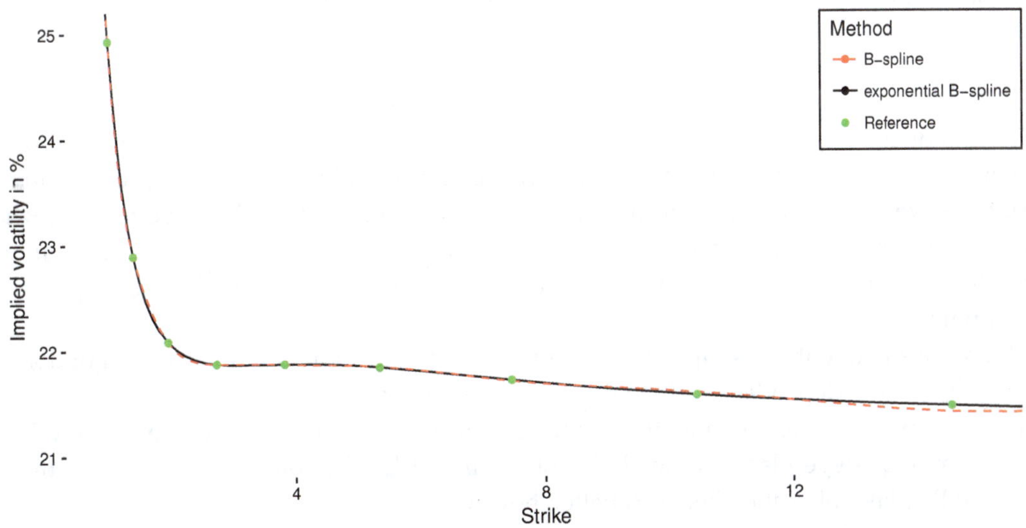

(**b**)Volatility smile for moneyness larger than one

Figure 5. Implied probability density and implied volatility for the spline collocations of the market data of Table A2 in appendix A.

Table 4. Root mean square error (RMSE) of the collocation method implied volatilities starting the calibration with the Bachelier, the convex, or the "best" initial guess, and using a small regularization constant.

Market Data	Collocation Method	Bachelier	Convex	Best
Peter Jäckel	B-spline	0.00063	0.00025	0.00001
	Exponential B-spline	0.00016	0.00006	0.00003
TSLA raw	B-spline	0.00330	0.00326	0.00322
	Exponential B-spline	0.00343	0.00345	0.00343
TSLA convex	B-spline	0.00054	0.00042	0.00034
	Exponential B-spline	0.00108	0.00118	0.00108

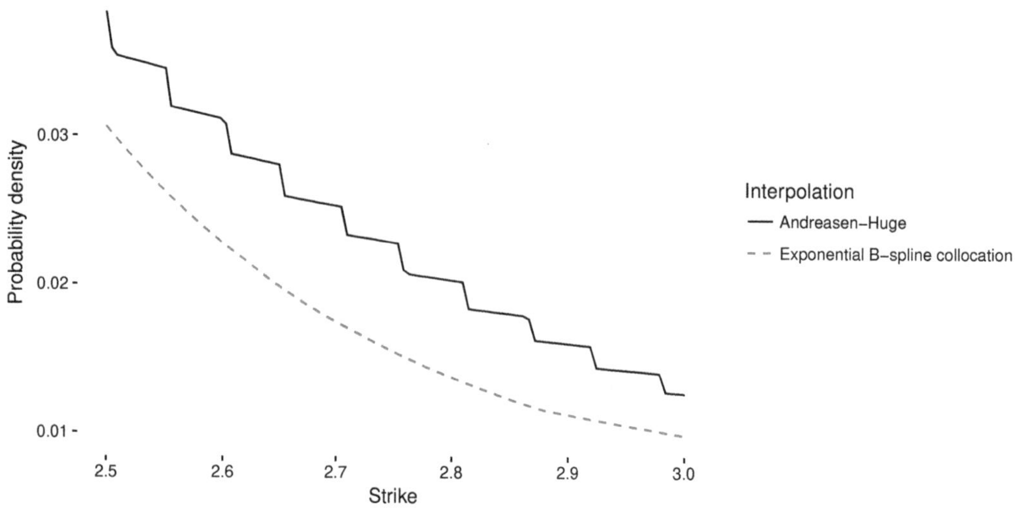

Figure 6. Implied probability density for the exponential B-spline collocation and Andreasen–Huge techniques, for strike moneyness $K \in [2.5, 3.0]$, calibrated to the market data of Table A2 in Appendix A. The B-spline has a knot located at $K = 2.679$.

9. Conclusions

The monotonic B-spline and exponential B-spline collocations allow a more flexible arbitrage-free representation as compared to the monotonic polynomial collocation. They can capture multi-modal distributions well. In practice, when the goal is to fit market option prices, we have shown that is important to add a regularization during the optimization in order to stabilize the calibration and produce a smooth implied probability density, and we have described which regularization is appropriate.

We have also presented a simple non-parametric technique to de-arbitrage a set of option prices, which may be used independently of the B-spline collocation method.

In some specific cases, such as the example from Jäckel (2014), the outcome of the B-spline calibration may be dependent on the choice of the initial fixed knots. In the latter example, the exponential B-spline collocation behaved better, however.

On actual market options quotes, corresponding to various equity or equity indices, we did not observe this strong dependence on the choice of initial knots. We observed a quality of fit in terms of implied volatilities similar to or better than the best non-parametric arbitrage-free methods, such as the technique of Andreasen and Huge (2011). Compared to the latter, the spline collocation has the advantage of providing a natural continuous interpolation and extrapolation. The technique from Andreasen and Huge is based on a fine discretization of the problem, and requires an additional careful arbitrage-free interpolation scheme to compute the prices for option strikes not placed on the discretization grid. The B-spline collocation is also less computationally intensive, as the Andreasen and Huge technique mainly works well on a dense grid, typically composed of thousand points or more.

An additional interesting property of the exponential B-spline representation is the simple analytical expression we obtain for the price of a variance swap. The latter is a linear combination of the B-spline parameters. This allows including the market prices of variance swaps very easily into the calibration and thus obtaining a better representation of the wings of the implied volatility.

Finally, the B-spline and exponential B-spline collocations can be used directly to price exotic derivatives within the collocated local volatility model of Grzelak (2016).

We leave for further research the definition of an algorithm for an automatic selection of the best B-spline knots, as well as an extension to B-splines of order four.

Author Contributions: Conceptualization, F.L.F. and C.W.O.; methodology, F.L.F. and C.W.O.; software, F.L.F.; writing–original draft preparation, F.L.F.; writing–review and editing, C.W.O.; visualization, F.L.F.; supervision, C.W.O.

Funding: This research received no external funding.

Conflicts of Interest: The authors declare no conflict of interest.

Appendix A. Market Data

Table A1. Implied volatilities against strikes K for TSLA options expiring on 17 January 2020 as of 15 June 2018. This corresponds to a maturity $T = 1.59178$ and the forward is $f = 356.73$.

Strike	Implied Volatility	Strike	Implied Volatility
20	1.217 45	330	0.507 12
25	1.152 97	335	0.504 29
50	1.001 35	340	0.501 40
55	1.008 70	350	0.496 19
75	0.905 59	360	0.491 45
100	0.819 65	370	0.485 71
120	0.779 70	380	0.482 10
125	0.753 93	390	0.477 66
140	0.725 53	400	0.468 23
150	0.703 70	410	0.469 13
160	0.687 09	420	0.465 20
175	0.663 15	430	0.462 10
180	0.654 28	440	0.459 70
195	0.631 00	450	0.456 14
200	0.623 20	460	0.454 18
210	0.615 45	470	0.451 55
230	0.586 62	480	0.445 42
240	0.578 38	490	0.445 28
250	0.562 50	500	0.443 04
255	0.562 55	510	0.439 39
260	0.557 23	520	0.441 32
270	0.548 52	550	0.433 63
275	0.545 61	580	0.429 71
280	0.540 06	590	0.428 44
285	0.538 48	600	0.424 11
290	0.532 53	650	0.422 27
300	0.522 24	670	0.420 34
310	0.520 24	680	0.419 34
315	0.516 84	690	0.419 35
320	0.512 74	700	0.417 59
325	0.510 04		

Table A2. Implied volatilities against moneyness $\frac{K}{F}$ for an option of maturity $T = 5.0722$, corresponding to the example 1 of Jäckel (2014).

Moneyness	Implied volatility
0.035 12	0.642 41
0.049 10	0.621 68
0.068 62	0.590 58
0.095 92	0.553 14
0.134 08	0.511 40
0.187 41	0.466 70
0.261 96	0.420 23
0.366 17	0.373 30
0.511 82	0.327 56
0.715 42	0.285 11
1	0.249 33
1.397 78	0.228 97
1.953 80	0.220 86
2.730 99	0.218 76
3.817 33	0.218 74
5.335 80	0.218 43
7.458 29	0.217 20
10.425 07	0.215 74
14.572 00	0.214 62
20.368 49	0.214 11
28.470 74	0.214 58

References

Andreasen, Jesper, and Brian Norsk Huge. 2011 Volatility interpolation. *Risk* 24: 76. [CrossRef]

Andersen, Martin S., Joachim Dahl, and Lieven Vandenberghe. 2013. CVXOPT: A Python Package for Convex Optimization. Available online: abel.ee.ucla.edu/cvxopt (accessed on 22 January 2019).

Aster, Richard C., Brian Borchers, and Clifford H. Thurber. 2018. *Parameter Estimation and Inverse Problems*. Amsterdam: Elsevier.

Breeden, Douglas T., and Robert H. Litzenberger. 1978. Prices of state-contingent claims implicit in option prices. *Journal of business* 51: 621–51. [CrossRef]

Carr, Peter, and Dilip Madan. 2001. Towards a theory of volatility trading. In *Option Pricing, Interest Rates and Risk Management, Handbooks in Mathematical Finance*. Cambridge: Cambridge University Press, pp. 458–76.

Carr, Peter, and Roger Lee. 2009. Robust Replication of Volatility Derivatives. Available online: www.math.uchicago.edu/~rl/rrvd.pdf (accessed on 22 January 2019).

Corlay, Sylvain. 2016. B-spline techniques for volatility modeling. *Journal of Computational Finance* 19: 97–135. [CrossRef]

De Boor, Carl. *A Practical Guide to Splines*. New York: Springer, vol. 27.

Demeterfi, Kresimir, Emanuel Derman, Michael Kamal, and Joseph Zou. 1999. More than you ever wanted to know about volatility swaps. *Goldman Sachs Quantitative Strategies Research Notes* 41: 1–56.

Dupire, Bruno. 1994. Pricing with a smile. *Risk* 7: 18–20.

Eilers, Paul H. C., and Brian D. Marx. 1996. Flexible smoothing with B-splines and penalties. *Statistical Science* 11: 89–102. [CrossRef]

Gatheral, Jim. 2004. A Parsimonious Arbitrage-Free Implied Volatility Parameterization With Application to the Valuation of Volatility Derivatives. In *Presentation at Global Derivatives & Risk Management, Madrid*. Available online: faculty.baruch.cuny.edu/jgatheral/madrid2004.pdf (accessed on 22 January 2019).

Glass, J. M. 1966. Smooth-curve interpolation: A generalized spline-fit procedure. *BIT Numerical Mathematics* 6: 277–93. [CrossRef]

Grzelak, Lech A., and Cornelis W. Oosterlee. 2017. From arbitrage to arbitrage-free implied volatilities. *Journal of Computational Finance* 20: 31–49. [CrossRef]

Grzelak, Lech A. 2016. The CLV Framework-A Fresh Look at Efficient Pricing with Smile. SSRN 2747541. Available online: papers.ssrn.com/sol3/papers.cfm?abstract_id=2747541 (accessed on 22 January 2019).

Hagan, Patrick S., Deep Kumar, Andrew Lesniewski, and Diana Woodward. 2014. Arbitrage-Free SABR. *Wilmott* 2014: 60–75. [CrossRef]

Hansen, Per Christian. 1992 Analysis of discrete ill-posed problems by means of the L-curve. *SIAM Review* 34: 561–80. [CrossRef]

Hansen, Per Christian, and Dianne Prost O'Leary. 1993. The use of the L-curve in the regularization of discrete ill-posed problems. *SIAM Journal on Scientific Computing* 4: 1487–503. [CrossRef]

Huynh, Hung T. 1993. Accurate monotone cubic interpolation. *SIAM Journal on Numerical Analysis* 30: 57–100. [CrossRef]

Hyman, James M. 1983. Accurate monotonicity preserving cubic interpolation. *SIAM Journal on Scientific and Statistical Computing* 4: 645–54. [CrossRef]

Jäckel, Peter . 2014. Clamping Down on Arbitrage. *Wilmott* 2014: 54–69. [CrossRef]

Kahalé, Nabil. 2004. An arbitrage-free interpolation of volatilities. *Risk* 17: 102–6.

Kanzow, Christian, Masao Fukushima, and Nobuo Yamashita. 2004. Levenberg-Marquardt methods for constrained nonlinear equations with strong local convergence properties. *J. Computational and Applied Mathematics* 172: 375–97. [CrossRef]

Klare, Kenneth, and Guthrie Miller. 2013. GN—A Simple and Effective Nonlinear Least-Squares Algorithm for the Open Source Literature. Available online: www.netlib.org/misc/gn/GN_ReadMe.pdf (accessed on 22 January 2019).

Le Floc'h, Fabien. 2016. Fast and Accurate Analytic Basis Point Volatility. SSRN 2420757. Available online: papers.ssrn.com/sol3/papers.cfm?abstract_id=2420757 (accessed on 22 January 2019).

Le Floc'h, Fabien, and Cornelis W. Oosterlee. 2019. Model-Free Stochastic Collocation for an Arbitrage-Free Implied Volatility, Part I. *Decision in Economics and Finance*. Available online: link.springer.com/article/10.1007/s10203-019-00238-x (accessed on 22 January 2019).

Le Floc'h, Fabien, and Gary J. Kennedy. 2017. Finite difference techniques for arbitrage-free SABR. *Journal of Computational Finance* 20: 51–79.

LeVeque, Randall J. 2007. *Finite Difference Methods for Ordinary and Partial Differential Equations: Steady-State and Time-Dependent Problems*. Philadelphia: SIAM, vol. 98.

Mathelin, Lionel, and M. Yousuff Hussaini. 2003. *A Stochastic Collocation Algorithm for Uncertainty Analysis*. CR-2003-212153. Hampton: NASA Langley Research Center, pp. 1–16.

Nonweiler, Terence R. 1968. Algorithms: Algorithm 326: Roots of low-order polynomial equations. *Communications of the ACM* 11: 269–70. [CrossRef]

Schumaker, Larry I. 1983. On shape preserving quadratic spline interpolation. *SIAM Journal on Numerical Analysis* 20: 854–64. [CrossRef]

Stellato, Bartolomeo, Goran Banjac, Paul Goulart, Alberto Bemporad, and Stephen Boyd. 2017. OSQP: An Operator Splitting Solver for Quadratic Programs. *arXiv*. Available online: http://xxx.lanl.gov/abs/1711.08013 (accessed on 22 January 2019).

Turlach, Berwin A., and Andreas Weingessel. 2007. quadprog: Functions to Solve Quadratic Programming Problems. CRAN-Package. Available online: https://cran.r-project.org/web/packages/quadprog/index.html (accessed on 22 January 2019).

Permissions

All chapters in this book were first published in RISK, by MDPI; hereby published with permission under the Creative Commons Attribution License or equivalent. Every chapter published in this book has been scrutinized by our experts. Their significance has been extensively debated. The topics covered herein carry significant findings which will fuel the growth of the discipline. They may even be implemented as practical applications or may be referred to as a beginning point for another development.

The contributors of this book come from diverse backgrounds, making this book a truly international effort. This book will bring forth new frontiers with its revolutionizing research information and detailed analysis of the nascent developments around the world.

We would like to thank all the contributing authors for lending their expertise to make the book truly unique. They have played a crucial role in the development of this book. Without their invaluable contributions this book wouldn't have been possible. They have made vital efforts to compile up to date information on the varied aspects of this subject to make this book a valuable addition to the collection of many professionals and students.

This book was conceptualized with the vision of imparting up-to-date information and advanced data in this field. To ensure the same, a matchless editorial board was set up. Every individual on the board went through rigorous rounds of assessment to prove their worth. After which they invested a large part of their time researching and compiling the most relevant data for our readers.

The editorial board has been involved in producing this book since its inception. They have spent rigorous hours researching and exploring the diverse topics which have resulted in the successful publishing of this book. They have passed on their knowledge of decades through this book. To expedite this challenging task, the publisher supported the team at every step. A small team of assistant editors was also appointed to further simplify the editing procedure and attain best results for the readers.

Apart from the editorial board, the designing team has also invested a significant amount of their time in understanding the subject and creating the most relevant covers. They scrutinized every image to scout for the most suitable representation of the subject and create an appropriate cover for the book.

The publishing team has been an ardent support to the editorial, designing and production team. Their endless efforts to recruit the best for this project, has resulted in the accomplishment of this book. They are a veteran in the field of academics and their pool of knowledge is as vast as their experience in printing. Their expertise and guidance has proved useful at every step. Their uncompromising quality standards have made this book an exceptional effort. Their encouragement from time to time has been an inspiration for everyone.

The publisher and the editorial board hope that this book will prove to be a valuable piece of knowledge for researchers, students, practitioners and scholars across the globe.

List of Contributors

Delia Coculescu
Institut für Banking und Finance, Universität Zürich, Plattenstrasse 32, 8032 Zürich, Switzerland

Freddy Delbaen
Departement für Mathematik, ETH Zürich, Rämistrasse 101, 8092 Zürich, Switzerland
Institut für Mathematik, Universität Zürich, Winterthurerstrasse 190, 8057 Zürich, Switzerland

Susanna Levantesi
Department of Statistics, Sapienza University of Rome, Viale Regina Elena, 295/G, 00161 Rome, Italy

Virginia Pizzorusso
Ernst and Young Advisory, Via Meravigli, 12, 20123 Milano, Italy

Mauricio Junca
Department of Mathematics, Universidad de los Andes, Bogotá 11711, Colombia

Harold A. Moreno-Franco
Department of Mathematics and Statistics, Universidad del Norte, Barranquilla 080003, Colombia

José Luis Pérez
Department of Probability and Statistics, Centro de Investigación en Matemáticas A.C., Guanajuato 36000, Mexico

Shuaiqiang Liu
Delft Institute of Applied Mathematics (DIAM), Delft University of Technology, Building 28, Mourik Broekmanweg 6, 2628 XE Delft, The Netherlands

Cornelis W. Oosterlee
Delft Institute of Applied Mathematics (DIAM), Delft University of Technology, Building 28, Mourik Broekmanweg 6, 2628 XE Delft, The Netherlands
Centrum Wiskunde & Informatica, Science Park 123, 1098 XG Amsterdam, The Netherlands

Sander M. Bohte
Centrum Wiskunde & Informatica, Science Park 123, 1098 XG Amsterdam, The Netherlands

Sel Ly, Kim-Hung Pho and Sal Ly
Faculty of Mathematics and Statistics, Ton Duc Thang University, Ho Chi Minh City 756636, Vietnam

Wing-Keung Wong
Department of Finance, Fintech Center, and Big Data Research Center, Asia University, Tai Chung 41354
Department of Medical Research, China Medical University Hospital, Taichung 40402, Taiwan
Department of Economics and Finance, Hang Seng University of Hong Kong, Shatin 999077, Hong Kong

Ravi Summinga-Sonagadu and Jason Narsoo
Department of Economics and Statistics, University of Mauritius, Réduit 80837, Mauritius

Apostolos Bozikas and Georgios Pitselis
Department of Statistics and Insurance Science, University of Piraeus, 18534 Piraeus, Greece

Florin Avram
Laboratoire de Mathématiques Appliquées, Université de Pau, 64012 Pau, France

Danijel Grahovac
Department of Mathematics, University of Osijek, 31000 Osijek, Croatia

Ceren Vardar-Acar
Department of Statistics, Middle East Technical University, Ankara 06800, Turkey

Martin Leo, Suneel Sharma and K. Maddulety
SP Jain School of Global Management, Sydney 2127, Australia

Mansi Jain, Gagan Deep Sharma and Mrinalini Srivastava
School of Management Studies, Guru Gobind Singh Indraprastha University, Sector 16C, Dwarka, New Delhi 110078, India

Fangyuan Dong
Paid Growth Analyst, Airbnb, Inc., 888 Brennan St., San Francisco, CA 94103, USA

Nick Halen
Strategy, Research and Analytics, New York Life, 51 Madison Avenue, New York, NY 10010, USA

Kristen Moore
Department of Mathematics, University of Michigan, 2074 East Hall, 530 Church Street, Ann Arbor, MI 48109-1043, USA

Qinglai Zeng
People Advisory Services, Ernst & Young LLP, 155 North Wacker Drive, Chicago, IL 60606, USA

Fabien Le Floc'h
Delft Institute of Applied Mathematics, TU Delft, 2628 XE Delft, The Netherlands

Index

A

Algorithm, 13-17, 19-20, 23-24, 26, 52, 57, 60-62, 64, 75-76, 78-79, 89, 95, 164-170, 173-175, 177-178, 209, 216, 226, 229

Arbitrage Free, 220

B

Backtest, 98-99, 104-105, 112-117

Backtesting Procedure, 98, 103, 105, 112-115, 117

Banking Risk, 158-159, 161, 163-165, 167, 169, 171, 173, 175, 177, 179

Brownian Motion, 52, 58, 154-155, 157

Buhlmann Credibility, 141

C

Capital, 1, 3-6, 8-11, 32-35, 37-39, 41, 43, 45-51, 53-55, 99-100, 117, 119, 145, 148, 159, 162, 165, 176, 180-181, 195

Capital Injection, 32-35, 37-39, 41, 43, 45-47, 49, 51, 53-55

Claim, 4, 6-7, 11, 122, 209

Copulas, 78-83, 85, 87, 89-97

Corporate Social Responsibility, 182-183, 195-197

Credibility Regression, 121-122, 125-126, 128-133, 135, 137-140

Credit, 12, 56, 80, 96, 158-160, 162-179

Credit Risk, 56, 158-160, 162-168, 170-179

Credit Risk Management, 160, 164, 167-168, 171, 173-174

Credit Scoring, 158, 165-166, 170-171, 173-178

D

Daily Variance, 99, 101-102, 106-109, 116

Decision Tree, 14-16, 20, 26, 166, 170, 173, 175

Density Function, 60, 81, 210-212

Dependence Structure, 80-82, 84, 89, 91-93, 95, 97

Distribution, 2, 4, 11, 13, 17, 52, 58-59, 67, 69-73, 78-85, 87-93, 95-98, 100-105, 108, 110-113, 117-118, 123-124, 156, 162-163, 171, 210-211, 215

Distribution Function, 84, 95, 103, 211

Dividend Payment, 32, 54

Drawdown, 143, 146, 148-155, 157

E

Error Distribution, 69-73, 98, 101-102, 108, 110, 117

Expected Shortfall, 98-105, 114, 116, 119-120, 160, 162

F

Financial Crisis, 98-99, 118, 158, 164, 171, 183, 195

Financial Market, 59, 98-99, 119-120, 183, 197

Financial Returns, 100, 117-118, 180-181, 183-185, 189, 191, 193-195, 197

Financial Risk, 56, 79, 95, 100, 160, 162, 171, 176-177, 179, 198

First Passage, 143-151, 153, 155-157

Fixed Coefficients, 122, 124-125, 128-129, 132-133, 138, 140

Forecasting, 13-15, 17, 19, 21, 23-27, 29, 31, 57, 77, 98-101, 103-104, 106-107, 116-117, 119-122, 124, 129-131, 135, 140-142, 161, 166-168, 176-177, 183

Fraud, 158, 160, 163-164, 169-171, 175-179

G

Gradient Boosting, 14, 16-17, 20, 26, 167

H

Heston Model, 59-60, 66-68, 71-75

Heteroskedasticity, 98-99, 106-107, 110-111, 120, 180, 182, 196

I

Implied Volatilities, 56-57, 59, 61, 63, 65, 67, 69-71, 73-75, 77, 209, 212, 216, 220, 222-228

Income Risk, 198-207

Injected Capital, 32-33, 39, 46-48, 50

Insurer, 3-12

K

Kupiec's Test, 98, 100-101, 103, 112-113, 117

Kurtosis, 59, 78, 88-92, 94, 99, 108-110, 117-118, 184-186

L

Levy Process, 154-155

Liability, 3-4, 12, 199

Life Insurance, 1, 3, 12-13, 122, 129-130, 137-139, 141, 198-203, 205-208

Liquidity, 158-160, 162, 168-169, 171-172, 174-176, 178, 198

Liquidity Risk, 158-160, 162, 168-169, 171-172, 174-176, 178

Loss Function, 16, 63, 66, 98-99, 104, 113, 117

M

Machine Learning, 13-15, 17, 19, 21, 23-27, 29, 31, 56, 64, 73, 75-76, 158-159, 161-173, 175-179

Machine Learning Algorithm, 15

Machine Learning Techniques, 13-15, 31, 163, 167, 169-172

Market Risk, 99, 119, 158-160, 162, 168, 171-172, 175-176, 199

Markov Process, 144, 148

Money Laundering, 160, 163, 169, 171, 175, 177-178

Monotonicity, 2, 5, 11, 58, 92, 210, 215-217, 229

Mortality Data, 15, 121-122, 129-130

Mortality Model, 14-15, 23, 26

Mortality Rate, 15, 21-22, 135

N

Neural Networks, 14-15, 56-57, 59, 61, 63-65, 67, 69, 71, 73-77, 165-168, 171, 174-175, 177-178, 195

Normal Distribution, 58, 69-70, 102, 112, 117-118, 211

Null Hypothesis, 103-105, 110-112, 114-115, 119, 185-186, 188

O

Operational Risk, 33, 158-160, 162, 164, 169-172, 175-176

Optimal Dividend, 33, 35, 47, 54-55, 153-154, 156

Option Pricing, 56-59, 64, 75, 77, 120, 156, 228

P

Plat Model, 14, 18-24, 26

Premium, 1, 3-10, 12, 32, 137, 155, 199-203, 207

Probability Of Default, 160, 162, 165, 167, 170, 178-179

R

Random Coefficients, 121-124, 126-129, 132-133, 138, 141

Risk Metric, 104, 115, 201

Risk Model, 32, 98, 103-104, 166

Risk Process, 37, 46, 48, 156

S

Scale Functions, 32-33, 35, 47, 52, 54-55, 143-144, 146, 148, 156

Skewness, 78, 88-92, 94-95, 109-110, 117-118, 120, 184-186

Spectrally Negative Levy Process, 154-155

Standard Deviation, 64, 78, 88-89, 91-92, 94, 118, 168, 184-186, 202

Stochastic Collocation, 209-211, 213, 215, 217, 219-221, 223, 225, 227, 229

Stochastic Mortality Model, 15

Stress Testing, 162, 167-168, 171-174, 176-177

Surplus, 1, 4-7, 9-11, 32-33, 54

Sustainable Investment, 180-181, 183-185, 189, 191, 193-197

T

Transaction Cost, 32-35, 37-39, 41, 43, 45, 47, 49, 51-55

U

Utility Functions, 1, 3, 5, 7, 9-12

V

Value At Risk, 98-103, 119-120, 162, 168, 175, 177

Volatility, 56-62, 67-76, 98-102, 106-109, 111-112, 117, 119-120, 159, 168, 171, 177, 180-185, 188, 194-197, 209-211, 213, 215, 217-229